THE GREAT RECESSION

Since publication of Robert L. Hetzel's *The Monetary Policy of the Federal Reserve* (Cambridge University Press, 2008), the intellectual consensus that had characterized macroeconomics has disappeared. That consensus emphasized efficient markets, rational expectations, and the efficacy of the price system in assuring macroeconomic stability. The 2008–2009 recession not only destroyed the professional consensus about the kinds of models required to understand cyclical fluctuations but also revived the credit-cycle or asset-bubble explanations of recession that dominated thinking in the nineteenth century and first half of the twentieth century. These "market-disorder" views emphasize excessive risk taking in financial markets and the need for government regulation. The present book argues for the alternative "monetary-disorder" view of recessions. A review of cyclical instability over the last two centuries places the 2008–2009 recession in the monetary-disorder tradition, which focuses on the monetary instability created by central banks rather than on a boom-bust cycle in financial markets.

Robert L. Hetzel is Senior Economist and Research Advisor in the Research Department of the Federal Reserve Bank of Richmond, where he participates in debates over monetary policy and prepares the bank's president for meetings of the Federal Open Market Committee. Dr. Hetzel's research on monetary policy and the history of central banking has appeared in publications such as the *Journal of Money, Credit, and Banking*; the *Journal of Monetary Economics*; the *Monetary and Economics Studies* series of the Bank of Japan; and the *Carnegie-Rochester Conference Series*. His writings provided one of the catalysts for the congressional hearings and Treasury studies that led to the issuance of Treasury Inflation Protected Securities (TIPS). Dr. Hetzel has given seminars or served as a visiting scholar at the Austrian National Bank, the Bank of England, the Bank of Japan, the Bundesbank, the European Central Bank, the National Bank of Hungary, and the Center for Research into European Integration in Bonn, Germany. He received his PhD in 1975 from the University of Chicago, where Nobel Laureate Milton Friedman chaired his dissertation committee. Dr. Hetzel is author of *The Monetary Policy of the Federal Reserve* (Cambridge University Press, 2008).

Studies in Macroeconomic History

Series Editor:
Michael D. Bordo, *Rutgers University*

Editors:
Marc Flandreau, *Institut d'Etudes Politiques de Paris*
Chris Meissner, *University of California, Davis*
François Velde, *Federal Reserve Bank of Chicago*
David C. Wheelock, *Federal Reserve Bank of St. Louis*

The titles in this series investigate themes of interest to economists and economic historians in the rapidly developing field of macroeconomic history. The four areas covered include the application of monetary and finance theory, international economics, and quantitative methods to historical problems; the historical application of growth and development theory and theories of business fluctuations; the history of domestic and international monetary, financial, and other macroeconomic institutions; and the history of international monetary and financial systems. The series amalgamates the former Cambridge University Press series *Studies in Monetary and Financial History* and *Studies in Quantitative Economic History.*

Other books in the series:

Howard Bodenhorn, *A History of Banking in Antebellum America* [9780521662857, 9780521669993]

Michael D. Bordo, *The Gold Standard and Related Regimes* [9780521550062, 9780521022941]

Michael D. Bordo and Forrest Capie (eds.), *Monetary Regimes in Transition* [9780521419062]

Michael D. Bordo and Roberto Cortés-Conde (eds.), *Transferring Wealth and Power from the Old to the New World* [9780521773058, 9780511664793]

Michael D. Bordo and Ronald MacDonald, *Credibility and the International Monetary Regime: A Historical Perspective* [9780521811330]

Claudio Borio, Gianni Toniolo, and Piet Clement (eds.), *Past and Future of Central Bank Cooperation* [9780521877794, 9780511510779]

Richard Burdekin and Pierre Siklos (eds.), *Deflation: Current and Historical Perspectives* [9780521837996, 9780511607004]

Forrest Capie, *The Bank of England: 1950s to 1979* [9780521192828]

Trevor J. O. Dick and John E. Floyd, *Canada and the Gold Standard* [9780521404082, 9780521617062]

Barry Eichengreen, *Elusive Stability* [9780521365383, 9780521448475, 9780511664397]

Barry Eichengreen (ed.), *Europe's Postwar Recovery* [9780521482790, 9780521030786]

Caroline Fohlin, *Finance Capitalism and Germany's Rise to Industrial Power* [9780521810203, 9780511510908]

(Continued after index)

The Great Recession

Market Failure or Policy Failure?

ROBERT L. HETZEL

Senior Economist and Research Advisor
Federal Reserve Bank of Richmond

CAMBRIDGE
UNIVERSITY PRESS

CAMBRIDGE
UNIVERSITY PRESS

Shaftesbury Road, Cambridge CB2 8EA, United Kingdom

One Liberty Plaza, 20th Floor, New York, NY 10006, USA

477 Williamstown Road, Port Melbourne, VIC 3207, Australia

314–321, 3rd Floor, Plot 3, Splendor Forum, Jasola District Centre, New Delhi – 110025, India

103 Penang Road, #05–06/07, Visioncrest Commercial, Singapore 238467

Cambridge University Press is part of Cambridge University Press & Assessment, a department of the University of Cambridge.

We share the University's mission to contribute to society through the pursuit of education, learning and research at the highest international levels of excellence.

www.cambridge.org
Information on this title: www.cambridge.org/9781107011885

© Robert L. Hetzel 2012

First published 2012
First paperback edition 2014

A catalogue record for this publication is available from the British Library

Library of Congress Cataloging-in-Publication data
Hetzel, Robert L.
The great recession : market failure or policy failure? / Robert L. Hetzel.
p. cm.
Includes bibliographical references and index.
ISBN 978-1-107-01188-5 (hbk.)
1. Recessions – United States.   2. Monetary policy – United States.
3. Business cycles – United States.   4. United States – Economic policy – 2009–
5. United States – Economic conditions – 2009–   I. Title.
HB3743.H48   2011
330.973–dc23   2011038742

ISBN   978-1-107-01188-5   Hardback
ISBN   978-1-107-45960-1   Paperback

Contents

Figures

Tables

Preface

Prior to the 2008–2009 recession, considerable professional consensus existed that a prolonged, deep recession required contractionary monetary policy. With the 2008–2009 recession, this consensus disappeared. Popular and professional discourse revived the view that dominated thinking in the nineteenth century and first half of the twentieth century. According to this view, the business cycle derives from excessive swings in risk taking by investors. Although popular expressions of this view ignore the operation of the price system, the implicit assumption is that these fluctuations in investor sentiment between optimism and pessimism overwhelm the ability of the price system and, especially, the real interest rate to maintain full employment.

In contrast to this market-disorder view, the monetary-disorder view is that the price system works well to equilibrate the economy, provided that money creation and destruction do not prevent the interest rate from adjusting. There is no inevitable movement from boom to bust. This view receives empirical content from the hypothesis that to prevent the monetary emissions and absorptions that destabilize the price level, the central bank must follow a rule that provides for a stable nominal anchor and that allows market forces to determine the real interest and, by extension, other real variables (Hetzel 2008b).

Historically, the term used here, "market-disorder," has represented several traditions. Prior to World War II, the term "credit-cycle" or "real bills" focused attention on speculative behavior in asset markets that led to asset "bubbles," whose bursting required debt liquidation and deflation. The Keynesian tradition emphasized swings in the animal spirits of investors that produced destabilizing fluctuations in investment. The contrasting monetary-disorder view summarizes variants of the quantity-theory tradition.

Over time, the intellectual climate has oscillated between the market-disorder and monetary-disorder views. The former in its credit-cycle manifestation dominated thinking in the Depression and returned with vigor in the 2008–2009 recession. According to this view, excessive risk taking of banks caused the Depression and the 2008–2009 recession. The change over time in the intellectual consensus about the cause of the Depression from a credit-cycle to a monetary-disorder view should make contemporary observers cautious about assigning causes to the 2008–2009 recession without the advantage of thorough debate and the perspective of time. In the spirit of such debate, this book runs a horse race between the market-disorder and monetary-disorder views of the most likely causes of recessions, including the 2008–2009 recession.

The explanation offered here for both the Depression and the 2008–2009 recession is in the monetary-disorder spirit. To a significant extent, the 2008–2009 recession arose because the Federal Reserve departed from a rule that allowed the price system to work.

The author is indebted to Michael Bordo for a combination of critical review and encouragement without implicating him in the arguments expressed in the book. The views in this book are those of the author, not the Federal Reserve Bank of Richmond or the Federal Reserve System.

ONE

The 2008–2009 Recession

Market or Policy Maker Failure?

After the end of the Volcker disinflation in 1983 and through the end of 2007, growth in the world economy proceeded steadily, interrupted only by two minor recessions starting in 1990 and in 2001. Economists talked about the Great Moderation. The Great Recession, which began in the United States in December 2007, came as a shock. Once again, economists and the public began to ask fundamental questions about the nature of free-market economies. Are they inherently unstable? What kind of government policy can stabilize economic fluctuations?

This chapter reviews what is at stake in understanding the cause of the 2008–2009 recession. Seemingly commonsensical but misguided responses to the distress suffered during recession not only can be ineffective, but also can harm long-term growth. Such responses can also direct public policy away from the institutional arrangements and policies required to prevent cyclical instability. The following chapters contrast two explanations of the business cycle. One explanation highlights market disorder resulting from swings in the psychology of financial markets from excessive risk taking to excessive risk aversion. The other explanation highlights monetary disorder based on central bank (Federal Reserve) interference with the operation of the price system.

THE LACK OF AN AGREED CONCEPTUAL FRAMEWORK FOR CENTRAL BANKING

There is no agreement over the conceptual framework to use in understanding what the central bank controls and how it exercises its control. This lack of agreement mirrors the lack of consensus within the economics profession about the reasons for economic instability. Economists differ over the efficacy of the price system in maintaining aggregate demand equal to potential output.

They also differ over the role played by expectations about the future. In the terminology employed here, there have been historically two broad schools of thought: the market-disorder view and the monetary-disorder view.

Adherents of the market-disorder view believe that sharp swings in expectations about the future from unfounded optimism to unfounded pessimism overwhelm the ability of offsetting changes in the real interest rate to stabilize economic activity. Those expectational swings arise independently of central bank actions and require discretion in the conduct of monetary policy. The failure of the price system to mitigate fluctuations in output provides an opening for the central bank and government to manage aggregate demand. The central bank can control the real expenditure of the public through controlling the flow of credit and its allocation – that is, through controlling the left (asset) side of its balance sheet.

Adherents of the monetary-disorder view believe that the real interest rate works well as a flywheel to stabilize fluctuations in aggregate demand around potential produced by real demand shocks. However, money creation and destruction can interfere with those self-equilibrating powers. The conduct of monetary policy by a rule providing a nominal anchor and allowing market forces to determine the real interest rate and real output makes expectations into a stabilizing force by causing the public to anticipate that shocks that produce divergences between real aggregate demand and potential output will be short-lived.

HAS MACROECONOMICS FAILED?

The 2008–2009 recession initiated a vigorous debate over the relevance of macroeconomics, which is above all the study of the business cycle. Since Keynes's *General Theory*, macroeconomists have engaged in a prodigious research effort aimed at understanding and ameliorating the business cycle. The knowledge gained obviously did not allow policy makers to avoid a major world recession. In some sense, macroeconomics failed, but how? Has it failed as a methodology for learning about the world? The answer offered here is that the methodology for learning is the correct one. However, there is a need for more emphasis on the empirical study of the shocks that have produced recurring cyclical fluctuations in output. That effort should guide the direction of model development.

Narayana Kocherlakota (2009, 1), president of the Minneapolis Federal Reserve Bank, wrote:

I believe that during the last financial crisis, macroeconomists (and I include myself among them) failed the country, and indeed the world. In September 2008, central bankers were in desperate need of a playbook that offered a systematic plan of attack to deal with fast-evolving circumstances. Macroeconomics should have been able to provide that playbook. It could not. Of course, from a longer view, macroeconomists let policymakers down much earlier, because they did not provide policymakers with rules to avoid the circumstances that led to the global financial meltdown.

Kocherlakota (2009, 19, 9, 7, and 9) asserted that there is no difference among economists about methodology. There is a shared ideal of avoiding policy "based on purely verbal intuitions or crude correlations as opposed to tight modeling." All economists recognize the ideal of models that yield numerical predictions and that are not susceptible to the Lucas critique.[1] Kocherlakota said that "modern macro models are designed to be mathematical formalizations of the entire economy" and thus to replace "verbal intuitions." Because such models are "grounded in more fundamental features of the economy, such as the *technology* of capital accumulation and people's *preferences* for consumption today versus in the future," their estimated relationships will not change in unpredictable ways when the "policy regime changes." Moreover, Kocherlakota emphasized the need to be "explicit about the shocks that affect the economy."

According to Kocherlakota, economists' models failed on both criteria: model building and shock identification. With respect to the first criterion, Kocherlakota (2009, 14, 7, and 16) emphasized the limitations in computing power that make solving models difficult. Economists now build models around only a single friction: financial, pricing, or labor market. "This piecemeal approach is again largely attributable to computational limitations." With respect to the second criterion, he wrote, "Finally, and most troubling, macro models are driven by patently unrealistic shocks.... Macroeconomists ... are handicapping themselves by only looking at shocks to fundamentals like preferences and technology."

If existing models cannot yield numerical implications for the behavior of macroeconomic variables based on a realistic description of shocks and policy in a way that both explains the historical experience with recession and predicts the consequences of alternative policy rules, what is their value in policy making? Does this gloomy prognosis mean that there exists no alternative to the conduct of policy within an ad hoc, judgmental framework? The answer given here is that economists can examine the historical record of central banking and can draw conclusions about which class of models is most likely to offer useful guidance for policy making. Even though the

---

[1] That is, according to Lucas (1976), the behavioral relationships used by models to forecast should not vary in an unpredictable way when policy makers change the way they make policy. See also Marschak (1953).

class of models chosen will not offer numerical guidance to policy makers, it will still impose useful discipline. That discipline will mitigate the problems inherent in the current practice of ad hoc policy making.

Consider the criticisms of purely judgmental policy making made by James Tobin and Milton Friedman. Tobin (1977 [1980], 41) wrote:

> There is really no substitute for making policy backwards, from the desired feasible paths of the objective variables that really matter to the mixture of policy instruments that can bring them about.... The procedure requires a model – there is no getting away from that. Models are highly imperfect, but they are indispensable. The model used for policymaking need not be any of the well-known forecasting models. It should represent the policymakers' beliefs about the way the world works, and it should be explicit. Any policymaker or advisor who thinks he is not using a model is kidding both himself and us. He would be well advised to make explicit both his objectives for the economy and the model that expresses his view of the links of the economic variables of ultimate social concern to his policy instruments.

Friedman (1988) wrote:

> Every now and then a reporter asks my opinion about "current monetary policy." My standard reply has become that I would be glad to answer if he would first tell me what "current monetary policy" is. I know, or can find out, what monetary actions have been: open-market purchases and sales and discount rates at Federal Reserve Banks. I know also the federal funds rate and rates of growth of various monetary aggregates that have accompanied these actions. What I do not know is the policy that produced these actions.... [T]he closest I can come to an official specification of current monetary policy is that it is to take those actions that the monetary authorities, in light of all evidence available, judge will best promote price stability and full employment – i.e., to do the right thing at the right time. But that surely is not a "policy." It is simply an expression of good intentions and an injunction to "trust us."

Tobin's point is that to understand the impact of their actions, policy makers must use models. That is, they make policy based on conditional rather than on unconditional forecasts. When they take a policy action by setting a value for the funds rate, they are making a conditional forecast about the effect of that action on the variables of ultimate concern to them. To make that forecast, they must necessarily draw on past experience. Specifically, they must abstract the essential characteristics of the current economic situation and then base their forecast on outcomes of past periods possessing the same essential characteristics. Such abstraction requires a rudimentary model.

Friedman's point is complementary to Tobin's point. To understand the impact of their actions, policy makers need to place their individual policy actions (funds-rate decisions) into a broader context of what is systematic about their behavior. In a similar spirit, Friedman and Schwartz (1963a, 252–3) criticized the section in the Federal Reserve Board's 1923 *Tenth Annual Report*, "Guides to Credit Policy," in which the Fed authors argued that policy "is and must be a matter of judgment." Friedman and Schwartz (1963a, 252) commented that "the section offers little beyond glittering generalities instructing the men exercising the judgment to do the right thing at the right time with only the vaguest indications of what is the right thing to do."

Friedman's point also concerns learning. Thinking about policy as a systematic procedure for responding to incoming information in a way designed to achieve ultimate objectives allows policy makers to summarize succinctly their behavior at different times. If their forecasts turn out to be wrong, they are then positioned to ask whether their understanding of the past was correct.

Models and systematic characterizations of policy discipline the learning that takes place in this ongoing dialectic between present and past. They aid policy makers in evaluating how well their understanding of the past conditions their contingent forecasts of current policy actions. When outcomes belie forecasts, policy makers then possess a framework for asking whether the failure lay with the model (the understanding of the world), with policy (the systematic response of policy makers to incoming information about the economy), or with unforeseen shocks. Models make manageable the task of asking whether adverse outcomes (inflation and recession) derive from powerful exogenous shocks or from destabilizing policy. There is a need for the systematic study of past recessions to determine how best to construct models that are useful for policy makers. The Federal Reserve especially needs to examine its past behavior in a way that summarizes how the evolution of the consistent part of its policy procedures has defined the evolution of the monetary standard.

To provide a continual vetting of the appropriateness of monetary policy, academic economists and monetary policy makers need to engage in an ongoing dialogue about the kinds of models most useful for understanding the historical experience with central banking. That dialogue would provide the context for an exchange of views about the appropriateness of current policy. What has been de-emphasized in modern macroeconomics is the methodology pioneered by Friedman and Schwartz (1963a; 1991) to use events and beliefs about appropriate policy at particular times in the past to identify shocks capable of distinguishing between classes of models. The economist must treat history as a series of event studies in which information outside the model is used to discipline the choice of shocks.

RULES VERSUS DISCRETION

The view that financial fragility produces real instability is associated with the belief that markets are inherently unstable. From this view, it follows that economic stability requires the regulation of markets through government intervention.[2] In contrast, the free-market tradition, which takes Adam Smith as its founding father, holds that markets are self-regulating provided that government allows competitive markets and the price system to allocate resources and gives individuals an incentive to monitor the use of their resources, physical and financial, through the protection of property rights. One manifestation of this free-market-versus-interventionist debate is the rules-versus-discretion debate.

Historically, the Federal Reserve has always argued for the conduct of policy based on ongoing discretion. For example, Allan Sproul (1963 [1980], 124 and 127), former president of the New York Fed, wrote with reference to the rule proposed by Milton Friedman (1960) for steady money growth:

I find it impossible to swallow his (Friedman's) prescription which would reduce monetary management to the definitive act of forcing a constant drip of money into the economic blood stream. It seems to me patent that the uncertain hand of man is needed in a world of uncertainties and change and human beings, to try to accommodate the performance of the monetary system to the needs of particular times and circumstances and people.... "Money will not manage itself." It needs managers who are aware of the fact that they are dealing primarily with problems of human motivation and human reactions.

The market-disorder explanation for the 2008–2009 recession, which blames the speculative excesses of financial markets and the inevitable collapse of this excess, naturally implies the desirability of discretionary monetary policy. The herd behavior of investors creates an amount of market power that overwhelms the self-equilibrating powers of the price system and the ability of fluctuations in the real interest rate to maintain aggregate demand at

---

[2] For example, Paul Krugman generalized from his interpretation of the Great Depression and placed the blame for the current recession on the excesses of unregulated banks. Krugman (2008) wrote, "What turned an ordinary recession into a civilization-threatening slump was the wave of bank runs that swept across America in 1930 and 1931. This banking crisis of the 1930s showed that unregulated, unsupervised financial markets can all too easily suffer catastrophic failure." More succinctly, Krugman (2009a) wrote of the current recession, "[F]inance turned into the monster that ate the world economy." More generally, the pro–free market management consulting firm McKinsey & Company (2009a) wrote in a newsletter, "The parallels between financial crises and natural disasters ... suggest that the economy, just like complex natural systems, is inherently unstable and prone to occasional huge failures that are very hard or impossible to foresee."

potential. In these psychological-factors explanations of the business cycle (the credit-cycle view), the emphasis is on the unpredictability of shifts in investor psychology between unrealistic levels of optimism and pessimism about the future. Similarly, the panicky, herd behavior of depositors can close banks indiscriminately through runs. Necessarily, policy makers require discretion to respond to these unpredictable shifts in psychology.

In contrast, explanations of the business cycle in the neoclassical tradition of economics stress an ongoing continuity in the structure of the economy that derives from the operation of the price system. In the two main schools in this tradition, the price system works well to maintain real aggregate demand at potential either unambiguously (the real business cycle model) or in the absence of monetary shocks that cause the price level to evolve in an unpredictable fashion (the monetary-disorder view). It is desirable to have a rule that allows the price system to work.

These contrasting views about the stabilizing properties of the price system yield different implications for the ability of policy makers to learn. If the price system works well apart from monetary shocks that interfere with its operation, significant benefits accrue to an effort to evaluate past policies by asking: "How has the systematic component of policy evolved over time?" and "What were the implications for macroeconomic and financial stability?" In contrast, in a world buffeted by the vagaries of investor psychology in a way that periodically overwhelms the stabilizing properties of the price system at unpredictable intervals, learning is difficult. With discretion, the monetary policy maker chooses the optimal setting of policy each period based on prevailing economic and financial conditions – that is, independently of past and future policy settings. A recession or inflation then naturally leads to the conclusion that powerful real forces have overwhelmed the stabilizing actions of policy. The adherence of the Fed to the rhetoric of discretion in its public communication can explain the observed lack of any attempt to institutionalize an effort to draw lessons for the conduct of policy from its past experience.

Contrasting views about the ability of the price system to stabilize economic fluctuations yield different implications about the role the central bank should play in stabilizing economic fluctuations. This difference in views arises from different ways of disentangling the historical joint association between instability of the real economy and financial markets as opposed to instability of the real economy and money creation. Do fluctuations in the business cycle originate in instability in financial markets due to excessive risk taking? Alternatively, do they originate in instability in money creation due to the failure of central banks to allow the price system to work? The first perspective focuses attention on central bank control over excessive risk taking in financial markets. The second perspective focuses attention on central bank control over money creation and the role of the real interest rate in mitigating fluctuations in real output around trend.

AN EMPIRICAL ROAD MAP

Do waves of optimism and pessimism overwhelm the working of the price system and prevent the real interest rate from serving an equilibrating role for economic activity? If so, periods of economic stability should correspond to behavior by the central bank that entails a vigorous response to the emergence of asset bubbles. The unpredictable nature of the shifts in psychology that trigger booms and busts will require the exercise of discretion and judgment on the part of the policy maker.

Alternatively, does the price system work well to equilibrate economic activity in the absence of monetary disorder that interferes with the market determination of the real interest rate? If so, the central bank exacerbates cyclical instability in downturns with money destruction that limits declines in the real interest rate and, similarly, during expansions, with money creation that limits increases in the real interest rate. Support for the monetary-disorder view of the world requires successful generalization across history of a monetary rule that allows market forces to determine real variables while providing a nominal anchor.

The presence or absence of such a rule should separate periods of economic stability from instability. Consistency in the operation of the price system implies that economic stability requires consistent application of such a rule without periodic departures in response to special events like perceived asset bubbles. Departures from the rule most often take the form of increases in interest rates that are exaggerated relative to strength in economic activity. Such increases precede business cycle peaks and for prolonged recessions entail inertia in declines in interest rates subsequent to cycle peaks. For the period prior to 1981, given the existence of a stable demand function for the monetary aggregates M1 and M2, monetary instability should serve as a "smoking gun" in the identification of instances in which the central bank induced a behavior of interest rates incompatible with steady growth of output around trend (Chapters 7 and 8).

Hetzel (2008b) attributed the Great Moderation to the overall consistency imposed on policy by the desire to stabilize the public's expectation of inflation at a low value corresponding to the Federal Open Market Committee's (FOMC) implicit inflation target. That consistent set of procedures, termed lean-against-the-wind (LAW) with credibility, entailed moving the funds rate in a measured, persistent way in response to sustained changes in the economy's rate of resource utilization, subject to the constraint that financial markets believed that funds-rate changes would cumulate to whatever extent necessary to maintain trend inflation unchanged in response to inflation shocks and aggregate demand shocks. The stabilizing properties of the rule derived from the way in which it conditioned expectations. Credibility for maintaining constant the expectation of trend inflation coordinated the price setting of firms setting prices for multiple periods. The discipline imposed on policy during economic recovery of maintaining nominal expectational stability required turning over the determination of real variables such as the unemployment rate to the operation of the price system. Markets believed that the funds-rate changes engineered by LAW would result in a level of real interest rates high enough or low enough to keep aggregate real demand equal to potential output.

Both the market-disorder and the monetary-disorder views offer an explanation for the historical record of recurrent recessions. Each must answer the question of why a low price of resources today (a low real interest rate) does not create sufficient demand to keep output at potential. As summarized in the market-disorder (credit-cycle) view, the herd behavior of investors overwhelms the stabilizing properties of the price system with alternating periods of greed and fear. Alternatively, as summarized in the monetary-disorder view, recessions manifest excess supply produced by central bank price fixing – that is, episodes in which the central bank set the real interest rate too high through money destruction. In short, does financial or monetary instability cause real instability?

How does one give predictive content to these contrasting views in such a way that one can use the historical record to distinguish them? What does one do in the contemporary world in which the monetarist assumption of a stable, interest-insensitive money demand function no longer allows money to serve as a useful measure of expansionary and contractionary monetary policy? What about the 2008–2009 recession? Does it represent a return to an earlier pattern of recessions epitomized by the Great Depression in which the risky behavior of banks purportedly overwhelmed the stabilizing properties of the price system? Alternatively, does it conform to the pattern highlighted by the monetary-disorder view in which the central bank imparts inertia to reductions in real interest rates despite deteriorating economic conditions? Perhaps also the 2008–2009 recession is a black swan sighting (a unique occurrence) that disproves the Smithian assumption of a price system that works well to clear markets both intertemporally as well as intratemporally.

WHAT IS AT STAKE?

Is there a trade-off between secular growth and the smoothing of cyclical instability? Since the Civil War, the growth rate of per capita output in the United States has averaged a little more than 2 percent a year. However, sustained declines in output below trend have punctuated secular growth. These declines are associated with enormous human suffering. Comparison of the U.S. economy with the numerous examples of economies that lack competitive markets demonstrates that competitive markets drive secular growth. The defining characteristic of a competitive market economy is the free entry and free exit (bankruptcy) of firms that allow the price system to control the allocation of resources. The desire to limit the high unemployment accompanying recession, however, leads governments to implement policies that prevent bankruptcy, especially for banks, and that supersede the working of the price system. A trade-off appears to arise between policies that engender secular growth and polices that mitigate cyclical fluctuations.[3] Moreover, government intervention into the economy, especially to bail out troubled banks, creates the impression that government is fixing a problem created by the private market.

The current regulatory system combines a financial safety net with government regulation of risk taking. Does the 2008–2009 recession demonstrate the need for increased government regulation of risk taking? Alternatively, does the moral hazard inherent in the existence of a financial safety net encourage excessive risk taking by skewing innovation toward strategies that provide high returns to financial institutions in good times while imposing losses to taxpayers in bad times (Hetzel 2009a)? Specifically, did moral hazard bias financial innovation toward finding ways to leverage portfolios of long-term, risky assets with short-term funding?

---

[3]   The direct limitation of all financial innovation through government regulation as a way of limiting risk taking in financial markets will impede the ability of financial innovation to increase living standards over time. In particular, families are better off to the extent that financial markets have allowed them to smooth consumption over time in response to transitory income shocks. As argued by Perri (2008), a broader availability of credit instruments has yielded a fall over time in the correlation between individuals' income and consumption.

TWO

Recessions

Financial Instability or Monetary Mismanagement?

Popular commentary on the 2008–2009 recession has revived the market-disorder view. According to the variant that dominated thinking in the nineteenth century and first half of the twentieth century, a combination of easy money and speculative greed creates asset bubbles, which when deflated require a purgative cleansing of debt that produces deflation and recession. This understanding of recession as the outcome of unrestrained financial speculation motivated the original Federal Reserve Act. Acting on the basis of this speculative-excess or real-bills view, the Fed's founders established the Fed to eliminate the periodic recessions they associated with excessively risky lending by banks and the subsequent forced liquidation of the resulting bad debt.[1]

According to the real-bills view, the business cycle originates in speculation that creates unsustainable asset bubbles. The monetary-disorder view instead emphasizes money creation and destruction that interferes with operation of the price system. To illustrate the perennial nature of the debate, this chapter reviews the contemporaneous commentary on the 1818–1819 deflation and recession in the United States and then contrasts this commentary with later analysis in the monetary-disorder (quantity theory) tradition.

These contrasting views give rise to contrasting views on the stability of the banking system. Does unrestrained speculation periodically lead to a cycle of boom and bust for banks that destabilizes the real economy? This chapter also reviews the record of financial stability in the

---

[1] As embodied in the Federal Reserve Act, the only commercial paper acceptable for discounting at the Reserve banks' discount windows was short-term, self-liquidating IOUs used to finance goods in the process of production. The intention of restricting the collateral acceptable for discount window lending to these "real bills" was to prevent the extension of credit for speculative purposes and thereby limit the creation of asset bubbles.

era before the establishment of the Fed, the National Banking era. Did the absence of a financial safety net turn the banking system into a source of economic instability?

SPECULATIVE MANIA VERSUS MONETARY DISORDER: THE 1819–1820 DEFLATION

An eternally popular explanation of the business cycle is the alternation in financial markets of periods of greed and fear. Speculative mania starts a boom phase, followed inevitably by bust and deflation. There is a credit cycle characterized by shifts in investor psychology. Washington Irving (1819–1820 [2008], 4]) wrote:

Every now and then the world is visited by one of these delusive seasons, when the "credit system"... expands to full luxuriance: everybody trusts everybody; a bad debt is a thing unheard of; the broad way to certain and sudden wealth lies plain and open.... Banks ... become so many mints to coin words into cash; and as the supply of words is inexhaustible, it may readily be supposed that a vast amount of promissory capital is soon in circulation.... Nothing is heard but gigantic operations in trade; great purchases and sales of real property, and immense sums made at every transfer. All, to be sure, as yet exists in promise; but the believer in promises calculates the aggregate as solid capital....

Now is the time for speculative and dreaming of designing men. They relate their dreams and projects to the ignorant and credulous, [and] dazzle them with golden visions.... The example of one stimulates another; speculation rises on speculation; bubble rises on bubble.... No "operation" is thought worthy of attention, that does not double or treble the investment.... Could this delusion always last, the life of a merchant would indeed be a golden dream; but it is as short as it is brilliant.

Commenting on the same event, William Graham Sumner (1874, cited in Wood 2006, 4) quoted from a report of the Pennsylvania legislature that attributed the distress of the 1819 recession to the prior excesses of an expansion in bank credit begun during the War of 1812.

In consequence ..., the inclination of a large part of the people, created by past prosperity, to live by speculation and not by labor, was greatly increased. A spirit in all respects akin to gambling prevailed. A fictitious value was given to all kinds of property. Specie was driven from circulation as if by common consent, and all efforts to restore society to its natural condition were treated with undisguised contempt.

As expressed in the spirit of the American populist tradition, speculation in financial markets creates paper wealth that does not correspond to an ability to produce goods. Bubbles in asset prices emerge detached from fundamental values. The speculation that drives up asset prices entails excessive debt creation. In the inevitable bust phase of the boom-bust cycle, debt liquidation creates deflation and recession through a disruption in financial intermediation for productive purposes. These explanations stress the increase in asset prices and the reduction in risk premia in boom periods and the decline in asset prices and the increase in risk premia in bust periods. Cycles propagate through the seeds sown by easy money during economic recovery that encourage the leverage that pushes asset prices to unsustainable levels. Still in the American populist tradition, the credit-cycle view personifies the forces that create recession in the form of the excessive, unrestrained greed of bankers.

Timberlake (1993, ch. 2) provided a different analysis of the 1818–1819 deflation. With the War of 1812, the government began to run fiscal deficits. Because the charter for the First Bank of the United States had lapsed in 1811, the Treasury financed these deficits with the issuance of Treasury notes. These notes constituted legal tender and served as a medium of exchange. Because banks used them as clearing balances (high-powered money), they allowed banks to expand their note issue, which the public used as currency. This expansion in the money stock fueled inflation. With inflation, the paper-money price of gold rose and banks suspended the convertibility of their notes into gold.

In 1816, after the end of the war, the government began to run surpluses. In order to achieve resumption of the gold standard, that is, the reestablishment of convertibility between bank notes and gold at the prewar parity, Treasury Secretary Crawford used these surpluses to retire the Treasury notes. High-powered money contracted and deflation replaced inflation. The monetary contraction that began in 1816 led to declines in the price level starting in 1817. By 1818, the country was in severe recession.

Timberlake (1993, 25) wrote, "The price level decline in 1818–1820 that resulted in full-scale resumption was accompanied by the usual symptoms of failing banks and business hardships." As Timberlake (1993, 25) noted, the banks then found that they were forced [in the language from an 1818 Treasury Report written by Treasury Secretary Crawford] "to contract their discounts for the purpose of withdrawing from circulation a large proportion of their notes. This operation, so oppressive to their debtors, but indispensably necessary to the existence of specie payments, must be continued until gold and silver shall form a just proportion of the circulating medium."

Although the Treasury forced the monetary contraction, the Second Bank of the United States, which had been chartered in 1816, received the blame. Wood (2005, 131) wrote, quoting the historian Bray Hammond:

There was a scramble for liquidity, and failures almost included the United States Bank, whose "grim efforts" to collect its debts aroused a popular hatred that "was never extinguished." ... Andrew Jackson's bank-hating adviser, William Gouge, wrote of this episode that "The Bank was saved and the people were ruined."

The Washington Irving and the Richard Timberlake explanations of the 1818–1819 recession stress different correlations with real instability, one financial and one monetary. Which of these correlations reflects symptom and which cause? The speculative-mania explanation derives its perennial popularity from the association of declining risk premia in periods of cyclical strength and rising risk premia in periods of cyclical weakness. But does that association imply causation? Do concentrated power and greed in financial markets overwhelm the self-equilibrating properties of the price system?

Charles Mackay (1841 [2009]) wrote, "Men think in herds ... [and] they go mad in herds." Of course, the calculating, optimizing agents in economists' models are human beings with emotions. During cyclical expansions, they feel optimistic about the future; during cyclical contractions, they feel pessimistic about the future. Over the business cycle, exuberance gives way to gloom and greed gives way to fear. Implicit in psychological explanations of the business cycle, however, is the assumption that this alternation in human emotions overwhelms the stabilizing properties of the price system.

In the monetary-disorder tradition, the real interest rate serves as a flywheel to moderate fluctuations in real GDP around its longer-run trend. When individuals are pessimistic about their future job and income prospects, a low real interest rate encourages real aggregate demand sufficiently to equal full-employment output. Conversely, when individuals are optimistic about the future, a high real interest rate constrains real aggregate demand sufficiently to equal full-employment output. Serious recessions occur only when central banks interfere with this operation of the price system through their ability to create and destroy money.[2]

---

[2] As pointed out by Friedman (1964 [1969]), if the credit-cycle view is correct, the magnitude of the preceding boom would predict the magnitude of the following bust. However, Friedman found that the magnitude of cyclical expansions in output fails to forecast the magnitude of subsequent cyclical declines in output. Using data on cyclical expansions and contractions from 1879 through 1961, Friedman (1964 [1969], 272) concluded that "there appears to be no systematic connection between the size of an expansion and of the succeeding contraction.... This phenomenon ... [casts] grave doubts on those theories that see as the source of a deep depression the excesses of the prior expansion. At the same

FINANCIAL PANICS AND RECESSIONS
BEFORE WORLD WAR I

The issue of whether an inherent fragility of banks requires a financial safety net and regulation or whether a financial safety net and regulation create systemic fragility is empirical. This section reviews the experience with banks in the era before the establishment of the Fed.

The historical evidence does not support the popular belief that the banking system was unstable because of panic-induced runs prior to the founding of the Fed. Bank runs did not start capriciously but rather originated with insolvent banks. Moreover, bank runs did not cause recessions in this period. In the clearinghouse era before the Fed, panics only occurred in the absence of prompt support for solvent banks from the clearinghouse. Although unit banking made the U.S. banking system susceptible to shocks, before deposit insurance, market discipline was effective in closing banks promptly enough to avoid significant losses to depositors.[3] As in the Depression, significant systemic problems occurred only against a backdrop of monetary contraction that stressed the banking system.

Calomiris and Gorton (2000) reviewed the literature on bank panics in the pre-FDIC deposit-insurance era. They pointed out that across countries over long periods, despite the commonality of demandable debt (bank notes or demand deposits), bank panics were not a universal feature (Calomiris and Gorton 2000, 106). There were no bank panics in Canada after the 1830s and none in England after the Overend, Gurney & Company panic in 1866. The authors cited the work of Bordo (1985), who surveyed the experience of six countries from 1870 to 1933. "Summarizing the literature, Bordo attributes the U.S. peculiarity in large part to the absence of branch banking" (Calomiris and Gorton 2000, 102). Haubrich (1990) attributed the stability in the Canadian bank market to the existence of branch banking and the ability of its smaller number of banks (10 by 1929) to respond in a coordinated way to threats to the system. Calomiris and Gorton (2000)

---

time, the magnitude of an economic contraction predicts the magnitude of the subsequent expansion." Morley (2009, 3) reconfirmed Friedman's results using quarterly data from 1947Q2 through 2008Q4: "[E]xpansions imply little or no serial correlation for output growth in the immediate future, while recessions imply negative serial correlation in the near term."

[3] Unit banking in the United States was a constitutional accident. Competition through free entry is protected in the Constitution through the interstate commerce clause that prevents states from erecting barriers to interstate trade. However, courts ruled that banking was distinct from commerce. States were then free to grant state bank charters in a way that created local monopolies without concern for competition from out-of-state banks.

and Bordo, Redish, and Rockoff (1994) attributed the absence of bank panics before 1914 in Canada to nationwide bank branching and the resulting ability to diversify geographically both the deposit base and assets.

As a counter to the conclusions drawn from work inspired by Diamond and Dybvig (1983), namely, that bank contracts "necessarily lead to costly panics," Calomiris and Gorton (2000, 107) advanced the asymmetric-information approach, which "identifies asset shocks as the source of panics and sees panics as an attempt by the banking system as a whole to resolve asymmetric information by closing insolvent banks." "[T]he asymmetric-information approach predicts unusually adverse economic news prior to panics, including increases in asset risk, declines in the relative prices of risky assets, increases in commercial failures, and the demise of investment banking houses" (Calomiris and Gorton 2000, 120). Although the approach of these authors leaves unspecified the nature of the macroeconomic shocks that rendered some banks insolvent (monetary or real), their empirical work supports the view that the relationship between instability in economic activity and in the banking system ran from the former to the latter.

The frequently expressed belief that bank failures historically have started with runs unprovoked by insolvency but rather precipitated by investor herd behavior has encouraged the view that free entry and exit is inappropriate for banks as opposed to nonfinancial businesses. That is, bankruptcy decisions for banks should be determined by regulators rather than through the market discipline imposed by depositors. Concern that free entry encourages fraud and excessive risk taking goes back to the "free banking systems" common from 1837 to 1865 in which banks could incorporate under state law without a special legislative charter. Rolnick and Weber (1984) and Dwyer (1996), however, showed that "wildcatting," defined as banks open less than a year, did not account for a significant proportion of bank failures. Moreover, the failures that did occur resulted not from "panics" but rather from well-founded withdrawals from banks whose assets suffered declines in value due to aggregate disturbances. An example of such a disturbance was the failure in the 1840s of Indiana banks that held the bonds used to finance the canals rendered uneconomic by the advent of the railroad.

Calomiris (1989) compared the success and failure of state-run systems of deposit insurance before the Civil War. Several systems operated successfully to prevent the closing of insured banks through depositor runs. The reason for their success was monitoring among banks to limit risky behavior and assurance to depositors of prompt reimbursement in case of bank failure. Both attributes depended on a mutual guarantee system among insured banks made credible by an unlimited ability to impose on member banks whatever assessments were required to cover the costs of reimbursing depositors of failed banks.

The National Banking era lasted from 1863, when the National Bank Act taxed state bank notes out of existence, until 1913 and the establishment of the Federal Reserve. It included six financial panics defined as instances in which the New York Clearing House Association (NYCH) issued loan certificates (Roberds 1995). Although it is difficult to generalize from this period because of a lack of good data, the literature allows the generalization that bank runs started with a shock that produced insolvency among some banks. In summarizing the research of Calomiris and Gorton (2000), Calomiris and Mason (2003, 1616) wrote, "[P]re-Depression panics were moments of temporary confusion about which (of a very small number of banks) were insolvent."

As dated by the National Bureau of Economic Research (NBER), there were eleven recessions during the National Banking era, 1864–1913. For these recessions, at least as concerns bank runs, there is no empirical evidence that financial market disturbances constituted an independent shock causing cyclical decline. However, monetary contraction always accompanied severe recession.[4] Gorton (2009, 16) presented data on these recessions. For four of the eleven recessions, there was no bank run. Furthermore, for the six countries (U.S., U.K., Germany, France, Canada, and Sweden) studied by Bordo (1985), only the United States experienced bank runs whereas all experienced recessions. Bordo (1985, abstract) summarized:

[F]or the six countries over the period 1870–1933, severe contractions in economic activity were in all cases accompanied by monetary contraction, in most cases with stock market crashes, but not, with the exception of the U.S., by banking crises. The unique performance of the U.S. can be attributed to the absence of a nationwide branch banking system compared to the five other countries examined, and the less effective role played by the U.S. monetary authorities in acting as lender of last resort.

Prior to the July 1890, January 1893, and December 1895 cycle peaks, free-silver agitation produced gold outflows and monetary contraction. In noting the defeat of Grover Cleveland by Benjamin Harrison in the 1888 presidential election, Timberlake (1993, 167) wrote, "Without a promise

---

[4]   Friedman and Schwartz (1963a, 677) wrote:

   [Prior to World War II] there have been six periods of severe economic contraction.... The most severe contraction was the one from 1929 to 1933. The others were 1873–79, 1893–94 – or better, perhaps, the whole period 1893 to 1897, ... 1907–08, 1920–21, and 1937–38. Each of those severe contractions was accompanied by an appreciable decline in the stock of money, the most severe decline accompanying the 1929–33 contraction.

to 'do something' for silver, Harrison would not have been elected.... Both houses of Congress proposed silver bills." These bills came to fruition in July 1890 with monetization of silver under the Sherman Act. Again, as Timberlake (1993, 170) wrote: "The national elections of 1892 seemed to be an unequivocal victory for the cheaper-money free-silver forces." Until the personal opposition of President Cleveland prevailed over congressional sentiment in early summer of 1893, uncertainty over the standard led to "external gold drains and an accumulation of silver in the Treasury" (Timberlake 1993, 170).

Friedman and Schwartz (1963a, 133) wrote, "The fear that silver would produce an inflation sufficient to force the United States off the gold standard made it necessary to have severe deflation in order to stay on the gold standard." Concerning the December 1895 cycle peak, Friedman and Schwartz (1963a, 111) wrote:

[T]he next three years [after 1893] were characterized by dragging deflation.... Speculative pressure on the dollar continued, as political agitation proceeded apace. The Treasury's gold reserves fell to a low of $45 million in January 1895. [The losses of gold reserves] were a link in the transmission of the external pressure to the domestic money stock.

Monetary contraction also preceded the start of the last recession of the National Banking era, in which the cyclical peak occurred in May 1907. Odell and Weidenmier (2004, 1002) wrote:

In April 1906 the San Francisco earthquake and fire caused damage equal to more than 1% of GNP. Although the real effect of the shock was localized, it had an international financial impact: large amounts of gold flowed into the country in autumn 1906 as foreign insurers paid claims on their San Francisco policies out of home funds. This outflow prompted the Bank of England to discriminate against American finance bills and, along with other European central banks, to raise interest rates. These policies pushed the United States into recession and set the stage for the Panic of 1907.

The National Banking era is especially important because it offers a laboratory for studying the stability of the banking system in the absence of a financial safety net in the form of deposit insurance and the policy of too big to fail. There are two assumptions embedded in the view that a financial system is inherently unstable when risk taking is regulated by creditors with their own money at risk as opposed to government regulators. First, creditors (depositors and debt holders) occasionally act unpredictably as a herd to close solvent and insolvent institutions alike. Second, banks either do not or cannot adjust their own risk taking to guard adequately against depositor runs.

Kaufman (1989; 1994), Benston et al. (1986, ch. 2), Benston and Kaufman (1995), and Goodfriend and King (1988, 16) concluded that such fragility is not inherent to banking. They pointed out that from the end of the Civil War to the end of World War I bank failures were relatively few in number and imposed only small losses because the fear of losses by both shareholders and depositors resulted in significant market discipline, high capital ratios, and prompt closure of troubled banks. In the period 1864 through 1913, there were three episodes of bank runs in which the number of suspensions was nontrivial. In 1873, 1.6 percent of national and state banks suspended payment. In the two most serious episodes, 1893 and 1907, 4.2 percent and 2.6 percent of banks suspended payment, respectively. Over the entire interval, only one national bank in New York City suspended, and that was in 1884.[5]

Apart from the first recession, October 1873 to March 1879, for the recessions in which there was a bank run, the run always occurred after the cycle peak with the average lag being 5.5 months.[6] Apart from the first panic in September 1873 in which losses amounted to two cents per dollar of deposits, losses to depositors resulting from a panic were quite small, averaging just less than half a penny per dollar of deposits.[7] For these recessions, only 0.7 percent of national banks failed (Gorton 2009, 16). The considerable stability of the banking system is especially significant because of the inflexibility of the National Banking System. Government control of the amount of bank note issue and reserve requirements on banks in central reserve cities (New York and Chicago) that immobilized reserves in the event of a bank run increased the fragility of a fractional reserve system in a gold standard.

The most extensive overview of bank panics in the National Banking era is in Wicker (2000). Like Sprague (1910) and Timberlake (1984), Wicker

---

[5] The numbers are from Wicker (2000, tables 1.2 and 1.4).

[6] For the first recession with cycle peak in October 1873, the dates for the cycle peak and bank run are basically contemporaneous. Gorton, however, dismissed this observation because of the absence of monthly data for this period. In this period, the government held the quantity of greenbacks fixed to encourage resumption of the gold standard at the pre–Civil War parity between gold and the dollar. Deflation set in after 1871. See Friedman and Schwartz (1963a, chart 3) and the discussion in their chapter "The Greenback Period."

[7] Wicker (2000, 26) commented, "[I]t is quite clear that bank failures per se did not cause a contraction of M (the money stock) because of the fewness of their numbers." In contrast, for the Depression, Friedman and Schwartz (1963a, 351) reported, "[F]ailures imposed losses totaling about $2.5 billion on stockholders, depositors, and other creditors of the more than 9,000 banks that suspended operations during the four years from 1930 through 1933. Slightly more than half the loss fell on depositors." The loss amounted to about 3.6% of nominal GNP calculated as an average of GNP for those four years (Balke and Gordon 1986, app. B, table 1).

emphasized that the NYCH acted like a central bank in financial crises by mobilizing the reserves of the money center banks and by creating clearing-house certificates, which banks used for clearing payments among them-selves. The NYCH had the power to prevent a bank run from spreading by lending to banks suffering runs. The willingness of the large banks to support a bank was a signal of the bank's solvency. Friedman and Schwartz (1963a, 329) wrote, apart possibly from the restriction in bank payments from 1839 through 1842, there were no "extensive series of bank failures after restriction occurred."

When runs did develop, it was because the clearinghouse was slow to respond. The problem was that among the NYCH clearing banks, an inherent conflict of interest existed because only a subset maintained cor-respondent balances with banks in the interior. Because it was that subset of banks that experienced reserve outflows to the interior in the event of financial crisis, the other banks could not always agree promptly to support this subset. Wicker (2000, 14) wrote, "Critical delays in responding to the onset of banking unrest in 1893 and 1907 exacerbated the panic symptoms." In 1893, the NYCH was slow to respond because the runs originated with the interior banks. In 1907, it was slow to respond because the problem originated with the trust companies.

The precipitating event in the 1907 Panic was the decision by the National Bank of Commerce on October 21, 1907, to stop clearing checks for the Knickerbocker Trust Company whose president had reportedly been involved in a scheme to corner the market in the stock of a copper com-pany. In 1907, the trusts were to banks as today investment banks are to commercial banks. Trusts operated like banks by accepting deposits and making loans, especially call loans to the New York Stock Exchange (NYSE). However, by forgoing the ability to issue bank notes, they avoided being sub-ject to reserve requirements. The trusts lacked access to lines of credit with banks: "The trusts operated under the impression that they could 'free ride' on the liquidity-providing services of the banks and the clearinghouses" (Roberds 1995, 26). Because they were not part of the NYCH, bankers were initially reluctant to come to their aid (Tallman and Moen 1990).

Only on October 26, 1907, did the NYCH issue loan certificates to off-set reserve outflows. Sprague (1910) "believed that by issuing certificates as soon as the crisis struck the trusts would have calmed the market by allowing banks to accommodate their depositors more quickly" (cited in Tallman and Moen 1990, 10). At the same time, stringency existed in the New York money market because of gold outflows to London (Tallman and Moen 1990; Bordo and Wheelock 1998, 53). As a result, a liquidity crisis propagated the initial deposit run into a panic. Like Wicker, Roberds (1995, 26) reviewed the panics during the National Banking era and attributed the severity of the 1873 and 1907 panics to provision of liquidity by the NYCH only after "a panic was under way." Overall, the mechanism for dealing with the forced multiple contraction of credit and deposits in a fractional reserve system caused by reserve outflows, namely, the issuance of clearinghouse certificates to serve as fiat money among banks, generally worked (Timberlake 1984). Calomiris and Gorton (2000, 158) argued, "Private bank coalitions were surprisingly effective in monitoring banks and mitigating the effects of panics, even if panics were not eliminated."

White (2010, abstract) summarized the change in regulatory regime that occurred with passage from the National Banking System to the Federal Reserve System:

[U]nder the National Banking System ... the cost of bank failures was minimal. Double liability induced shareholders to carefully monitor bank managers and voluntarily liquidate banks early if they appeared to be in trouble.... The arrival of the Federal Reserve weakened this regime.... When the Great Depression hit, policy-induced deflation and asset price volatility were misdiagnosed as failures of competition and market valuation. In response, the New Deal shifted to a regime of discretion-based supervision with forbearance.

It is hard to find convincing evidence in the historical record that past recessions arose from dysfunction in credit markets arising from a credit cycle.[8] Of course, there may be something special about the 2008–2009 recession that explains a failure of financial markets to perform their function of intermediation, but the general presumption that financial markets have worked well in the past raises the hurdle that a special explanation must satisfy. Moreover, the considerable stability in financial markets in the pre-Fed era does not mean that regulators today should allow runs to close insolvent banks in a way that requires immediate liquidation. However, it does conflict with the belief that placing a bank into conservatorship with haircuts on large depositors and debt holders would generate a systemwide run on all banks, solvent and insolvent. The fragility of the current system

---

[8] Until the 2008–2009 recession, there was never any presumption that recessions in the post–World War II period originated in speculation that created bubbles in asset prices. Koller (2010, 2) wrote:

The performance of equity markets shows that they have not been a good predictor of past recessions. Indeed, during every major recession since the early 1970s, most of the decline in the S&P 500 index occurred *after* the economy had already slowed.... Moreover, when the index's value does drop during nonrecessionary periods, this rarely signals a downturn.... Even an extreme case, such as the 20 percent drop during a couple of days in 1987, didn't portend a systematic downturn.

requires an explanation other than an appeal to "inherent" instability. The other side of the too-big-to-fail coin is regulatory forbearance for under-capitalized banks. A macroeconomic shock that causes widespread losses among banks then can leave a significant number of banks insolvent and, as a result, can render the system prone to systemwide runs.

WHAT IS THE APPROPRIATE ROLE OF A CENTRAL BANK?

Is there an inherent fragility to the banking system produced by the fact that its liabilities are payable on demand and its assets are illiquid? Does this maturity transformation render banks susceptible to panic-induced runs in which depositors withdraw funds simply because they believe that others might withdraw their funds? Based on these assumptions, government has created an elaborate financial safety net that prevents market forces from closing banks. That protected status contrasts strongly with nonbank businesses, which are subject to market discipline.

Policy makers espoused the inherent-fragility view in fall 2008. Bernanke (2009b) stated:

[T]he disorderly failure of AIG would have put at risk not only the company's own customers and creditors but the entire global financial system. Historical experience shows that, once begun, a financial panic can spread rapidly and unpredictably; indeed, the failure of Lehman Brothers a day earlier, which the Fed and Treasury unsuccessfully tried to prevent, resulted in the freezing up of a wide range of credit markets, with extremely serious consequences for the world economy.

The opposite view is that, by removing market discipline, the financial safety net has created financial fragility. The financial safety net undercuts the incentive of banks' creditors (debt holders and depositors) to monitor the risk taking of banks and to require capital proportionate to asset riskiness. A concomitant of the financial safety net and the policy of too big to fail is capital forbearance by regulators for troubled banks. A macroeconomic shock then brings into question the solvency of large numbers of banks along with confusion about which banks remain solvent. Any hesitation on the part of government about bailing out all banks can create a run.

THREE

The Great Contraction

1929–1933

The Great Depression remains the most horrific economic event in the twentieth century. In the 1948 edition of *Economics: An Introductory Analysis*, Paul Samuelson wrote, "It is not too much to say that the widespread creation of dictatorships and the resulting World War II stemmed in no small measure from the failure to meet this basic economic problem [the Great Depression] adequately" (cited in University of Chicago 2009).[1] The Depression gave birth to modern macroeconomics. Sorting out the causes of the Depression remains essential to achieving professional agreement within monetary economics about the appropriate model of the economy to use for the design of stabilization policy in general and monetary policy in particular.

This chapter complements Hetzel (2008b, ch. 3) by using historical narrative to distinguish between the market-disorder (credit-cycle) and monetary-disorder views of the cause of the Depression. Strong similarities exist in the way that policy makers in the Depression and policy makers in the 2008–2009 recession understood the causes of cyclical downturns. A cyclical downturn begins with the bursting of a speculative asset bubble and propagates through the dysfunction in financial markets produced by the forced liquidation of the excessive debt acquired in the prior boom. The

---

[1] Earlier, Warren and Pearson (1933, 299) wrote:

In order to function, an economic society that is based on the private ownership of property must have a reliable medium of exchange. When the medium of exchange rises in value, the chaos that results leads persons to challenge this economic order. The thing that has broken down is not "capitalism," which is another name for private enterprise, but merely the medium of exchange.... When serious deflation occurs, the party in power is usually voted out or revolution comes. As a result of the deflation in 1929, most of the political powers that were in power were thrown out and in many countries revolutions occurred. Probably we have not seen the last of these. Popular demand is usually for a dictator. The assumption is that democratic government is a failure.

issue then arises of how the Great Depression and the 2008–2009 recession could have been so intense if policy makers had the correct understanding of the business cycle as a manifestation of financial market dysfunction as opposed to monetary disorder.

THE FED AS SYSTEMIC RISK REGULATOR

In today's terminology, the Fed was established as a systemic risk regulator to control asset-market speculation. The 1907 recession created a political movement to limit the dominance of the large New York City banks and the concentration of finance epitomized by J. P. Morgan. Speaking of the "Money Trust" issue, Woodrow Wilson, governor of New Jersey, stated that "the greatest monopoly in the country is the money monopoly. So long as it exists our old variety of freedom and individual energy of development are out of the question" (cited in Grant 1992, 125). The authors of the Federal Reserve Act agreed on the desirability of a system that controlled money and credit automatically as a way of preventing both Wall Street financiers and Washington politicians from using money creation for their own purposes.

To this end, the Federal Reserve Act contained provisions codifying the gold standard. In particular, the act specified for the Federal Reserve banks the minimum amount of gold that had to be held against the deposits of their member banks and against the Federal Reserve notes they created. If the act had required the New York Fed to change its discount rate inversely in response to gold flows influencing these ratios, the United States could in principle have continued as part of the international gold standard. The advent of World War I in 1914 and the controls imposed by the combatants on gold flows, however, rendered the gold standard inoperable. When the United States entered World War I in 1917, like the central banks of other countries, the Fed monetized Treasury debt issuance to finance the war effort.

Also, in the same spirit of automaticity, but in contradiction to the provisions enforcing the gold standard, the Federal Reserve Act contained provisions codifying the real-bills doctrine (also known as the commercial loan theory of banking). The act legislated the requirement that the Reserve banks discount only short-term commercial paper (real bills) with the intent of automatically allocating credit toward productive uses and away from speculative uses. As Alvin Hansen (1941, 75 and 71), American apostle of Keynesianism, summarized:

The Reserve System had been established on the commercial banking theory. The member banks ideally were to extend credit only on the basis of self-liquidating loans. They were to "monetize" the credit of producing and marketing units. Bank loans work to refinance goods during the process of production or marketing. And when the process was completed, the sale of the goods would supply the funds to repay the loans. Thus, the process of production would be facilitated by bank credit accommodation.

The central basis of stabilization policy rested upon the firm belief that the boom was the progenitor of the depression and, if it could be controlled, stability would result. It would not do to wait until depression was already upon us to introduce control measures. The time for action was in the preceding phase of the cycle. Once the boom had been allowed to run its course, depression was regarded as inevitable and it, in turn, would perforce have to be permitted to run its course. Preventive, not remedial, measures were required.

In practice, without any specification of the rule to be followed for setting the discount rate, the contradictory gold-standard and real-bills objectives legislated in the Federal Reserve Act robbed the monetary system of the intended automaticity and left the conduct of monetary policy to the discretion of policy makers. Policy makers used that discretion in different ways at different times. In fall 1919, the Fed raised the discount rate to bring down the high level of commodity prices it attributed to a speculative bubble in world commodity markets. The country experienced a sharp recession with a cycle peak in January 1920 and trough in July 1921. Policy makers interpreted the ensuing years of prosperity as validation of a policy of deflating speculative bubbles through contractionary monetary policy.

Russell Leffingwell (1932b), a partner at J. P. Morgan who had been Assistant Secretary of the Treasury during World War I, wrote to Carter Glass, who was Treasury Secretary:

[I]n January 1920, as soon as the Treasury's maturities had been got into manageable shape, on my recommendation and by your deciding vote as Chairman of the Federal Reserve Board, the 6% discount rate was established.... It was your ... decisive acceptance of the sound doctrine of control by use of the discount rate ... that set the country's house in order for seven years of as unbroken and magnificent prosperity as was ever known.

Elihu Root, senator from New York and earlier secretary of war under McKinley and secretary of state under Roosevelt, had opposed creation of the Fed on grounds that it would initiate boom-bust cycles through easy money. In 1928, when the Fed raised interest rates to deflate what it considered to be a bubble in equity prices on the New York Stock Exchange, the Fed was acting as if Root had prophetically forecast exactly such a failing. In a speech in 1913, Root (cited in Grant 1992, 143) stated:

With the exhaustless reservoir of the government of the United States furnishing easy money, the sales increase, the businesses enlarge, more new enterprises are started, the spirit of optimism pervades the community. Bankers are not free from it. They are human. The members of the Federal Reserve Board will not be free of it. They are human. All the world moves along upon a growing tide of optimism. Everyone is making money. Everyone is growing rich. It goes up and up, the margin between costs and sales continually growing smaller as a result of the operation of inevitable laws, until finally someone whose judgment was bad, someone whose capacity for business was small, breaks; and as he falls he hits the next brick in the row, and then another, and then another, and down comes the whole structure.

That, sir, is no dream. That is the history of every movement of inflation since the world's business began, and it is the history of many a period in our own country. That is what happened to greater or less degree before the panic of 1837, of 1857, of 1873, of 1893, and of 1907. The precise formula which the students of economic movements have evolved to describe the reason for the crash following this universal process is that when credit exceeds the legitimate demands of the country the currency becomes suspected and gold leaves the country.

According to this view, once a speculative asset bubble had burst, the country had to endure the resulting painful adjustments. Wilbur Aldrich (1903, 96–7, cited in Wood 2009b, 161), coauthor of the Aldrich-Vreeland Act of 1908, which authorized the National Monetary Commission whose recommendations resulted in creation of the Federal Reserve, wrote in his monetary treatise:

When over-production and inflation of credit have brought on a crisis, no currency juggle can prevent losses.... Any permanent plan of extending credit in face of crises would simply be discounted and used up before the pinch of a succeeding crisis.... The true time for banks to begin to prepare for a panic and provide for their reserves, is before a careless extension of credit in the mad industrial race which invariably precedes a panic.

Root's misgivings reappeared in the blame assigned to the Fed for the presumed speculation that led to a stock market bubble and resulting crash in 1929 and the presumed fallout that appeared as the Depression. As background, note that in the 1920s the Fed had developed open-market operations as a way of controlling money-market rates indirectly by forcing banks through open-market sales into the discount window and by pushing them out of the window through purchases (see Chapter 4). According to the views of Fed critics, open-market purchases undesirably circumvented the automatic regulation of credit in response to the needs of business by forcing on markets unwanted credit, which spilled over in the form of speculation.

In 1927, New York Fed Governor Benjamin Strong lowered the discount rate to provide financial conditions conducive to Britain's return to the gold standard. The consensus formed that this "easy money" policy produced a speculative increase in the value of the New York Stock Exchange.[2] Meltzer (2003, 289) quoted San Francisco Fed President Calkins, "The 1927 experiment [is] now quite generally ... admitted to have been *disastrous*" (italics in original). Later, Adolph C. Miller (1935, 442), who had been a governor at the board since the founding of the Fed, blamed the New York Fed for the speculative rise in the NYSE: "The 1927 easy money policy was initiated by the New York reserve bank to encourage domestic business and strengthen European exchanges. The policy ... gave a dangerous impetus to stock market speculation." Garet Garrett (1931, 79, 81) wrote in the *Saturday Evening Post*:

[T]he Federal Reserve System has failed to cast out the besetting evil of American banking. That is the reckless lending of bank credit for purposes of Wall Street speculation.... [I]f the Federal Reserve System had not existed, this mad episode would have ended much sooner for want of bank credit.... What the Federal Reserve System did was to force into the hands of the banking world a vast amount of surplus credit and money – much more than there was any legitimate need for – and this was done with full intent to make interest rates fictitiously low in New York. The effects were far reaching, uncontrollable, and at last disastrous.... The banks did not need this credit and had not asked for it.... Naturally, they loaned it to Wall Street brokers and speculators, and what these did with it was to foment a speculation nobody was able afterward to stop.

Fed policy makers interpreted the elevated P/E ratio on the NYSE as deriving from a speculative bubble.[3] That is, they believed that the price of stocks (P) derived from the self-fulfilling expectation that a price rise today would generate a price rise tomorrow. Irving Fisher presented the counter argument. He argued that the price of stocks was high because investors expected high earnings (E) in the future because of high productivity growth.

On October 29, 1929, Irving Fisher (1929 [1997], 6–9) gave a speech arguing that the NYSE was not overvalued. He emphasized the future effects on productivity of the change from scientific invention as the haphazard discoveries of individuals like Watt (steam engine), Arkwright (spinning machine), and Cartwright (power loom) to the systematic pursuit of scientific invention and its application in industry:

There has been a changed expectation on the part of the investor as to future earnings, for many reasons. The first reason for expecting future earnings is that we are

---

[2] On August 1925, M1 reached $26.2 billion. At the cyclical peak on August 1929, four years later, M1 was only $26.7 billion, an annualized growth rate of 0.5%. In 1927 and 1928, M1 grew at -1.1% and -0.1%. In those years, the CPI fell -1.9% and -1.2%. By these measures, monetary policy was contractionary.

[3] "At the end of 1927, the price-dividend ratio [of the NYSE] was around 23.... The stock market peaked in the first week of September [1929]" at 32.8 (Cogley 1999, 1).

now applying science and invention to industry as we never applied it before.... Invention is a profession.... [T]here is a "hook-up" between the university and business.... The most important mass production today is the mass production of inventions in the American Telephone & Telegraph Company laboratory, and in the General Electric Company's laboratory, in the laboratory of the Allied Chemical and Dye Corporation.... [I]n the automobile business, obsolescence is the life of trade, which merely means that old inventions are being superseded by new.... All the resources of modern chemistry, metallurgy, electricity, are being utilized.

Fisher (1929 [1997], 12) also emphasized the importance of price stability in the 1920s:[4]

[W]e have had an immense impulse towards prosperity through a stable price level.... If the physical yardstick by which we measure cloth were to vary, evidently contracts in terms of cloth would be confused.... The same is true of money, only a hundred times as true.... Dollars are used wherever yards are used, or kilowatts, or any other unit, and yet the dollar is the only unit of commerce that has been essentially unstable.

Starting in 1928, the Board of Governors and the New York Fed debated how to prick the presumed bubble in equity prices. The board wanted to use quantitative measures to restrict credit used for speculative purposes. That is, it wanted to restrict use of the discount window for banks making loans to brokers for the purchase of stocks on margin. In opposition, the New York Fed argued that, because credit is fungible, banks would circumvent quantitative restrictions. The New York Fed won the debate and began to raise the discount rate in early 1928 to engineer asset price deflation. In 1927, the New York Fed discount rate was 3.5 percent and the commercial paper rate 4 percent (Figure 4.3). In September 1929, the discount rate was 6 percent and the paper rate 6.25 percent. A business cycle peak occurred in August 1929.[5]

If Fisher was correct, the P/E ratio on the NYSE was high because the expectation of high future real returns justified a contemporaneously high price. If so, the attempt by the Fed to lower the nominal value of stocks was

[4]   Tavlas (2011) pointed out that the economists William T. Foster and Waddill Catchings were also contemporaneous critics of the Fed and predicted that the Fed's contractionary policy would lead to recession. Like Fisher, Foster and Catchings argued that the level of equity prices was an inappropriate target for the Fed. Similarly, they argued that the Fed should target stability of the price level and believed that the death in 1928 of Benjamin Strong, governor of the New York Fed, caused the Fed to move away from the control of the quantity of bank credit to the real-bills objective of preventing the speculative use of credit.

[5]   The best critique of monetary policy in this period remains Currie (1934). See also Roberts (2000) and Burgess (1964).

comparable to a central bank like the Bank of England in the post–World War I period lowering the pound price of gold to its prewar parity. The price level had to fall.

After the October 1929 stock market crash, the New York Fed steadily lowered its discount rate and, as a result, money-market rates. The discount rate went from 6 percent in October 1929 to 2 percent in January 1931. However, the Fed did not push down rates in a forceful, determined way with the intention of taking whatever action was required to revive economic activity. Why? The reluctance of the Fed to undertake open-market purchases and to lower the discount rate in a dramatic way reflected the majority opinion that low rates of interest would revive the speculation that had created the stock market bubble and would impede the required liquidation.

Wheelock (1991, 101) cited Harris (1933, 622), who referred to the 20 percent increase in the stock market from November 1929 to April 1930 as an explanation for why the Fed was reluctant to ease sufficiently to revive economic activity:

The hesitation on part of reserve authorities can be easily condoned. The incipient stock market boom, which set in in the spring of 1930, necessarily was followed by hesitation.

Wheelock (1991, 101) also cited Hayek (1932 [1984], 130), who criticized the reduction in interest rates after the October 1929 market crash as

preventing the normal process of liquidation, and that as a result the depression has assumed more devastating forms and lasted longer than before.... It is quite possible that we would have been over the want long ago and that the fall in prices would never have assumed such disastrous proportions, if the process of liquidation had been allowed to take its course after the crisis of 1929.

Most famously, Friedman and Schwartz (1963a) chronicled the policy debate within the Fed in this period. Those advocating monetary ease to stimulate bank lending and economic activity included Winfield Riefler and Carl Snyder, staff members at the New York Fed and, initially, the directors of the New York Fed. In June 1930, the latter criticized a proposal to make only a modest open-market purchase and noted "that our difficulties of credit administration have grown largely out of our disposition to postpone action and to administer remedies in homeopathic doses" (cited in Friedman and Schwartz 1963a, 369). George Harrison, governor of the New York Fed, appeared to have no clear beliefs of his own but rather tried to find common ground between those advocating easing and those opposing easing. In his notes from June 1930, Harrison noted a "real difference of opinion among those deemed capable of forming a judgment, as to the power of cheap and abundant credit, alone, to bring about improvement in business and commodity prices" (cited in Friedman and Schwartz 1963a, 370).

In September 1930, Eugene Meyer replaced Roy Young as governor on the board. Meyer advocated the open-market purchases that started in April 1932. However, Meyer was also irrevocably committed to maintenance of the gold standard. As documented by Butkiewicz (2008, 298), Meyer "delayed pursuing open-market purchases due to concerns about the high level of foreign deposits relative to United States monetary gold." Open-market purchases lowered market interest rates and encouraged the exodus of foreign deposits in New York banks and gold from the United States. Meyer supported the dramatic increases in the discount rate made in October 1931 and February and March 1933 to arrest gold outflows.

Within the Fed, critics of expansionary monetary policy to stimulate economic activity predominated. They opposed the monetary easing undertaken by the New York Fed after the stock market crash in October 1929 as delaying the necessary "natural liquidation" (cited in Friedman and Schwartz 1963a, 367). The governors of the regional Reserve banks were especially vocal. As a result, the Fed lowered interest rates only reluctantly out of fear that ease in credit markets would reignite the speculation universally held responsible for the boom-bust cycle. Meltzer (2003, 294) quoted a policy statement of the Federal Reserve's Open Market Committee in January 1930:

[It] is inexpedient [to] attempt to stimulate business when it is perhaps on a downward curve ... in a vain attempt to stem an inevitable recession.... The majority of the Committee is not in favor of any radical reduction in the bill rate or radical buying of bills which would create an artificial ease or necessitate a reduction in the discount rate.

Friedman and Schwartz (1963a, 372) reported that in November 1930:

The Philadelphia Bank objected to "the present abnormally low rates for money" as an interference "with the operation of the natural law of supply and demand in the money market ..." and concluded ... "We have been putting out credit in a period of depression, when it was not wanted and could not be used."

Many in Congress pressured the Fed for monetary stimulus. Especially, Reserve bank governors (later called presidents) resisted in part because of concerns about the limited amount of their free gold.[6] In response,

---

[6] By law, the regional Reserve banks had to hold a reserve in gold of at least 40% against Federal Reserve notes, and currency outflows had increased the amount of Federal Reserve

Congress passed the Glass-Steagall Act on February 27, 1932. The act loosened the gold cover requirement against Federal Reserve notes by including government securities as eligible collateral. It also provided for discounting by the Reserve banks of a wider class of bank assets including government securities.

In April 1932, the Fed began large-scale purchases of government securities. Although as Friedman and Schwartz (1963a, 363) wrote, "The open market operation of 1932 was acceded to largely under Congressional pressure and with the new Glass-Steagall Act ostensibly permitting release of the System's expansionary powers. The operation was terminated in August, shortly after Congress adjourned." Although Fed policy makers were split over the desirability of open-market purchases, with most regional Reserve bank presidents very much opposed, they all agreed that the transmission mechanism for monetary policy was through bank lending.[7] In his diary, Governor Hamlin quoted Governor Meyer as saying, "[I]f damned hoarders would cease hoarding and the damned banks begin loaning, all would be well" (cited in Butkiewicz 2008, 288).

When banks accumulated excess reserves in response to the open-market purchases without increasing lending, Fed policy makers agreed that stimulative monetary policy had failed.[8] *Time* (May 30, 1932, 12) wrote:

[M]ember banks were not carrying out their end of this credit-expansion scheme. They let the Reserve's funds stack up unused at the Reserve banks instead of piping it out to customers.... Charged with economic cowardice, the banks defended themselves with the assertion that no good borrowers were now seeking loans.

Butkiewicz (2008, 290, 293) supported this interpretation of Fed thinking and cited evidence that a renewed outflow of gold "probably destroyed

---

notes outstanding. The remainder of the backing for notes could either be more gold or the eligible paper the Reserve banks received as collateral in their rediscounting of paper offered by member banks using the discount window. Open-market purchases, however, reduced rediscounting at the window and thus reduced the amount of eligible paper available for backing Federal Reserve notes. Because banks then had to pledge more of their gold against notes, they had less free (unpledged) gold.

[7] *Fortune* (1934, 122) magazine wrote:

[A]s a backing for currency [the Federal Reserve] held $2,129,000,000 of governments as of the end of last August [1932].... The whole Reserve was, in other words, engaged in the most flagrant interference with the Economic Law [the real-bills criterion for discounting].

[8] Writing in 1938 and commenting on the growth of bank excess reserves, Johnson (1939, 221) concluded that "a volume of excess reserves undreamed of before 1933" meant "the complete breakdown of the quantitative, monetary approach to the depression phase of the business cycle."

the nerve of the Federal Reserve authorities." The board's *Annual Report* (1932, 22) wrote that "steps should be taken to enlist the cooperation of bankers and business men in an effort to develop ways and means of making effective use of the funds which were being made available by the open-market operations of the System" (cited in Todd 1996, 107).

As *Time* (May 30, 1932, 12) reported, the regional bank governors organized committees of businessmen to encourage banks to make loans:

It was decided to continue open market operations.... The Board's decision meant that Governor Harrison would now try to buck his district's banks into line for credit expansion. Back in his Manhattan office Governor Harrison summoned a dozen big bankers and industrialists for a heart-to-heart. Governor Meyer bustled over from Washington to attend. It was forcefully explained that some method had to be found to get the Reserve's credit through the banks and out to the country. The Government had moved. The next move was up to private enterprise and initiative.... The businessmen were to canvass their fields for worthy borrowers and present such applications as they could find to their banking colleagues on the committee.

Friedman and Schwartz (1963a, 348) wrote:

[A]ccumulation [of excess reserves] contributed to adoption of the policy of keeping total government securities at the level reached in early August [1932]. Excess reserves were interpreted by many as a sign of lack of demand for bank funds, as meaning that monetary authorities could make "credit" available but could not guarantee its use, a position most succinctly conveyed by the saying, "monetary policy is like a string; you can pull on it but you can't push on it."

In summer 1932, policy makers believed that banks accumulated excess reserves passively in response to open-market purchases providing them with reserves and, as a result, monetary policy had no ability to influence the economy. However, banks had good reason to accumulate excess reserves after the additional stress imposed on the banking system by the increase in the New York Fed discount rate from 1.5 percent to 3.5 percent in October 1931 in response to the gold outflows triggered by Britain's departure from the gold standard. Starting in October 1931, member banks began borrowing heavily at the discount window. However, such borrowing carried the stigma of a bank suffering from reserve outflows. Starting in February 1932, banks began reducing their borrowed reserves and building up their excess reserves. Excess reserves went from $44 million in February 1932 to $526 million in December 1932.[9]

---

[9] Figures are from table 105, "Member Bank Reserve Balances, Required Reserves, Excess Reserves, and Borrowings by Class of Bank," Board of Governors (1943

Because Fed policy makers believed that the emergence of significant excess reserves demonstrated the impotence of monetary policy, they froze the size of the Fed's holdings of securities. Henceforth, the size of the monetary base and money creation would be subject to the vagaries of international gold flows and domestic currency drains from banks. As Leffingwell (1932c) from J. P. Morgan wrote in December 1932 to Harrison, governor of the New York Fed:

[T]he striking thing is that total reserve bank credit is down about 10% from the peak in July [1932], and is about the same as it was at the beginning of the year.... [H]aving sailed your ship across the Atlantic [undertaken open-market purchases of government securities] I fear you may scuttle her in sight of Sandy Hook.

BLAMING THE BANKERS

The public blamed the large banks for the Depression. Referring to the congressional investigation of 1933 into the causes of the financial collapse named after the chief investigator, Ferdinand Pecora, an assistant district attorney for New York County, Leffingwell (1933), referred to "an hysterical wave of banker-baiting." *Time* (1934) quoted the "political inflationist" Senator Thomas' reference to the "private selfish interests whose manipulations of our money and credit brought on the most destructive and costly panic in history." *Harpers Magazine* (Greer 1933, 539 and 544) contained the following commentary:

[T]he large banks which got into difficulties and failed, or barely escaped failure, did so solely because of the kind of business they transacted. They deliberately extended their activities beyond the proper function of commercial banking, not because they were driven to do so by the necessity of obtaining adequate earnings but because of the inordinate greed of their managers for profits. They used the funds of their depositors for speculation, whether in the form of purchasing high-yield but low-grade securities, or making long-term loans against real estate mortgages.... If the lending activities of the banks are limited to operations arising out of the production of goods and services ... then the purchasing power created by the banks will correspond exactly to the needs of the economic community.

The *Northwestern Banker* (1932, 1) reproduced the complaint of an Iowa banker:

Most of our financial difficulties past and present have been due to "easy credits." We know from long experience that far too many people buy automobiles and luxuries on the installment plan, which they can not afford to buy, and would not think of buying if they had to pay the full purchase price at one time.

A *Fortune* magazine article in December 1932 (cited in Grant 1992, 222) commented on the nation's desire to punish the "banksters:"

Out of wrath come none but misbegotten offspring. Our danger now is that we shall legislate in wrath, letting the desire to punish our present banks outstrip our efforts to obtain a better banking system.

Grant (1992, 222–3) wrote of the congressional demand for the Reconstruction Finance Corporation (RFC) to disclose publicly the names of the banks to which it had lent and of the congressional pillorying of Charles E. Mitchell, chairman of the National City Bank, who had earned more than $1 million in salary and bonus in 1929:

Never had a banker, any banker, seemed less worthy of 1 million tax-free dollars than Mitchell did in February 1932. Standing in cold lines outside in closed banks, Americans had ample time to reflect on the difference between their lot and his. In the *American Mercury*, Clifford Reeves had written a few months earlier: "The title of banker, formerly regarded as a mark of esteem in the United States, is now almost a term of opprobrium."

The public associated the Fed with Wall Street bankers, whom it blamed for the Depression. Rep. Louis McFadden (1932), who was chairman of the House Committee on Banking & Currency, (D-PA), stated:

[W]e have in this country one of the most corrupt institutions the world has ever known. I refer to the ... Fed.... This evil institution has impoverished and ruined the people of these United States, has bankrupted itself, and has practically bankrupted our government. It has done this ... through the corrupt practices of the moneyed vultures who control it.

DEBATE OVER THE MONETARY STANDARD

Fed policy makers in the Depression could not throw off the tradition of real bills and abandon the gold standard by actively creating money to stimulate the expenditure of the public. Policy makers were bankers whose views on the monetary standard derived from the post–Civil War debates over how to respond to the deflation produced by the return to the gold standard in 1879. Figure 3.1 shows how adherence to the gold standard forced deflation in the late nineteenth century.[10] With the international gold standard, the

[10] The graph was prepared as part of the late nineteenth-century debate in Japan over whether to adopt the gold standard. It is figure 9 from a report by the Research Committee for the Reform of the Currency System (貨幣制度調査会) The Meiji government created the committee in 1893 to evaluate whether Japan should adopt the gold standard. The committee published the report in March 1895. Ukichi Taguchi created the figure

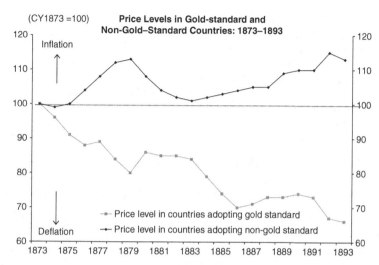

Figure 3.1. Price levels in gold-standard and non-gold-standard countries: 1873–1893. *Source(s)*: Research committee for reform of currency system, DB Global Markets Research.

level of prices among the gold-standard countries moved inversely to the real value of gold, which rose as the demand for gold reserves increased as countries joined the gold standard in the last part of the nineteenth century (Friedman and Schwartz 1963a, ch. 3; Friedman 1992, ch. 5).

The Depression era debates over the monetary standard pitted the eastern business establishment against the combination of forces composed of populists, western agrarian interests, and free-silver forces. Fed policy makers viewed the attack on the gold standard by this latter group as a threat to property rights and the established social order. Attempts to reflate through "managed money" revived the emotions raised by the late nineteenth-century debates over the monetary standard.

Calomiris (1992, 1) offered a succinct summary of the older debates:

Uncertainty regarding future monetary regimes was a central feature of American political and economic life in the second half of the nineteenth century. From 1862 to 1879 the U.S. operated on a greenback standard with no convertibility maintained between the greenback and gold. Following a decade of bitter political struggle over resumption of convertibility, the greenback became convertible into gold

to support his opposition to the gold standard. He succeeded in persuading the finance minister, Masayoshi Matsukata, and Japan did not join at that time. The graph and this information came from Seiji Adachi, senior economist at Japan Deutsche Securities Inc., Tokyo Branch.

in January 1879. But after resumption of convertibility, a new threat to the dollar emerged in the form of the "free-silver" movement. The goal of this movement was to re-establish a bimetallic standard, which would have led to a de facto switch to a depreciated silver dollar standard. These struggles were the defining characteristics of party platforms and national political campaigns. The soft- and hard-money wings of the Democratic party were described in terms of their positions on Greenback resumption in the 1870s and free coining of silver during the years of silver controversy.... William J. Bryan's famous speech at the Democratic convention in 1896 decried the "cross of gold" that threatened the crucifixion of America.

The defeat of Bryan by McKinley in the 1896 presidential election "settled" the issue of the monetary standard in favor of the gold standard and the monetary orthodoxy advocated by the eastern financial establishment. The Federal Reserve Act of 1913 contained gold cover provisions that required Federal Reserve notes to have 40 percent gold backing. At the same time, the reason for the creation of the Federal Reserve was to end bank panics like the one that had occurred in 1907. These two standards had different and conflicting criteria for money creation, but policy makers did not understand the contradictions. Because policy makers did not understand the responsibility for the determination of the price level under any monetary standard, they did not have to confront the contradictions.

Policy makers possessed only a legalistic not an economic understanding of the operation of the international gold standard. Free gold was the gold that each Federal Reserve bank held beyond what was required to back the currency it issued (Federal Reserve notes). After the United States returned to the gold standard with the end of World War I, the only time that the gold standard exercised any influence on domestic monetary policy was in fall 1919, fall 1931, and winter 1933 when gold outflows reduced free gold. In each instance, the Fed raised the discount rate sharply. The legal convertibility of the dollar into gold then exercised a sporadic, deflationary impact on the price level. Maintenance of the gold standard understood in this legalistic fashion along with balancing the federal budget was the bedrock of financial orthodoxy going into the Depression.

Apart from Governor Strong, who ran the New York Fed, and his staff member Carl Snyder, there was no understanding of the monetary standard created with the establishment of the Federal Reserve. The founders of the Fed had no intention of creating a central bank with the ability to create money. They wanted only to centralize reserves holdings at each of the regional Reserve banks. Through the discounting exclusively of real bills, the demand for credit would automatically regulate the supply of credit in a way that accommodated the needs of business while also limiting speculative excess. In reality, when the Fed gained its independence after World

War I, Governor Strong ran monetary policy discretionarily. That fact escaped public recognition.

A *Fortune* (1934, 115, 118) article offered a review of Fed history stressing departures from the real-bills doctrine:

The whole theory of the separation of bank and state was based upon the alleged necessity of removing the control of credit from the hands of individuals [financiers and politicians] who might exert it for ulterior purposes.... So far as volume of credit was concerned it was as automatic as human ingenuity could make it....

When the stock market started up in August, 1918, in anticipation of victory, Governor Strong ... would have liked to raise the discount rate.... But the Treasury still had its Victory Loan to float and Secretary Glass would not permit the step. The immediate result was the "veritable orgy of extravagance, waste, and speculation" which reached its height – or its depth – in the summer of 1920.... Governor Strong, convinced that the boom constituted a potential threat to the entire American economy, decided as soon as the dead hand of the Treasury was removed, to fight it.... [T]he country was saved from what might very well have been a precocious 1929....

From 1920 to 1925, the Federal Reserve Banks conducted their open-market operations and their rate changes with a view to the stabilization of the American economy ... forcing money into the market [with open-market purchases].

[In 1925] Governor Strong made his ... greatest effort to interfere willfully and humanly in the operation of the Economic Law [the real-bills criterion for discounting].... He determined to aid the United Kingdom to return to the gold standard.... It was a gallant effort. And it failed.... [In] early 1927 ... the stock market started on the rocket ride which ended with the gorgeous explosion and the beautifully falling flares of October, 1929.

Despite the unsettled character of the monetary standard in the United States after the world went off the gold standard in 1914, the legal adherence to the gold standard obscured the actual operation of the standard and prevented public discussion of it. The Depression revived the debate over the monetary standard that had occurred prior to 1896.

In the House of Representatives, various groups wanted government action to reverse deflation and to raise prices. Leffingwell (1932a) wrote Senator Glass, "I am fearful that the greenbackers and bimetallists and managed-money-men will run away with it. I am fearful that a suffering people will not tolerate a banking and currency system which ... failed them." The influence of the "greenbackers" appeared in the Thomas Amendment of the Agricultural Adjustment Act, passed May 12, 1933, which authorized the Fed to buy $3 billion in government securities to add to its holdings acquired in spring and summer 1932. The influence of the "bimetallists" also appeared in the Thomas Amendment. It authorized the president to direct U.S. mints to purchase all silver that was newly mined domestically at a price significantly above the market price. The Silver Purchase Act of June 19, 1934, required the secretary of the Treasury to purchase sufficient silver to raise its dollar price to $1.29 an ounce (Friedman and Schwartz 1963a, 483–5).

Financial orthodoxy opposed such experimentation with the monetary standard. However, this orthodoxy rested on numerous misconceptions. It held that market forces determined the price level as an agglomeration of factors reflecting the determination of various relative prices. Imbalances in production and the structure of prices inextricably linked recession and deflation. In recession, government needed to allow the working of the marketplace to correct the accumulated imbalances that depressed output and prices. Benjamin Anderson (1931, 4–10, 14), economist at Chase National Bank of New York, expounded this "equilibrium" view.

Equilibrium in economic life involves ... a proper balance between the prices of goods and the costs of production, including wages.... In credit matters, the equilibrium doctrine is far more interested in having a good *quality* of credit than it is in having a large *quantity* of credit.... The equilibrium doctrine looks upon periods of reaction and depression as periods of liquidation of credit and improvement of the quality of credit, as times for the paying of debts.... The equilibrium doctrine, calling upon individuals to work out their own problems and make their own adjustments and shifts, is a doctrine of hard work.

The great depression is due to an unbalanced economic situation: 1. Production is unbalanced.... 2. Prices are unbalanced.... 3. Costs have not fallen as much as prices.... In periods of crisis and depression the general rule has been that both prices and costs yield, and that, in the reduction of prices and costs, and in the restoration of a proper relation of prices to costs ... the foundation of recovery is laid.

H. Parker Willis (1933, 233, 245–6), who had advised Carter Glass in the writing of The Federal Reserve Act, criticized succinctly the

unsound and dangerous revival of the heresies of past generations in money and banking.... The root evil, as is now apparent in our whole programme of "recovery," whether under the Hoover or the Roosevelt Administration, is that of seeking to restore something that should never have existed – the price and business situation of pre-panic days, say, of 1926 or 1929.... [B]anking can never be safe or solvent under an artificial price level, and that the effort of assumed necessity to control or maintain prices is always the deadly foe of wise and safe credit extension. A prerequisite to the restoration of banking soundness is, in short, the total abandonment of any and all attempts to direct prices through what is termed "credit control."

Fed policy makers objected to the idea that the Fed could control the price level. In congressional hearings in 1928 on the Representative Strong bill requiring the Fed to stabilize the price level, Governor Adolph Miller (U.S. Congress 1928, 109, 348, 180, and 193) from the Board of Governors objected on the grounds that the Fed could not control prices and that it needed to retain discretion in the conduct of policy:

DR.MILLER: One of those assumptions [of the Representative Strong bill] is that changes in the level of prices are caused by changes in the volume of credit and currency; the other is that changes in the volume of credit and currency are caused by Federal [R]eserve policy. Neither of those assumptions is true of the facts or the realities. They are both in some degree figments – figments of scholastic invention – that have never found any very substantial foundation in economic reality, and less to-day in the United States than in other times.

[U]ndertaking to regulate the flow of Federal [R]eserve credit by the price index is a good deal like trying to regulate the weather by the barometer. The barometer does not make the weather; it indicates what is in process.

The total volume of money in circulation is determined by the community. The Federal [R]eserve [S]ystem has no appreciable control over that and no disposition to interfere with it.

REPRESENTATIVE STRONG: You think the law, then, could be changed so that it would read for the accommodation of commerce and business or at the will of the Federal Reserve Board?

DR.MILLER: It is the same thing.

REPRESENTATIVE STRONG: I am afraid it is.

In congressional hearings on the Goldsborough bill in April 1932, which would have required the Fed to return the price level to its higher level of the 1920s, Representative Strong urged George Harrison, governor of the New York Fed, to stabilize the price level (U.S. Congress 1932b, 513):

We have given them [members of the Federal Reserve Board] the powers to regulate the volume of money in circulation.... We have given them the greatest powers ever given to any group of men except in matters of life and death and liberty.... [Y]ou ought to now use the powers Congress has given you to stabilize the purchasing price of the dollar.

Harrison (U.S. Congress, 1932b, 485) refused, arguing that it was more important to retain flexibility to prevent asset price speculation (2008, 17):

[S]uppose ... the price level is going down, and the Federal [R]eserve [S]ystem begins to buy government securities, hoping to check the decline, and that inspires a measure of confidence, and a speculation is revived in securities, which may in turn consume so much credit as to require our sales of Governments. There was that difficulty in 1928 and 1929.

Governor Miller (U.S. Congress 1932c, 250) repeated this view that any attempt to control the price level would interfere with the Fed's responsibility to control speculation (the motivating factor in the reluctance with which the Fed lowered interest rates in 1930):

The average of commodity prices does not mean anything.... The price level is wholly metaphysical. It is a statistical summation of the movements of an infinite variety of commodities in a vast number of markets scattered over the face of the world.... [T]he commodity price level, with the stability it showed during those years [the 1920s], was a cover for one of the most vicious and costly, disastrous and destructive inflations this country or any country in a state of solvency had ever experienced.... [T]he thing to be expected in this country if we operated under a stabilization philosophy would be inflations.

THE ORIGINAL QUANTITATIVE EASING DEBATE: THE GOLDSBOROUGH BILL

The debate in the 1932 hearings on the Goldsborough bill presaged the debates among FOMC participants over quantitative easing in fall 2010. A relevant question arises: What have policy makers learned about the responsibilities of a central bank since 1932? How do central bankers, then and now, understand what they control and how they exercise that control? Because none of the participants in the current debate have articulated publicly their view of how the Fed controls inflation, the outside observer has no way of answering these questions. Nevertheless, there are strong similarities in the way in which Fed policy makers in 1932 and in the present day understood their powers.[11]

In two central respects, the testimony of Fed policy makers in the hearings over the Goldsborough bill displays continuity in views with the present. First, Fed officials firmly rejected any association between monetary policy and money creation. They viewed monetary policy through the perspective of financial intermediation. Second, they rejected the idea of conducting monetary policy within the framework of a rule as opposed to discretion.

---

[11] In one respect, the debate over the responsibilities of a central bank changed in the post–World War II period. After the war, a professional consensus existed that the government was responsible for the management of aggregate demand. By the 1970s, the consensus view, represented by Keynesian economics, had changed to admit monetary policy as a central influence on aggregate demand. With the rise of inflation in the postwar period, the distinction between nominal and real aggregate demand became relevant. However, how to give that distinction relevance in terms of what the central bank can and should control remains controversial within the economics profession. In the postwar period, the dominant Keynesian view favored a hard-wired relationship between nominal and real aggregate demand over the relevant policy-making horizon. Current debate suggests that FOMC participants have made no progress in reconciling these "Phillips curve" issues among themselves.

Rep. T. Alan Goldsborough (D-MD) revived the 1920s collaboration between Irving Fisher and Rep. James F. Strong (R-KS). With the support of Irving Fisher, in hearings in 1926, 1927, and 1928, Representative Strong had promoted a bill requiring the Fed to stabilize the price level.[12] On May 2, 1932, the House of Representatives passed the Goldsborough bill legislating that "the average purchasing power of the dollar ... for the years 1921 to 1929 ... shall be restored and maintained by the control of the volume of credit and currency." That is, the bill directed the Fed to raise commodity prices to their 1921–1929 average and to stabilize them at that level.[13] Goldsborough advocated that the Fed commit to a policy of steady money creation through open-market purchases until the price level returned to its 1926 level.

Spokesmen for the Fed argued that monetary policy exercised its influence over the way in which it influenced financial intermediation, but the Fed was only one influence on that intermediation. Governor Meyer (U.S. Congress 1932c, 214) testified of the Fed's open-market operations, "We are exercising a power which is designed to make funds available to the member banks more freely and thereby help to improve business conditions." Governor Miller (U.S. Congress 1932c, 247) explained, "Credit is created in increasing volume only as the community wishes to use more credit." Willford King (U.S. Congress 1932b, 187), economics professor at New York University, responded critically:

[W]e have heard over and again, that the Federal [R]eserve banks have been doing everything possible to meet the present emergency, because they have lowered the interest rates, and nobody wants to borrow.... [However] the only way you can put money into circulation is to buy something. If they [the Federal Reserve banks] buy Government bonds, the man that got the money ... is going to buy something else with it.

Irving Fisher (U.S. Congress 1932c, 26) continued the criticism:

The people for and against this bill are composed, to my mind, of two classes: the banker-minded who uses money as a commodity for making profit, and those who believe that money should be used as a measure of value and for the purpose of exchange between the people who buy and sell their labor and their goods.

---

[12] See Hetzel (1985) and U.S. Congress (1926; 1927; 1928).

[13] This effort was quixotic given the political environment at the time, especially the opposition of Carter Glass in the Senate. Benjamin Anderson (1932) wrote:

I do not believe that the Goldsborough Bill, with its absurd proposal to restore the price level of 1921–29, has any chance at all legislatively. It is opposed by the President of the United States, who would undoubtedly veto it if it were presented to him, and there is evidence that the Senate does not take it seriously.

The exchange between Representative Goldsborough and Governor Harrison in the House hearings on the Goldsborough Bill on April 13, 1932, illustrated the fundamental disagreement over whether to conduct policy disciplined by a rule or subject to the ongoing discretion of the policy maker. Goldsborough argued that an articulated, explicit policy would render monetary policy potent through its constructive influence on expectations. In contrast, Harrison (U.S. Congress 1932b, 462–71) argued that the impact of individual actions (open-market purchases) undertaken by the Fed had been overwhelmed by adverse events that made bankers pessimistic about the future:

HARRISON: [T]hat pressure [excess reserves] does not work and will not work in a period where you have bank failures, where you have panicky depositors, where you have a threat of huge foreign withdrawals, and where you have other disconcerting factors such as you have now in various sorts of legislative proposals which, however wise, the bankers feel may not be wise. You then have, in spite of the excess reserve, a resistance to its use which the reserve system can not overcome.

GOLDSBOROUGH: [I]n anything like normal times, specific directions to the Federal [R]eserve [S]ystem to use its power to maintain a given price level will tend to decrease very greatly these periods, or stop these periods of expansion and these periods of deflation which so destroy confidence and produce the very mental condition that you are talking about.... I do not think in the condition the country is in now we can rely upon the *action* of the Federal [R]eserve [S]ystem without the announcement of a *policy*. A banker may look at his bulletin on Saturday or on Monday morning and see that the Federal Reserve [S]ystem has during the previous week purchased $25,000,000 worth of Government securities. But that does not restore his confidence under present conditions because he does not know what the board is going to do next week.... If this legislation ... were passed, the Federal Reserve Board could call in the newspaper reporters and say that Congress has given us legislative directions to raise the price level to a certain point, and to use all our powers to that purpose, and we want you to announce to banks and public men at large that we propose to go into the market with the enormous reserves we now have available under the Glass-Steagall Act and buy $25,000,000 of Governments every day until the price approaches the level of that of 1926.... [I]f the bankers and business men knew that was going to be the policy of the Federal [R]eserve [S]ystem, ... it would restore confidence immediately ... and the wheels of business would turn [italics supplied].

HARRISON: [W]e have bought since the crash in the stock market approximately $800,000,000 to $850,000,000 of additional Government securities.... [H]owever, when after all the huge withdrawals of currency for hoarding purposes ... we had in the system a relatively small proportion of free gold.... [W]hile I would have liked to proceed further and faster last year, I was adverse to doing so till we had the protection of the Glass-Steagall bill.... Perhaps we could have gone a little faster without clogging the banks by giving them too much excess reserve. If you give them too much excess reserve when they lack confidence it is just like flooding the carburetor of an automobile.

[D]iscounts in the system have gone down.... [I]n our experience in the Federal Reserve [S]ystem such a reduction in discounts or borrowings from the [R]eserve banks operates as a real relaxation in the attitude of lending banks.... Let us suppose we should go ...

GOLDSBOROUGH: [interrupting] No; not whether you had determined to go so many millions further, but that you had announced a policy after the passage of this bill that you were going to raise the price level to a certain point and you were going to buy till that was done. That is a very different proposition.

HARRISON: Yes; I think so. I think it is a very much more difficult proposition because I do not think there is any one power or authority in the world that can say they are going to raise the price level. There are so many factors to be taken into consideration; unless you have control of all of them (even human psychology), you cannot be assured you can raise it.... I think to make a statement of that character [raise the price level] to the public and to the world would be one of the most unfortunate things the system could do, because primarily they would not be able to deliver all by themselves.

Representative Strong (U.S. Congress, 1932c, 28) testified:

[I]f the people of this country knew that through the Federal [R]eserve [S]ystem they were going to pour money out until there was a reaction, they would have a restoration of confidence.... I do not think they [powers given to the Fed by Congress] ought to be used to regulate the price of stocks and bonds. I think they ought to be used to stabilize the purchasing power of the dollar.

In Senate hearings on the Goldsborough bill, Governor Meyer expressed misgivings similar to his colleagues. Meyer (U.S. Congress 1932c, 216) believed that the control of the price level required control of individual prices: "If you want to fix a price level or fix prices you have got to control production." Meyer also opposed the reflation mandate. *Time* (1932) reported:

The gist of his [Meyer's] opposition was that the measure imposed an impossible order upon the Federal Reserve because prices depend upon many factors beyond its control.... Said he: "I don't think any small group of men should be entrusted with fixing price levels. I wouldn't want to be entrusted with such a power."

Governor Meyer argued that speculation in the housing market had driven the 1926 price level to an unsustainable level. Financial innovation increasing capital market funding for housing promoted the speculation. What was important in reviving economic activity was the confidence of the businessman, and for that a balanced budget was paramount. Any explicit mandate from Congress would limit the desirable discretion necessary in the exercise of monetary policy. Meyer (U.S. Congress 1932c, 167, 175, 186, 191, and 217) testified:

In this period [after 1921] a very important financial development occurred which was the means by which the construction activity passed from the legitimate stage into the speculative stage.... That was the development of a new channel to large amounts of capital through the real-estate bond market. Real-estate bonds had been known previously on a small scale, locally. But in this period of rapid development and profitable activity there was found a way to large amounts of the savings of the country, through the real-estate bond market, on a scale which had never existed before. That led to speculative building where the business was carried on for the profit of the people who were doing it rather than to meet legitimate need; and to overbuilding....

[W]hen you talk of this operation as sufficient to control a price level at any particular point, you are thinking in terms of a price level which was established by the greatest building activity in the history of the country. It may be that it is the right price level, but it was a price level established with a very extraordinary background of building activity.

An economically youthful country ... is likely to have periods of extreme activity and of speculation at the end of it, and reactions and depressions after it.... [S]ometimes a large number of people, en masse, get optimistic and overdo things; then they get pessimistic and overdo things on the other side....

I feel that the balancing of the Budget is becoming a fundamentally important factor in rebuilding confidence in business.... I do not think a resolution of Congress can contemplate all the circumstances under which that judgment [about monetary policy] must be exercised, and therefore any definite policy laid down by a congressional enactment, in my opinion, is inappropriate and unwise.

Governor Meyer resisted any commitment about the extent of the Fed's open-market purchases (U.S. Congress 1932c, 210–11):

SENATOR COUZENS: What is your program for the next few weeks?
GOVERNOR MEYER: It is to continue at a rate to be determined as conditions, which have to be judged from time to time, justify.
SENATOR COUZENS: In other words, it is a secret?
GOVERNOR MEYER: No; [T]here is not any fixed schedule, and there ought not to be, because it is a question of fine judgment as to what the best policy is.

POLITICAL IMPASSE OVER THE MONETARY STANDARD

In the Senate, in contrast to the House, there was no willingness to change the monetary standard. Any banking legislation would have to pass through the Banking and Currency Committee, and Carter Glass, who was a member, wanted to reinforce the real-bills aspects of the Federal Reserve, the circumvention of which he blamed for the stock market crash and

Depression. In March 1932, he introduced a bill to limit severely the ability of the Federal Reserve banks to discount securities as opposed to real bills "to prevent the undue diversion of funds into speculative operation" (U.S. Congress March 1932a). The deep divisions within Congress meant that Roosevelt could decide on his own how to change the monetary standard.

FOUR

Monetary Policy and Bank Runs in the Great Depression

The Great Depression launched macroeconomics as a major discipline within economics. Nevertheless, after more than seventy years, economists continue to argue over the shocks that caused it. The issue is one of "identification." The identification scheme used throughout this book is quantity-theoretic in spirit. For a monetary regime to be sustainable and to avoid imparting shocks to the economy, the central bank must follow a rule that provides a nominal anchor and that allows market forces to determine real variables like real GDP and employment.

The two most important monetary experiments of the twentieth century were the real-bills experiment of the Great Depression and the full-employment experiment of the stop-go era. Both began with considerable expectational stability over the behavior of prices. In both episodes, the Fed failed to provide a nominal anchor, in the first case through pursuit of the control of presumed speculative behavior on Wall Street and by banks and in the second case through pursuit of the control of the unemployment rate. Neither monetary regime was sustainable. This chapter first summarizes monetary policy in the Great Contraction (August 1929 to March 1933). It then concludes with a review of the literature on bank runs in the Great Depression and the findings of this literature with regard to the issue of whether banks regulated only by market discipline are inherently unstable.

THE FED'S PROCEDURES FOR CONTROLLING THE INTEREST RATE

Essential to understanding monetary policy in the Great Contraction is an understanding of how the Fed controlled the nominal interest rate by controlling the marginal cost of funds to banks (Riefler 1930; Wheelock 1991). Likewise, an understanding of how monetary contraction turned to monetary expansion after March 1933 requires an understanding of the collapse of these procedures and their replacement by exogeneity of the monetary base expanded through gold inflows.

An understanding of the nature of the monetary regime is essential to the identification of the shock that produced the Great Contraction. Monetarists have used a reserves-money-multiplier framework with exogeneity of reserves to attribute to money a role as an independent shock. Within this framework, bank runs and an increase in the currency/deposit ratio acted as independent forces affecting money. However, that scheme for identification has lacked universal appeal because of the endogeneity of reserves when the central bank uses an interest rate as its instrument.

The quantity-theory critique of monetary policy advanced here is more radical. In a monetary regime characterized by the exogeneity of reserves, whereas monetary policy can be highly contractionary, it is a sustainable regime. In the spirit of the real-bills critique of Mints (1945), the argument advanced here is that the monetary regime was not sustainable because it lacked a nominal anchor. The Fed created a deflationary spiral of self-reinforcing increases in real interest rates and monetary contraction that ended only with the change in the monetary regime that occurred with the inauguration of Franklin Roosevelt in March 1933.

Figure 4.1 illustrates diagrammatically the monetary policy procedures of the Fed during the Great Contraction. With them, through open-market purchases, the New York desk supplied an amount of nonborrowed reserves (NBR_0) less than the demand for reserves by the banking system (R_0). Banks had to obtain the difference through recourse to the discount window (BR_0). The Reserve banks rationed use of the discount window by making surveillance of the borrowing bank increase with the duration and size of borrowing. As a result of the stigma associated with use of the discount window, the marginal cost of borrowing rose above the discount rate in a way that depended on the collective amount of borrowing by banks.[1] In sum, the marginal cost of funds to banks was the sum of the discount rate plus a markup that varied positively with the amount of borrowing at the discount window.

With the Fed's borrowed-reserves operating procedures, reductions in the discount rate lowered money-market interest rates directly. Also,

---

[1] These procedures for controlling the interbank (funds) rate were similar to the nonborrowed reserves operating procedures adopted by the Fed October 6, 1979 (Goodfriend 1983; Hetzel 1982). For a discussion of the discount window in the 1930s, see Bordo and Wheelock (2010, especially the section "The Discount Window – A Flawed LLR Mechanism").

The Market for Bank Reserves

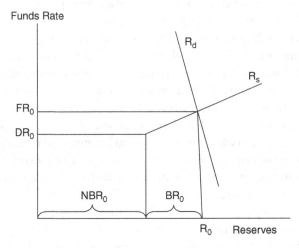

Figure 4.1. The market for bank reserves.
Note: The market for bank reserves. R is bank reserves. R_d is the reserves demand schedule of the banking system and R_s is the reserves supply schedule. FR is the funds rate. DR is the discount rate. NBR and BR are nonborrowed and borrowed reserves. The 0s denote particular values.

open-market purchases increased the nonborrowed reserves of banks, reduced their borrowed reserves, and reduced money-market interest rates by lowering the cost to banks of obtaining the marginal dollar of reserves. Figure 4.2 illustrates a reduction in money-market rates achieved through a reduction in the discount rate (from DR_0 to DR_0') and an increase in nonborrowed reserves from NBR_0 to NBR_0'. The increase in nonborrowed reserves lowers the cost of obtaining reserves by reducing borrowed reserves and, as a result, the excess of market rates over the discount rate. The discount rate remains as a floor for interest rates.

The regional Fed banks were free to set their discount rates independently. Figure 4.3 displays the discount rate set by the New York Fed and the average of the discount rates set by the other regional Feds. As shown, during the Great Contraction, the regional Reserve banks set their discount rates at significantly higher levels than New York. For example, in November 1930, the discount rate in New York was 2.5 percent while the discount rate at all other regional Reserve banks was at 3.5 percent. As a result, the discount rates for the regional Reserve banks other than New York set a floor on the marginal cost of funds for banks, a floor that was significantly in excess of the discount rate in New York. In principle, the

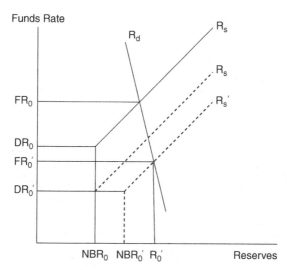

Figure 4.2. Increase in nonborrowed reserves and decrease in discount rate.
Note: R_s' shows a reduction in the discount rate. R_s'' shows the combined effects of a reduction in the discount rate and an open-market purchase by the Fed that increases nonborrowed reserves (NBR).

regional banks with a correspondent relationship with a bank in New York could have borrowed from their New York banks, which in turn could have borrowed at their lower discount rate.

That arbitrage did not happen. Starting with the stock market crash of October 1929, the New York City banks reduced and then basically eliminated discount-window borrowing by early 1930. The New York Fed had pressured the New York City banks to limit their borrowing, which it believed financed the call money loans that it held responsible for speculation on the NYSE (Grant 1992, 194). Moreover, "The regional Fed Banks interpreted the uniform excess of money market rates over the discount rate not as evidence of contractionary monetary policy but as evidence of an incentive for banks to borrow and speculate" (Hetzel 2008b, 16, citing Chandler 1958, 455–9). Some combination of the stigma for weakness attached to borrowing, the onset of recession in August 1929, Fed supervisory pressure, and the absence of loan demand caused the New York City banks to abandon the discount window. The important fact, however, is that outside New York banks continued to obtain reserves through the discount window. The marginal cost of funds to the banking system remained elevated because of the high level of discount rates at the regional Fed banks.

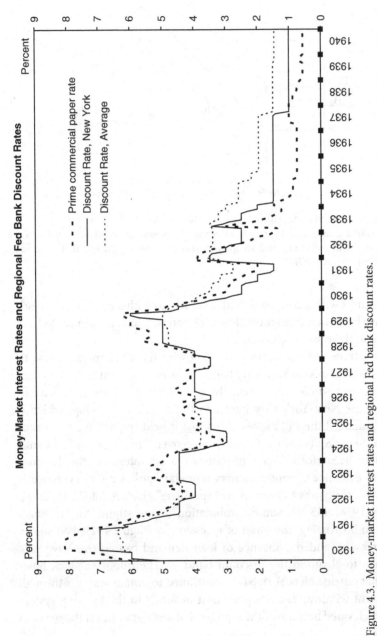

Figure 4.3. Money-market interest rates and regional Fed bank discount rates.

Note: Monthly observations of the prime commercial paper rate and the discount rate from Board of Governors, *Banking and Monetary Statistics* (1943), tables 115 and 120. The solid line is the discount rate set by the New York Fed, and the dotted line is the average of the discount rates set by all the other regional Fed banks. Heavy tick marks indicate fourth quarter.

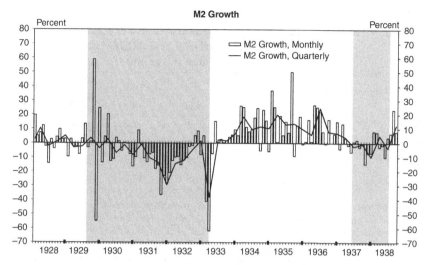

Figure 4.4. M2 growth.

Note: The bar chart shows monthly observations of annualized percentage changes in the monetary aggregate M2. The solid line shows annualized quarterly changes. Shaded areas indicate NBER recessions. Data from Friedman and Schwartz (Table 1, 1970). Heavy tick marks indicate December.

Figure 4.4 shows annualized monthly observations of M2 growth for the Great Contraction (the shaded area between the business cycle peak of August 1929 and trough of March 1933). The issue is whether the negative growth rates are evidence of an independent monetary shock or are a consequence of a negative real shock. The argument here is that negative money growth was required to maintain the excessively high level of nominal interest rates set by the Fed. The intensification of the monetary contraction in 1931 came about because of the way in which the expectation of deflation raised the real interest rate to which nominal market rates corresponded.

Table 4.1, reproduced from Hetzel (2008b), shows the commercial paper rate plotted in Figure 4.3. Because it fell below the discount rates set by the regional Reserve banks other than New York starting in 1930, it is a lower estimate of the marginal cost of reserves facing the majority of Fed member banks. The table constructs a measure of the real interest rate as the sum of the nominal interest rate and the measure of expected deflation from Hamilton (1992, table 7). The striking fact that emerges from the table is the high real interest rates that coincided with strong declines in real GNP starting in 1930. Those high real interest rates were much higher than the real interest rates consistent with the growth rate of output at its

Table 4.1. *Nominal and real rate*

Year	Commercial paper rate	Expected inflation	Real rate of interest	Real GNP growth	M1 growth	M2 growth
1929	5.8	−0.9	6.7	6.6	0.9	0.2
1930	3.6	−2.1	5.7	−9.6	−3.5	−2.0
1931	2.6	−7.1	9.7	−7.7	−6.6	−7.1
1932	2.7	−4.1	6.8	−13.8	−12.4	−15.4
1933T1	2.1	−6.1	8.2	−21.3	−17.8	−31.6
1933T2&T3	1.6	5.1	−3.5	14.2	6.0	4.9

Note: Commercial paper rate is from Board of Governors, Banking and Monetary Statistics (1943, table 120). Expected inflation is from Hamilton (1992, table 7). Hamilton's figures are for trimesters. The figures are the average of expected inflation for the three trimesters of the individual years. The real rate of interest is the commercial paper rate minus expected inflation. Real GNP growth is annual growth rates from Balke and Gordon (1986, appendix B). M1 and M2 growth are annual growth rates from Friedman and Schwartz (1970). 1933T1 is the first trimester (4 months) of 1933 and 1933T2&T3 is the last two trimesters (8 months) of 1933. For 1933T1, real GNP growth is for 1933Q1. For 1933T1&T2, it is the average of annualized quarterly growth rates for 1933Q2, 1933Q3, and 1933Q4. For 1933T1, M1 and M2 growth are the annualized growth rates from December 1932 through April 1933. For 1933T2&T3, they are the annualized growth rates from April 1933 through December 1933. The table is reproduced from Hetzel (2008b, table 3.1).

longer-run trend value. The identification of the shock that caused the Great Contraction then requires answering the question of how such high real interest rates arose.

As chronicled by Friedman and Schwartz (1963a) and Chandler (1958), starting in early 1928, the Fed initiated a contractionary monetary policy to burst the presumed speculative bubble on the NYSE. In terms of Figure 4.2, the Fed forced market rates up from FR_0' to FR_0 through open-market sales of securities to force banks into the discount window and through increases in the discount rate. Figure 4.5 shows member bank borrowed reserves as the difference between Federal Reserve credit (solid line) and Federal Reserve credit minus discounting (dotted line). Borrowed reserves went from $465 million in January 1928 to $1 billion in June 1928 and remained near that level until August 1929. As shown in Figure 4.3, the Fed raised the cost of those borrowed reserves by raising the discount rate. The New York Fed discount rate went from 3.5 percent in May 1928 to 6 percent in August 1929. Hamilton (1987, 145) wrote:

[I]n terms of the magnitudes consciously controlled by the Federal Reserve, it would have been difficult to design a more contractionary policy than that adopted in January of 1928.

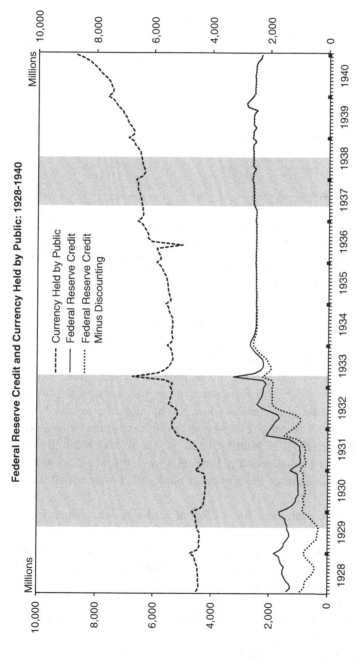

Figure 4.5. Federal Reserve credit and currency held by public: 1928–1940.

Note: "Federal Reserve bank credit outstanding" is the sum of the securities held by the Federal Reserve plus discount-window borrowing. The difference between the solid line (Federal Reserve credit) and the dotted line (Federal Reserve credit minus discounting) is discount-window borrowing. "Currency held by public" is money in circulation. All series from Board of Governors, *Banking and Monetary Statistics, 1943,* table 101, "Member Bank Reserves, Reserve Bank Credit and Related Items." Shaded areas indicate NBER recessions. Heavy tick marks indicate December.

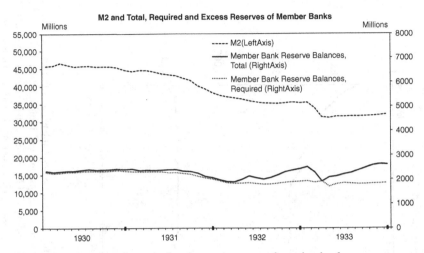

Figure 4.6. M2 and total, required and excess reserves of member banks.
Note: The level of M2 and total and required reserves of member banks. The difference between total and required reserves is excess reserves. Data are from Friedman and Schwartz (1970, table 1) and from Board of Governors, Banking and Monetary Statistics (1943, table 101). Heavy tick marks indicate December.

Following the stock market crash in October 1929, the Reserve banks lowered their discount rates, but never aggressively enough to maintain money creation and aggregate spending (see Chapter 3).

What role did bank runs play in the monetary contraction? Wicker (1996) argued for an empirical measure of the public's concern for the viability of the banking system based on the holding of currency by the public. By this measure, the public retained confidence in the banking system until summer 1931. In June 1931, the public held $4,463 million in currency, basically unchanged from June 1928 when it held $4,449 million (Figure 4.5). Until summer 1931, member bank reserves remained steady (Figure 4.6).

The evidence is weak for a direct effect of bank runs on declines in the money stock. Figure 4.7 plots monthly observations of the dollar change in M2 and in the deposits of suspended banks. The latter is an upper estimate of the deposit loss due to bank runs because it includes deposits in banks closed voluntarily by their owners and banks closed by regulators in the absence of a run. Deposits in suspended banks never amounted to a significant fraction of the decline in M2. The significant numbers for deposits in suspended banks for November and December 1930 arose from the failure of Caldwell and Company with headquarters in Tennessee.

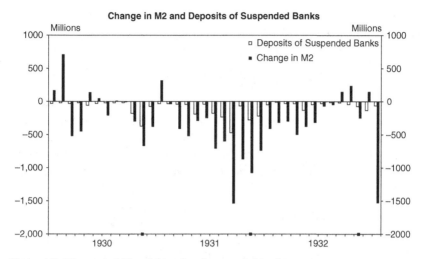

Figure 4.7. Change in M2 and deposits of suspended banks.
Note: Monthly observations. Data on M2 are from Friedman and Schwartz (Table 1, 1970). Data on suspended deposits are from *Federal Reserve Bulletin* (1937, table 13, 909). Heavy tick marks indicate December.

Starting in summer 1931, a significant outflow of currency from the banking system began. That outflow may have been a manifestation of a lack of depositor confidence in the banking system extending beyond the prior regional disturbances. Until July 1931, there had been no currency drains to the interior as measured by the stability in the "balances with domestic banks" of the weekly reporting Fed member banks in New York City. However, starting in August 1931, these balances declined sharply.[2] That outflow made monetary policy more contractionary.[3]

Note first that the size of the Federal Reserve's asset portfolio (Federal Reserve credit) began to increase in August 1931 and continued to increase, albeit irregularly, through early 1933 (Figure 4.5). The framework summarized in Figure 4.1 explains why this increase in the size of the Fed's

---

[2]   In the first seven months of 1931, these correspondent bank deposits had averaged $100 million. In the last five months, they averaged $73 million (Board of Governors *Banking and Monetary Statistics* 1943, table 49, "Weekly Reporting Member Banks in New York City").

[3]   The deposits/currency ratio did decline starting in October 1930, but because of a decline in deposits rather than an increase in currency (Friedman and Schwartz 1970, table 1). The decline in deposits reflected the stress on the banking system from contractionary monetary policy. As noted, both currency in circulation and bank reserves were stable through summer 1931.

portfolio nevertheless accompanied an increasingly restrictive monetary policy stance.

From July 1931 through February 1932, currency held by the public increased by $791 million, which member banks largely met through increased discount-window borrowing of $679 million (Figure 4.5). At the same time, the discount rates of the regional Reserve banks remained elevated.[4] Moreover, in response to gold outflows precipitated by the departure of Britain from the gold standard in September 1931, all the regional Reserve banks raised their discount rates.[5] Initially in summer 1931 with given discount rates and then with even higher discount rates in October 1931, increased discount-window borrowing raised the marginal cost of reserves to the banking system. Starting in August 1931, a significant increase occurred in the rate of decline in M2 (Figure 4.4).

Starting in spring 1932, monetary policy became less contractionary as a result of open-market purchases by the Fed (see Chapter 3). Government securities held by the Fed increased by somewhat more than a billion dollars from March 1932 through August 1932. An increase in free reserves (excess reserves minus borrowed reserves) registered the decline in pressure on the banking system to contract. Over the March through August interval, excess reserves increased by $211 million and borrowed reserves fell by $263 million.

However, because Fed policy makers interpreted the increase in the excess reserves of banks as evidence of the inability of monetary policy to stimulate growth in bank credit, they ceased making open-market purchases in August 1932. Nevertheless, stress on the banking system stabilized through early 1933. From July 1932 through January 1933, gold inflows and a reduction in currency in circulation somewhat more than offset an increase in excess reserves and a reduction in borrowed reserves. As shown in Figure 4.4, M2 stopped contracting by the end of 1932. In early 1933, the calm came to an end for two reasons: statewide bank closures (termed "holidays" because of their temporary nature) and gold

---

[4] In August 1931, the New York Fed had the lowest discount rate at 1.5%. Of the remaining regional Reserve banks, one had a rate of 2%, four had a rate of 2.5%, six had a rate of 3%, and one had a rate of 3.5%.

[5] The discount rate at the New York Fed went from 1.5% in September to 3.5% in October 1931. As of November 1931, ten of the regional Reserve banks had discount rates of 3.5% and two had discount rates of 4%. Wicker (1996, 93), using notes made by Governor Harrison, summarized remarks by Governor Meyer of the Federal Reserve Board to the directors of the New York Fed on October 15, 1931, "[A]n advance in the rate was called for by every known rule, and [he] believed that foreigners would regard it as a lack of courage if the rate were not advanced."

outflows motivated by fear the United States would abandon the gold standard.

When did the Fed's borrowed-reserves procedures actually end and a monetary regime based on exogeneity of the monetary base emerge? In principle, one can answer this question precisely. The old regime ended when banks accumulated sufficient excess reserves and reduced their discount-window borrowing to the point at which they no longer obtained the marginal dollar of reserves they demanded through the discount window. Banks began to accumulate excess reserves and reduce borrowed reserves in April 1932 (Figures 4.5 and 4.6).

The problem with setting a precise date is to know when borrowed reserves became frictional in the sense that the only banks in the window were distressed banks not representative of the banking system. After a spike in March 1933, borrowed reserves fell rapidly. In May 1933, M2 ceased falling; and in October 1933, it started growing. It is probable that the banking system became detached from Fed procedures for determining the cost of funds to the banking system through use of the discount window sometime in summer 1933. Not until the increases in reserve requirements in 1936 and 1937 would the Fed again actively influence monetary policy.

BANK RUNS IN THE GREAT DEPRESSION: SYMPTOM OR CAUSE OF MONETARY CONTRACTION?

Friedman and Schwartz (1963a) attributed the severity of the monetary contraction in the Depression to panic-induced bank runs of solvent but illiquid banks. According to Friedman and Schwartz (1963a, 308–9), a mild recession became the Great Contraction when bank runs exacerbated a moderate contraction in money:

In October 1930, the monetary character of the contraction changed dramatically.... A contagion of fear spread among depositors, starting from the agricultural areas.... [S]uch contagion knows no geographical limits.... [T]he most dramatic [failure] being the failure on December 11, 1930 of the Bank of the United States.

Given their assumption of a general banking panic, Friedman and Schwartz have to explain the failure of banks to declare a restriction of deposit withdrawals as occurred in the pre-Fed era. Friedman and Schwartz (1963a, 311) blame the Fed for the failure of banks to suspend deposit withdrawals:

[U]nder the pre-Federal Reserve banking system, the final months of 1930 would probably have seen a restriction, of the kind that occurred in 1907, of convertibility of deposits into currency. By cutting the vicious circle set in train by the search for liquidity, restriction would almost certainly have prevented the subsequent waves of bank failures that were destined to come in 1931, 1932, and 1933, just as restriction in 1893 and 1907 had quickly ended bank suspensions arising primarily from lack of liquidity.... [T]he existence of the Federal Reserve prevented concerted restriction.

An understanding of the role played by bank runs during the first cyclical downturn of the Depression is essential to a broader understanding of the cause of the Depression. Did those runs turn a moderate recession into the Great Depression, as argued by Friedman and Schwartz? Did the runs arise because of the inherent fragility of a financial system prone to panicked runs? An affirmative answer points to an error of omission by the Fed. Through its lender-of-last-resort role, it should have prevented the bank runs. A negative answer points to an error of commission by the Fed. The bank runs arose as a concomitant of the fundamental shock – a contractionary monetary policy.

There are three problems with the Friedman/Schwartz attribution of the severe monetary contraction during the Great Contraction to bank panics. First, their assertion that the recession intensified after the start of bank runs is at odds with the behavior of the decline in output. Second, the money-multiplier framework they use to explain the determinants of the money stock is inconsistent with the prevailing monetary regime of interest-rate targeting. Third, detailed studies of bank failures during the Great Contraction do not support their assertion of geographically widespread runs due to bank panics.

Pertinent to the first Friedman and Schwartz contention, the first bank runs began in November 1930 (1930Q4) with the failure of Caldwell & Company, which was headquartered in Nashville, Tennessee. As shown in Table 7.1, from the onset of the recession in 1929Q3 through 1930Q3, real GNP fell at an average annualized rate of -12.9 percent. This rate of decline, which predated the onset of bank runs, was hardly moderate and was comparable to the annualized decline in real output that occurred over the interval containing bank runs. Over this latter interval, which lasted from 1930Q4 through 1933Q1, real GNP declined at the annualized rate of -11.6 percent. In the two quarters that followed the initial bank run in 1930Q4 (1931Q1 and 1931Q2), annualized real GNP growth was actually positive at 4 percent (Balke and Gordon 1986, appendix B historical data, table 2).

Pertinent to the second Friedman and Schwartz contention, when the central bank uses the interest rate as its policy instrument, the reserves-money-multiplier framework is not a useful analytical framework for understanding money stock determination.[6] As explained previously, the currency drains from the banking system, which began in earnest in summer 1931, exercised their contractionary influence on money by forcing banks into the discount window and thereby increasing the marginal cost of reserves to the banking system. The Friedman and Schwartz argument about the failure of banks to restrict deposit withdrawals as they did in the pre-Fed era when the United States lacked a central bank is irrelevant. Given that the Fed maintained the level of interest rates at a level that required monetary contraction, restriction was an impotent tool for preventing monetary contraction.

Pertinent to the third Friedman and Schwartz contention, subsequent detailed studies of bank closings during the Great Contraction do not support their contention that panic-induced bank runs closed illiquid and solvent banks alike.[7] Unfortunately, the resulting literature attempted to infer, from the finding that closed banks were more likely insolvent than illiquid, something about the nature of the primal shock. Although relevant for the issue of whether an unregulated banking system is stable or inherently unstable, this literature had nothing to say about the source of the shock (real or monetary) that produced the stress on the banking system.

Peter Temin (1976) challenged the Friedman and Schwartz premise that the Depression originated in monetary contraction by arguing that a decline in autonomous expenditures rendered banks insolvent and that insolvency not illiquidity produced bank runs. Eugene White (1984) used bank balance sheet data to infer the causes of bank runs. Although White noted the stress placed on banks by the Fed's tight money policy starting in 1928, he documented the similarities between the banks failing in 1930 and those that failed in the 1920s. White's (1984, 119) conclusion does not support Friedman and Schwartz's bank panic hypothesis: "The bank failures in this crisis do not seem to have been different in character from failures in previous years."

The stress on the banking system of the high real interest rates produced by the deflation trap evidenced in Table 4.1 wreaked havoc with both bank liquidity and bank solvency. Given unit banking, the monetary contraction

---

[6] Friedman and Schwartz (1963a, 346) wrote:

It was the necessity of reducing deposits by $14 in order to make $1 available for the public to hold as currency that made the loss of confidence in banks so cumulative and so disastrous. Here was the famous multiple expansion process of the banking system in vicious reverse.

[7] For an overview of the relevant literature, see Wicker (1996) and Bordo and Landon-Lane (2010b).

required by high real interest rates occurred in part through bank failures. Depositors withdrew their deposits from smaller banks and redeposited them in larger banks, which they considered safer (Calomiris and Mason 1997 and 2003; Kaufman 1994; and Walter 2005). "[T]he failure rate was inversely related to bank size" (Mengle 1990, 7).[8] Kaufman (1994, 131) found little evidence in written sources before late 1932 of "concern with nationwide contagion."

What is remarkable is the stability of the banking system given the magnitude of the monetary shock inflicted on it. Currency outflows from the banking system did not appear to a significant extent until summer 1931. Between the business cycle peak of August 1929 and August 1931, industrial production had already declined by 34 percent.[9] The existence of bank runs in the Depression does not support the inherent-fragility view of banking that runs appear as a self-fulfilling prophecy among depositors closing banks indiscriminately regardless of their solvency.

The stability exhibited by the U.S. banking system also appeared internationally. Grossman (1994) demonstrated support for the hypothesis that causation ran from macroeconomic stress to financial market instability rather than conversely. Not all countries suffering from the Depression experienced financial crises. For example, Britain, Canada, Czechoslovakia, Denmark, Lithuania, the Netherlands, and Sweden escaped bank runs yet experienced high rates of unemployment. Grossman found that economic factors caused bank runs. He attributed the banking instability to stress placed on the financial system by the gold outflows and deflation forced by adherence to the gold standard (the delay in abandoning the gold standard).[10] After monetary stringency, the most important factor was

---

[8] Wicker (1996, 102) cited in support of this characterization of bank failures the increase from December 1929 to December 1932 in the ratio of member bank deposits to nonmember bank deposits and the ratio of the 101 weekly reporting member banks to all commercial banks, with the former categories of banks being larger and stronger.

Wicker (1996) and Temin (1989) contended that the first two sets of bank failures in 1930 and 1931 did not result from a national panic but rather were confined to specific regions and the insolvent banks within those regions. Calomiris and Mason (2003, 1616) also challenged the blame that Friedman and Schwartz placed on the Fed for the failure of clearinghouses to deal with runs through suspension and certificate creation. Their explanation is that solvent (large) banks were not threatened by the failure of insolvent (small) banks.

[9] See *Historical Statistics of the United States* 2006, table Cb28–31, "Indexes of industrial production: 1884–2003," Federal Reserve Board.

[10] Eichengreen and Portes (1987) also stressed the importance for bank failures of deposit withdrawals spurred by international capital flight due to overvaluation of exchange rates.

banking structure, in particular, the absence of nationwide branch banking. The willingness of the central bank to provide lender-of-last-resort assistance to banks was not a factor.

Calomiris and Mason (2003) constructed a model using panel data from individual bank balance sheets to explain the probability of bank failure over the interval from January 1930 to December 1933. Their explanatory variables fell into two groups. The variables that measured "fundamental bank attributes" served as proxies for insolvency and included measures of asset risk and leverage. The remaining variables served as proxies for "panic/contagion/illiquidity" and included indicator variables for the waves of bank runs dated by Friedman and Schwartz and measures of local contagion. Calomiris and Mason (2003, 1636) concluded "that prior to January 1933, the effects of panics – whether national, regional, or local – contributed little to the failure risk of Fed member banks in the nation as a whole.... [P]anic effects were not potentially important until January 1933."

Calomiris and Mason (1997) used a bank run in Chicago in June 1932 as a case study. They concluded that the cause of the run was a common shock to the value of bank assets, not contagion. Despite the run, mutual assistance among banks prevented the failure of solvent banks. The description of the events that led to the run by Calomiris and Mason (1997, 868) is consistent with "fears of bank insolvency" rather than contagion:

[B]y June 23, Chicago bank depositors had witnessed, in a matter of only two weeks, the collapse of some of the largest businesses in their city, several enormously costly cases of bank fraud, and a deepening of the municipal financial crisis as the result of the denial of relief to their city government by federal authorities. All of these stories were front-page news day after day in the two weeks leading up to the banking crisis, and the news grew progressively worse. In this light, it is not surprising that depositors became increasingly concerned about the ability of banks to pay out their deposits, and transferred bank deposits to riskless postal savings accounts.

Wicker (1996) supported the hypothesis that runs did not close banks indiscriminately regardless of their financial health but rather closed weaker banks. Wicker identified four windows of relatively intense run-induced bank closings: November 1930 to January 1931, April to August 1931, September to October 1931, and February to March 1933. According to Wicker, the two initial banks runs were regional in character. The first one was concentrated in the St. Louis Fed district; the second one occurred in the Chicago, Minneapolis, Cleveland, and Kansas City Fed districts with Toledo and Chicago especially affected; and the third one occurred in Pittsburgh, Philadelphia, and Chicago. "What are perhaps most conspicuous by their absence in 1930 and 1931 are crises in the New York money market. The banking panics of the Great Depression had their origin in the interior of the country with minimal repercussions in the central money market" (Wicker 1996, 22).

The epicenter of the first wave of bank suspensions was the failure of Caldwell and Company of Nashville, Tennessee, in November 1930. Caldwell controlled the largest chain of banks in the South and through a correspondent business held the deposits of many smaller banks. "The juxtaposition of the failure of Caldwell and Co. and its bank affiliates together with the prolonged drought captures the principal ingredients of an explanation of the high incidence of bank suspensions in the St. Louis Federal Reserve District" (Wicker 1996, 35). It is true that the Bank of United States (BUS) failed in New York City in December 1930, but Wicker (1996, 37) concluded "that the failure of BUS had negligible effects in contributing to the increased number of bank suspensions in December."

Contemporary commentary did not indicate that the failure of the Bank of United States resulted in runs that closed banks. Daiger (1931, 515) wrote:

When announcement was quietly made in December that the billion dollar merger [intended to save the Bank of United States] was not to be, every bank in New York suspected what was coming, and every possible preparation had been made to meet a descent of frightened depositors even upon the city's most highly solvent banks. Never had the banks of New York been in more liquid condition than they were then; never had they so much currency heaped high in their vaults, with as much more as should be needed ready to be rushed in armored trucks from the Federal Reserve. In one week the New York member banks of the Federal Reserve System obtained from it $170,000,000 of additional currency.... The failure of the Bank of United States caused runs on many other banks, but only one of them, a tenth of the size of the bank of United States and not a member of the Federal Reserve System, was unable to meet the emergency.

In the second wave of bank suspensions, Chicago banks were especially vulnerable because of strict unit banking laws that prevented branching into the suburbs. As a result of these laws, all the demand for real estate lending associated with the growth of the suburbs was met by newly created banks with portfolios heavily concentrated in mortgages. In Wicker's (1996, 69) words, "The vulnerability of Chicago banks to failure was idiosyncratic."

When describing the concentrated closing of banks due to runs, Wicker was careful to use the term "mini panic." For example, for the September–October 1931 wave of bank runs, Wicker (1996, 84, 99) identified Pittsburgh, Philadelphia, and Chicago as the "major centers of disturbance:"

The panic failed to engulf the largest banks in all three cities. In Pittsburgh and Philadelphia, the largest and the strongest banks mobilized support for some of the troubled banks and thereby contributed to allaying the fear and uncertainty. We have described the banking crises in each of the three cities as a mini panic since the brunt of the crisis was geographically constrained to certain parts of the city and mainly to specific bank classifications, namely savings banks including trust companies. Deposit losses amounted to no more than 8 percent of total bank deposits in each city.... The loss of confidence was confined to a particular class of banks and usually those located on the periphery rather than in the central city.... [T]here was no *indiscriminate* run on banks by depositors whose confidence in banking institutions in a given area had been shattered. (italics in original)

Only once did Wicker (1996, 85) refer to a "full scale panic." The reference was to Toledo, Ohio, in August 1931 where four of nine banks closed, including the third largest bank (Wicker 1996, 69).

Richardson (2007) examined documentary evidence from Federal Reserve bank examiners who compiled a database listing the cause of bank suspensions during the Depression. Based on examiner evidence, he concluded that banks closed for reasons both of illiquidity and insolvency. Richardson and Van Horn (2009, 462) attributed the bank liquidations in New York City in summer 1931 to "An intensified inspection regime, which was a delayed reaction to the failure of The Bank of United States."

According to Wicker (1996, 108), the last wave of bank suspensions was "an anomaly among U.S. financial panics" because of the importance of statewide moratoria on cash withdrawals from banks. On February 14, 1933, the governor of Michigan ordered the statewide suspension of cash payments by Michigan banks when negotiations broke down between the Reconstruction Finance Corporation and the Guardian Group of banks in Detroit wounded by a heavy commitment to real estate lending. Wicker (1996, 108–9) described how the politics of statewide bank closures created a genuine national banking panic:

Bank moratoria created additional uncertainty among depositors about when and if state banking officials would close all the banks in a particular state.... The bank holiday was the mechanism for transmitting banking unrest from state to state. The declaration of a banking holiday in one state motivated depositors to withdraw deposits from out-of-state banks to meet their immediate transactions needs thereby transmitting withdrawal pressures to contiguous states and to the New York and Chicago money markets. Moreover, depositors in surrounding states became alarmed that similar deposit restrictions would be imposed in their states and would therefore rush to withdraw deposits in anticipation of a bank moratorium.... A sequence of uncoordinated bank moratoria describes how the panic was disseminated throughout the country.

The second crisis that brought to an end the monetary regime of interest-rate targeting was the fear that the newly elected president, Franklin Roosevelt, would take the country off the gold standard. As a result of this fear, gold began to flow out of the New York banks. As Wicker (1996, 27) demonstrated, "[T]here was no panic in the central money market in each of the four banking crises of the Great Depression." Nevertheless, gold out-flows threatened the gold cover of the New York Fed, which lost 60 percent of its gold reserve between February 1 and March 8 (Wigmore 1987; Wicker 1996, 130; Eichengreen 1995). In March 1933, the New York Fed raised its discount rate from 2.5 percent to 3.5 percent. After increasing moderately in January 1933, M2 fell dramatically in February and March 1933.

MONETARY OR FINANCIAL MARKET DISORDER

Financial stress inevitably accompanies recession. However, that associ-ation does not demonstrate anything about the nature of the shock that precipitated the recession. In the National Banking era, the fact that bank runs when they did occur, with one possible exception, followed peaks in the business cycle pointed to a primary shock other than a bank run. In the post–World War I period, there are seventeen business cycle peaks. In their table 1, for each cyclical peak, Bordo and Haubrich (2010) iden-tified whether a banking crisis occurred and whether monetary policy was contractionary. For each cyclical peak, they identified the existence of a "tight monetary policy." Only for the Great Contraction from August 1929 to March 1933 did they identify "banking crises." The argument made here is that the primal shock was contractionary monetary policy insti-tuted by the Fed to control a perceived asset price bubble. Until 1933, the banking system was amazingly robust given the severity of contractionary monetary policy.

FIVE

Vigorous Recovery and Relapse

1933–1939

As *Fortune* (1934, 122) wrote, "[T]he fundamental conviction upon which the New Deal was based was the conviction that Something Can Be Done About It [the Depression] – that it is not necessary to submit to the natural laws of economics as an animal submits to the chances of the weather." The "natural laws of economics" did not require "liquidation" to restore a balanced structure of prices and costs. The common objective of the initiatives undertaken by Roosevelt in 1933 was to raise "prices." He did not distinguish between the price level and relative prices like commodity prices and real wage rates. Some programs like the National Industrial Recovery Act passed in June 1933, with its price-fixing provisions, undoubtedly hindered recovery. However, the change in the monetary standard, which replaced monetary contraction with expansion, created the economic recovery that began in March 1933.

In early 1933, rumors that the incoming Roosevelt administration would devalue the dollar engendered outflows of gold. George Harrison, governor of the New York Fed, told his directors that the crisis "represents in itself a distrust of the currency and is inspired by talk of devaluation of the dollar" (cited in Eichengreen 1995, 328). Just as in 1893, fear of dollar devaluation and inflation was deflationary through the monetary contraction created by the loss of gold, given that the Fed did not sterilize the depressing effect of the outflows on bank reserves but rather raised the discount rate in February 1933 from 2.5 percent to 3.5 percent. In contrast, with the floating of the dollar in March 1933, the resulting expectation of dollar devaluation and inflation created monetary stimulus instead of contraction, albeit initially in a fitful way.

GOING OFF GOLD

Ferguson (1981) argued that Roosevelt's decisions about the monetary standard reflected his decision to put together a new political coalition to replace the one organized around the financial orthodoxy of the banking community. The adverse reaction in the banking community to the decision to leave the gold standard appeared in the comments of Elliot Bell (1934), a financial columnist for *The New York Times*:

The suspension of the gold standard in April, 1933, a deliberate, cold-blooded act of repudiation, as most bankers saw it, bewildered the "Street." The President, yielding apparently to the inflationist sentiment in Congress, threw away the results of all the work that had so won their admiration, shattered his campaign promises, burned the planks of his Democratic platform and unloosed the terrible threat of inflation.

In a reflection of the new coalition formed around the New Deal, Roosevelt scapegoated the bankers. Bell (1934, 258) summarized Roosevelt's inaugural address on March 4, 1933:

[B]ankers had "failed through their own stubbornness and their own incompetence," and had "admitted their failure and abdicated," adding that "practices of the unscrupulous money-changers stand indicted in the court of public opinion, rejected by the hearts and minds of men.... Stripped of the lure of profit by which to induce our people to follow their false leadership, they have resorted to exhortation, pleading tearfully for restored confidence. They know only the rules of a generation of self-seekers.... They have no vision.... The money-changers have fled from their high seats in the temple of our civilization."

A biography by Ronald Steel (1981, cited in Ferguson 1981, 754) of Walter Lippman portrayed the political choice faced by Roosevelt through recounting a lunch between Lippman and J. P. Morgan partners Russell Leffingwell and Thomas Lamont:[1]

Lamont and Leffingwell ... agreed that the steady erosion of commodity prices, which was causing open revolt on the farms, could not be halted unless the Administration gained full control over the currency. It was simply no longer possible, as in the previous depressions, to let farm prices collapse.... "Walter," Leffingwell told Lippman ... "You've got to explain to the people why we can no longer afford to chain ourselves to the gold standard." ... The next morning, April 18, [1933] millions of Americans found Lippman calling for an abandonment of the gold standard.

Bratter (1941) detailed how industrialists with companies dependent on exports organized as The Committee for the Nation to devalue the dollar (Ferguson 1981, 763). They worked with free-silver and agricultural

---

[1] Russell Leffingwell had probably first advanced the idea, incorporated into the 1932 Glass-Steagall Act, of allowing the Fed to back Federal Reserve notes with government securities (Butkiewicz 2008, 287).

interests and with the agricultural economists from Cornell, George F. Warren and F. A. Pearson, who advocated devaluation of the dollar against gold as a means of reflation. In spring 1933, the Committee for the Nation advocated raising the price of gold from $20.67 per fine ounce to $36.17 "to re-establish promptly the 1926 price level" (Bratter 1941, 535).

Johnson (1939, 14) described Roosevelt's gold policy in 1933:

The vehemence of the Administration's intention to raise prices is evident, not only in the statements of the President and other prominent officials, but also in the various items of its legislative program other than the gold policy, such as NRA [National Recovery Administration] with its aim of boosting wages and maintaining prices in general, the farm program with its restriction of production in order to restore a profitable market for farm products, the silver program resulting in the inflation of currency reserves, and the Thomas Amendment to permit the issuance of greenbacks.... It became the emphatically expressed determination of the Administration to raise prices substantially, and, to that end, cutting loose from gold appeared to the President to be necessary and the depreciation of the dollar contributory.

Perhaps the best popular account of Roosevelt's reflation policies is contained in the Metro-Goldwyn-Mayer movie "Inflation," released June 15, 1933.[2] The movie begins with two newspaper headlines: "US Goes off Gold Standard" and "Inflation Seen as US Salvation." An actor portraying a fictional Professor Gordon Watkins shows a graph of the purchasing power of the dollar (the inverse of the price level), which is stable before 1929 but then begins to increase. He illustrates by explaining the additional amount of steel pipe a dollar could purchase in 1933 compared to 1929. Professor Watkins refers to the Agricultural Adjustment Act, with the Thomas amendment allowing for the issuance of $3 billion in currency unbacked by gold, and he notes that with money more plentiful it will be worth less.

Still according to Professor Watkins, the expectation that money will fall in value over time will cause people to start spending again. The value of debt for farmers will fall and their crop prices will increase. The "wheels of industry" will begin turning again. The film ends with the song Happy Days Are Here Again.

Going off gold was the prerequisite to ending deflation, and the various actions of the administration created the expectation of dollar devaluation and inflation. Johnson (1939, 15) wrote:

[A]t that time [1933] adherence to the gold standard appeared to be a definitely deflationary factor. From September 1931, when England left the gold standard,

[2] See http://www.imdb.com/title/tt0194041/combined

until March 1933, wholesale prices in that country had remained approximately stable, despite a sterling devaluation of 30–35 per cent in terms of dollars; while on the other hand, during the same period, wholesale prices continued to decline in the gold-standard countries, the drop amounting to around 10 per cent in France and 15 per cent in the United States.

The bank holiday promulgated by Roosevelt on March 6, 1933, imposed capital controls on the export of gold. That suspension of the gold standard was incidental to preventing currency outflows from banks and was not interpreted as a change in the monetary standard. However, that interpretation changed with the executive order extending the gold embargo on April 20, 1933. According to Friedman and Schwartz (1963a, 464–5), in his press conference on April 19, 1933, Roosevelt

made it clear that the administration intended to permit the dollar to depreciate in terms of foreign currencies as a means of achieving a rise in domestic prices.... [T]he Thomas amendment to the Agricultural Adjustment Act was ... enacted into law on May 12, and explicitly directed at achieving a price rise through expansion of the money stock, contained a provision authorizing the President to reduce the gold content of the dollar to as low as 50% of its former weight. The dollar price of gold immediately started rising, which is to say that so also did the dollar price of foreign currencies.

Government abrogation of gold clauses reinforced the impression that the government would devalue the dollar to create inflation. In legislation passed on June 5, 1933 (introduced earlier as a joint resolution on May 6, 1933), Congress abrogated gold clauses in contracts. The continued existence of gold clauses in government and private contracts requiring payment in gold or in dollars equal to a specified weight in gold would have left unchanged the real value of this indexed debt given an increase in the price level. That windfall was unacceptable politically. "In 1933, it was estimated, $100 billion of gold-denominated contracts were outstanding in the United States" (Grant 1992, 228).

With its float on April 19, 1933, the dollar fell "steadily until July when it had declined between 30 and 45% against the currencies of most trading partners" (Temin and Wigmore 1990, 489). Dollar depreciation increased the dollar prices of commodities whose gold prices were determined in international markets. By reversing the decline in the price level, these actions turned expected deflation into the expectation of short-term inflation and almost overnight changed the short-term real interest rate from a high positive number to a negative number (Table 4.1).[3] M1 growth went

---

[3] To explain the economic recovery after the cyclical trough in March 1933, Eggertsson (2008) emphasized the change in monetary regime with the advent of Roosevelt's inauguration and

from (an annualized rate of) -12.4 percent in 1933Q2 to -2.0 percent in 1933Q3, to 9.3 percent in 1933Q4 (Friedman and Schwartz 1970, table 1). Economic recovery replaced economic decline with the cyclical trough occurring on March 1933. Expenditures on the interest-sensitive categories of business investment and consumer durables, especially, revived rapidly (Temin and Wigmore 1990, 493).

Tellingly, as Eichengreen (1995, 333) described, when rumors emerged from The World Economic Conference in London in April 1933 that the United States was again going to peg its currency to the pound and franc:

The effects were devastating. Financial and commodity markets, which had strengthened dramatically following the suspension of convertibility, reversed course. Stock prices tumbled. Commodity prices turned down. Observers were unanimous in attributing the reaction to investors' fears that the Fed and the Treasury ... would have to renew their restrictive policies.... [In response] the U.S. Delegation conveyed Roosevelt's position ... [that] "We are interested in American commodity prices.... What is to be the value of the dollar in terms of foreign currencies is not and cannot be our immediate concern." [After this statement] The dollar resumed its fall.

The public associated recession with deflation. Floating the dollar along with the expectation of inflation created by dollar depreciation created optimism about the future that revived economic activity (Temin and Wigmore 1990). However, floating the dollar did not in itself provide for a monetary policy of sustained expansion in aggregate nominal demand. The monetary base remained unchanged in 1933. Industrial production spurted initially, growing by 57 percent from March 1933 to July 1933.[4] It then declined, falling by 20 percent from July 1933 to September 1934.

Johnson (1939, 20) wrote:

In late July [1933] the prices of farm products broke sharply, and the rise in wholesale prices generally tapered off; industrial production began to slacken, and the dollar

---

its effect on inflationary expectations. That explanation accords with the one offered here. However, his monetary transmission mechanism does not accord with a variety of facts. Eggertsson offered no explanation for the Depression, instead simply assuming a negative shock that required for full employment a negative real interest rate persisting through 1939. According to Eggertsson, recovery arose because the public believed that after 1939 the Fed would create inflation by a nominal interest rate lower than what would be consistent with price stability. However, U.S. government bond yields displayed no increase indicative of an increase in long-term expected inflation after March 1933, remaining in the neighborhood of 3.2% (Board of Governors *Banking and Monetary Statistics: 1914–1921*, table 128). As shown in Figure 5.1, long-term interest rates declined steadily after March 1933 until 1940. Evidently, the public thought of the inflation that arose after March 1933 as short-term, perhaps reflecting a return of the price level to a more normal level.

[4] *Historical Statistics of the United States* (2006, table Cb28–31, "Indexes of Industrial Production: 1884–2003. Federal Reserve Board, seasonally adjusted.")

showed increasing strength on the foreign exchanges. The inflationists renewed their clamor, reinforced by the wheat and cotton belts with their agitation for higher prices. Pressure began to be exerted on the President to utilize his power to reduce the weight of the gold dollar by 50 percent, and sentiment appeared in Congress and elsewhere in favor of issuing additional, unsecured United States notes.

As Johnson (1939, 21ff) described, in October 1933, Roosevelt instructed the Reconstruction Finance Corporation (RFC) to begin buying gold as a way of raising the dollar price of gold and domestic prices. For a while the dollar depreciated, but then it strengthened starting in the last half of November 1933. The RFC program was a commodity stabilization program in that it financed its gold purchases by issuing debt rather than by monetizing it, as would have occurred if the Fed had made unsterilized purchases. Over the last half of 1933, it became clear that manipulation of the foreign exchange value of the dollar was not raising domestic prices and reviving economic activity in a sustained way. Moreover, the attempts to manipulate the dollar created dissension with U.S. trading partners and domestic bankers.

Through a one-time, significant devaluation of the dollar, Roosevelt could not only carry out a policy of raising the domestic price level but also quiet foreign and domestic critics through a renewed "stabilization" of the dollar and apparent return to the gold standard. Given the resulting undervaluation of the dollar and the continued embargo on the export of gold, the devaluation was in fact only a commodity stabilization scheme for raising the price of gold carried out in a way that was self-financing through monetization of gold inflows.

On February 1, 1934, the United States raised the price of gold from $20.67 an ounce to $35 an ounce. In combination with the political unrest in Europe caused by Hitler and renewed fears of war, this dollar devaluation created gold inflows, which through monetization augmented the monetary base and money. M1 had stabilized in 1933Q3 and began to grow vigorously in 1933Q4. Industrial production, after declining from July 1933 through September 1934, began to grow strongly. From 1933Q2 to 1936Q3, M1 grew at an annualized rate of 14.3 percent and M2 at 11.4 percent and the economy grew vigorously until 1937Q2. Romer (1992, 757) wrote, "[N]early all the observed recovery of the U.S. economy prior to 1942 was due to monetary expansion."

At the same time, gold inflows into the United States forced deflation on countries like Belgium and France that remained part of the gold bloc. The Federal Reserve could have achieved the same monetary expansion through open-market purchases without forcing deflation on the remaining gold standard countries. As Eichengreen (1995, 347) wrote, "American policy seemed expressly designed to maximize the drain of gold from the rest of the world and to intensify the pressure on the gold bloc countries."

However, Fed policy makers watched with concern as bank excess reserves grew along with gold inflows. In their view, the gold inflows created the same "tinder" for speculative extension of credit as open-market purchases. Worry about antagonizing Congress and the administration initially kept the Fed from sterilizing the gold inflows. "[W]ith the banking act in Congress, the government could change the entire financial system, including the central bank" (Meltzer 2003, 493). With a new Board chairman, Marriner Eccles, and with the centralization of authority in the Board of Governors provided for in the Banking Act of 1935 accomplished, the Fed in 1936 decided again to become an active central bank.

Eccles held the conventional view that monetary policy had no power to stimulate the economy because, as he said in his 1935 congressional testimony, "you must have borrowers who are willing and able to borrow" (Meltzer 2003, 478).[5] However, the Fed could still forestall the ability of banks to resume speculative lending by neutralizing their excess reserves through an increase in reserve requirements. Without a cushion of excess reserves, a resumption of bank lending would again require bank recourse to the discount window, which would produce an increase in interest rates. As the board's research director, Emanuel Goldenweiser, told the FOMC at their January 26, 1937, meeting, "An increase in reserve requirements ... would restore the System to the position in relation to the market which it normally would occupy" (this quotation and the following are cited in Orphanides 2004b, 107). The Board of Governors press release of July 14, 1936, announced the initial increase in required reserves:

This action eliminates as a basis of possible injurious credit expansion a part of the excess reserves.... The part of excess reserves thus eliminated is superfluous for all present or prospective needs of commerce, industry, and agriculture.... [L]ater action when some member banks may have expanded their loans and investments and utilized their excess reserves might involve the risk of bringing about a severe liquidation and of starting a deflationary cycle. It is far better to

---

[5] Eccles (1935, 17, 48, and 55) testified to Congress:

At the present time we are still in the depths of a depression and, beyond creating an easy money situation, there is very little, if anything, that the Reserve organization can do toward bringing about recovery. One cannot push on a string.... In my judgment it is impossible at the present time to force out and to keep in circulation more currency than is now outstanding.... You may create excess reserves through open-market operations, but unless the borrowers are willing to borrow from the banks, and the banks are willing to lend to the borrowers, you would not create a further increase in the money supply.

sterilize a part of these superfluous reserves while they are still unused than to permit a credit structure to be erected upon them and then to withdraw the foundation of the structure.

Between August 15, 1936, and May 1, 1937, the Board of Governors raised reserve requirements on demand deposits by 100 percent and the Treasury sterilized gold inflows. The interest rate on newly issued nine-month Treasury bills climbed from around 0.1 percent in early 1936 to a peak above 0.7 percent in May 1937. A decline in the level of money (M1) replaced vigorous expansion. With the cyclical peak in May 1937, economic decline began anew.

The Board of Governors miscalculated. It considered the excess reserves of banks to be superfluous and an indication of monetary ease. However, banks wanted that level of reserves to protect themselves against the reserve outflows they had experienced in the first years of the Depression. In January 1935, Jackson E. Reynolds, president of First National Bank in New York City, defended the level of excess reserves his bank held in response to a shareholder question asking whether that level of reserves conflicted with the exhortations of the Roosevelt administration for bankers to lend to businesses (cited in Grant 1992, 240):

[Jackson] replied, in reference to the First's own indelible experience in the 1933 panic, "Two years ago, deposits in this bank were $447,000,000. Two weeks later, deposits had declined to $172,000,000. We don't suggest that there is a possibility of another such wallop, but it would be simple to have one-half of this proportion.... A large proportion of the deposits represented by our excess reserves is placed here for safety ... and we don't want to put it where we can't get at it when we want it."

Keynesian economists blamed the return to contraction with the May 1937 cyclical peak on the attempt by the Roosevelt administration to balance the budget. For example, Krugman (2010b) wrote, "Many economists, myself included, regard this turn to austerity [attempted deficit reduction in Europe in 2010] as a huge mistake. It raises memories of 1937, when F.D.R.'s premature attempt to balance the budget helped plunge a recovering economy back into severe recession." It is true that given evidence of sustained recovery Roosevelt hoped to balance the budget in 1938. However, even casual inspection of the numbers creates doubt as to whether restrictive fiscal policy could have ended the cyclical recovery underway.

Table 5.1 shows the annual budget deficit for the federal government in billions of dollars. It is true that the deficit fell by $1.6 billion between 1936

Table 5.1. *Federal government budget deficit*

1932	1933	1934	1935	1936	1937	1938
−2.7	−2.6	−3.6	−2.8	−4.4	−2.8	−1.2

Note: *Historical Statistics of the United States* (2006, table Ea584–7, "Federal Government Finances – Revenue, Expenditure, and Debt: 1789–1939.")

and 1937, which amounted to a swing of 1.8 percent of GNP.[6] The swing came from a veterans' bonus payment in 1936, which increased the deficit, and the start of social security payroll taxes in January 1937, which lowered the deficit (Stein 1996, 99). However, the large deficit in 1936 appears like an anomaly with the $2.8 billion deficit in 1937 in line with earlier years. Moreover, it is hard to reconcile the assumption that fiscal policy exercised an important influence on output given that the deficit again declined by $1.6 billion from 1937 to 1938 and the economy began growing again with the cyclical upturn in 1938Q2.[7]

MONEY CREATION OVERWHELMS
FINANCIAL MARKET FRICTIONS

The credit-channel view that frictions in financial markets propagate macroeconomic shocks constituted the basis for the government and central bank interventions in credit markets in fall 2008. Particularly since Bernanke (1983), economists have attempted to identify frictions in credit markets that caused bank runs to exacerbate the severity of the Depression. Ex-Fed Governor Frederic Mishkin (2008) wrote:

In late 1930 ... a rolling series of bank panics began. Investments made by the banks were going bad.... Hundreds of banks eventually closed. Once a town's bank shut its doors, all the knowledge accumulated by the bank officers effectively disappeared.... Credit dried up.... And that's when the economy collapses.

---

[6] *Historical Statistics of the United States* (2006, table Ea584–7, "Federal Government Finances – Revenue, Expenditure, and Debt: 1789–1939"). The GNP number is from Balke and Gordon (1986, appendix B, table 1).

[7] For the 1920s and 1930s, Romer (1992, 766) estimated a small value for the effect of the fiscal multiplier on output as opposed to the money multiplier on output:

The magnitude of the fiscal policy multiplier is quite small. It implies that a rise in the surplus-to-GNP ratio of one percentage point lowers the growth rate of real output relative to normal by 0.23 percentage points.... [I]t would be very difficult to attribute most of the declines in output in 1921 and 1938 to fiscal policy.

The inauguration of Franklin D. Roosevelt as president on March 4, 1933, initiated a remarkable experiment allowing a comparison of the effectiveness of aggregate demand management of intervention into credit markets and of money creation. The intervention of the Roosevelt administration and regulators into the banking system restrained the ability of the banking system to make loans. In contrast, the change in the monetary regime to a pegged exchange rate with an undervalued exchange rate (without the sterilization of reserves inflows) produced double-digit growth in money. Money creation trumped credit restriction. The following discussion begins with a review of the bank holiday proclaimed by Roosevelt on March 5, 1933.

The credit-channel view of how a negative macroeconomic shock propagates to the real economy implies that its depressing effects must have continued well after the cyclical recovery that began March 1933. According to this view, bank failures depress economic activity by destroying the specialized knowledge required for bank lending. Given the occurrence of widespread bank failures in winter 1933 and the additional permanent closing of banks after the bank holiday in March 1933, economic activity should have continued to stagnate. Between the call dates December 31, 1932, and June 30, 1933, the loans of Fed member banks fell 15.4 percent.[8]

In the bank holiday, which lasted from March 6 through March 13 to 15, the government closed all commercial banks including the Federal Reserve banks. Before the holiday, there were 17,800 commercial banks. Afterward, "fewer than 12,000 of those were licensed to open and do business" (Friedman and Schwartz 1963a, 425). Calomiris and White (2000, 191) cited statistics from Friedman and Schwartz (1963a, 426–8):

Between December 1932 and 15 March 1933, deposits in banks open for business fell by one-sixth, and 70 percent of this decline was accounted for by the deposits on the books of banks not licensed to open.... In the earlier episodes [of bank suspensions], banks had continued most activities except the unlimited payment of deposits on demand, and sometimes were able to expand loans under these circumstances. In 1933, access to all deposits was denied. Friedman and Schwartz [1963a, 330] conclude that "the 'cure' was close to being worse than the disease."

Silber (2009) explained how Roosevelt restored depositor confidence in banks. Silber (2009, 20) began by noting that in the short window offered

---

8   Table 18 – All Member Banks – Principal Assets and Liabilities, from Board of Governors of the Federal Reserve System (1943).

by the holiday "only the financially naïve would have believed that the government could examine thousands of banks in one week to identify those that should survive." Silber (2009, 24) quoted the contemporary social commentator Frederick Lewis Allen (1939 [1972], 110):

The banks opened without any such renewed panic as had been feared. They might not have done so had the people realized that it was impossible, in a few days, to separate the sound banks from the unsound.

What restored depositor confidence in banks? Roosevelt delivered his first Fireside Chat on March 12, 1933, and assured listeners that the banks that reopened would be sound. Silber argued that Roosevelt's success rested on the Emergency Banking Act of 1933, which Congress passed on March 9. Title IV of the act gave the Fed authority to issue currency backed by whatever collateral a bank offered. The implication was that "the government would guarantee all depositors against loss, without limit" (Silber 2009, 25). At the time, the heads of the regional Reserve banks did not see the Federal Reserve System as a central bank capable of creating money but rather as repositories for the reserves of member banks with a need to safeguard those reserves through protecting their own liquidity and solvency. Roosevelt's Treasury secretary encouraged the Reserve banks to lend freely without concern for their own credit losses by stating that "there is definitely an obligation on the federal government to reimburse the 12 regional Federal Reserve Banks for losses which they may make on loans made under these emergency powers" (Silber 2009, 26). Silber (2009, 29) concluded:

Congress passed the Emergency Banking Act of 1933, giving the President the power to restore confidence in the banking system by establishing 100 percent guarantees for bank deposits.

Ending the bank runs and the bank suspensions due to state moratoria ended the immediate threat to the viability of the banking system. Nevertheless, the ending of the runs did nothing to repair the enormous damage imposed on the banking system by the closings resulting from the earlier bank runs starting in February 1933 and from the closings resulting directly from regulator decisions during the bank holiday. As Willis (1933, 237) noted, Congress rejected the proposal to substitute for the closed banks by allowing branch banking. The extent of bank distress in 1933 appears in Friedman and Schwartz (1963a, table 16, 438) in the measure of "Losses to Depositors per $100 of Deposits Adjusted in All Commercial Banks." In 1930, 1931, and 1932, the numbers were, respectively, 0.6 percent, 1.0 percent, and 0.6 percent. For 1933, the number rose to 2.2 percent. The banking system required a long time to work through its bad debts. "Net profits as percentage of total capital accounts" were for the indicated years: -1.5 (1931), -5.0 (1932), -9.6 (1933), and -5.2 (1934).[9]

Moreover, the regulatory environment in which banks operated continued to force the termination of good loans. In the real-bills environment of the time, regulators believed that risky lending in the form of long-term, illiquid loans rather than in the form of short-term, self-liquidating loans to finance goods in the process of production had caused bank insolvency, which then produced bank runs and suspensions.[10] Friedman and Schwartz (1963a, 456) cited a study by C. O. Hardy and Jacob Viner "of the availability of bank credit in the Chicago Federal Reserve district during the period from the bank holiday to September 1, 1934." The authors concluded:

That there exists a genuine unsatisfied demand for credit on the part of solvent borrowers, many of whom could make economically sound use of working capital.... That one of the most serious aspects of this unsatisfied demand is the pressure for liquidation of old working-capital loans, even sound ones. That this pressure is partly due to a determination on the part of bankers to avoid a recurrence of the errors to which they attribute much of the responsibility for the recent wave of bank failures.

Bankers, burned by loan losses and depositor withdrawals, restricted relatively illiquid loans to business and instead favored liquid securities. Grant (1992) recounted their chastened mood:

The American banking system – indeed, the whole credit structure – had just passed through the ordeal of the Great Depression and the trial by fire of the 1933 panic. If the surviving lenders knew anything, it was that it was better to be safe than sorry.... Francis H. Sisson, vice president of the Guaranty Trust Company of New York and president of the American Bankers Association, reminded them [bankers] of their prudential duty to be liquid. Sisson warned particularly of the dangers of real-estate lending.

---

[9] *Historical Statistics of the United States* (2006, table Cj238–250, "National banks – number, earnings, and expenses: 1869–1998").

[10] In dealing with bank runs, Epstein and Ferguson (1984) documented the Fed's focus on the portfolio problems of individual banks. For example, they cited J. B. McDougal, governor of the Chicago Reserve Bank, who in July 1932, shortly after runs on Chicago banks, opposed open-market purchases because they "have resulted in creating abnormally low rates for short-term government securities" and depressed bank earnings (Epstein and Ferguson 1984, 977). Richardson and Van Horn (2009) attributed the wave of failures of New York banks that began in summer 1931 to intensified regulatory scrutiny. That intensified scrutiny was in reaction to the widespread criticism of the New York Superintendent of Banks Joseph Broderick for keeping The Bank of United States open for more than a year after it developed problems and closing it only in December 1930.

Having restored the National City Bank to strength, Perkins [president of National City] refused to take new losses.... For all Perkins knew, the depositors might again run for their money, as they had in March 1933, and he took precautionary measures. The bank did make some loans ... but mostly it laid in Treasury securities. It favored Treasury bills, which entailed no risk at all, not even the risk of rising interest rates.

The supply-side constriction of bank lending appeared in the figures on bank loans. Between the call report dates June 30, 1933, and June 30, 1936, the loans of Fed member banks fell slightly from $12.8 to $12.5 billion. They declined significantly in real terms given that the price level rose 11.4 percent from 1933 through 1936.[11]

Despite the sustained effort of bankers to make their portfolios more liquid by replacing loans with securities and despite the destruction to banking relationships from the wholesale closing of banks in the first three months of 1933, real output grew vigorously after the March 1933 cyclical trough. Real GNP grew at an annualized rate of 10.7 percent from the 1933Q1 cyclical trough to the 1937Q2 cyclical peak (Balke and Gordon 1986, appendix B, table 2). Although it seems plausible that there was a credit channel that depressed economic activity, the commencement of vigorous economic recovery after the business cycle trough implies that another force overcame its effect. The obvious candidate for this other force is the revival of money growth that occurred roughly coincident with the cyclical trough of March 1933.

The implications of the credit-cycle view also conflict with the timing of the 1937Q2 cycle peak. Prior to the peak, banks had recovered significantly from their 1933 nadir. In 1935, 1936, and 1937, as evidenced by "net profits as percentage of total capital accounts" of 5.1 percent, 10.0 percent, and 7.1 percent, respectively, banks had returned to good health.[12] That fact is inconsistent with the restriction of credit occurring as an independent shock. In addition, prior to the business cycle peak, bank credit continued to grow while money growth declined. After the initial increase in required reserves and up to the date of the cycle peak, banks sold securities and *increased* lending. In contrast, after the beginning of the increases in required reserves in August 1936, the vigorous, double-digit M1 growth that had accompanied economic recovery slowed steadily and the level of M1 declined over the last three quarters of 1937.[13]

---

[11] See citation in fn. 8. GNP deflator is from Balke and Gordon (1986, appendix B: Historical Data).

[12] *Historical Statistics of the United States* (2006, table Cj238–250, "National banks – number, earnings, and expenses: 1869–1998").

[13] Over the four-quarter interval prior to the increase in required reserves (between the call dates from June 1935 to June 1936), for all Fed member banks, lending increased by

The monetary shock produced by the increases in required reserves between August 15, 1936, and May 1, 1937, and the resulting decline in excess reserves below desired levels dissipated when banks had restored the level of excess reserves that had existed prior to the reserve-requirement increases.[14] At that point, in 1938Q2, money again began to increase steadily and the economy resumed growing. A chastened Fed once more retreated from its attempt to become an active central bank and continued to freeze its holdings of government securities. Monetary base and money growth resumed with gold inflows and the end of Treasury sterilization of gold inflows.[15]

Empirical evidence that a credit channel propagated the monetary shocks that produced the Great Depression is elusive.[16] Bernanke (1983) argued for a cost-of-credit intermediation channel because of an external finance premium, which raises the cost of funding to small firms more than to large firms during periods of monetary stringency. Hori (1996, 5),

---

$0.61 billion and securities increased by $2.86 billion. Over the next four-quarter interval including the required-reserves increase and ending with the cycle peak in May 1937 (between the call dates June 1936 to June 1937), their loans increased by $1.74 while their securities fell by $1.26 billion. For the weekly reporting member banks, for which monthly data are available, from August 1935 through August 1936, loans increased by $0.52 billion and investments increased by $1.95 billion. From August 1936 through May 1937, their loans increased $1.16 billion and investments declined by $1.25 billion. In contrast, annualized growth in M1 fell as shown by the numbers in parentheses: 1936Q2 (24.1%), 1936Q3 (14.1%), 1936Q4 (7.6%), 1937Q1 (5.0%). From March 1937 through December 1937, M1 fell at an annualized rate of 8.2%.

The numbers are from Board of Governors *Banking and Monetary Statistics* (1943, table 122, "Yields on Short-Term United States Government Securities;" table 18, "Member Banks–Principal Assets and Liabilities on Call Dates;" table 49, "Weekly Reporting Banks in New York City;" and table 50, "Weekly Reporting Member Banks Outside New York City") and Friedman and Schwartz (1970, table 1).

14 In August 1936, excess reserves were $2.5 billion, and in May 1938 they were again $2.5 billion. (Board of Governors *Banking and Monetary Statistics* 1943, table 105, "Member Bank Reserve Balances, Required Reserves, Excess Reserves and Borrowings").

15 Because inflation (CPI) turned to deflation in 1937Q4, the trough in real M1 occurred in 1937Q4. The return of growth after the business cycle trough in June 1938 is consistent with the increase in real M1 stimulating expenditure through portfolio rebalancing, that is, through a stimulative real-balance effect (Patinkin 1948; 1965).

16 Flandreau (2011) made a persuasive case that by discrediting the old, prestigious investment banks like J. P. Morgan, New Deal politics and legislation, especially Glass-Steagall, which separated commercial and investment banking, ended the relationship banking that had fostered the issuance of international debt. Because of the specialized knowledge in assessing risk and in handling restructuring and the reputational capital involved in certifying credit worthiness, the discrediting of these investment banks contributed to a disruption in international debt markets. Flandreau (2011, 25) concluded, "The short term effect of New Deal financial acts was a dramatic disruption of well-tried international financial roads and a global dislocation that was without precedent."

however, found "that the statistical evidence that substantiates the story by Bernanke is driven by just one monthly average observation, and that the observation itself is rather contradictory to his story." Hori (1996, 7 and 52) also failed to find evidence of a credit channel in cross-section data either by industry or by state:

[T]he damage to the industries populated by small firms was not noticeably more severe than that to the industries with larger firms during the Great Depression.... In the 1930s, the states that experienced the severest depression were not necessarily suffering the severest financial crisis.

MONEY CREATION OVERWHELMS UNCERTAINTY AND GOVERNMENT INTERVENTION

A common contention in recession is that uncertainty over the fiscal and regulatory regime retards recovery.[17] As *Time* (1932, 12) wrote in May 1932 under the heading of "Blame&Congress:"

Widespread was the financial opinion last week that the bad state of U.S. business was in no small part due to Congress and its vagaries on the Budget & Taxation. Washington tipster services hinted darkly of a "dictatorship." Bankers and industrialists complained bitterly of "uncertainties" at the Capitol. They were quite positive that if Congress passed an equitable tax law, approximately balanced the Budget and adjourned by June 10, their immediate troubles would be over.

H. Parker Willis (1933, 234–5) reviewed the uncertainties produced in the financial life of the country as of December 1933:

Our legislation of the past epoch-making year in finance may be grouped under three main heads: first, that which provides for a change in the standard of value and of the basis of contracts; second, that which alters the fundamental protection of our note currency and which threatens the inclusion of a new additional element of money; and third, that which imposes on our banks the requirement of radical business transformation.

These vast innovations open an immense field of division. Leaving entirely aside the questions of economic and social morality involved in the repudiation of our gold contracts, we may say that the great evil of that phase of our legislation, from

---

[17] An example is the comments of Dallas Fed President Richard Fisher (2010, 3–4):

[A]mong the CEOs I regularly survey before every FOMC meeting ... the prevailing sentiment is that politicians and officials who craft and enforce taxes and rules have been doing so in a capricious manner that makes long-term planning, including expanding payrolls, difficult, if not impossible.... The retarding effect of heightened uncertainty over the fiscal and regulatory direction of the country makes it difficult to kick-start the transmission mechanism of the economy.

the sole point of banking, lies not in the change itself or even the accompanying repudiation, but in the fact that no substitute standard has been provided. There may be sentiment for what is termed "devaluation" of the dollar but little or none for postponing an announcement of the conclusion arrived at therewith. Such postponement not only confuses and delays business recovery and renders impossible the raising of new capital but it weakens the banks and chills their activity by making them over-sensitive to danger, and too acutely distrustful of certain classes of advances and investments which they must feel reasonably free to make if the banking mechanism is to function with success.

A year later, Elliott Bell (1934, 261), financial writer for *The New York Times* wrote:

[I]n midsummer [1934] the money question rose again to plague the bankers. The passage of the Silver Purchase Act and the nationalization of silver, accompanied by widespread rumors of renewed devaluation of the dollar, induced in the bankers a sense of betrayal.... A new wave of inflation fear swept the financial markets.

The Willis and Bell citations referred only to uncertainty in financial markets. Friedman and Schwartz (1963a, 495–9) summarized the uncertainty introduced by direct intervention into the economy to raise wages and prices by New Deal measures such as the National Industrial Recovery Act (passed June 16, 1933), the National Labor Relations Act, minimum wage laws, the Guffey Coal Act, the agricultural price-support program, and the National Labor Relations Act.[18] They also referred to attacks on business ("economic royalists") by the administration, an unbalanced federal budget, and the expansion of government programs such as the Tennessee Valley Authority. Friedman and Schwartz (1963a, 499) argued that these measures created an exogenous increase in wages and prices that reduced the cyclical increase in output after March 1933.[19]

Nevertheless, by the end of 1934, the sustained money creation engendered by the January 1934 dollar devaluation created sustained growth in

---

[18] Cole and Ohanian (2004) attempted to quantify the Friedman-Schwartz hypothesis that New Deal policies limited the pace of the recovery in output from the March 1933 cyclical trough.

[19] The fundamental uncertainty faced by business was evidenced by the debate over the very nature of the economic organization desirable for an economy. Todd (1996, 120) cited Schlesinger (1959, 166–7):

[The] theorists of the managed society also continued to consider an NRA [National Recovery Administration] as indispensable.... "Industrial laissez-faire is unthinkable," said Raymond Moley, who argued that something had to be done "to satisfy the need for government intervention and industrial cooperation.... [T]he interests involved in our economic life are too great to be abandoned to the unpredictable outcome of unregulated competition."

aggregate nominal demand. Uncertainty created by government fiscal and regulatory policy did not overwhelm the impact of that growth in nominal demand on the growth of output.

HAVE POLICY MAKERS LEARNED THE RIGHT LESSONS?

In the same way that the Depression created the impression of monetary impotence, it also created the presumption that the economy is inherently unstable. However, in the Depression, after each cyclical trough, there was a snap-back in output. In the four quarters ending in 1933Q1, real GNP fell 14.1 percent, whereas in the four succeeding quarters it rose 13.5 percent. Similarly, in the four quarters ending 1938Q2, real GNP fell 10 percent, whereas in the four succeeding quarters it rose 7.4 percent. Given the depth of the first cyclical decline and because the second cyclical decline followed fairly closely on the first, the unemployment rate remained high throughout the 1930s. Because of the widespread association of the Depression with high unemployment, popular discourse held that World War II deficit spending ended the Depression. In fact, the ending of contractionary monetary policy ended both of the cyclical downturns and allowed the price system to work.

There is a striking overlap between the views of policy makers during the Depression and during the 2008–2009 recession defined both by what they considered relevant and what they considered irrelevant. In both cases, policy makers attributed recession to the collapse of an asset price bubble and to the resulting dysfunction in credit markets. That dysfunction arose from the insolvencies associated with defaults on the excessive issue of debt in the prior speculative boom. As a result, in both instances, policy focused on the disruption to credit flows. In neither instance did policy makers make any association between a central bank and money creation.

In the Depression, the focus by monetary policy makers was on financial intermediation. In 1932 during the Hoover administration, Congress created the Reconstruction Finance Corporation (RFC) to recapitalize banks. Bordo (2008, 16) cited Richard Sylla's figure that the RFC's recapitalization of 6,000 banks amounted to $200 billion in today's dollars. "At one point in 1933, the RFC held capital in more than 40 percent of all banks, representing one-third of total bank capital" (Hoenig 2009, 7). Also in 1932, Congress created the Federal Home Loan Bank System to encourage housing finance. The Roosevelt administration created numerous additional government entities to revive credit intermediation, for example, Fannie Mae, the Federal Housing Administration, the Federal Farm Mortgage

Corporation, and the Federal Credit Union system. Many states adopted laws preventing the foreclosure of homes and farms.

To limit excessive risk taking by banks in the future, Congress strengthened regulatory oversight of banks. The Banking Act of 1933 (the Glass-Steagall Act) gave the Fed the power to regulate the extension of credit to purchase stocks through margin requirements. It authorized the Fed to prohibit banks from use of its discount window "for the speculative carrying of or trading in securities, real estate, or commodities, or for any other purposes inconsistent with the maintenance of sound credit conditions." The act also separated commercial and investment banking. The Securities Exchange Act of 1934 established the SEC to regulate the issue of securities. The United States enforced rigorous limitations on bank entry to restrict the competition held responsible for excessive risk taking.[20]

In both the Depression and the 2008–2009 recession, policy makers interpreted a high level of excess reserves as evidence of an accommodative monetary policy. The coexistence of these excess reserves and the absence of bank lending supposedly indicated a breakdown in the transmission mechanism for monetary policy. The low level of market interest rates rather than the behavior of the money stock reinforced the belief in a central bank "out of ammunition."[21]

Given this continuity in the understanding of economic contractions, what have policy makers learned that is new? In the Depression, policy makers viewed the closing of banks through runs as a manifestation of the insolvencies created by risky lending, especially in real estate. They believed that a period of debt liquidation including bank failures and, as a result, economic contraction was inevitable. The Keynesian Revolution began with a challenge to this pessimism. Although "animal spirits" could create an unsustainable boom, government could still offset the ensuing contraction by making up the shortfall of spending from the full employment level through deficit spending.

---

[20] The long-running debate over how to end bank runs between proponents of unit banking who favored deposit insurance and proponents of interstate branch banking who opposed deposit insurance concluded with the former victorious (see Daiger 1931). On regulatory reform in this period, see Calomiris and White (2000), Fischer and Golembe (1976), Flood (1992), Mengle (1990), and Todd (1996).

[21] In summer 2010 when the economic recovery appeared to stall, the financial press was full of commentary captured by the title of an op-ed piece by Alan Blinder, former vice chairman of the Board of Governors, "The Fed is Running Low on Ammo." Blinder (2010, A15) wrote, "The bad news is that the Fed has already spent its most powerful ammunition; only the weak stuff is left." The implication was that sustained high rates of growth of money creation would not increase the dollar expenditure of the public.

Figure 5.1. U.S. long-term interest rates.
Note: Yields on long-term government securities from 1920 until 1953 are from the Board of Governors *Banking and Monetary Statistics*, 1914–1941 (1943) and 1941–1970 (1976). Thereafter, Treasury 10-year constant maturity bonds from Board of Governors "Selected Interest Rates," statistical release G.13 are used. The railroad bond yields are from Macaulay (1936). The shaded regions represent NBER recessions.

In a way analogous to the Keynesian focus on using fiscal policy to rectify the shortfall in *spending* from full employment spending in a recession, Fed policy in the 2008–2009 recession focused on using credit policy to rectify the shortfall in *lending* from full employment lending. *The Washington Post* (2010) wrote, "The primary lesson [of the Great Depression] – espoused by Ben S. Bernanke as an academic before acting on it as Fed chairman – was "Don't let the financial system collapse." The response of policy makers in the 2008–2009 recession went well beyond this injunction. They implemented measures to maintain intermediation in financial markets through supporting troubled individual banks and through the use of the Fed's asset portfolio to boost the availability of credit in various markets.

Just as the era of stop-go monetary policy represented a Keynesian experiment in the management of aggregate demand to assure full employment, the response to the 2008–2009 recession represented an experiment in using the direct intervention of central banks into credit markets to assure full employment. Despite the alacrity and the enormous scale of this intervention, an extraordinarily virulent world recession still occurred. This reality demands a reappraisal of the efficacy of credit policy similar to the one that occurred in the 1970s for fiscal policy. This reappraisal should start with the issue of whether cyclical fluctuations arise from credit cycles that disrupt financial intermediation or from monetary disorder that prevents the real interest rate from serving its equilibrating role as part of the price system.

In his First Inaugural Address on March 4, 1933, Roosevelt said:

We are stricken by no plague of locusts.... Nature still offers her bounty and human efforts have multiplied it. Plenty is at our doorstep, but a generous use of it languishes in the very sight of the supply. Primarily this is because the rulers of the exchange of mankind's goods have failed through their own stubbornness and their own incompetence.... [I]n our progress towards a resumption of work we require two safeguards against a return of the evils of the old order: there must be a strict supervision of all banking and credits and investments, so that there will be an end to speculation with other people's money; and there must be provision for an adequate but sound currency.

Following the 2008–2009 recession, public debate has centered on Roosevelt's admonition for "strict supervision of all banking" as opposed to "provision for an adequate but sound currency." Again, the challenge is to determine whether we have learned the right lessons.

SIX

Interwar International Monetary Experiments

As a professor at Princeton, Ben Bernanke (2000, 149, 165) criticized the Japanese central bank for a lack of decisive action to address its economy's "deep slump" in the 1990s by contrasting its inaction with the action of President Roosevelt in the Depression.

> Franklin D. Roosevelt was elected president of the United States in 1932 with the mandate to get the country out of the Depression.... In the end, his most effective actions were the same ones that Japan needs to take – namely, rehabilitation of the banking system and devaluation of the currency. But Roosevelt's specific policy actions were, I think, less important than his willingness to be aggressive and to experiment – in short, to do whatever it took to get the country moving again.

Bernanke (2002) returned to the issue of leadership when he wrote about the death of Benjamin Strong in 1928, governor of the New York Fed:

> [T]he central bank ... was essentially leaderless.... This situation led to decisions, or nondecisions, which might well not have occurred under either better leadership or a more centralized institutional structure. And associated with these decisions, we observe a massive collapse of money, prices, and output.

Based on this analysis of Roosevelt's leadership and of the absence of Fed leadership after Governor Strong's death, in a way allowed by Section 13(3) of the Federal Reserve Act that made possible lending by a single regional Fed bank, Bernanke and New York Fed President Timothy Geithner centralized decision making within the Fed and acted decisively after the financial turmoil following the Lehman bankruptcy in September 2008. However, as illustrated by the first quotation in this chapter, even assuming the need to centralize decision making, there remains an ambiguity about the appropriate lesson policy makers should have learned from the Depression applicable to the 2008–2009 recession. The reference to "rehabilitation of the banking system" focuses attention on strengthening bank balance sheets to improve financial intermediation. In contrast, the reference to "devaluation of the currency" focuses attention on the money creation made possible by abandonment of the gold standard. In fall 2008, Bernanke made the choice to focus on the former policy of strengthening bank balance sheets rather than on the latter policy of creating money.

Later, as a member of the Board of Governors, Bernanke (2002) alluded to his study of the Depression when he said on the occasion of Milton Friedman's ninetieth birthday, "I would like to say to Milton and Anna: Regarding the Great Depression. You're right, we did it. We're very sorry. But thanks to you, we won't do it again." Did Bernanke learn the right lesson from the Depression and, as a result, make the correct choice in 2008? Was Bernanke (1983, 257) right in his analysis of the Depression?

As the real costs of intermediation increased, some borrowers (especially households, farmers, and small firms) found credit to be expensive and difficult to obtain. The effects of this credit squeeze on aggregate demand helped convert the severe but not unprecedented downturn of 1929–30 into a protracted depression.

In the 2002 speech, Bernanke explained how Friedman and Schwartz treated the Depression as a controlled experiment useful for learning. Through the use of historical narrative to highlight the Fed's episodic actions, Friedman and Schwartz stressed the importance of monetary contraction rather than real forces as the cause of the Depression. Because they emphasized bank failures as the source of monetary contraction, however, their analysis left open the possibility of dysfunction in financial intermediation as the mechanism through which monetary disorder spread to the real economy rather than through monetary nonneutrality produced by sticky prices.[1]

---

[1] Examples of economists who blame the 2008–2009 recession on dysfunction in financial markets are Gjerstad and Smith (2009), who wrote:

It appears that both the Great Depression and the current crisis had their origins in excessive consumer debt – especially mortgage debt – that was transmitted to the financial sector.... [A] financial crisis that originates in consumer debt ... can be transmitted quickly and forcefully into the financial system. It appears that we're witnessing the second great consumer debt crash, the end of a massive consumption binge.

At least as concerns the Depression, the assertion appears implausible. In 1929Q3, the quarter of the cyclical peak leading to the Depression, Fed member banks held only 12.0% of their loans in mortgages (real estate loans) and 8.8% as a percentage of loans and investments (Board of Governors 1943], table 19 "All Member Banks-Classification of Loans on Call Dates" and table 18 "All Member Banks-Principal Assets").

IDENTIFICATION

Macroeconomics is about assigning the direction of causation to correlations among macroeconomic variables. This exercise in identification allows economists to advise policy makers about how to conduct policy. The methodology of identification entails constructing a model. A macroeconomic model aggregates individual behavior that is rational in the sense that agents use resources efficiently either to consume in the case of individuals (households) or to maximize profits in the case of firms. In particular, a model imposes the constraint that all markets clear – agents make all the trades that would leave them better off.

For a model to be useful to policy makers, it must yield implications that are supported by observed experience. Policy makers then have a basis for using the model to predict the future based on an assumption about their own behavior. Testing a model requires identification of shocks – the forces that arose in the past that affected the ability and willingness of agents to make trades and that required adjustment of prices. The difficulty in macroeconomics and a major source of the inability of macroeconomists to arrive at consensus over fundamental issues is that economists cannot agree on the shocks that produced recessions.

As suggested by the choice of the term, a shock is some force that originates outside of the working of the price system summarized by the model. Testing how well a model explains the behavior of the variables it determines (the endogenous variables) requires a choice of shocks capable of discriminating among models rather than a choice based on improving the fit of a given model. The role of historical narrative is critical in that it allows identification of information about policy and about other forces like wars specific to particular times.

The 1920s and 1930s offer numerous observations within and across countries on the timing of cyclical declines (cycle peaks) and cyclical recoveries (cycle troughs). The changes in the monetary regimes of countries and the actions of central banks rather than the independent occurrence of bank runs explain the timing of the business cycle. These various monetary phenomena took the form of deflation forced on countries like Britain and Japan by the return to the gold standard at parities that overvalued their currencies, by the Fed's attempts to control asset prices through increases in interest rates and in reserve requirements, and by the way in which the gold standard transmitted the deflationary monetary policies of the United States and the gold hoarding of France.

The timing of these changes in the monetary standard reflected a large number of political factors rather than a common, systematic response to the economy. For that reason, the changes represented the closest that economics gets to controlled experiments. Yeager (1976, 334) summarized the operation of the attempted return to the gold standard in the 1920s:

Gold-standard methods of balance-of-payments equilibration were largely destroyed and were not replaced by any alternative.... With both the price-and-income and the exchange-rate mechanisms of balance-of-payments adjustment out of operation, disequilibriums were accumulated or merely palliated, not continuously corrected. Too much depended on ad hoc policies and switches in policies.

Bernanke (1995, 2, 10) wrote:

[T]he evidence that monetary shocks played a major role in the Great Contraction, and that these shocks were transmitted around the world primarily through the workings of the gold standard, is quite compelling.... [D]eclines in inside money stocks, particularly in 1931 and later, were naturally influenced by macroeconomic conditions; but they were hardly continuous, passive responses to changes in output. Instead, money supplies evolved discontinuously in response to financial and exchange-rate crises, crises whose roots in turn lay primarily in the political and economic conditions of the 1920s and in the institutional structure as rebuilt after the war. Thus, to a first approximation, it seems reasonable to characterize these monetary shocks as exogenous with respect to contemporaneous output, suggesting a significant causal role for monetary forces in the world depression.

Using a discrete time duration model for twenty-four countries for the period 1928–1936, Wandschneider (2008, 151) summarized empirically the length of time a country spent on the gold standard:

High per capita income, international creditor status, and prior hyperinflation increased the probability of continuation [on the gold standard]. In contrast, democratic regimes left early. Unemployment, sterling group membership, higher inflation, and the experience of banking crises reduced the time a country remained on the gold standard.

The monetary experiments carried out in the 1920s and 1930s yielded results conformable to quantity-theoretic implications. Negative monetary shocks that forced deflation arose from going onto the gold standard at a par value that overvalued the currency. They also arose from capital outflows due to gold absorption by the United States and France or due to international political instability. Going off the gold standard relieved the pressure of deflation. Countries like Germany had to deflate to stay on the gold standard given capital outflows. Countries that went off the gold standard gained control over their own price levels.

Monetary shocks both negative and positive explain the timing of the business cycle across countries and over time within countries. This view does not accord with the contemporaneously held perception during the Depression. That perception highlighted the collapse of excessive speculation undertaken by the banking system and, more generally, "imbalances" created during the prior period of prosperity in the "roaring" 1920s (see Chapter 3).

Gustav Cassel (1932, cited in Wood 2009a) criticized the conclusion in a League of Nations report attributing the breakdown of the gold standard in 1931 to imbalances ("maladjustments") in the 1920s:

The way in which the [League of Nations] Gold Delegation presents the causes of the breakdown of the gold standard seems to me entirely unacceptable. What we have to explain is essentially a monetary phenomenon, and the explanation must therefore be essentially of a monetary character. An enumeration of a series of economic disturbances and maladjustments which existed before 1929 is no explanation of the breakdown of the gold standard. In fact, in spite of existing economic difficulties, the world enjoyed up to 1929 a remarkable progress. What has to be cleared up is why the progress was suddenly interrupted.

The remainder of the chapter highlights how the differing timing across countries regarding their entry into depression and their subsequent exit derived from differing decisions about whether to adopt the gold standard and, if adopted, when to abandon it. Of course, financial stress accompanied depression, but the independent shocks came from central banks and monetary arrangements, not from financial markets. The timing of the decisions determining whether to adopt or to relinquish the discipline over internal price levels imposed by the gold standard varied by country and for political reasons.[2] These political reasons derived especially from the experience with inflation after World War I and from the corrosive politics of German reparations imposed by the victorious Allies after World War I. Wolf (2010, 14) wrote, "The experience of inflation during the 1920s would prove to be one of the best predictors of which countries would allow their

---

[2] The literature on the timing of the exit of countries from the gold standard includes Wolf (2008), who estimated a hazard function model predicting the date of exit. One finding from Wolf (2008, 396) is that "[T]he more a country had devalued relative to pre-war parity when it entered the gold-exchange standard, the less independent the central bank, the less democratic the political regime and the longer the main economic partners stay on gold, the later exit will occur." More idiosyncratic factors included, for example, in the case of Poland, which did not leave gold until March 1936, the desire to arrange loans from France to rearm and the way in which adherence to the gold standard facilitated access to French capital markets.

currencies to depreciate in the 1930s." Also, remaining on the gold standard was a precondition of maintenance of the capital flows necessary for the viability of the reparations payments (Bordo et al. 1999). The case of Germany illustrates the essentially political character of the choice of monetary regime and the resulting usefulness of Germany as a controlled experiment for understanding inflation and recession.

HYPERINFLATION AND THE RETURN TO THE GOLD STANDARD IN THE WEIMAR REPUBLIC

In 1913, currency in Germany amounted to six billion marks. In November 1923 in Berlin, a loaf of bread cost 428 billion marks and a kilogram of butter almost 6,000 billion marks. From the end of World War I until 1924, the price level rose almost one trillionfold.[3] The economic cause of this hyperinflation was the monetization of public and private debt by Germany's central bank, the Reichsbank.[4] The political cause lay in the inability of a fragile democracy to impose the taxes necessary to pay war reparations.[5]

Germany entered World War I believing that the war would be like the Franco-Prussian war of 1870–1871. The government could finance a short war by issuing bonds, which a defeated France would redeem in gold (Marsh 1992, 77). In fact, the combatants devoted half of their economic output to the fighting. Germany, which did not impose income taxes, financed the war almost completely by issuing debt. With the deficits that followed the end of the war, the Reich's debt amounted to half of national wealth. Interest on the debt amounted to four times its 1913 revenues.[6]

At Versailles, the Allies imposed a punitive settlement on Germany. They stripped Germany of its colonies and the Alsace-Lorraine. The Treaty of Versailles required that Germany pay for the damages caused by the war without stipulating an upper limit. France especially, embittered by the appalling human cost of retaking Alsace-Lorraine, demanded heavy reparations. In May 1921, the London Ultimatum set an aggregate amount for reparations of 132 billion gold marks. However, the Reparations Commission could demand interest on the unpaid amount when it judged that German

---

[3] The figures are from Webb (1989, 3) and Bresciani-Turroni (1937, 25).

[4] Among others, Bresciani-Turroni (1937), Keynes (1923 [1971b]), Cagan (1956), and Webb (1989) present this quantity-theory view.

[5] Among others, Holtfrerich (1986) and Webb (1989) present this view. The earliest criticism of the punitive character of the Versailles Treaty by an economist is Keynes (1919 [1971a]).

[6] These figures are from Holtfrerich (1986), 102, 109, and 126.

finances had recovered. Uncertainty about the total reparations payments and the disincentive that uncertainty created for Germany to run fiscal surpluses probably weighed more heavily than even the huge magnitude of the total (Holtfrerich 1986, 143, 145, and 154).

Holtfrerich (1986, 153) argued that Germany could not have raised through direct taxation the amounts necessary "to effect a foreign transfer regarded from the outset as beyond fulfillment, unjust and indeed morally reprehensible by almost the entire population." He explained the resort to an inflation tax by quoting Friedrich Bendixen, a Hamburg bank director:

Only in taxation do people discern the arbitrary incursions of the state; the movement of prices, on the other hand, seems to them sometimes the outcome of traders' sordid machinations, more often a dispensation which, like frost and hail, mankind must simply accept. The statesman's opportunity lies in appreciating this mental disposition.

Unable to cover its expenditures through explicit taxes, the German government ran deficits exceeding 50 percent of its expenditures from 1919 through 1923 (Holtfrerich 1986, 173). Reichsbank purchases of government debt made the printing press the ultimate source for funding these deficits.[7] In the London Schedule of Payments of May 1921, the Allies threatened to occupy the Ruhr unless Germany transferred four billion marks annually and made additional payments as its economy grew. The Reichstag refused to impose additional taxes. Inflation rose when the prospect of ultimate budget balance receded. As inflation rose, collection lags in the tax system reduced real revenues. In October 1921, the Allies further weakened the political standing of the German government by annexing Upper Silesia to Poland.

Only the United States could have brokered a compromise by forgiveness of war debts owed it by France and Britain in return for moderation of their reparations demands on Germany. However, the United States retreated into isolationism. Contradictorily, Allied governments made it hard for Germany to run the surplus on its external account necessary to pay reparations by imposing high duties on its exports. Many Germans adopted the fatalistic attitude that only German economic ruin would demonstrate the wrongfulness of reparations. They argued that only when the Allies scaled back demands for reparations could Germany bring order to its domestic finances.

France never confronted the inherent contradictions in its policy toward Germany. It wanted a weak German economy incapable of supporting

---

[7] Keynes (1923 [1971b], chapter 2) explained inflation as a tax.

remilitarization, and it wanted the payment of reparations, which required a strong Germany economy. On January 11, 1923, France occupied the Ruhr when Germany failed to make in kind deliveries of coal. Germany responded with a policy of passive resistance. Workers in the Ruhr went on strike to prevent France from obtaining the region's coal and steel. Without coal, German railroads could not run, and without railroads the German economy could not run. The government also had to pay striking workers in part to prevent them from joining the Communist movement and starting a Bolshevik revolution. As the government deficit widened to 22 percent of net national product, the money stock soared (Ferguson and Granville 2000, 1068). By year-end 1922, the mark-dollar exchange rate had fallen to 1,500 to 1 from its prewar level of 4.2. By the end of November 1923, it had fallen to 4,200,000,000,000 to 1.

The actual breakdown of German economic life came because of interventions of the German government to maintain the paper mark as the medium of exchange. Holtfrerich (1986, 313) wrote of hyperinflation Germany, "The economy had already largely turned over to a foreign, hard-currency standard.... The crisis arose out of the reluctance of the Reich to permit business to employ foreign means of payment in domestic transactions as desired; indeed the Reich could not permit the practice ... as long as inflation remained as a 'tax' source."

Although the government ignored the price setting of the large industrial cartels, it imposed price controls on professionals and the retail trades to prevent "profiteering." The combination of price controls and hyperinflation threatened imminent economic and social collapse. The November 1923 stabilization program committed Germany to exchange 1,392 Reichsmarks for a pound of gold. The reform worked because of the political consensus that it had to work. The economic disruption had pushed Germany to the edge of social disintegration. Revolts, including Hitler's Beer Hall Putsch and attempted march on Berlin on November 9, 1923, challenged the survival of the government. Faced with chaos, Germany restored order. A social and political consensus emerged that the Reichsbank had to maintain the dollar-mark exchange rate.

Germany ended hyperinflation and restored social peace with its commitment to the gold standard (Sargent 1993). However, German economic stability then depended on the stability of the international gold standard. Starting in 1928, the deflationary monetary policies of France and the United States forced deflation and economic depression on Germany. Short-run salvation led to longer-run doom.

HOW THE GOLD STANDARD SPREAD DEFLATION
AND DEPRESSION

A historical antecedent for the debate over the nonneutrality of money exists in the criticism of Chancellor of the Exchequer Winston Churchill by Keynes for the decision to force a deflation by returning to the gold standard in 1925 at the prewar parity. In the language of economics, Churchill (1924–1925) questioned why a change in a nominal variable (the parity price of gold) would affect a real variable (the unemployment rate):[8]

Let us see exactly what [Keynes' policy] means. Currency is to be the medium of adjustment – the shock absorber [for unemployment]. How foolish to have any disputes with workmen about their wages! All you have to do is to inflate, to manipulate the currency. Immediately, you depreciate the exchange, immediately you give a bounty on exports, immediately prices at home are raised, and what does that mean? ... It means a diminution, in exact mathematical ratio, of the real wages which are received by the working classes.

D. H. Robertson (1928[1948], 2, 13, and 16), who was commenting on the British experience with the deflation required to return to the gold standard at the pre–World War I parity, offered the contrasting monetary nonneutrality view:

[A]ny violent or prolonged exhibition of instability in the value of money affects not only the distribution but also the creation of real wealth; for it threatens to undermine the basis of contract and business expectation on which our economic order is built up.... [M]en trained and willing to work find no work to do, and tramp the streets with ... growing rancor in their hearts.

By the end of 1927, it appeared that Europe had successfully returned to the gold standard. However, Germany and Britain especially had little cushion in the way of free gold to deal with gold outflows. Beginning in 1928, the monetary policies of France and the United States created deflationary pressures by absorbing gold that caused the gold standard to collapse in the 1930s.[9]

---

[8] The citation is from the material referenced in footnote 5 of Wolcott (1993).

[9] In criticizing the sterilization of gold inflows by France and the United States, on September 12, 1931, just before Britain left the gold standard, Keynes (1931 [1971d], 600, cited in Irwin 2010) wrote:

The whole world is heartily sick of the selfishness and folly with which the international gold standard is being worked. Instead of being a means of facilitating trade, the gold standard has become a curse laid upon the economic life of the world.... It is necessary only to look at the present distribution of the world's gold supplies.

After the war, France had counted unrealistically on German reparations to balance its budget. When those reparations did not materialize,
it used inflation as a tax to finance expenditures. In 1926, France pulled
back from the brink of hyperinflation. Unlike Britain, in France, inflation
had put the old parity hopelessly out of reach. As a consequence, France
returned to gold at a parity that undervalued the franc. Scarred by its experience with inflation, France sterilized the resulting gold inflows to prevent
a rise in prices. Irwin (2010, 4, 8) noted that by a measure of excess gold
reserves, that is, gold beyond that legally required to back the currency,
the excess reserves of France and the United States amounted to 6 percent
of the world's monetary gold stock in 1929 and 12 percent in 1930–1932.
In 1932, the two countries held 60 percent of the world's monetary gold
stock.[10] This growing maldistribution of the world's monetary gold stocks
made the newly restored gold standard into an instrument of deflation.

Allied war debts and reparations added to the inherent fragility of the
international gold standard. They required the transfer of resources from
Germany to France and England and then from these countries to the
United States. To accomplish these transfers, Germany would have had to
run a trade surplus with France and Britain. In turn, France and Britain
would have had to run a trade surplus toward the United States. In the protectionist environment of the 1920s, that trade pattern was politically unacceptable. Only capital outflows from the United States made the system
work (Yeager 1976, 333; Holtfrerich 1986, 151).[11]

In 1928, the Federal Reserve turned capital outflows into inflows with
a restrictive monetary policy to stop presumed stock market speculation.
High rates of interest in the United States disrupted the capital outflows that
had offset the international imbalances that would otherwise have arisen
from German reparations.[12] In 1920 and 1921, a floating exchange rate had
insulated countries like Germany from deflationary U.S. monetary policy.
In these earlier years, German industrial production rose 46 and 20 percent,

---

[10]   On the absorption of gold by France and the sterilization of gold inflows to prevent an
       increase in French prices, see also Eichengreen (1986) and Johnson (1997).
[11]   Eichengreen (1995, 224) calculated that most of the $2 billion in reparations paid by
       Germany between 1924 and 1929 went to the United States for payment of Allied war
       debts. America then returned the funds to Germany through capital flows. Not until 1929
       did reparations payments exceed those capital flows.
[12]   By the last half of 1929, foreign debt issued in New York was less than a third of its 1927
       level (Chandler 1958, 456). "Net portfolio lending by the United States declined from more
       than $1000 million in 1927 to less than $700 million in 1928 and turned negative in 1929"
       (Eichengreen 1995, 226). Eichengreen (1995, 226) also documented the corresponding
       decline in German bond flotations in New York.

respectively.[13] At the end of the decade, in contrast, a revived international gold standard transmitted U.S. deflation to Germany.

As a result, in 1928, the United States began attracting gold from Europe.[14] Foreign central banks had to raise their domestic interest rates to offset gold losses. The *Federal Reserve Bulletin* (Board of Governors 1930, 655) talked about "Money rates abroad, which had been kept up largely to protect the reserves of foreign countries against the attraction of speculative and high-money conditions in the United States." George Harrison, governor of the Federal Reserve Bank of New York, informed Secretary of the Treasury Andrew Mellon that "our high money rates ... continue to act as a pressure upon all the European bank reserves."[15] At the same time, France, with its undervalued franc, also absorbed gold from the rest of the world. In 1928 and the first half of 1929, France absorbed 3 percent of global gold reserves (Eichengreen 1995, 216).

To reverse their gold outflows, other countries had to run a trade surplus with the United States and France. Because both the Fed and the Banque de France sterilized gold inflows, those countries had to achieve trade surpluses through deflation. That is, to make their goods cheaper on international markets, their price levels had to fall. By creating obstacles to trade, protectionism exacerbated the extent of the required deflation.[16] The gold standard became an engine of worldwide deflation. The most visible sign of the stress of deflation took the form of bank failures as depositors withdrew funds from banks for gold and currency.

Both international and domestic considerations compelled Germany to deflate rather than to abandon the gold standard. The Banking Act, created in 1924 as part of the Dawes reparations plan, required Germany to back its currency with gold and foreign exchange reserves equal to 40 percent of its currency. A foreign member of the General Council, set up to oversee the Reichsbank, could stop note issue if he believed gold convertibility was threatened (James 1999, 25). The foreign loans from the Morgan syndicate used to finance reparations payments required Germany to stay on gold. Germany also believed that adherence to the gold standard provided

[13] The figures are from Holtfrerich (1986, table 38).
[14] From August through December 1928, the United States imported $44.5 million in gold; in 1929, $120 million; in 1930, $278 million; and from January through September 1931, $336 million (valued at $20.67 per fine ounce). Data are from table 156, "Analysis of Changes in Gold Stock of United States, Monthly, 1914–1941," Board of Governors (1976). Also, in 1929, Germany's scheduled reparations payments rose.
[15] Harrison memo, "Conversation over the telephone with Secretary Mellon," April 29, 1929, Harrison papers, Federal Reserve Bank of New York archives.
[16] The U.S. Congress passed the Smoot-Hawley Tariff Act June 13, 1930.

it with a reputation for financial conservatism that would make credible its efforts to renegotiate reparations obligations. Most important, seared by the memory of hyperinflation, German public opinion supported the gold standard. Germans associated abandonment of the gold standard with inflation (Bresciani-Turroni 1937, 402; Eichengreen 1995, 270; James 1999, 25). Politicians had difficulty supporting a possibly inflationary policy without appearing to favor large industry and agriculture, which as debtors had profited from the earlier inflation (Feldman 1997, 853).

In April 1929, with the near collapse of reparations negotiations in Paris, reserve outflows threatened the Reichsbank's legally required gold cover. In May 1929, calm reappeared with the successful resumption of the negotiations leading to the Young Plan signed in June. In September 1930, when elections gave Hitler's party the second largest majority in the Reichstag, gold outflows from the Reichsbank resumed. Aid from an international consortium relieved the crisis. In May 1931, the gold cover had risen to a comfortable 60 percent and capital markets had again become receptive to German debt issue (Ferguson and Temin 2003; Schnabel 2004).

However, any lasting restoration of investor confidence in the gold parity of the mark required settlement of the reparations issue.[17] In turn, settlement of the reparations issue required amicable relations among Germany's major trading partners, especially with France. According to Ferguson and Temin (2004), such a positive outcome appeared possible in spring 1931, but forces of nationalism within Germany forced aggressive actions on the Brüning government that upset the needed international cooperation. These nationalist forces emerged out of the discontent produced by high rates of unemployment.[18]

---

[17] See Bank of England Governor Montagu Norman telephone conversation with Harrison, June 18, 1931, Harrison papers. See also Shepard Morgan, "Memorandum on German Short-Dated Debt Reduction," July 6, 1931, Harrison papers, Federal Reserve Bank of New York.

[18] Shepard Morgan, partner in J. P. Morgan, was critical of the French. He wrote a memorandum placed in Governor Harrison's files arguing that the United States should reject the policy of allowing the deposits of its banks to flee German banks. The only purpose of allowing such a runoff would be to initiate an economic collapse that would "oblige the French to step in, either for the purpose of saving Germany from Hitlerism or communism or to protect their reparations revenues." Morgan (Shepard Morgan, "Memorandum on German Short-Dated Debt Reduction," July 6, 1931, Harrison papers, Federal Reserve Bank of New York) wrote:

German unity dates only from 1871, and forces of disruption latent in tradition and the German character have always to be reckoned with. If disintegration should occur, the main objective of the French foreign policy would be served, that is, the advance of national security. Germany in a condition corresponding to that at the close of the Thirty Years' War would not threaten French security for a generation or more.

Wolf (2010, 24–5) summarized, "The already fragile Weimar Republic had been further destabilized with a significant rise in unemployment during the winter 1928/29. … The September election in 1930 showed a massive radicalization of the electorate … the Nazi's [share of the vote increased] from 2.6% in 1928 to a spectacular 18.3%." The Reichsbank had pushed up the overnight rate of interest from 6.7 percent in 1928 to 7.5 percent in 1929. After a reduction in 1930, it pushed the rate up to 7.2 percent in 1931. The growth rate of money (currency, demand, and time deposits) declined over this period and then the level of the money stock fell by 6.1 percent, 15.3 percent, and 9.7 percent, respectively, in the years 1930, 1931, and 1932. In those three years, respectively, the CPI declined by 3.8 percent, 8.1 percent, and 11.4 percent and real GNP declined by 1.4 percent, 7.7 percent, and 7.5 percent. The unemployment rate rose steadily from 6.7 percent in 1928 to 28.1 percent in 1932.[19]

As detailed by Ferguson and Temin (2004) and Schnabel (2004), the emerging possibility of international cooperation and settlement of the reparations issue ended when internal forces pushed the German government into a confrontational foreign policy. Germany announced its intention to engage in naval rearmament and to forge closer cooperation with Austria through a customs union. On May 25, 1931, German Chancellor Brüning announced that Germany would no longer pay reparations (referred to as "tribute"). Foreign holders of deposits in German banks feared that Germany would repudiate all its foreign debts. They began to flee German banks, and at the beginning of June 1931, the Reichsbank began to lose gold.[20] The Reichsbank's gold cover fell from a comfortable 59.5 percent on May 30, 1931, to near the legal minimum of 40 percent on June 19, 1931. From 2,577 million reichsmarks on May 30, 1931, the Reichsbank's reserves then fell to only 1,610 million reichsmarks on July 31, 1931.[21]

On June 20, 1931, President Hoover proposed a one-year moratorium on reparations and Allied debt payments. Financial markets worldwide responded positively (Eichengreen 1995, 277). However, French concern

---

[19] The overnight interest rate is an annual average of monthly figures of "Day-to-day money" in table 172, "Money Rates in Selected Foreign Countries," Board of Governors (1976. The unemployment rate is from Bundesarbeitsblatt 7–8 (1997), Bundesanstalt für Arbeit, Bundesministerium für Arbeit und Sozialordnung (1997). The other series are from Deutsche Bundesbank (1976), "Ausgewählte Daten zur Wirtschaftsentwicklung 1879–1974," table 1.01, "Monetäre Entwicklung 1924–1974," and table 1.02, "Allgemeine Wirtschaftsentwicklung 1924–1974."

[20] Eichengreen (1995, ch. 9) and Yeager (1976, ch. 17) contain a chronological account of the 1931 financial crisis.

[21] Table 167, "Reichsbank-Principal Assets and Liabilities, Monthly, 1924–1941," in Board of Governors (1976).

about aggressive German foreign policy doomed the negotiations until a debt moratorium was too late to help. French reluctance to agree to the Hoover moratorium created an investor nervousness that allowed financial panics in Austria and Hungary to jump the border to Germany.[22]

Central banks had cooperated to maintain the gold standard in the twenties. The New York Fed and the Banque de France, the central banks with ample gold reserves, could have lent to the Reichsbank. In this event, it is possible that monetary contraction and the fall in the German price level necessary to improve Germany's trade balance could have occurred without bank failures. However, Governor Harrison of the New York Fed demanded that the Reichsbank cut its discount-window lending to German banks as a condition for a loan.[23] The head of the Reichsbank, Hans Luther, acceded to Harrison's demand that the Reichsbank cease discounting the commercial paper of banks.

As a result, the Reichsbank had to allow its banking system to collapse.[24] Closing its discount window to new discounts was the Reichsbank's last desperate attempt to meet the escalating demands that Governor Harrison set for a loan to replace the gold outflows. Despite having encouraged the Reichsbank to believe the New York Fed would organize a loan provided it met stringent conditions, under no condition was Harrison willing to lend to the Reichsbank (Hetzel 2002a, appendix). Because foreigners held half of German bank deposits, financial stability required that foreign investors retain confidence in the maintenance by Germany of its gold parity (Eichengreen 1995, 272). Only American leadership could have achieved that result, and Harrison failed to provide it.

The financial panic in Europe began with the failure of the Austrian Credit-Anstalt bank in mid-May 1931. At the time, commentators attributed the subsequent flight of foreign depositors in German banks to a contagion resulting from this failure of the Credit-Anstalt bank, which spread to the German Danat Bank. According to this "banking" view of the crisis, depositors first came to see German banks as insolvent. They withdrew their funds, and a foreign exchange crisis then developed. Most scholarship

---

[22] Cablegram Dreyse to Harrison, July 11, 1931, Harrison papers, Federal Reserve Bank of New York.

[23] Cablegram Harrison to Luther, July 10, 1931, Harrison papers. See also telephone call Dr. Dreyse, vice president Reichsbank, to Harrison, July 10, 1931, Harrison papers, Federal Reserve Bank of New York.

[24] On the restriction of discount-window lending, see Cable from Berlin to Murnane, July 6, 1931, Harrison papers, Federal Reserve Bank of New York. See also Eichengreen and Temin (1997, 28).

since then has assigned priority to a "currency" crisis view, emphasizing the concerns of foreign investors for the continued adherence of Germany to the gold standard with its free movement of capital and absence of exchange controls.

On the basis of an examination of deposit withdrawals at German banks, Balderston (1994) argued that the banking crisis emerged out of a foreign exchange crisis. In his view, foreign depositors withdrew funds from German banks as political developments both made a negotiated settlement of reparations less likely and brought into question the ability of the Reichsbank to maintain the discipline of the gold standard by not monetizing government debt. Pontzen (1999, 79) backed Balderston's view. He pointed out that capital outflows abroad set in before withdrawals by domestic depositors. Balderston also pointed to foreign investor nervousness caused by a more aggressive stance toward reparations by the German government. Ferguson and Temin (2003; 2004) argued for a currency crisis (depositor doubts over maintenance of the gold standard) rather than a banking crisis (depositor fears over solvency of the banking system).[25]

In summer 1931, Britain also experienced bank gold outflows. In response, the Bank of England raised its discount rate from 2.5 percent to 4.5 percent in July 1931. Like Germany, the run on sterling ultimately derived from the way in which world recession limited the ability of the central bank to implement the contractionary monetary policy necessary to defend an overvalued exchange rate. "The slump had led to an alarming deterioration in the current account of the balance of payments.... The scramble for liquidity on the Continent intensified the pressure on London, and when the Labour and National Governments were unable to decide on a concerted response, the banking crisis was transformed into a political crisis" (Cairncross and Eichengreen 1983, 73). After remaining basically unchanged in 1929, the retail price index fell by 3.8 percent in 1930 and 6.2 percent in 1931. Real GDP fell by 0.9 percent in 1930 and by 5 percent in 1931. The unemployment rate went from 10.4 percent in 1929 to 21.3 percent in 1931.[26] Britain suspended convertibility on September 19, 1931.

---

[25] Schnabel (2004) emphasized the currency crisis caused by political events in Germany related to reparations. She argued that only large Berlin banks (not the German banking system) had solvency problems. Lending to these banks reduced the available gold cover for the Reichsbank.

[26] The retail price index is from table III.(11), "Retail Price and Cost of Living Index, 1914–1982" (Capie and Webber 1985). Real GDP is from the "balanced" figures, table 3: "Annual Growth Rate Comparisons" (Solomou and Weale 1996). The unemployment rate is from table 160, "Percentage of Insured Workers Unemployed Each Month September 1912 to December 1939," *British Labor Statistics, Historical Abstract 1886–1968* (1971).

Morrison (2010) blamed the Bank of England's concentration on budget balance to reassure investors rather than on a fundamental overvaluation of the pound for its unwillingness to defend the pound through increases in the bank rate. In September, a National Government (a coalition among parties) led by Prime Minister MacDonald had passed a deeply divisive budget imposing cuts on unemployment benefits, public sector employee wages, and public works projects. Fundamentally, Keynes must have been right that Britain was no longer willing to bear the unemployment cost of the deflation required to defend the pound and the gold standard. These spending cuts exacerbated class divisions. Keynes feared further class divisions that would be created by the deflation required to remain on the gold standard.

In August 1931, Keynes (1931 [1971d], 591, cited in Morrison 2010) wrote MacDonald that the issue was whether "to make a definite decision... in favour of making deflation effective:"

The cut in money incomes which would be required to reach equilibrium by this route [deflation] ... might well be 30 per cent.... It would be impossible to obtain the public consent to such measures unless bondholders, etc., were treated in the same way. I know of no practical means to ensure this or to secure even a modicum of public justice.... [It] is now nearly *certain* that we shall go off the existing gold parity.... [W]hen doubts as to the prosperity of a currency ... have come into existence, the game's up.... I suggest that you should consult a Committee consisting of all living ex-Chancellors of the Exchequer, whether they believe that deflation *a outrance* is possible.

The economic fortunes of countries depended on whether adherence to the gold standard forced deflation on them or, alternatively, on whether a floating-exchange-rate regime allowed them to escape deflation. Deflation began in the 1920s when countries that had experienced wartime inflation announced an intention to return to prewar parities. Cassel (1928, 18–19, cited in Wood 2009a, 10) wrote of Denmark and Norway:

When once international speculation came to believe that a restoration of the old gold standard was to be expected, it took the currency into its own hands, and the authorities lost all control over developments. They were simply obliged to precipitate the deflation in order that the purchasing power of the currency should be made to correspond with its international value. In this way both currencies have been practically restored to their old gold parity, but the deflation which had to be gone through seriously affected the economic life of the countries. The losses were heavy, and unemployment became a most distressing factor.

China offers an especially striking example of the importance of how the monetary regime determines prices and, as a result, the course of the business cycle.[27] Because China was on a silver standard, it effectively maintained

---

[27] The following is from Friedman (1992) and Yeager (1976).

a floating-exchange-rate regime with the gold standard countries. The silver yuan had depreciated mildly against the dollar after 1925. Yeager (1976, 355) wrote that China experienced a:

mildly inflationary boom from about 1926 on.... This boom continued for some two years after the start of the world depression in 1929; the abundance of its depreciating silver-standard currency insulated China from the contagion of worldwide deflation.

China's economic fortunes crashed with the silver purchase program initiated by the United States as authorized by the Thomas Amendment to the Farm Relief Bill of 1933. To appease senators from the seven western silver states, the U.S. government purchased silver to raise its price. The resulting export of silver from China forced deflation on it. Friedman (1992, 158, 174) wrote:

U.S. silver policy imposed a major deflation on China in 1934–36.... While most of the rest of the world was beginning to recover from the Great Depression, China was, according to contemporary observers, entering into the severest phase of its internal depression.

Spain is the other example of a major country that entered the Depression with a floating exchange rate relative to the gold-bloc countries. Choudhri and Kochin (1980) contrasted the experience over the interval from 1928 through 1932 of Spain with the small gold-bloc countries Belgium, Italy, the Netherlands, and Poland. These gold-standard countries all experienced a decline in industrial production and in wholesale prices practically identical to the decline exhibited by the United States. In contrast, output and prices remained basically unchanged in Spain.

ABANDONING GOLD AS A PREREQUISITE FOR RECOVERY

Starting in 1931 with the departure of Germany and Britain from the gold standard, countries adopted a range of monetary standards. Eichengreen (1995, table 10.1) provided a useful classification of countries into four types: countries that remained on the gold standard, countries that formally remained on the gold standard but effectively departed because of exchange controls, countries in the sterling area, and a collection of other countries that depreciated their currencies.

Abandonment of the gold standard was a prerequisite for ending deflationary monetary policy. However, monetary stimulus generally came haltingly. Eichengreen (1995, 292) explained:

To a remarkable extent, their [central banks] actions were still conditioned by attitudes formed during the last episode when the gold standard had been in abeyance.

The early 1920s had been marked by inflation, social turmoil, and political insta-bility. Only when domestic interest groups had agreed to compromise over the dis-tribution of incomes and the burden of taxation and had sealed their compact by reimposing the gold standard had this chaos subsided. Central bankers hesitated to capitalize on the suspension of the gold standard until they were convinced that the same would not happen again.

Even after Germany left the gold standard in summer 1931 through impo-sition of foreign exchange controls, Germany did not adopt an expansion-ary monetary policy. "Haunted by memories of hyperinflation ..., [German Chancellor] Brüning continued to pursue policies designed to compress spending and preached the deflationary rhetoric of the gold standard. His famous decree reducing all prices was issued in December 1931, six months after Germany effectively had abandoned gold" (Eichengreen and Temin 1997, 31). Fearful of sterling depreciation, the Bank of England actually increased the bank rate from 4.5 percent to 6 percent the day after aban-doning the gold parity on September 21, 1931, while the government main-tained an austere budget. The Bank of England began pushing the bank rate down only in February 1932.

Despite the qualification that abandonment of the gold standard was not synonymous with adoption of a stimulative monetary policy, as Temin (1993, 92) wrote, "The single best predictor of how severe the Depression was in different countries is how long they stayed on gold." For example, Britain left the gold standard in 1931. Thereafter, as measured by wholesale prices, the price level began to increase slightly after mid-1932.[28] Also in mid-1932, industrial production stopped falling and started rising by year-end. Again, as noted in the Grossman (1994) reference in Chapter 4, because Britain never experienced bank runs, there is no obvious connection between financial market crises and cyclical instability. In Germany, wholesale price deflation ended at the start of 1933 and prices rose moderately starting in mid-1933. Industrial production began to rise in mid-1933.

In commenting on France as of 1937, Yeager (1976, 363) wrote:

The story so far shows how much economic misery and political turmoil over sev-eral years stemmed from the inappropriateness of one single pegged price – that of the French franc. This sacred price, so long and painfully defended, finally had to be adjusted anyway.

As referenced by Yeager, France devalued the franc in September 1936. However, the franc remained overvalued, and France had to float the franc

---

[28] Figures on prices and industrial production in this paragraph and the following one are from Wolf (2010), figures 1 and 3. See also Temin (1993), figures 1 and 2.

in June 1937. With its Stabilization Fund, France continued to support the franc. In spring 1937, economic recovery took hold and practically restored full employment. However, the Popular Front government of Leon Blum pursued policies that kept industrial production not far from its post–World War I level (Yeager 1976, 365).

Japan illustrated the way in which output contracted in response to the deflation forced by adherence to the gold standard and rebounded after the stimulative monetary policy made possible by its abandonment. Japan went onto the gold standard in January 1930 (Shizume 2007). "The consequences, economically, were abrupt deflation and a severe contraction of economic activities in 1930 and 1931" (Shizume 2009, 5). Japan went off the gold standard in December 1931. "[T]he yen was allowed to depreciate by 60 percent against the U.S. dollar and by 44 percent against the pound sterling, from December 1931 to November 1932" (Shizume 2009, 6). In both 1930 and 1931, the money stock (currency in circulation) fell by about 10 percent while wholesale prices fell almost 20 percent and 15 percent. In 1932 and 1933, after abandonment of the gold standard, output (industrial production) stopped falling and rose at rates of about 5 percent and 15 percent.[29]

Like other European countries, Sweden had inflated in World War I. It decided to return to the gold standard at the prewar parity. Jonung (1979, 463) wrote:

[T]he Swedish money stock was reduced by 29 percent between 1920 and 1925, and the price level by 35 percent during the same period. During these years of deflation, unemployment reached the highest level ever recorded in Sweden.

After Britain left the gold standard on September 19, 1931, speculators attacked the Swedish krona, and Sweden then left the gold standard on September 27, 1931.[30] Influenced by Wicksell, Sweden adopted a price level target.[31] However, the Riksbank remained attached to pegging the foreign exchange value of the krona. After breaking the link between the krona and gold in September 1931, the Riksbank raised the discount rate from 6 percent to 8 percent. After a

---

[29] The figures are from Shizume (2009), charts 6 and 7.

[30] This account is from Jonung (1979) and Jonung and Berg (1999).

[31] Jonung (1979, 460) quoted a speech given by Swedish economist Knut Wicksell in 1898:

There is no need to waste words proving how important it is that the exchange value of money or, what is the same thing seen from the opposite view, the general level of commodity prices, remains as stable and constant as possible. Money is the standard of all values, the basis of all property transactions, and daily becomes more and more so. All commodities are exchanged for money, and, moreover, we produce only in order to exchange, and to exchange for money. What then can be more important that that what constitutes the standard of everything else should itself retain a constant magnitude?

dirty float in which the krona at first appreciated against the British pound and then depreciated, in July 1933, the Riksbank pegged the krona to the pound at a rate about 7 percent above the former gold parity. Given stability in British prices, Swedish prices remained stable. The depreciation of the krona relative to the dollar and to the currencies of gold-bloc countries allowed industrial production to climb steadily starting in mid-1932. Beginning in early 1933, the unemployment rate fell steadily but from an elevated value of about 23 percent (Berg and Jonung 1999, figures 1, 2 and 3).

Eichengreen and Sachs (1985) wrote the pioneering article comparing differing experiences across countries with the gold standard. Their figure 1 plotted observations for countries of industrial production in 1935 relative to 1929 against the change in the exchange rate over that period ("the gold price of domestic currency in 1935 as a percentage of the 1929 parity"). For the gold-bloc countries like France, the exchange rate index remained at 100. For countries that had gone off the gold standard like Britain, the exchange rate index fell, in the case of Britain, to 60. Eichengreen and Sachs (1985, 936) wrote:

There is a clear negative relationship between the height of the exchange rate and the extent of the recovery from the Depression. The countries of the Gold Bloc, represented here by France, the Netherlands, and Belgium, had by 1935 failed to recover to 1929 levels of industrial production. Countries which devalued at an early date (the United Kingdom, Denmark, and the Scandinavian countries) grew much more rapidly.

Campa (1990) repeated the Eichengreen and Sachs experiment for Latin American countries, which left gold in discrete waves. Argentina, Uruguay, Paraguay, and Brazil had left gold by early 1930 in response to outflows in foreign capital. Countries tied to sterling devalued after September 1931, in particular, Argentina, Bolivia, Mexico, Costa Rica, Columbia, and Peru. When the United States abandoned the gold standard in 1933, the Central American countries, which pegged to the dollar, experienced depreciation relative to countries that remained on the gold standard. Using these countries and the same calculations performed in the figure 1 of Eichengreen and Sachs (1985), Campa found the identical striking relationship – the greater the currency depreciation from 1929 to 1935, the greater the recovery in output relative to the 1929 base.

REESTABLISHING CONVERTIBILITY: THE CONTRAST WITH THE POST-WORLD WAR II EXPERIENCE

The grandest experiment for evaluating the way in which the choice of monetary regime creates behavior of the price level useful for disentangling causation between common variability in prices and in output occurred through the contrasting way in which the world reestablished convertibility between currencies after World War I and World War II. The West succeeded in establishing a peaceful Europe after World War II, where it had failed after World War I.[32] That success depended in part on the establishment of a monetary system that did not entail the deflation of the late 1920s and early 1930s. The United States and Germany behaved in a way that allowed movement toward free trade with a system of pegged exchange rates while avoiding a forced deflation by countries with overvalued exchange rates.[33]

Immediately after World War II, an undervalued dollar created a "dollar shortage" and the United States ran a huge balance of trade surplus. In part, the United States recycled the resulting reserve inflows through unilateral transfers to the rest of the world.[34] Equally important, in 1949, the United States encouraged its trading partners to devalue their currencies (revalue the dollar).[35] By removing the overvaluation of their currencies, these countries eliminated pressures to either deflate or resort to protectionism and capital controls.

After a small deficit in 1951 and surplus in 1952, Germany began to run persistent current account surpluses (Giersch et al. 1992, table 28). Left alone, the surpluses would have widened because of the increasing

[32] This section excerpts material from Hetzel (2002b).

[33] The rejection by the United States of isolationism was also of central importance. U.S. aid replaced punitive reparations. The resulting cooperation between European countries in the form of the Organization for European Economic Cooperation (OEEC) facilitated the re-entry of Germany into the European community. With the establishment of the General Agreement on Tariffs and Trade (GATT), the United States encouraged an open, multilateral trading system.

[34] The sum of government and private unilateral transfers and capital outflows was $6.8 billion in 1949. The figure fell to around $4 billion in the mid 1950s but rose again to almost $7 billion in 1957 (Bureau of the Census. *Historical Statistics of the United States, Colonial Times to 1970*, Part 2, 1975. Series U 1–25, "Balance of International Payments: 1790 to 1970.")

[35] On September 18, 1949, after a sterling crisis and with U.S. encouragement, Britain devalued the pound by 30.5%. Thirty other countries, accounting for approximately two-thirds of all world trade, followed in devaluing relative to the dollar (Yeager 1976, 444–5). Those devaluations left the dollar somewhat overvalued for most of the 1950s. Giersch et al. (1992, 93) present a graph of the difference between the free market DM exchange rate on the Zürich market and the official exchange rate. According to this measure, the DM was about 20% overvalued in early 1950. By the end of 1953, the overvaluation disappeared.

Starting in 1950 and for the remainder of the 1950s, the United States incurred a deficit on current account (with the exception of 1956 and 1957 when the United States benefited from special factors related to the Suez crisis). From 1950 through the end of the Bretton Woods system in 1973, the United States persistently lost gold. (In 1949, the U.S. gold stock was $24.6 billion. It declined steadily and reached $10.5 billion in 1972, the last full year of the Bretton Woods system.) The willingness of the United States to allow reductions in its gold stock allowed other countries to rebuild their reserves without deflating.

competitiveness of German industry. After the war, western European countries purchased their capital goods exclusively from the United States; however, in the 1950s, Germany replaced the United States as the major exporter of capital goods to European countries (Giersch et al. 1992, 88–9; Yeager 1976, 486). Germany responded to balance-of-payments surpluses by liberalizing its trade faster than other countries (Holtfrerich 1999, 331).[36] After 1955, liberalization of its capital controls allowed Germany to become a significant exporter of capital (Yeager 1976, 490–6; Giersch et al. 1992, table 28). Germany granted significant amounts of credit to cover the deficits of other countries (Yeager 1976, 412). In the 1960s, Germany pursued a large-scale foreign aid program and encouraged capital exports (Holtfrerich 1999, 377 and 393).

LESSONS LEARNED FROM THE MONETARY EXPERIMENTS OF THE DEPRESSION

A striking feature of the decisions in the 1930s by governments to stay on gold and endure deflation followed by the reluctance to reflate once having abandoned gold was the extraordinary willingness of governments to tolerate high unemployment. Eichengreen and Temin (1997) attributed that willingness to a "gold standard mentality." In the case of Britain, they cited the way in which advocates of the gold standard blamed high unemployment on a social unwillingness to force wage cuts. As evidence of this "mentality," Eichengreen and Temin (1997, 28) cited Lionel Robbins (1934, 186) who argued that "if it had not been for the prevalence of the view that wages must at all costs be maintained in order to maintain the purchasing power of the consumer, the violence of the present depression and the magnitude of the unemployment which [h]as accompanied it would have been considerably less." Eichengreen and Temin (1997, 29) also cited the famous remark of Tom Johnson, former parliamentary secretary for Scotland and Lord Privy Seal, "Nobody told us we could do that [devalue]!"

This gold standard mentality, which possessed political and historical roots, made the 1920s and 1930s into a laboratory for understanding the implications of the monetary standard for the behavior of prices and for the causal relationship between forced deflation and high unemployment. The differing experience across countries with respect to the willingness to submit to

---

[36] Germany became a "pioneer of European [trade] liberalization" in an effort to "become a respected member of the Western world" (Giersch et al. 1992, 108–9).

deflation and the resulting differing experience with unemployment demonstrated that monetary contraction caused high unemployment.

Bernanke and James (1991, 41–42, 63) expressed the consensus that emerged by the 1990s espousing a monetary explanation of the shocks that caused the Depression:[37]

> For the positive question of what caused the Depression, we need only note that a monetary contraction began in the United States and France, and was propagated by the international monetary standard.... The basic proposition of the gold standard-based explanation of the Depression is that, because of its deflationary impact, adherence to the gold standard had very adverse consequences for real activity. The validity of this proposition is shown rather clearly by table 2.4.... Between 1932 and 1935, growth of industrial production in countries not on the gold standard averaged about seven percentage points a year better than countries remaining on gold.... With respect to the effect of banking panics on the price level ... the appropriate conclusion appears to be that countries with banking panics did not suffer worse deflation than those without panics.

Furthermore, the price system is a powerful equilibrating force – provided that monetary instability does not disrupt its operation. As Eichengreen and Temin (1997, 37) wrote:

> The world economy ... is endowed with powerful self-correcting tendencies. When activity turns down, its inner workings provide a tendency for it to bounce back. Only sustained bad policies can drive the world economy so far off path that it loses its capacity to recover.

MONETARY STABILITY AS A PREREQUISITE FOR FREE MARKETS

Because of the unseen way in which monetary disorder disrupts markets and robs individuals of control over their own destiny, it undermines support for free enterprise and creates a demand for scapegoats and a strongman to punish those scapegoated. Keynes described how inflation destroys the social foundation of a market economy:

> By a continuing process of inflation, governments can confiscate, secretly and unobserved, an important part of the wealth of their citizens. By this method they not

---

[37] Bernanke (1995, 25) strengthened that conclusion:

Comparative studies of a large set of countries have greatly improved our ability to identify the forces that drove the world into depression in the 1930s. In particular, the evidence for monetary contraction as an important cause of the Depression, and for monetary reflation as a leading component of recovery, has been greatly strengthened.

only confiscate, but they confiscate *arbitrarily*; and, while the process impoverishes many, it actually enriches some.... Those to whom the system brings windfalls ... become profiteers (Keynes 1919 [1971a], 148–9). (italics in original)

To convert the business man into a profiteer is to strike a blow at capitalism, because it destroys the psychological equilibrium which permits the perpetuance of unequal rewards (Keynes 1923 [1971b], 24).

Lenin was certainly right. There is no subtler, no surer means of overturning the existing basis of society than to debauch the currency. The process engages all the hidden forces of economic law on the side of destruction, and does it in a manner which not one man in a million is able to diagnose.... By combining a popular hatred of the class of entrepreneurs with the blow already given to social security by the violent and arbitrary disturbance of contract ... governments are fast rendering impossible a continuance of the social and economic order of the nineteenth century (Keynes 1919 [1971a], 149–50).[38]

Later, Warren and Pearson (1933, 124–5, cited in Irwin 2010) offered the same commentary about deflation in the Depression:

The chief explanation of any human ill whose cause is unknown has always been personal sin or error.... [However] The sufferer ... often attributes the results to witchcraft ... or to Congress. Most of the discussions in every period of deflation fall in this class. The man who has failed in business or who is out of work is blamed for it, and he often blames himself.... The present depression is not an act of God.... It is not due to extravagant living. It is not due to unsound business practices. It is not due to overproduction. It is not due to too great efficiency. It is not due to lack of confidence, but is the cause of lack of confidence....

It teaches the devastating effects of deflation, but teaches no other lesson that is good for society. The one lesson to be learned is that, if we are to have deflation, the miser is the wise man. The modern version of the miser who sells short is even wiser. The man who engages in business, producing things that the world needs, is foolish.

The generalization carried over from the world Depression of the 1930s is not particular to the gold standard. The general lesson is that central banks through contractionary monetary policy can disrupt the operation of the market economy. In the Depression, the gold standard forced central banks into undercutting the operation of the price system through the requirement to raise interest rates at times of falling output and prices.

[38] In the 1920s, Germans desired a return to a world where wealth came through hard work, not financial transactions. Feldman (1997, 657–8) wrote that with hyperinflation Germans wanted to reestablish a social order in which:

[T]he public good should take precedence over private gain.... It was not only Hitler who appealed to these sentiments.... [I]nflation ... caused the [Weimar] Republic to be identified with ... violations of law, equity and good faith.... No less offensive ... was the sense that there had been a misappropriation of spiritual values.

In the post–World War II period, the same phenomenon occurred in a different context. After allowing inflation to increase, central banks increased nominal and real interest rates to levels that required recession. As a consequence of their desire to restore noninflationary expectations of interest rates, they introduced significant inertia in that level of interest rates. This inertia, imparted at times of falling output and prices, again undercut the operation of the price system and disrupted the operation of the market economy.

SEVEN

Identifying the Shocks that Cause Recessions

Policy makers base their understanding of how the economy works on their understanding of how the economy has responded to shocks. Most commonly, identification of these presumed shocks has not rested on the systematic study of history but rather on subjectively formed impressions.

HOW WELL DOES THE PRICE SYSTEM WORK
TO OFFSET SHOCKS?

As shown in Figure 7.1, since the Civil War, real output per capita has grown on average at an annualized rate of 2.2 percent. The figure also shows periods of sustained declines in output – recessions. Do these declines represent a failure of the price system? If so, can governments and central banks rectify that failure? The dotted line, which uses an H-P filter (a two-sided moving average) to fit a trend line, proxies for potential output.

In Figure 7.1, if the smoother (dotted) line represents aggregate supply (potential output) and the more volatile (solid) line represents aggregate demand, then the issue is: Why does the price system (the real interest rate) not work to prevent recessions by making aggregate demand equal aggregate supply? Why does not a low real interest rate, which makes the use of resources today inexpensive in terms of foregone future resources, prevent sustained shortfalls of aggregate demand below potential output by stimulating contemporaneous demand?

One possible response is that the question is ill posed. The real business cycle (RBC) view contends that real productivity shocks impart the observed volatility to real output (Kydland and Prescott 1982). Potential output and actual output move in tandem. There are no negative output gaps, that is, situations in which actual minus potential output is negative. A recession is a period of low productivity growth in which workers

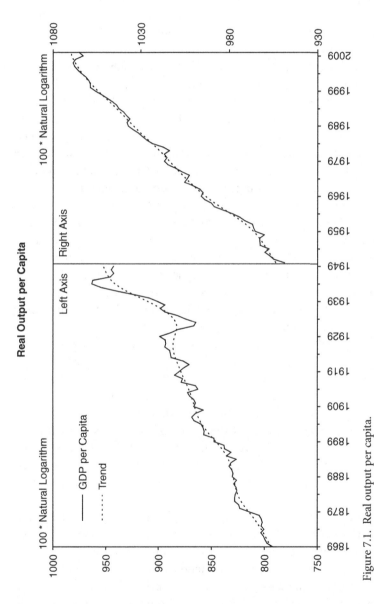

Figure 7.1. Real output per capita.

Note: Series are 100 times the natural logarithm of real output per capita and the HP-filtered trend. Real output is real GNP from Balke and Gordon (1986) until 1929. Thereafter, it is real GDP from the Commerce Department. Series before 1950 are plotted on the left axis; series after 1950 are on the right axis.

choose to work less. That is, they work less today when they are less productive in the expectation that they will work more tomorrow when they are more productive. Because of the widespread distress associated with recessions and the resulting demands placed on the political system for remedial action, the RBC view remains confined to a small number of academic economists.

The alternative to the RBC view is that periodically the price system (equilibrating movements in the real interest rate) does not work well to maintain aggregate demand equal to potential output. Here, there are two classes of explanations: the market-disorder and the monetary-disorder views. According to the market-disorder view, swings in investor sentiment from excessive optimism to excessive pessimism about the future overwhelm the ability of a low real interest rate to sustain demand by providing an incentive to transfer spending from the future to the present.

One variant of the market-disorder view is the "credit-cycle" view in which the collapse of an asset-price bubble leads to dysfunction in financial intermediation that prevents savers from transferring resources to investors. The resulting decline in investment depresses aggregate demand. A second market-disorder variant is the Keynesian view in which pessimism about the return on investments causes a decline in investment. Multiplier effects amplify this decline through a fall in output and income sufficiently large to make savings fall to the lower level of investment.

Both the credit-cycle views that dominated policy making in the Depression and the Keynesian views that dominated academic thinking in the post–World War II period derived from the assumption that in recession pessimism about the future overwhelms the stabilizing properties of the price system. For Keynesians, the persistent high unemployment in the Depression provided evidence of the failure of the price system. The low unemployment in World War II was the experiment showing that government expenditure could make up for the chronic shortfall in demand produced by a price system operating only feebly to assure the full employment of resources.

In contrast to the market-disorder view, the monetary-disorder (quantity-theory) view holds that recessions result from monetary disturbances that interfere with the equilibrating role of the real interest rate. In the event of a recession, monetary contraction is a manifestation of central bank price fixing in the sense of maintaining a price (the interest rate) at an above-market-clearing level. In the absence of money creation and destruction that impede determination of the real interest rate by market forces, the real interest rate will vary to determine a market-clearing intertemporal price of resources (consumption) just as markets clear intratemporally in the absence of price fixing.

From the monetary-disorder perspective, if the central bank maintains an above-market-clearing interest rate, the counterpart to the resulting excess supply in the goods market is the monetary contraction produced by open-market bond sales to offset the corresponding excess demand in the bond market. Interference by the central bank with the determination of the interest rate by market forces implies that money creation does not follow real money demand; therefore, the price level must fall.

IDENTIFYING SHOCKS: WHAT IS AT STAKE?

The general issue is how to identify the nature of the shocks that initiate recessions.[1] In the spirit of the monetary-disorder (quantity-theory) tradition, identification of monetary shocks rests on the principle that the self-equilibrating properties of the price system provide continuity over time to the behavior of the economy. George Stigler (1965, 23 and 30) wrote:

[T]he elements of an economic system which economists believe to be basic have been present for a long time. The nature of economic systems has changed relatively little since [Adam] Smith's time. ... A discipline which was in intimate and continuous dependence upon the current output of events ... would simply not be a discipline; it would be a temporary collection of subjects. It could have no specialists – who would be pathetically obsolete in a few years – nor any accumulated theoretical corpus, for its theory would change with each new liaison or external development. It would not be a science.

Furthermore, as an empirical matter, since the establishment of the Fed, the contemporaneous intellectual and political environment in which it

---

[1] The generation of testable implications ideally requires a model capable of yielding numerical implications. Also, the choice of shocks generating those implications must not derive from information used to fit the model. Kocherlakota (2009, 17) noted that Smets and Wouters (2003) "demonstrated that a sufficiently rich New Keynesian model could fit European data well." However, he added, "I believe statistical fit is overemphasized as a criterion for macro models." Smets and Wouters incorporated ten shocks and allowed the data to choose the shocks to improve model fit. Shocks such as changes in consumer preferences are not observable and cannot serve as a basis for using the model to predict. Shocks such as the central bank's inflation target are in principle observable. However, the authors modeled the inflation target as an empirical process in which the estimation procedures chose the target so that the model fitted the data. That is different from using information apart from the observed behavior of the model's variables to identify changes in the objective function of the central bank and then asking whether the model can explain the resulting behavior of observed variables. For a critique of choosing shocks to make dynamic-stochastic-general-equilibrium (DSGE) models fit the data, see Morley (2010).

operated imposed considerable consistency on its objectives and its strategy for achieving those objectives. As a result, there was a consistency to monetary policy defined as the systematic way in which the Fed responded to the behavior of the economy. Changes in the intellectual and political environment produced changes in monetary policy in this sense. There is, then, a natural laboratory for identifying monetary shocks. Over the lifetime of the Fed, it has implemented monetary policies that have worked better (worse) than others at allowing the self-equilibrating powers of the price system to work. Similarly, different policies have encouraged (limited) the ability of the expectations of the public to stabilize economic activity.

As a result, over time, the different monetary policies have created natural event studies. Assuming that the price system works continually to equilibrate the economy in response to shocks, episodic and infrequent large changes in the central bank's policy instrument are disruptive and make changes in money into an independent source of disturbances through forcing unanticipated changes in the price level. In the pre–World War II era, episodic attempts to control asset prices produced the relevant experiments. In the stop-go era, episodic attempts to lower the inflation engendered by stimulative monetary policy produced the relevant experiments.

Central to understanding the nature of the monetary experiments undertaken by the Fed is an understanding of how monetary policy makers have understood at different times the kind of expectational stability targeted by the central bank. Central bankers operate in financial markets and, as a result, understand policy in terms of achieving expectational stability. However, what sort of expectational stability do they pursue?

William Lidderdale, governor of the Bank of England in the 1890s at the time of the international gold standard, wanted stability in the expectation that the par value of gold would remain unchanged. George Harrison, governor of the Federal Reserve Bank of New York from 1928 to 1940, wanted stability in expected future asset prices as a way of avoiding speculation that would push asset prices to unsustainable levels. William McChesney Martin, FOMC chairman from March 1951 to February 1970, wanted stability in the expectation of the price level. Arthur Burns, FOMC chairman from February 1970 to February 1978, wanted stability in the expectation of businessmen about the future level of real wages (Hetzel 1998). Paul Volcker and Alan Greenspan (FOMC chairmen from August 1979 to August 1987 and August 1987 to January 2006, respectively) wanted stability in a low level of expected inflation. Harrison and Burns wanted stability of a real variable, whereas Martin, Volcker, and Greenspan wanted stability of a nominal variable.

Milton Friedman (1960) used stability in money growth (a k-percent rule) as a benchmark for assessing monetary policy. Volatility in money growth provided evidence of monetary shocks. This identification scheme for shocks required a stable, interest-inelastic money demand function. The benchmark employed here is in the spirit of Friedman's k-percent rule, but it is more general in that it allows for instability and interest sensitivity of money demand.

A stabilizing rule for the central bank should both provide a stable nominal anchor and allow market forces to determine the real interest rate and, by extension, other real variables like unemployment. The derivation of such a rule comes from comparison of monetary policy in the stop-go era with monetary policy in the Volcker-Greenspan era (Hetzel 2008b). The consistency in monetary policy that characterized the latter era is aptly termed "lean-against-the-wind (LAW) with credibility." According to this rule, the FOMC moves the funds rate away from its prevailing value in a measured, persistent way in response to sustained changes in the economy's rate of resource utilization subject to the constraint that bond markets believe that changes in the funds rate will cumulate to whatever extent necessary to maintain trend inflation unchanged after shocks.

The issues at stake are the most fundamental in macroeconomics. How well do the self-equilibrating powers of the price system work to maintain output at potential? In the monetary-disorder (quantity-theory) tradition, they work well in the absence of monetary shocks that interfere with the determination by market forces of real variables, especially the real interest rate. The central bank should follow a rule that provides for a stable nominal anchor but should stand back and allow the price system to determine real variables.[2]

In the market-disorder tradition, the central bank should supersede the working of the price system so as to maintain output at potential. The central bank should actively intervene to control real variables, either to limit the formation of bubbles in asset prices or to limit the magnitude of negative output gaps (excess unemployment). In a recession, the central bank can stimulate private spending through taking over private lending to make up for the shortfall in lending from the full-employment level. Also, the

---

[2] The real-business-cycle view holds that the self-equilibrating powers of the price system work well to maintain output at potential regardless of the nature of the monetary regime. Although the RBC view is consistent with such a rule, its primary message is one of central bank irrelevance. The historical correlation between the variability in prices and output is either an irrelevant artifact or evidence of causation going exclusively from output to prices.

government can stimulate private spending through deficit spending to make up for the shortfall in spending from the full-employment level. In this tradition, economic stability depends on the degree of active intervention by the central bank and government in credit markets and in the economy.

IDENTIFYING MONETARY SHOCKS THROUGH EVENT STUDIES

An implication of the monetary-disorder view is that a correlation will exist between money growth and inflation. Famously, Friedman (1964 [1968], 39) wrote, "Inflation is always and everywhere a monetary phenomenon." Figure 7.2 shows the relationship between money (M2) per unit of output and the price level.[3] Over the interval for which M2 demand is stable (1915 through 1989), the common movements in money and prices are consistent with this monetary-disorder hypothesis.

Friedman (1960, 9) also wrote: "In almost every instance, major instability in the United States has been produced or, at the very least, greatly intensified by monetary instability." As a measure of monetary instability, Friedman and Schwartz (1963b, chart 3) used changes in the steps of a step function fitted to money growth rates. Following Friedman and Schwartz, Figure 7.3 plots a step function fitted to money growth with recessions shown as shaded areas. Apart from the 1945 recession, declines in the level of the M1 steps (monetary contraction) accompanied recessions.[4] Although monetary deceleration preceded business cycle peaks, temporal precedence does not assure causation.

To endow the monetary-disorder view with empirical relevance requires generalizing about the Fed behavior associated with the fluctuations in the money steps shown in Figure 7.3. In the spirit of the quantity theory, monetary instability arises when the central bank sets market interest rates in a way that is adventitious to the equilibrating role played by the real interest rate in moderating output fluctuations around trend. The twentieth

---

[3] Even if the public's money demand function remains stable, the two series can diverge through predictable changes in velocity. In the Depression, for example, the low level of market interest rates increased real money demand and caused the money series in Figure 7.2 to be high relative to the price series (Hetzel 2008b, figure 3.6). The public's demand for real M1 became unstable after 1980, and the demand for real M2 became unstable after 1989.

[4] Monthly observations begin in 1907 when monthly data on M2 become available. Earlier, only a single mid-year observation exists.

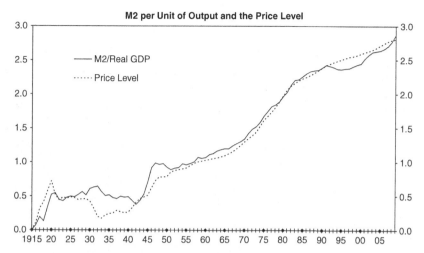

Figure 7.2. M2 per unit of output and the price level.
Note: The series are the price level and M2 divided by real output. Observations are annual values of the natural logarithm of an index number that uses 1915 as a base value. From 1915 to 1929, real output is real GNP and the price level is the GNP deflator from Balke and Gordon (1986). After 1930, real GDP is from the Commerce Department. From 1915 to 1958, M2 is from Friedman and Schwartz (1970). Over this period, it is their M4 series, which corresponds most closely to the current definition of M2. From 1959 on, M2 is from the Board of Governors.

century offered an extraordinary variety of monetary experiments useful for identifying such monetary shocks. These experiments began with two events. First, the world went off the gold standard in World War I and then attempted to reconstruct it in the 1920s. Second, the United States established the Federal Reserve System. Monetary policy in the United States then lurched between very different objectives at different times.

In World War I, the Fed monetized the issuance of government bonds. In 1919–1920, it raised interest rates to lower the price level, presumed to be elevated by speculation in commodity markets. In the 1920s, it sterilized gold inflows to prevent inflation and moved toward the lean-against-the-wind procedures developed in the post–World War II period. After 1928, the Fed concentrated on raising interest rates and then maintained them at levels high enough to suppress presumed speculation, especially on the New York Stock Exchange (Figure 7.4). On two occasions, October 1931 and February 1933, the Fed raised its discount rate to prevent gold outflows.

In March 1933, the Roosevelt administration took control of monetary policy, relegated the Fed to the sidelines, and made monetary policy a function of international gold inflows. By freezing the amount of securities in its

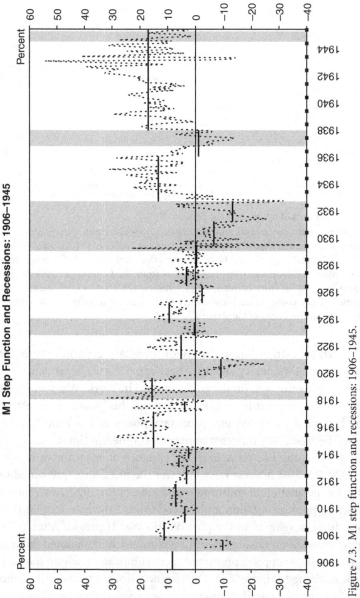

M1 Step Function and Recessions: 1906–1945

Figure 7.3. M1 step function and recessions: 1906–1945.

Note: Series are a three-month moving average of the annualized monthly money growth rates and a step function fitted to monthly annualized growth rates of money. Step function before May 1907 uses annual growth rates based on June observations of M2 from 1900 to 1907. Observations for money from June 1900 to May 1914 are for M2; observations from June 1914 to December 1945 are for M1. Data are from Friedman and Schwartz (1970). Shaded areas indicate NBER recessions. Heavy tick marks indicate December.

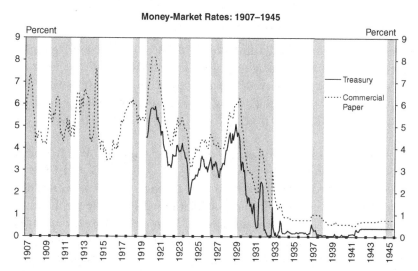

Figure 7.4. Money-market rates: 1907–1945.

Note: Treasury yields on 3-month Treasury bills from Board of Governors *Banking and Monetary Statistics* (1943 and 1976), "Yields on Short-term United States Government Securities," tables 122 and 12.9, respectively. Commercial paper rate on 4–6 month maturities from Board of Governors *Banking and Monetary Statistics* (1943 and 1976), "Short-term Open Market Rates in New York City," tables 120 and 12.5, respectively. Shaded areas indicate NBER recessions. Heavy tick marks indicate December.

portfolio along with minimal discount-window borrowing (Federal Reserve credit), the Fed ceded control over monetary policy to the Treasury, which manipulated gold inflows and the monetary base through setting the dollar price of gold discretionarily in 1933 and at a fixed, devalued exchange rate in January 1934. In 1936 and 1937, the Fed attempted to reassert itself as a central bank with increases in required reserves intended to sterilize the excess reserves of banks.

After World War I, different countries and at times the same country floated their currencies against the dollar or pegged them as a consequence of returning to the international gold standard. Given the preponderant size of the U.S. economy in the world economy, these contrasting international monetary arrangements possessed different implications for the extent to which the United States exported contractionary monetary policy to other countries. As a result, the pre–World War II era offers a rich panel data across time and countries characterized by differences in monetary regimes that emerged in a way adventitious to the working of the price system (see Chapter 6).

RISING REAL RATES AND PERSISTENTLY FALLING OUTPUT

For serious recessions, the declines in the M1 steps observed in Figure 7.3 corresponded to purposeful tightening by the Fed (Hetzel 2008b). However, the Fed responded to observed events in the economy. Perhaps the Fed's tightening facilitated the equilibrating property of the real interest rate, but an adverse real shock still overwhelmed the stabilizing properties of the price system.

Consider the three most serious recessions in the pre–World War II period: the recessions with cycle peaks in 1920Q1, 1929Q3, and 1937Q2. In the first, the Fed raised rates to squelch inflation it considered was due to commodity speculation. In the second, it raised rates to lower the value (P/E ratio) of the NYSE. In the third, when the monetary base had replaced money-market rates as the instrument of monetary policy, the Fed increased required reserves to neutralize the high levels of bank excess reserves, which it believed encouraged speculative investment (Hetzel 2008b). Table 7.1 shows observations of the commercial paper rate and annualized quarterly growth rates of real GDP, the Consumer Price Index (CPI), and M1 with dates measured relative to cycle peaks for the recessions with cycle peaks in 1920Q1, 1929Q3, and 1937Q2. High real interest rates accompanied sustained declines in real GDP – a relationship counterproductive for the working of the price system.

Prior to the 1920Q1 cyclical peak, the Fed began raising rates to suppress what it considered speculative excess in commodity markets produced by the suspension of real-bills principles in World War I. It pushed up the discount rate and maintained it at a high level well after the cyclical peak. The resulting shock was monetary because no banking crisis occurred and "there is no narrative evidence for a credit crunch" (Bordo and Haubrich 2010, 7). Real GNP, which had barely started growing again after the 1918Q3 cyclical peak, fell sharply starting in 1920Q2.

Although Table 7.1 shows nominal rates of interest, experience with a commodity standard induced the expectation that the price level would rise in wartime and then decline after the war. Edwin Kemmerer (1932, 87), professor of economics at Princeton, wrote, "In late 1920 and early 1921 the expected price collapse came," and wrote of the "inevitable post-war deflation of late 1920." Without inertia in inflation due to inertia in expected inflation, the appearance of recession immediately turned double-digit inflation into severe deflation starting in 1920Q3. Given expectations conditioned by the gold standard, the public did not extrapolate actual inflation

Table 7.1. *Behavior of selected series at NBER turning points*

Time	1920Q1 Peak				1929Q3 Peak				1937Q2 Peak			
	Commercial Paper Rate	Real GNP	CPI (NSA)	Nominal M1	Commercial Paper Rate	Real GNP	CPI (NSA)	Nominal M1	Commercial Paper Rate	Real GNP	CPI (NSA)	Nominal M1
	Yield (%)	%	%	%	Yield (%)	%	%	%	Yield (%)	%	%	%
t−6					4.04	3.1	−3.8	2.5				
t−5					4.54	5.0	−0.8	0.8				
t−4					5.38	9.5	0.8	−4.6				
t−3					5.42	4.2	0.0	6.4	0.75	11.9	7.0	14.0
t−2	5.38	2.7	20.4	17.7	5.59	8.4	−2.3	−2.1	0.75	13.9	1.0	7.7
t−1	5.46	−0.2	21.2	20.2	6.00	17.5	−1.6	−0.3	0.75	−1.3	3.9	4.9
t=0	6.42	−3.3	23.4	8.7	6.13	2.6	7.2	5.1	1.00	10.5	6.8	−1.7
t+1	7.38	−18.6	24.5	2.0	5.67	−17.5	−0.8	3.4	1.00	−1.5	4.7	−4.9
t+2	8.13	−6.6	−4.5	−2.8	4.63	−13.7	−6.0	−10.3	1.00	−25.7	−0.9	−12.2
t+3	8.09	−20.1	−12.5	−6.8	3.71	−2.3	−2.3	−6.7	0.96	−15.9	−9.7	2.1
t+4	7.71	−17.0	−21.1	−15.6	3.08	−18.2	−7.7	−4.9				
t+5					2.92	−17.3	−5.5	−2.6				

Note: Quarter-over-quarter percent change at annual rate unless noted. NSA is not seasonally adjusted. Commercial Paper Rate and Real Gross National Product (GNP) are from Balke and Gordon (1986). Consumer Price Index (CPI) is from the Bureau of Labor Statistics. M1 is from Friedman and Schwartz (1970).

and deflation into an expectation of sustained inflation and deflation. The behavior of nominal rates, therefore, was close to that of real rates.

Prior to the 1929Q3 cyclical peak, the Fed began raising interest rates to suppress what it believed to be speculative excess in the NYSE (see Chapters 3 and 4; Hetzel 2008b, ch. 3). Because the price level measured by the CPI had remained unchanged over the interval 1924 through 1928, it is likely that this increase in rates corresponded to an increase in real rates. Real GNP began double-digit declines in 1929Q4. The coexistence of high real interest rates with falling GNP appears most dramatically in the real rates calculated from the measures of expected inflation (deflation) from Hamilton (1992) shown in Hetzel (2008b, table 3.1) and reproduced earlier as Table 4.1. For example, for 1931, a real rate of interest of 9.7 percent coexisted with a decline of real GNP of -7.7 percent, while M1 declined by 6.6 percent.[5]

By 1931, the short-term real rate consistent with the return of real output to trend was very likely negative. This natural rate of interest is a measure of the optimism, or in this case pessimism, of the public about the future. Tobin (2007) commented:

When you go into 1931 and the British devaluation, I think that expectations changed in a very pessimistic direction. People began to think that this is not something temporary that is going to reverse itself the way previous downturns did. This is the way it is going to be. As soon as people thought they could not make economic decisions on the basis of things getting better, but they make economic decisions based on things continuing the way they are and worse, then it is a whole new ball game.

The only way for the Fed to have broken out of the deflation trap that it had created would have been for it to pursue a sustained policy of reserves and money creation sufficient to stimulate nominal expenditure. That change in policy happened only when the Roosevelt Treasury took control of monetary policy and abandoned the gold standard (see Chapters 4 and 5).

In August 1936, the Fed began a phased increase in reserve requirements. Its intention was to sterilize bank excess reserves, which it viewed as kindling for renewed speculative lending. At that time, the Fed was not setting the market interest rate, which rose with the reduction in bank excess reserves. However, the return of deflation in 1937Q4 probably revived the expectation of deflation, especially against the backdrop of the deflation and cyclical downturn prior to 1933Q2. The short-term real rate of interest would then have risen.

---

[5]   Romer (1992, 778) estimated ex ante real interest rates as high as 15% in the early 1930s.

How can one explain this correlation of high real interest rates with persistent declines in real output? Because the RBC model explains fluctuations in output in a framework that excludes monetary frictions and emphasizes persistent real productivity shocks, it is an implausible candidate. In such a model, there is no way to break the link between low real interest rates and persistent, and presumably expected, declines in output due to persistent, negative productivity shocks. The New Keynesian (NK) model, which adds a nominal friction in the form of sticky prices to the RBC model, possesses a similar deficiency.[6]

However, in the previously mentioned episodes, there remains the fact of an increase in the real rate of interest produced by the actions of the Fed – an increase that was large relative to the contemporaneous growth rate of real output. High real rates then coexisted with sustained declines in real output and consumption. At the same time, there occurred a monetary contraction. The most plausible explanation for these correlations is the existence of some monetary or financial friction not incorporated into the NK model.

In the first two episodes cited previously, the increase in market interest rates reflected a reduction in the nonborrowed reserves of the banking system from open-market sales of securities by the Fed. Given the discount rate, the resulting increased borrowing of banks from the discount window, whose use the Fed rationed, forced the interbank rate higher (Chapter 4). In the third episode, the elimination of bank excess reserves left banks vulnerable to reserve outflows.[7] The banking system needed to replace those reserves by some means other than the Fed's discount window. Banks either had to attract currency domestically or gold internationally. Collectively, they had no immediate way to do so.

To gain reserves, individual banks wanted to sell liquid assets like Treasury bills and commercial paper; however, the market was other banks. Collectively, because such an effort was stymied, the price of these liquid assets had to decline sufficiently to induce banks to hold them. The flip side of that price decline was an increase in yield. Over the longer run, the consumption smoothing of households determined the real interest rate, but in the short run, market segmentation broke that link and created the correlation of high real rates and falling output. Over time, banks called loans to increase reserves. That action contracted deposits, thereby raising the reserves/deposits ratio.

[6]   For expositions of this model, see Goodfriend and King (1997) and Woodford (2003).
[7]   Member banks could borrow from the Fed, but only for a limited duration.

The correlation documented in the discussion of Table 7.1 of increasing real interest rates and persistent declines in real output is compatible with a monetary shock or a financial shock. When banks under stress call loans, the simultaneous decline in loans and deposits confounds efforts to disentangle monetary from financial shocks. How then does one differentiate between them? The period of the 1920s and 1930s offered an extraordinarily rich panel data set of countries that differ with respect to the timing of adopting and leaving the gold standard. These changes in the monetary standard occurred independently of changes in the financial system. Of course, gold outflows stressed the banking system, and deflationary monetary policies produced bank runs in a few countries. Still, shocks induced by changes in the monetary standard rather than financial market stress are the simple touchstone for identifying differing kinds of shocks (Chapter 6).

Historically, monetary instability has accompanied real instability. Quantity theorists give causal content to this correlation by arguing that the behavior of the central bank causes destabilizing monetary emissions and contractions by creating unsustainable divergences between the values of real macroeconomic variables and the values determined by the working of market forces. In the language of economics, the price system determines well-defined equilibrium (natural) values of real variables like output and unemployment in the absence of monetary disturbances. In the NK model, the real-business-cycle (RBC) core of the economy determines these values. In a monetary economy, discrepancies in these natural values and the prevailing real values create monetary emissions and absorptions that turn money into an independent negative shock by requiring destabilizing changes in the price level.

A SUMMARY OF THE PROCEDURE FOR IDENTIFYING SHOCKS

To understand the behavior of the price level, one needs to understand the arrangements of a country for controlling money creation. The question then emerges of how market forces discipline the way in which the central bank controls money creation to prevent money from becoming a destabilizing influence. The quantity theory of money advances two general hypotheses about this discipline. First, because of the intrinsic worthlessness of paper (fiat) money, the central bank must give money (more generally, any nominal variable) a well-defined value. Individuals, whose welfare depends only on real variables, cannot perform this function. The central bank must provide a nominal anchor. Second, the market works well because market forces determine well-defined (natural) values of real variables, and the central bank must permit market forces to perform this function. A corollary of this hypothesis is that when the central bank interferes with the operation of the price system in its determination of real variables, the resulting money creation and destruction become an independent source of disturbance by forcing unanticipated changes in the price level.

The first quantity-theoretic criterion for identification of shocks as monetary in origin is whether the monetary regime is sustainable. If it does not meet the two criteria listed previously of providing a nominal anchor and of allowing market forces to determine real variables, it is not sustainable. The second criterion is that the role played by changes in the price level as part of the price system depends on how the central bank chooses its nominal anchor. Given the choice of a nominal anchor, the central bank must respect the resulting role of the price system. With the gold standard, changes in the price level made the parity (nominal) price of gold consistent with the market-determined real price of gold. With a fixed exchange rate, changes in the price level make the nominal exchange rate consistent with the market-determined real exchange rate that clears the market for internationally traded goods. With floating exchange rates and an inflation target, changes in the price level make the nominal quantity of money equal to the real purchasing power demanded by the public.

The three monetary regimes described in the preceding paragraph are sustainable in that they provide a well-defined value for the price level and allow the price system to work. Two examples in U.S. history of monetary regimes that were not sustainable were the Great Contraction from 1929 until March 1933 and stop-go monetary policy from 1965 until 1979. These two monetary regimes did not provide for a nominal anchor and did not allow market forces to determine real variables. They began with a period of price stability and stability in the expectation of the price level. In both instances, the attempt to control a real variable destroyed the monetary regime. In the first episode, the Fed attempted to control asset bubbles with no understanding of the consequences for the price level. In the second episode, it attempted to control the unemployment rate.

How does the choice of a nominal anchor affect the role played by changes in the price level and thereby discipline the behavior of the central bank? With the gold standard, the nominal anchor is the parity price of gold. With fixed exchange rates, the nominal anchor is the fixed value of the foreign exchange value of the currency. The international gold standard that existed prior to World War I combined the features of both of these regimes. Because countries set a value (parity) of their currency in terms of gold, they also set an exchange rate between their currencies. Overall, the world price level determined by the average price level in different countries had to conform to the real price of gold. At the same time, the relative price levels among countries had to adjust to produce balance-of-payments equilibrium.

A third monetary regime is one of floating exchange rates in which the central bank targets price stability. Given an objective of price stability, the central bank must choose procedures that make changes in the price level unnecessary. Under the Volcker and Greenspan FOMCs, the Fed desired to avoid sustained changes in the price level: persistent inflation or deflation. It was, however, willing to allow random movements in the price level provided that they did not cumulate over time to sustained increases or decreases. That is, it allowed bygones to be bygones with respect to the price level but not with respect to sustained changes in the inflation rate. The Fed used the short-term interest rate (the Fed funds rate) as its instrument. The nominal anchor became the policy the Fed followed to stabilize the public's expectation of inflation. The real variable that it had to allow market forces to determine was the real interest rate (natural interest rate).

The Fed's objective was to stabilize inflation, although it was willing to allow transitory fluctuations. One can think about the discipline this objective places on the central bank in two parts. First, the central bank must follow a rule that moves its interest-rate target in line with changes in the natural rate of interest. Second, it must maintain credibility in that the public must expect a stable inflation rate. Various shocks to the economy can impart movements to the contemporaneous price level. However, the public must assume that such movements will impart only one-time changes to the price level. Those shocks do not cause the public to expect any sustained change in the growth rate of the price level (see Hetzel 2008b, ch. 13, 14, 15, and 21).[8]

---

[8] Formula 7.1 expresses the (gross) nominal interest rate $(1+R_t)$ as the product of the (gross) expected inflation rate $(1+\pi^e)$ and the (gross) real interest rate $(1+r_t)$. The price level the public expects in period t+1 is $P_{t+1}{}^e$. P_t is the period t price level. Expected (gross) inflation is $\dfrac{P^e_{t+1}}{P_t}$.

$$1+R_t = (1+\pi^e)(1+r_t) = \frac{P^e_{t+1}}{P_t}(1+r_t) \tag{7.1}$$

Formula 7.1 can be reformulated as Formula 7.2, in which the nominal interest rate is the central bank's policy instrument R_t^T. The bar over the symbol e means that the central bank desires to maintain expected inflation unchanged. The replacement of the real interest rate r_t with the expression r_t^N indicates that the central bank must allow market forces to determine the real interest rate.

$$1+R_t^T = (1+\pi^{\bar{e}})(1+r_t^N) = \left(\frac{P_{t+1}}{P_t}\right)^{\bar{e}}(1+r_t^N) \tag{7.2}$$

To maintain low, stable inflation, the central bank must obviate the role played by changes in the price level in converting the nominal money stock into the real amount of purchasing power desired by the public. Hetzel (2008a; 2008b) described these procedures as lean-against-the-wind with credibility. According to the lean-against-the-wind component, the Fed raises the funds rate in a persistent way in response to sustained declines in the rate of resource utilization, and conversely for reductions in the funds rate. In effect, if the rate of growth of output is above trend, the price for resources today in terms of resources foregone tomorrow is too low. The real rate of interest must increase. If the Fed is credible, expected inflation stays constant and changes in the interest-rate target reflect only the way in which market forces change the natural interest rate.

This quantity-theoretic view emphasizes the conduct of monetary policy by a credible rule. As new information arrives, the real yield curve adjusts in a way that causes real output to fluctuate around potential output. Changes in the yield curve are entirely real, that is, not due to changes in expected inflation. A key corollary of the assumption that markets work well in the absence of monetary disturbances is that markets use information efficiently in that participants in markets form their expectation of inflation in a way that is consistent with the systematic behavior of the central bank (Hetzel 2008a).

CONCLUDING COMMENT

The relevant monetary experiments for testing the monetary-disorder (quantity-theory) view are threefold. First, is the monetary regime sustainable? Second, do changes in the monetary regime produce the predicted changes in the role played by changes in the price level? Third, do shocks that require large, unpredicted changes in the price level precede instability in real output?

Heuristically, as shown in Formula 7.2, the central bank must follow a rule for changing R_t^T that causes R_t^T to track r_t^N and that stabilizes π^e. Also, shocks that cause changes in the price level P_t must pass through to an expectation of the future price level only one for one. That is, $\left(\dfrac{P_{t+1}}{P_t}\right)^{\overline{e}}$ is stable (invariant to shocks). More specifically, to control the price setting of the firms that set prices for multiple periods in order to maintain trend inflation unchanged, the central bank must maintain expected inflation unchanged. To do that, it requires a rule that causes it to change its interest-rate target in line with changes in the natural interest rate. In doing so, it prevents undesired monetary emissions or absorptions that force changes in the price level. Also, the rule must be credible.

EIGHT

From Stop-Go to the Great Moderation

In 2004, Governor Bernanke gave a speech stating his understanding of the reasons for the improved performance of the economy starting in the early 1980s known as the Great Moderation. He attributed the better economic performance to an improvement in monetary policy. Bernanke (2004, 9) expressed optimism about future economic activity based on a belief "that monetary policymakers will not forget the lessons of the 1970s."

What are those "lessons?" This chapter first presents the critique made by monetarists of the alternations in the stance of monetary policy in the late 1960s and the 1970s labeled contemporaneously as "stop-go." The chapter concludes by arguing that this monetarist view is a better starting point for understanding the change in monetary policy from the 1970s to the 1980s than the more recent characterization offered by John Taylor.

Bernanke's understanding of appropriate policy, based on the work of Taylor, foreshadowed the monetary policy of the FOMC in spring and summer 2008. At this time, inflation (especially headline inflation but also core inflation) had persistently exceeded the FOMC's unstated inflation target. From spring through fall 2008, the FOMC left its funds rate target unchanged despite the steady growth in a negative output gap (Chapter 12). The FOMC countered inflation directly through the attempted manipulation of a negative output gap. The argument here is that it misunderstood the lessons offered by the contrasting experience of the Great Inflation and the Great Moderation.

THE "VAST EXPERIMENT" OF STOP-GO

Just as the pre–World War II real-bills era represented an experiment in central bank control of asset prices, the stop-go era represented an experiment in control of the unemployment rate. One reason for the powerful impact of stop-go on the professional consensus within economics derived from this characteristic of an identifiable experiment (Hetzel 2008b).

In 1960, Paul Samuelson and Robert Solow (1960 [1966]) published a paper called "Analytical Aspects of Anti-Inflation Policy," which read like a position paper for the Kennedy campaign for president. The unstated issue was how to defend Kennedy against attacks that a 4 percent target for full employment would be inflationary.[1] Samuelson and Solow plotted a Phillips curve with U.S. data showing nominal wage inflation on the vertical axis and the unemployment rate on the horizontal axis. With nominal wage inflation adjusted by trend increases in output per worker (productivity growth), their graph yielded a relationship between inflation and the unemployment rate. The "problem" was that this latter Phillips curve intersected the horizontal axis (the price stability level) at about a 6 percent unemployment rate. Specifically, in 1956 and 1957, when the unemployment rate was 4 percent, inflation had risen to 3 percent.

Samuelson and Solow argued that if 4 percent unemployment was full employment, then the 3 percent inflation that arose in 1956 and 1957 was cost-push inflation. As careful economists, they said that the data did not allow such a determination. They said only a "vast experiment" could determine whether 1956 and 1957 represented the combination of an unsustainably low unemployment rate with demand-pull inflation or full employment with cost-push inflation. As they surely hoped, the country did indeed run that experiment.

In the *1962 Economic Report of the President*, the Walter Heller Council of Economic Advisors for President Kennedy wrote that "4% is a reasonable and prudent full employment target for stabilization policy." The *Economic Report* also highlighted a graph, which displayed a significant negative output gap (real GDP minus potential GDP) persisting from mid-1957 onward (reproduced in Hetzel 2008b, figure 6.2). Based on its estimate of the fiscal multiplier, the council recommended a fiscal deficit sufficient to eliminate the output gap and achieve 4 percent unemployment. Finally, the *Report* contained wage guidelines based on assumed productivity growth to encourage constant unit labor costs and, as a result, price stability. President Kennedy, however, was focused on international tensions. Desirous of avoiding a dollar crisis, he was hesitant to sign on to an aggressive fiscal policy, although in spring 1963 he proposed a tax cut (Hetzel 2008b).

The Keynesian consensus in the economics profession after World War II did not affect either fiscal or monetary policy until the mid-1960s.

---

[1]   In early 1960, the unemployment rate was above 5%. With the onset of recession in April 1960, the unemployment rate rose to a cyclical peak of 7% in early 1961.

Lyndon Johnson, who succeeded John Kennedy in November 1963 as president, was a populist from Texas who hated "high" interest rates. More important, war and social tensions created deep social fissures. Flag-burning, long-haired demonstrators against the Vietnam War angered the patriotic generation, which had won World War II. A black militant civil rights movement frightened the white middle class. The political system wanted the social balm of low unemployment, and Keynesian economics promised to provide it with only a reasonable cost in terms of inflation. The political system adopted a 4 percent unemployment rate as a national objective based on the assumption that aggregate-demand manage-ment would deliver full employment while incomes policies would mit-igate the inflation-unemployment trade-offs of the Phillips curve (Hetzel 2008b, ch. 7).

The resulting monetary policy earned the moniker of stop-go, although go-stop would have been more apt. The experiment undertaken was that monetary policy could control the unemployment rate with predictable consequences for inflation given by the empirical correlations of the Phillips curve. The Phillips curve promised that, coming out of recession, monetary policy could be stimulative without exacerbating inflation. A large negative output gap indicated by an unemployment rate in excess of 4 percent meant that the Phillips curve was flat – significant reductions in the unemploy-ment rate would lead to minimal increases in inflation.

At the end of the 1960s, Keynesian macroeconomics appeared vindicated. The *1969 Economic Report of the President* contained a plot of a Phillips curve for the years 1955 through 1968. It displayed a clear negative relationship between the unemployment rate and inflation. Friedman (1968) sounded a discordant note in his 1968 American Economics Association (AEA) presi-dential address. He argued that the inverse correlations of the Phillips curve came from unanticipated changes in inflation. Once the public accepted inflation as the norm, the correlation would disappear. Friedman, however, represented a small minority of economists.

The year 1970 started the intellectual ferment that led to modern macro-economics. In that year, both the unemployment rate and the inflation rate rose to 6 percent. Had not the Phillips curve promised that policy makers could achieve low unemployment with only moderate inflation? In 1963, Samuelson (1963 [1966], 1543) had written the following about the empiri-cal correlations of the Phillips curve:

[T]he first duty of an economist is to describe correctly what is out there: a valid description without a deeper explanation is worth a thousand times more than a clever explanation of nonexistent facts. The late Sumner Slichter said: "If some price creep is the price we must pay for growth and prosperity, and perhaps it often is, then it is the lesser evil to pay this price."

On August 15, 1971, with the imposition of wage and price controls, President Nixon completed the "vast experiment" that Samuelson and Solow had envisaged a decade earlier. They had argued that validation of the number 4 percent as representing full employment would involve the following policy: the use of aggregate-demand management to achieve an unemployment rate of 4 percent and government involvement in private price setting to prevent the exercise of the market power that produced cost-push inflation. If 4 percent did represent full employment, such a combination of aggregate-demand and incomes policies would be consistent with sustained price stability.

The experiment failed. The combination of high unemployment and high inflation of the 1970s became known as stagflation. Although stagflation created intellectual turmoil within the economics profession, the Keynesian consensus remained in place until after the Volcker disinflation. Samuelson (1977a, 802; 1977b, 58) wrote:

One is forced by the facts of experience into an eclectic position.... [E]xplanation of the varied pattern of ongoing experience [with inflation] calls for bold combination of causations.... Microeconomic commodity inflation – whether in food, in fuels, or indeed in any important sector of the domestic or international economy – refuses to remain microeconomic.... Monetary expansion ... is typically more the result than the cause of sustained general inflation, simply because ... central bankers ... must be accommodative and avoid policies that would acutely worsen short-run unemployment and stagnation problems.

What the nation hopes for in governor Burns and his colleagues is discrimination between price inflation induced by an over employed and overheated economy and that induced by OPEC, juntas or worldwide crop shortages.

In 1979, a warning by Samuelson (1979 [1986]) captured the drama and high stakes of the Volcker policy of attempting to use monetary policy to achieve low, stable inflation.

Today's inflation is chronic. Its roots are deep in the very nature of the welfare state. [Establishment of price stability through monetary policy would require] abolishing the humane society [and would] reimpose inequality and suffering not tolerated under democracy. A fascist political state would be required to impose such a regime and preserve it. Short of a military junta that imprisons trade union activists and terrorizes intellectuals, this solution to inflation is unrealistic – and, to most of us, undesirable.

Modern macroeconomics arose out of the intellectual turmoil of the 1970s and the failure of Keynesian aggregate-demand policy. However, just as important as the failure of Keynesian fine-tuning was the success of the Volcker disinflation policy. The Volcker-Greenspan FOMCs brought about low, stable inflation without the anticipated need for a periodic recourse to Fed-engineered high unemployment.

The consensus that had formed around discretionary aggregate-demand management ceded to the belief that such attempts to manipulate the economy only introduced uncertainty and worked undesirably through monetary "surprises." As summarized by Lucas (1996, 679):

The main finding that emerged from the research in the 1970s is that … anticipated monetary expansions … are not associated with … stimulus to employment and production…. Unanticipated monetary expansions on the other hand can stimulate production as, symmetrically, unanticipated contractions can induce depression.

A TAXONOMY OF STOP-GO

The Keynesian tradition started from the prevailing real-bills view in the Depression that the business cycle originates in investor mood swings from excessive optimism to excessive pessimism about the future. According to the real-bills view, the violence of these swings overwhelms the self-equilibrating properties of the price system. The phase of excessive optimism is characterized by speculation that creates bubbles in asset prices. The inevitable collapse of these bubbles leads to a period of liquidation of debts, deflation, and recession.[2] Keynesians challenged this pessimistic resignation to prolonged recession (purging) and argued that government deficit spending could make up for the shortfall in private spending from its full-employment level.

The inspiration for deficit spending came from the assumption that recession was evidence of a failure in the price system that government could correct. Because pessimism about the future in recession overwhelms the

---

[2] Robert Shiller (2009b) recently repeated these views:

Keynes … knew first-hand the great difficulties that come from unregulated, unfettered capitalism…. [C]apitalist economies, left to their own devices, without the balancing of governments, were essentially unstable…. The key to this insight was the role Keynes gave to people's psychological motivations…. To a remarkable extent we have got into the current economic and financial crisis because of a wrong economic theory – an economic theory that itself denied the role of the animal spirits in getting us into manias and panics.

In the above excerpt, the reference to "a wrong theory" is to rational expectations, the hypothesis that market participants do not repeatedly make the same mistakes as a consequence of making forecasts inconsistent with the predictable part of monetary policy or of government policy more generally. Krugman (2009b) also denied the ability of the central bank to control expectations by following a consistent policy (a rule).

stimulative effects of a low real interest rate, firms and households spend too little or, equivalently, save too much. As summarized by *New York Times* (2010b) columnist David Leonhardt:

The policy mistakes of the 1930s stemmed mostly from ignorance.... [H]is [John Maynard Keynes'] central insight about depressions – that governments need to spend when the private sector isn't – was not widely understood.

The era of stop-go monetary policy reflected the Keynesian temper of that time. The presumed failure of the price system to maintain full employment implied the chronic persistence of a negative output gap. The go phases of policy represented an attempt to eliminate a negative output gap defined by potential output consistent with 4 percent unemployment. In the go phases, the FOMC raised the funds rate only well after cyclical troughs and then only cautiously in an attempt to reduce a negative output gap in order to lower unemployment. In response to the inflation that resulted from the stimulative monetary policy in the go phases, in the stop phases, the FOMC lowered the funds rate only after the cyclical peak and again only cautiously in an attempt to lower inflation through maintenance of a negative output gap. The overall result was that monetary policy imparted significant cyclical inertia to nominal and real short-term interest rates in the conduct of its lean-against-the-wind (LAW) procedures.

This inertia produced the same alternation between low and high rates of growth of money shown in Figure 7.3 in Chapter 7 for the pre–World War II period and the same association between recession and the initiation of monetary contraction as measured by low rates of growth of money. Figure 8.1 shows the analogous M1 step function and periods of recession for the post–World War II period.[3] That cyclical inertia in interest rates created procyclicality in money and resulted in the fluctuation in the steps in M1 growth shown in Figure 8.1.

Table 8.1 and Figure 8.2, reproduced from Hetzel (2008b, ch. 23, table 23.1 and figure 23.1), display the cyclical inertia that characterized the funds rate in the stop-go era and that led to the procyclical fluctuations in the M1 step function shown in Figure 8.1.[4] For example, as shown in Figure 8.2 by the arrows running from the black dots to the hollow dots and recorded in

---

[3] The series ends in 1981 when the public's real M1 demand function became unstable.

[4] Table 8.1 begins with the mini stop-go cycle with the peak and trough for nominal GDP set at 1966Q1 and 1966Q4, respectively. The FOMC interrupted the stop phase as part of a deal with the Johnson administration in which President Johnson would seek a tax increase from Congress. In doing so, it initiated the era of monetary policy known as stop-go (Hetzel 2008b, ch. 7).

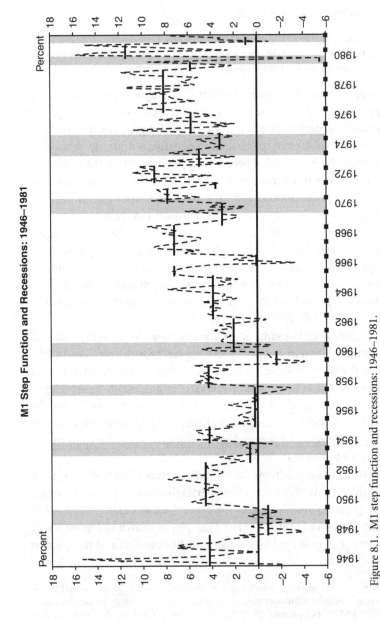

Figure 8.1. M1 step function and recessions: 1946–1981.

Note: Series are a three-month moving average of the annualized monthly money growth rates and a step function fitted to monthly annualized growth rates of money. Data on money (M1) from January 1946 to December 1958 from Friedman & Schwartz (1970). From January 1959 to December 1980, data from Board of Governors. January 1981 to December 1981 M1 is "shift-adjusted M1" (Bennett 1982). Shaded areas indicate NBER recessions. Heavy tick marks indicate December.

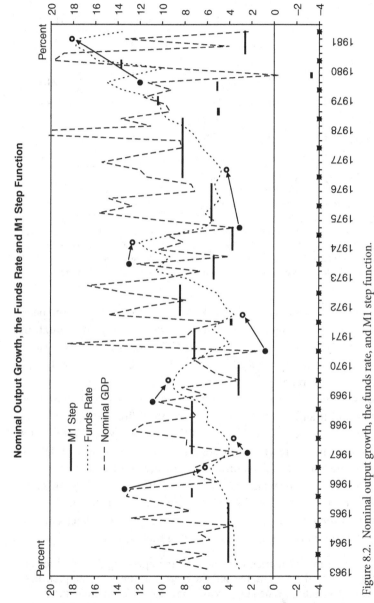

Nominal Output Growth, the Funds Rate and M1 Step Function

Figure 8.2. Nominal output growth, the funds rate, and M1 step function.

Note: Observations of annualized, quarterly nominal GDP growth and the funds rate. The M1 steps are an average of the annualized quarterly M1 growth rates. In 1981, M1 is "shift adjusted" (Bennett 1982). Dark circles mark changes in nominal output growth. Light circles mark significant turning points in the funds rate. Reproduced from Hetzel (2008b, figure 23.1). Heavy tick marks indicate fourth quarter.

Table 8.1. *M1 steps, nominal output growth, and funds rate*

	Nominal GDP peak, trough	Funds rate peak, trough	Lag in quarters	Change in M1 step
P	1966 Q1 (12.8%)	1966 Q4 (5.6%)	3	−5.2
T	1967 Q2 (3.1%)	1967 Q4 (4.2%)	2	5.2
P	1969 Q1 (10.7%)	1969 Q4 (8.9%)	3	−4.2
T	1970 Q4 (1.4%)	1972 Q1 (3.5%)	5	5.3[1]
P	1973 Q4 (13.2%)	1974 Q3 (12.1%)	3	−3.7[2]
T	1975 Q1 (2.4%)	1977 Q1 (4.7%)	8	4.5[3]
P	1980 Q1 (11.5%)	1981 Q3 (17.6%)	6	−5.6[4]

[1] From 1969Q2–1970Q2 step to 1972Q1–1973Q1 step.
[2] From 1972Q1–1973Q1 step to 1974Q2–1975Q1 step.
[3] From 1974Q2–1975Q1 step to 1976Q4–1978Q4 step.
[4] From 1976Q4–1978Q4 step to 1981Q1–1981Q4 step.
Note: The dates correspond to the turning points in the series shown in Figure 8.2. The numbers in parentheses are the values at turning points. The lags show the quarters elapsed between the turning points in nominal GDP growth and in the funds rate. The "Change in M1 Step" refers to the difference between the M1 steps in Figure 8.1. Table reproduced from Hetzel (2008b, table 23.1).

Table 8.1, for the 1970 recession, the peak in the funds rate lagged the peak in nominal GDP growth by three quarters. In the recovery, the trough in the funds rate lagged the trough in nominal GDP growth by five quarters. The resulting fluctuations produced in the height of the successive M1 steps were −4.2 and +5.3 percentage points, respectively.

In response to the inflation created in the go phases, the FOMC raised the funds rate over time sufficiently to create recession.[5] With the appearance of recession, the FOMC remained concerned that markets would interpret a reduction in the funds rate as a diminution in its resolve to lower inflation. The view that the behavior of the funds rate conveyed the stance of monetary policy constrained the willingness of the FOMC to lower the funds rate after business cycle peaks when the Fed was trying to lower the inflationary expectations of the public. Stephen Axilrod (1971, 23), who later became staff director at the Board of Governors, argued that:

[C]oncentration on money market conditions in the operating paragraph of the directive has led both the Committee and the market at times to interpret these conditions as policy itself.... When this occurs, the System often tends to get locked in, because it feels that any change in money market conditions will be interpreted

[5] For a characterization of the evolution of monetary policy across the business cycle during the stop-go era, see Hetzel (2008b, ch. 23–25).

as a change in policy and, therefore, lead to overreactions by market participants and others. This is particularly true in periods, such as 1969, when abatement of inflationary psychology appeared to be the ultimate aim of monetary policy. With that aim, there seemed to be fear that any change in money market conditions would be interpreted itself as signaling a change in policy and thus would fuel inflationary psychology.

Similarly, in fall 1974 even as the recession intensified and even with high real rates of interest, FOMC members resisted reductions in the funds rate. Al Hayes (Board of Governors *FOMC Minutes*, October 15, 1974, 1125–7), president of the New York Fed, stated:

Policy had to remain basically restrictive.... The Committee continued to be up against the old danger that modest slackening of monetary restraint might be over-interpreted by the market and might lead to an unwanted acceleration of inflationary expectations.... It was of crucial importance that the System not undermine the belief that it meant business about combating inflation.

As a result, in the stop phases of stop-go monetary policy, the FOMC imparted inertia to downward movements in the funds rate. The FOMC's intention was to allow a negative output gap of sufficient magnitude to develop to lower expected inflation and thus to restrain actual inflation. The intention was always to allow a moderate amount of excess capacity to develop without causing a recession. The attempt left correlations in the data between reductions in inflation and a negative output gap. However, the attempt to produce a controlled amount of excess capacity to lower inflation in a moderate but sustained way failed. Interpreted as an experiment in exploiting Phillips curve correlations, stop-go monetary policy is consistent with the quantity-theory hypothesis that the central bank cannot control real output in a predictable way. As documented in Chapter 12, similar behavior appeared in the 2008–2009 recession.

This inertia in short-term rates imparted by the central bank is a key characteristic of recessions. Figures 8.3 and 8.4 make this point. Figure 8.3 fits a trend line between cyclical peaks to real personal consumption expenditures (real PCE). Figure 8.4 shows how consumption falls below trend in recession (the dashed minus the solid line in Figure 8.3). Despite a growing negative output gap, the real interest rate remained elevated. Because of its concern about inflation, the Fed maintained the funds rate at a high level. That disruption to the working of the price system produced the monetary decelerations associated with recessions shown in Figure 8.1.

In the 1970 recession, the contrast between the decline in consumption below trend and high real interest rates is clear. In the 1974 recession, high real rates preceded the cyclical peak in October 1973 and then fell. However,

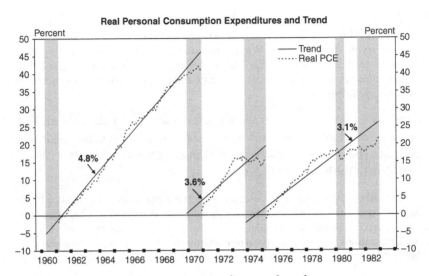

Figure 8.3. Real personal consumption expenditures and trend.

Note: Observations are the natural logarithm of monthly observations on real personal consumption expenditures (PCE) normalized using the value at the prior business cycle peak. Using peak-to-peak values, trend lines are fitted to these observations between cycle peaks and the trend line is extended through the subsequent recession. Data from the Commerce Department via Haver Analytics. Shaded areas indicate NBER recessions. Heavy tick marks indicate December.

real rates increased again in late summer and fall 1974 when FOMC chairman Burns overrode FOMC procedures for setting the funds rate as part of bargaining with Congress. Burns was reluctant to cut the funds rate without congressional action to restrain spending increases (Hetzel 2008b, ch. 10). The Volcker disinflation era is confusing because of the brief stop-go cycle set off by the Carter credit controls announced March 15, 1980, and then withdrawn in July 1980. However, the overall pattern is clear over the period of disinflation from 1980 through 1982. Despite a clear decline in real economic activity, the Fed maintained a high level of short-term real interest rates.

The Volcker-Greenspan era contained two echoes of the prior stop-go policy. Each originated out of concern for the behavior of the foreign exchange value of the dollar (Hetzel 2008b, ch. 14 and 17). First, after the Louvre Accord in early 1987, the FOMC became reluctant to raise the funds rate out of a desire to encourage stimulative policy in Germany and Japan. As shown in Figure 8.5, inflation trended down in the first part of the 1980s but rose starting in 1987. In 1988, FOMC chairman Alan Greenspan initiated the policy of moving to price stability. As shown in Figure 8.5, in early

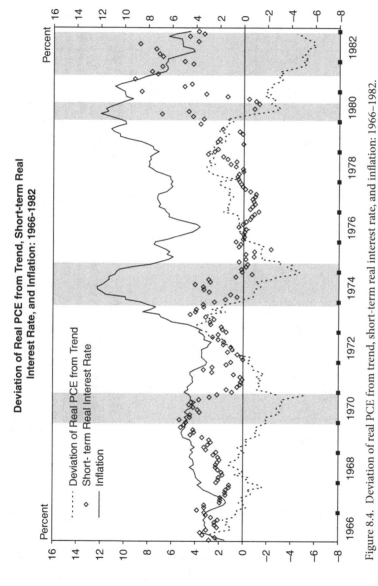

Figure 8.4. Deviation of real PCE from trend, short-term real interest rate, and inflation: 1966–1982.

Note: "Deviation of Real PCE from Trend" is the difference between the actual values and trend lines shown in Figure 8.3. Inflation is twelve-month percentage changes in the personal consumption expenditures deflator. The "Short-term Real Interest Rate" is the commercial paper rate minus the corresponding inflation forecast made by the staff of the Board of Governors. It is the real interest rate series labeled "Overall Inflation Forecast" shown in Figure 11.2. Data on inflation from the Commerce Department via Haver Analytics. Shaded areas indicate NBER recessions. Heavy tick marks indicate December.

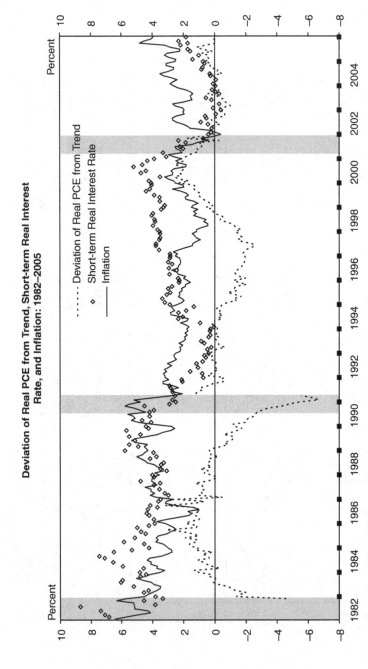

Deviation of Real PCE from Trend, Short-term Real Interest Rate, and Inflation: 1982–2005

Figure 8.5. Deviation of real PCE from trend, short-term real interest rate, and inflation: 1982–2005.

Note: For the series "Deviation of Real PCE from Trend," observations are calculated using the natural logarithm of monthly observations on real personal consumption expenditures (PCE) normalized using the value at the prior business cycle peak. Using peak-to-peak values, trend lines are fitted to these observations between cycle peaks and the trend line is extended through the subsequent recession. Deviation of real PCE from trend is the difference between the actual values and trend lines. Inflation is twelve-month percentage changes in the personal consumption expenditures deflator. The real interest rate is the commercial paper rate minus the corresponding inflation forecast made by the staff of the Board of Governors. It is the real interest rate series labeled "Overall Inflation Forecast" series in Figure 11.2. Data on PCE and the PCE deflator from Commerce Department via Haver Analytics. Shaded areas indicate NBER recessions. Heavy tick marks indicate December.

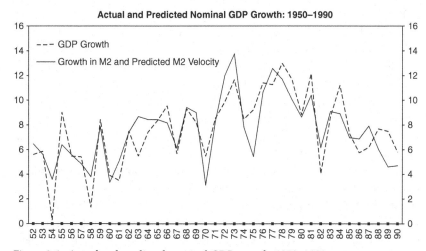

Figure 8.6. Actual and predicted nominal GDP growth: 1950–1990.
Note: Actual and predicted nominal GDP growth using a velocity-adjusted M2 indicator variable: $\Delta\ln M2 + \Delta\ln V^p$. See Appendix to Chapter 8.

1988, the FOMC began to raise the funds rate and the real interest rate. Short-term real rates remained high until after the cyclical peak of the business cycle in July 1990.

With the deregulation of interest rates in 1981, the monetary aggregate M1 lost its value as an indicator of monetary policy. Real M1 demand became highly interest sensitive so that when the economy weakened and market rates fell, real M1 demand increased. The corresponding increased growth in M1 then gave the wrong signal about the desirable direction of short-term rates. However, until 1990, real M2 demand remained reasonably stable (Hetzel and Mehra 1989; Mehra 1993). One could then construct an indicator of monetary policy using the growth rate of M2 adjusted for the change in velocity produced by the change in the opportunity cost of holding M2 (the difference in the market rate of interest and an average of the interest rates paid on the components of M2). After 1990, none of the monetary aggregates served any longer as useful indicators of the stance of monetary policy.[6]

---

[6] The Board of Governors does not collect adequate statistics on the money stock. It either does not collect or only partially collects data on the amount of deposits that banks remove from their balance sheet solely as a bookkeeping artifact to avoid the payment of interest on demand deposits and the tax imposed by noninterest-bearing reserve requirements before the initiation of payment of interest on reserves in October 2008. First, to an unknown extent, banks remove the deposits of corporations at the end of the day when they are

For the period 1950 through 1990, Figure 8.6 shows annual observations of nominal GDP growth and values predicted from an M2 indicator variable. The latter is the sum of annual percentage changes in M2 and predicted changes in M2 velocity based on changes in the opportunity cost of holding M2 (see Appendix: M2 Indicator Variable, which is at the end of this chapter). Figure 8.6 displays the downward trend in nominal aggregate demand produced by monetary policy in the decade of the 1980s. After 1990, M2 velocity increased and M2 no longer offered much useful information as an indicator for monetary policy (Darin and Hetzel 1994).

As shown in Figure 8.5, starting in 1997, the economy grew above potential. As shown by the dashed line, consumption went from below trend to above trend from 1997 to 2000. The FOMC departed from its lean-against-the-wind procedures, which called for increases in the funds rate, out of concern that an increased value of the dollar in the foreign exchange markets would disrupt International Monetary Fund (IMF) programs being implemented in response to the Asia crisis (Hetzel 2008b, ch. 16–19). The short-term real interest rate remained steady from 1997 through August 1998. The FOMC lowered the funds rate in September 1998 in an attempt to offset capital outflows from emerging markets into the United States. Only by the end of 1999 did the real rate exceed its summer 1998 value. In mid-2000, the real rate averaged close to 5 percent. Starting in December 2000, when it became apparent that the economy was going into recession, the FOMC lowered the funds rate sharply. Hetzel (2008b) argued that monetary policy mimicked a mini go-stop cycle in this period.

---

measured for purposes of determining reserve requirements and place them overnight in off-balance-sheet instruments like RPs. Because corporations still have the full amount of their deposits available for clearing purposes, they do not perceive any reduction in their balances. Using information in trade publications, Anderson (2002) estimated the amount of business-related swept balances at $270 billion in 2000.

Since January 1994, the board has also allowed banks to sweep funds out of retail customer transactions accounts. If the sweep program is set up to transfer funds to a money-market-deposit account (MMDA), the Fed collects the number for the initial amount swept out. The cumulative value of this number is available. It is available as "Sweeps of Transaction Deposits into MMDAs" (initial amount swept in $ billions). As of July 2010, the number amounted to $801.1 billion. However, the number is misleading in that banks do not report any subsequent transfers from the account, only the initial one.

It is likely also that with financial innovation the reduction in transactions costs of shifting among liquid assets rendered problematic the use of any single monetary aggregate as a measure of the liquidity services offered by liquid assets. In principle, one could construct a broad monetary services indicator using all liquid financial instruments. The proliferation of these instruments due to financial innovation probably renders any such measure infeasible.

FROM STOP-GO TO LAW WITH CREDIBILITY

The second half of the "vast experiment" in aggregate-demand management was the adoption in the Volcker-Greenspan era of a monetary policy that abandoned the attempt to manipulate an output gap. For the Volcker-Greenspan era, a time known as the Great Moderation, Hetzel (2008a; 2008b) distilled the consistent part of the FOMC's reaction to the economy as "lean-against-the-wind (LAW) with credibility," that is, abstracting from the two go-stop "echoes" discussed in the preceding section (the episodes concerning the Louvre Accord and the Asia crisis). The FOMC raised the funds rate in a measured, persistent way in response to sustained increases in rates of resource utilization (declines in the unemployment rate) provided that bond markets anticipated that the rate increases would cumulate to a degree necessary to avoid an increase in inflation. Of course, there is a converse statement for sustained decreases in resource utilization. These procedures caused the real funds rate to track the natural rate of interest generated by market forces. Sustained increases in resource utilization rates indicated a real interest rate below the natural rate, and conversely.

The back-to-back occurrence of stop-go with the Volcker disinflation moved the intellectual consensus away from the belief that inflation was a real phenomenon powered by cost-push and real aggregate-demand shocks and toward the belief that inflation was a monetary phenomenon, which required that central banks follow a rule to discipline money creation. That discipline occurred through the Fed's rule-like behavior, which created a nominal anchor in the form of stability of expected inflation. The central event, comparable in importance to the failure of the Depression to return after World War II, was the ability of the Fed through this consistency in its behavior to deliver low, stable inflation without recourse to periodic, engineered bouts of high inflation.

The sustained effort of Volcker and Greenspan to create an expectation of inflation that was both low and stable and that remained unchanged in periods of above-trend real growth forced the implementation of consistent procedures that effectively allowed market forces to determine the real interest rate and, as a result, the unemployment rate (Hetzel 2008b). By allowing the price system to work, these procedures largely removed monetary policy as a source of shocks. However, the failure of the Fed to communicate the systematic character of policy necessary to achieve low, stable inflation (a rule) created a vacuum about the kind of monetary policy required to maintain economic stability. There was then no publicly understood benchmark against which to assess the departure of the Bernanke FOMC in 2008 from the earlier Volcker-Greenspan procedures.

THE PHILLIPS CURVE BECOMES THE TAYLOR CURVE

In a 2004 speech, Governor Bernanke argued that in the 1970s, the Fed had an unduly pessimistic view of the Taylor version of the Phillips curve. Plotted as an inverse relationship between variability of the output gap on the y-axis and variability of inflation on the x-axis, the Fed understood the trade-off as steeper than it actually is. According to Bernanke, this pessimism about the trade-offs offered by a Taylor curve caused the Fed to respond too weakly to realized inflation. The Taylor principle, in contrast, calls for the Fed to respond to an increase in realized inflation with a more-than-commensurate increase in the funds rate. Bernanke (2004, 8) stated:

[I]f policymakers do not react sufficiently aggressively to increases in inflation, spontaneously arising expectations of increased inflation can ultimately be self-confirming and even self-reinforcing. ... The finding that monetary policymakers violated the Taylor principle during the 1970s but satisfied the principle in the past two decades would be consistent with a reduced incidence of destabilizing expectational shocks.

In the 1990s, economists attempted to explain the contrast between the stagflation of the 1970s and the Great Moderation that followed the Volcker disinflation. In the latter period, not only did trend inflation decline, but also the variability of both output and inflation declined. Some economists argued that this outcome emerged because the exogenous shocks that impinged on the economy lessened in the 1980s. Among economists who accepted the existence of monetary nonneutrality and who attributed the contrasting economic outcomes to a change in monetary policy, debate continued between the heritors of the earlier Keynesian and monetarist traditions. Hetzel (2008b, ch. 22) termed the associated contrasting views of the appropriate role of the central bank as "inflation fighter" versus "inflation creator."

Both groups accepted the responsibility of the central bank for the control of trend inflation and rejected the existence of a trade-off between the level of the unemployment rate and trend inflation. However, the division continued over the existence of an exploitable Phillips curve trade-off. Specifically, the Keynesian successors argued for a menu of choices allowing the central bank to reduce the variability of output around potential by increasing the variability of inflation around its long-run target value, and conversely. This group coalesced around the ideas of John Taylor.

Taylor (1998a, 38, 40–41) expressed his views succinctly. There is a Phillips curve trade-off in variances of output and inflation. Also, there are two shocks whose existence forces this trade-off on the central bank – an aggregate-demand shock and an inflation shock. Taylor did not consider monetary shocks:

> [T]here is a trade-off between the size of the fluctuations in inflation and the size of the fluctuations in real GDP. ... [A]ggregate demand shocks, such as a shift in government purchases or change in demand for exports from abroad ... cause real GDP to fluctuate around ... potential GDP. ... The response of monetary policy to these shocks helps determine how large the effects on real GDP or inflation will be. ... [E]xactly the same type of trade-off occurs in the case of a price shock due perhaps to an oil price shock. ... [P]olicymakers ... must choose a policy rule that takes a position on the importance of one measure of stability versus the other.

In addition to a reformulation of the Phillips curve as a menu of choice between output and inflation variability, Taylor advanced a monetary policy rule, which requires the central bank to respond directly to inflation. That is, the Taylor rule posits that the central bank possess a reaction function according to which it moves the funds rate around a constant benchmark value based on a response to deviations of realized inflation from target and an output gap (the difference between actual and potential output). Using ex post, revised data, Taylor (1993) showed that such a functional form could broadly trace out the behavior of the funds rate over long periods of time. Moreover, estimated as a regression equation, Taylor (1998a; 1998b) showed that the coefficient on the inflation term increased from less than one to more than one after Paul Volcker became FOMC chairman in 1979. Using the Taylor principle, Taylor (1999b) argued that the improvement in monetary policy during the Great Moderation resulted from a more aggressive response by the Fed to the appearance of inflation.

In a general sense, the last statement is certainly true. However, the stop-go era showed that responding directly to high inflation through creation of a negative output gap is destabilizing. Moreover, the empirical Taylor rule literature is an illustration of measurement without theory. Its adherents treat a reduced-form regression equation as equivalent to a structural relationship expressing a reaction function, that is, the response of the Fed to the economy (see Hetzel 2008b, ch. 22 and appendix: Taylor Rule Estimation).

From 1971 until 1979, the funds rate and the inflation rate moved together at the same height. Thereafter, until 2002, the funds rate significantly exceeded the inflation rate (Hetzel 2008b, figure 13.3).[7] Taylor (1999a) captured this behavior in a regression equation of the funds rate on inflation and a measure of the output gap fitted as the deviation of output from a trend line. In such a regression, starting in 1979, the estimated coefficient on inflation exceeds one, whereas prior to that date it is less than one.

Taylor (1998b) imbued this reduced form with a structural interpretation as the reaction function of the FOMC. He drew the normative implication, later termed the Taylor principle, that a central bank should raise short-term interest rates more than commensurately with changes in inflation. This one reduced form replaced the earlier monetarist critique of monetary policy based on the empirical generalization of Friedman (1960) that responding directly to inflation causes the central bank to destabilize economic activity. According to Friedman, the central bank should follow a rule that prevents the emergence of sustained inflation.

Examination of the period of monetary policy known as stop-go, which lasted from 1965 until 1979, vindicates the original monetarist critique. Sustained inflation arises from undesirably expansionary monetary policy. Inflation shocks do occur, but they do not propagate in an environment of nominal expectational stability.[8] Monetary policy should prevent the emergence of sustained inflation rather than having to respond to its emergence,

[7] Sorting out the behavior of monetary policy from the behavior of the public in a Taylor rule regression is probably impossible. In the 1970s, inflation increased marginal tax rates on individuals and corporations (Hetzel 2008b, ch. 12 and appendix: Revenue from the Inflation Tax). Capital flowed out of the corporate sector into real estate. General uncertainty about the course of inflation made investors unwilling to issue and hold long-term debt. These factors must have lowered the short-term real interest rate.

With The Economic Recovery Tax Act of 1981, which lowered marginal tax rates for personal income taxes, and the sustained fall in inflation, which began in 1983, optimism replaced pessimism about the productivity of the U.S. economy. Short-term and long-term real interest rates increased in the decade of the 1980s (Hetzel 2008b, figure 14.2). A Taylor rule regression captures this change in the relationship between realized short-term real interest rates and inflation in moving from the decade of the 1970s to the decade of the 1980s. However, any inference about a structural relationship capturing the response of the FOMC to the economy is problematic. That is so, not only because of the reduced-form nature of estimated Taylor rules, but also because of misspecification of their functional form. Most important, they ignore the central variable of concern to the FOMC in the Volcker-Greenspan era, namely, inflationary expectations (Hetzel 2008b, ch. 21).

[8] See Hetzel (2008b, ch. 4) for a discussion of two inflation shocks, which did not propagate into sustained inflation. The first occurred with the end of price controls in 1946 after World War II. The second occurred with the expansion of the Korean War in November 1950 and the resulting expectation of another world war. More recent examples come from countries initiating significant devaluations of their currencies in the context of central bank credibility. For example, in 1992, the United Kingdom and Italy engineered significant devaluations while experiencing declining inflation.

which can only come from a prior inflationary monetary policy. As shown in Figure 8.4, the FOMC did raise the real interest rate in response to the appearance of realized inflation. Such a policy was destabilizing.

A major source of confusion in the Taylor rule literature is the failure to distinguish the real interest rate, which depends on expected inflation, and the realized real interest rate, which depends on realized inflation. The expansionary monetary policy that characterized the go phases of stop-go monetary policy produced real effects because it exploited the historical experience of significant price stability interrupted only by wartime. In the 1970s, actual inflation significantly exceeded forecast inflation. That fact appeared in the underprediction of inflation from the Livingston survey and the losses suffered by bond holders with the brief exception of 1976 (Hetzel 2008b, Figure 4.4).

In the stop-go period, inflation rose with about a two-year lag after monetary acceleration (Friedman 1989; Hetzel 2008b, figure 23.2). As inflation rose and became more of a concern than the unemployment rate, the FOMC raised the funds rate (Hetzel 2008b, figures 24.1, 24.2, and 24.3). When inflation increased significantly, the FOMC raised the funds rate significantly. Using expected rather than realized inflation, the real interest rate did increase. As a result, monetary policy became contractionary as measured by the decline in the growth rate of money (Hetzel 2008b, figure 24.1).

Contrary to the impression left by the Taylor rule literature, increased inflation led to the stop phases of stop-go monetary policy. Indeed, one can argue that the era of stop-go monetary policy represented the high point of monetary policy conducted in the spirit of a Taylor rule. Given the consensus that 4 percent represented full employment, the FOMC believed that it could give operational content to the concept of an output gap. Moreover, the FOMC responded directly to realized inflation.

With replacement of stop-go monetary policy with lean-against-the-wind with credibility, the FOMC moved to the control of inflation with a rule that conditioned the expectational environment in which price setters operate. With the control of trend inflation assured by nominal expectational stability, the FOMC could then allow inflation shocks to pass through into random movements in the price level. The FOMC allowed the price system to operate by moving the funds rate in response to sustained changes in the rate of resource utilization, subject to the constraint that financial markets believed that funds rate changes would cumulate to the extent necessary to maintain trend inflation unchanged. That procedure eliminated the measurement error inherent in trying to estimate the level of potential output.

Table 8.2. *Regression equation predicting M2 velocity*

$\Delta \ln V_t = 9.4^*$ Korea $+ 1.57^* \Delta(R_t\text{-}RM2_t) + \varepsilon_t$
$\quad\quad (5.0) \quad\quad\quad (6.3)$
CRSQ = .65　SEE = 1.85　DW = 1.7　DoF = 39　Dates: 1950 to 1990

Note: Observations are annual averages. V is the ratio of GDP (gross domestic product) to M2. Korea is a shift dummy with the value of 1 in 1951 and 0 elsewhere. R is the 4–6 month commercial paper rate before 1964 and the 6-month CD rate thereafter; RM2 is a weighted average of the own rates of return paid on components of M2; these data are from Federal Reserve Bank of St. Louis FRED database. Before 1959, M2 is M4 in table 1 of Friedman and Schwartz (1970). ln is the natural logarithm; Δ is the first-difference operator. t-statistics are in parentheses. CRSQ is corrected R-squared; SEE is standard error of estimation; DW is Durbin-Watson statistic; DoF is degrees of freedom.

Letting the price system work was the precondition to the monetary control that obviated the need for destabilizing changes in prices.

APPENDIX: M2 INDICATOR VARIABLE

The M2 indicator variable used for predicted nominal GDP growth in Figure 8.6 derives from the quantity equation:

$$\Delta \ln M2 + \Delta \ln V^p = \Delta \ln Y^p. \tag{1}$$

Adding annual percentage changes in M2, $\Delta \ln M2$, to annual percentage changes in predicted M2 velocity, $\Delta \ln V^p$, creates an indicator variable of annual nominal GDP growth, $\Delta \ln Y^p$ ($\Delta \ln$ is the change in the natural logarithm or percentage change). Table 8.2 shows the regression of percentage changes in M2 velocity, $\Delta \ln V_t$, on changes in the opportunity cost of holding M2 (the difference between a short-term money-market interest rate and the own rate on M2), $\Delta(R_t - RM2_t)$. The regression yields predicted values of percentage changes in M2 velocity, $\Delta \ln V^p$. The solid line in Figure 8.6 shows the resulting measure of the monetary (M2) determinants of annual percentage changes in nominal output: $\Delta \ln M2 + \Delta V^p$. The dashed line shows percentage changes in actual nominal output (GDP) growth.

NINE

Controlling Bank Risk Taking

Market or Regulator Discipline?

The financial safety net that protects the debt holders and depositors of financial institutions from losses came sharply into view on March 15, 2008, with the bailout of Bear Stearns' creditors. The New York Fed assumed the risk of loss for $30 billion (later reduced to $29 billion) of assets held in the portfolio of the investment bank Bear Stearns as inducement for its acquisition by JPMorgan Chase. In addition, it opened the discount window to primary dealers in government securities, some of which were part of investment banks rather than commercial banks. The rationale for the bailout was prevention of the systemic risk of a cascading series of defaults brought about by wholesale withdrawal of cash investors from money markets. At the same time, there was also recognition of how a financial safety net creates moral hazard, that is, an increased incentive to risk taking (Lacker 2008). Given the twin goals of financial stability and mitigation of moral hazard, what regulatory regime should emerge from the 2008–2009 recession?

Such a regime must address the consensus that financial institutions took on excessive risk in the period from 2003 to summer 2007. They did so through the use of leverage involving borrowing short-term, low-cost funds to fund long-term, illiquid, risky assets. However, should the limitation of risk taking come from increased oversight by government regulators or should it come from the enhanced market discipline that would follow from sharply curtailing the financial safety net? Each alternative raises the issue of trade-offs. Does the optimal mix of financial stability and minimal moral hazard lie with an extensive financial safety net and heavy government regulation of the risk taking encouraged by moral hazard? Alternatively, does the optimal mix lie with a limited financial safety net and the market monitoring of risk taking that comes with the possibility of bank runs but combined with procedures for placing large financial institutions into conservatorship with losses imposed on debt holders?

This chapter argues for the latter alternative. Its feasibility requires that the financial system not be inherently fragile in the absence of an extensive financial safety net. Such a premise involves contentious counterfactuals. There is no shortcut to the use of historical experience to decide between two contrasting views of what causes financial market fragility. On the one hand, do financial markets require regulation because they are inherently fragile? Are they inherently subject to periodic speculative excess (manias) that results in financial collapse and panicky investor herd behavior so that in the absence of a safety net depositors would run solvent banks out of fear that other depositors will run? On the other hand, have financial markets become fragile because of the way that the financial safety net has exacerbated risk taking? In the absence of the risk taking induced by the moral hazard of the safety net, would market discipline produce contracts and capital levels sufficient to protect all but insolvent banks from runs? Would regulators then be able to place insolvent banks into conservatorship (with mandatory haircuts to debtors and large depositors) without destabilizing the remainder of the financial system?

The first section of this chapter summarizes the unwillingness of the Fed to allow market discipline to close financial institutions. That unwillingness springs from an assumption that failure of a single institution with losses to creditors could precipitate a wholesale run on all financial institutions regardless of their solvency. The second section summarizes the rise of the policy of too big to fail (TBTF). The third section explains how banks take risk through lack of portfolio diversification. The fourth section illustrates the trade-offs created by a financial safety net through the example of the run on prime money-market funds that occurred after the failure of Lehman Brothers on September 15, 2008. The fifth section of this chapter applies the time-inconsistency principle of Kydland-Prescott (1977) to regulatory bail-out policy. The general conclusion reached is that a steadily expanding financial safety net even combined with heavy regulation has increased financial instability. There is a need for more regulation of the risk taking of banks, but that regulation should come from the market discipline imposed through severe limitation of the financial safety net, especially elimination of TBTF.

THE FED VIEW: CREDITOR LOSS AS THE TRIGGER
FOR FINANCIAL PANIC

An assumption motivating the Fed's adherence to discretion in policy making has been that the expectations of financial markets are inherently unpredictable and potentially destabilizing. Implicitly, the assumption is that the conduct of policy based on an articulated rule would not discipline expectations to behave in a stabilizing way. Compare, for example, the following statement of Chairman Burns (1974, 13) with the similar statement of Chairman Martin (reproduced in Hetzel 2008b, ch. 9) about the destabilizing character of floating exchange rates:

With floating exchange rates ... a more rapid rate of inflation in the United States than abroad would tend to lead to a depreciation of the dollar in exchange markets. Such a depreciation ... results ... in higher prices. ... Speculative anticipations of further weakness in the exchange value of the dollar could intensify this vicious circle of domestic inflation and exchange depreciation.

In the context of financial markets, the counterpart is a conjectured unreasoning panic triggered by the default of a financial institution on its debt that causes debtors to withdraw funds from banks regardless of their solvency. Greenspan (2001a, 1) commented:

Bank creditors ... either in response to adversity or ... any reason might decide to withdraw their funds. What is different about leveraged financial intermediaries [from other businesses] is ... the possibility ... of a chain reaction, a cascading sequence of defaults that could culminate in financial implosion.[1]

DEPOSIT INSURANCE AND TBTF

Fischer and Golembe (1976) and Flood (1992) examined the politics of the 1933 and 1935 banking acts, which created deposit insurance. President Roosevelt as well as many bankers and congressmen opposed deposit insurance on the grounds of moral hazard. In its July 1933 newsletter, National City Bank (predecessor of Citibank) wrote that with deposit insurance (cited in Grant 1992, 234),

the element of character in the choice of a bank is eliminated and the competitive appeal is shifted to other and lower standards, such as liberality in making loans. The natural result is that the standards of management are lowered, bankers may take greater risks for the sake of larger profits and the economic loss which accompanies bad bank management increases.

Although opponents of deposit insurance feared that well-managed banks would have to subsidize mismanaged, risk-taking banks, at the time, the

---

[1] Greenspan (2001a, 6), however, disowned the idea of a credit channel as a propagation mechanism for shocks: "As weak intermediaries contract, the markets can, and do, quickly replace the profitable services of the displaced intermediary."

alternative to deposit insurance offered to restore stability to the banking system was nationwide branch banking, which would have favored large urban banks to the detriment of small country banks. Not only did that alternative run into the long-standing populist hostility to large money center banks and the opposition of small community banks to competition from branching (Mengle 1990, 6), but it also seemed to reward the bankers held responsible for creating the Depression. A common explanation of the Depression was that through correspondent balances the large New York banks had drained funds away from the small banks and had used those funds to promote speculative excess on the New York Stock Exchange.

This political animus toward large banks not only doomed branch banking but also resulted in the separation of commercial banking and investment banking in the Banking Act of 1933 (Glass-Steagall). Because depositors running banks were taking their money out of small banks and redepositing it in large banks, deposit insurance favored small banks. In return for accepting deposit insurance, large banks received both the prohibition of payment of interest on demand deposits including the correspondent deposits small banks held with them and Regulation Q, which imposed price-fixing ceilings on the payment of interest on savings deposits (Haywood and Linke 1968; Kaufman and Wallison 2001).

The banking acts contained provisions designed to limit moral hazard in the form of restrictions on bank entry and insurance coverage restricted only to depositors with small balances. Flood (1992) argued that erosion of these safeguards led to the banking problems of the 1980s. After the enactment of deposit insurance and, continuing through the early 1970s, strict unit banking and restrictive entry assured high net worth for individual banks by limiting competition. High net worth militated against the moral hazard of the safety net, that is, asset bets large enough to place taxpayers at risk. However, technological advances in the 1970s, for example, ATM machines and computerized record keeping that made possible money-market mutual funds, effectively ended the ability of regulators to limit entry into the financial intermediation industry. From the early 1960s through the early 1980s, capital-to-asset ratios (measured by market values) for the fifteen largest bank holding companies fell from about 13 percent to 2 percent (Keeley 1990). The recurrent crises in the financial system since 1980 are consistent with financial system fragility produced by the resulting incentives of the social safety net to risk taking.

The moniker "too-big-to-fail" is not an adequate description of the financial safety net that surrounds financial institutions. A more accurate characterization would be "too-leveraged-to-fail." Since the Depression, regulators and especially the Fed have not been willing for any financial institutions beyond small community banks to fail with losses to creditors (uninsured depositors and debt holders). The fear of regulators has always been that if a debt holder suffers a loss, a general financial panic will ensue. Of course, the fear is more intense with a large institution, but the Fed has always feared the spread of a financial contagion precipitated by any failure regardless of the size of the institution. Likewise, the expression "bank bail-out" is misleading. The bailouts involved are really aimed at the creditors of banks (the uninsured depositors and debt holders).

Given its attachment to discretion as opposed to commitment in policy, the Fed has never articulated TBTF as an explicit policy. Politically, given the perverse wealth transfers involved from the general public to the financially sophisticated debt holders of banks, explicit formulation of such a policy would not have been feasible. Nevertheless, this policy emerged through the consistency with which regulators and the Fed have bailed out troubled financial institutions – not only regulated banks but also unregulated investment banks. The following offers a brief history.[2]

Congress had intended that FDIC deposit insurance be used only to compensate holders of insured deposits at failed banks. There was no intention for the FDIC to bail out uninsured depositors and debt holders. In the 1950 Federal Deposit Insurance Act, Congress added an "essentiality" condition to *restrict* FDIC bailouts. This condition gave the FDIC authority to make an insolvent bank solvent by transferring funds to the bank only if it "is essential to provide adequate banking services in its community." Ironically, the FDIC used that language to justify expanding its mandate to one of bailing out all creditors of insolvent banks (Sprague 1986, 27ff).

According to Sprague (1986, 48 and 38), the FDIC set the precedent for bailouts and the move "away from our historic narrow role of acting only after the bank had failed" in 1971 with the black-owned bank, Unity Bank, in inner-city Boston out of fear that its failure would "touch off a new round of 1960s-style rioting." The systemic-failure rationale for bailouts first arose in 1972 in connection with the failure of the Detroit Commonwealth Bank, which had a billion-dollar asset portfolio. According to Sprague's account, the Fed always vociferously supported bailouts. In reference to Detroit Commonwealth Bank, Sprague (1986, 53, 70) cited Fed Board Chairman Arthur Burns' fear that "the domino effect could be started by failure of this

---

[2] The best history of TBTF remains the 1986 book *Bailout* by Irvine Sprague, who was chairman of the FDIC from 1979 through 1981 and continued as a board member through 1985.

large bank with its extensive commercial loan business and its relationships with scores of banks.... Nobody wanted to face up to the biggest bank failure in history, particularly the Fed."

The Fed bailout of Franklin National Bank, which went into receivership in October 1974, set the standard for TBTF. First, a troubled bank relies heavily on short-term funding. Second, when the holders of short-term debt become concerned about the bank's solvency, they withdraw their funds. The Fed makes fully collateralized loans to the troubled bank to allow this withdrawal. When the regulator closes the bank, the FDIC arranges for a purchase that makes insured and any remaining uninsured depositors whole and takes the Fed out to prevent it from suffering any loss.[3] The FDIC insurance fund absorbs the cost of closing the insolvent bank.

Franklin National had a large number of troubled loans in its portfolio and significant losses in foreign exchange trading. Its largest stockholder, Michele Sindona, later went to jail for fraud. Sindona had also earlier tried unsuccessfully to contribute $1 million to President Nixon's 1972 campaign fund (*The New York Times* 1980). Andrew Brimmer (1976), a member of the Board of Governors in 1974, stated the issues raised by Franklin's use of the discount window along with the rationale for the Fed's bailout:

Why did the Federal Reserve Board let Franklin borrow $1.7 billion of the public's money when System officials had concluded as early as June, 1974, that the bank would ultimately fail? Why did the Federal Reserve permit Franklin to use at least $352 million of the loan to meet deposit run-off at its London branch? Why did the Federal Reserve Bank of New York (on the eve of Franklin's failure) assume $725 million of the latter's foreign exchange commitments?

The answers to these questions can be stated directly: ... [T]his nation's central bank saw itself as having a fundamental responsibility to help assure the health and stability of the financial system as a whole – not only in terms of domestic money markets but also in terms of the international financial system as well.

In testimony before the House Banking Committee, the following exchange occurred between Burns and two congressmen (U.S. Congress 1974 [August 8], 290, 327):

REPRESENTATIVE STARK(CA): Franklin National ... was bankrupt by any standard accounting practice. If you are willing to value their assets at market value, and not at book, they would have to be liquidated.

---

[3] Walter and Weinberg (2002, 380) pointed out:

When troubles in large banks have surfaced in the past, uninsured holders of short-term liabilities frequently have been able to withdraw their funds from the troubled bank before regulators have taken it over. Bank access to loans from the Federal Reserve has allowed short-term liability holders to escape losses.

BURNS: It [valuing assets at book value] is an accounting convention. ... What reason is there for dropping the accounting convention?

STARK: Because we may have to liquidate loans to meet outflow.

PATMAN: [Y]ou furnished the money; it would appear that that money was really used to "bail out" the big fellows. They got their money.

In a comparison of the bailout of Franklin National by the Fed with a contemporaneous decision by the Bundesbank to allow the failure of Herstatt Bank, which also incurred large losses in foreign exchange trading, a *Wall Street Journal* editorial (reprinted in U.S. Congress 1974 [August 8], 298) summarized the moral hazard issues raised by the bailout of Franklin National:

In May, when the Franklin National Bank was on the verge of collapse, the Federal Reserve rushed into action with a $1.2 billion rescue operation. In June, when the largest private bank in West Germany – Herstatt – was on the verge of collapse, the Bundesbank considered a rescue operation and turned thumbs down. ... The Fed ... believes a bank, at least a big bank, shouldn't be allowed to go under or the public's confidence in banks generally will be undermined. The Bundesbank, on the other hand, believes that the public will have "confidence" in banks when banking is sound, and that banking diverges from "soundness" when those who run banks know there is a net under them. Isn't it strange that the Socialists who run the West German economy insist that their banks meet the test of the market-place, and the free enterprisers at the Fed want their banks, at least the big ones, kept out of harms way in the market? ... Franklin National should have been permitted to sink, victim of its excesses in "unauthorized currency trading." Its loan portfolio would have been peddled and its depositors paid off.... [T]he market system cannot function without downside risk to discipline managers.... On the assumption that central banks will bail out big banks, depositors are pulling out of small banks and regional banks and going with the big fellows.... All the distortions are perverse. A risky bank that is "big" is to be preferred to a sound bank that is small.... What can be done to correct this situation? There are only two alternatives. The Bundesbank can announce, along with the Bank of England and the Fed, that all banks, big and small, will be rescued when parlous conditions occur. Of course, this will invite ... a string of Franklin Nationals. The other alternative is for the other central banks to join the Bundesbank in pulling the net from under all the banks, big and small, inviting lenders to search out not big banks, but sound ones.

Burns (1978, 367–71; U.S. Congress 1974 [July 30], 263) utilized a public rhetoric favoring the market allocation of capital that failed to match his private practice of superseding the market allocation of capital in favor of bank bailouts. Publically, he criticized the nonmarket allocation of credit:

Decisions as to social priorities in the use of credit are inherently political in character. If such decisions are to be made at all, they should be made by Congress – not by an administrative and nonpolitical body such as the Federal Reserve.

The concept of credit allocation implies a degree of knowledge of social priorities that I for one am quite certain that we at the Federal Reserve Board do not have. I think the Congress would not be well advised to give us a power that we simply do not know how to exercise properly. If we are to have credit allocation in this country, then I think credit allocation should proceed according to the rules devised by the Congress. But there again, I must say, in all humility, that I am not at all sure that Congress has the wisdom to substitute its rules for the workings of the marketplace.

The systemic-risk argument appeared again with the 1980 bailout of First Pennsylvania Bank with $9 billion in assets and whose "loan quality was poor" and whose "leverage was excessive" (Sprague 1986, 85 and 89):

> The domino theory dominated the discussion – if First Pennsylvania went down, its business connections with other banks would entangle them also and touch off a crisis in confidence that would snowball into other bank failures here and abroad. It would culminate in an international financial crisis.... Fed Chairman Paul Volcker said he planned to continue funding indefinitely until we could work out a merger or a bailout to save the bank.

The only bank of any size closed with losses to uninsured depositors was Penn Square, which had $365 million in deposits and which suffered from large loan losses in the energy sector. As detailed in *International Currency Review* (1982, 31–32):

> [In 1982, the FDIC departed from its] purchase and assumption technique [with which] no depositors actually lose money – even those having deposits above the $100,000 insurance limit. ... [T]he comptroller ... wanted the Penn Square Bank to be bailed out. The Federal Reserve, fearing a general crisis of confidence, also argued this case. ... [T]he predictable consequence of the Penn Square shock was to precipitate frantic deposit withdrawals from smaller banks, regardless of their financial standing – since markets are now differentiating *not* between well-and-badly-run banks, *but between those that are likely to be bailed out, and those that might not be.* (italics in original)

The policy of TBTF really took off in the early 1980s during the LDC (less-developed country) debt crisis. When Argentina, Brazil, and Mexico effectively defaulted on their debt, almost all large U.S. money center banks became insolvent (Hetzel 2008b, ch. 14). Regulator unwillingness to close large, insolvent banks became publicly apparent in 1984 with the bailout of the debt holders and uninsured depositors of Continental Illinois and of its bank holding company. As shown in the following commentary by Sprague, Continental presaged the 2008 bailouts of financial institutions that used short-term funding to leverage portfolios of long-term risky assets.

"Although Continental Illinois had over $30 billion in deposits, 90 percent were uninsured foreign deposits or large certificates substantially exceeding the $100,000 insurance limit.... First Pennsylvania had a cancerous interest-rate mismatch; Continental was drowning in bad loans" (Sprague 1986, 184 and 199). Continental held a "shocking" $1 billion in loan participations from the Oklahoma bank Penn Square, which had "grown pathologically" and had made "chancy loans to drillers" (Sprague 1986, 111–3). Penn Square had in turn grown rapidly with wholesale money. "The Penn Square experience gave us a rough alert to the damage that can be done by brokered deposits funneled in the troubled institutions" (Sprague 1986, 133).

At the time, regulators claimed that they had no choice but to bail out Continental because of the large number of banks holding correspondent balances with it.[4] Subsequent research showed that even with losses significantly greater than estimated at the time, only two banks would have incurred losses greater than 50 percent of their capital (Kaufman 1990, 8).[5] After the Continental bailout, the Comptroller of the Currency told Congress that eleven bank holding companies were too big to fail (Boyd and Gertler 1994, 7). Regulators also extended TBTF to small banks. For example, in 1990, regulators bailed out the National Bank of Washington, which ranked 250th by size in the United States (Hetzel 1991).

Regulators were unwilling to let Continental fail with losses to creditors because of the fear of systemic risk. "Volcker raised the familiar concern about a national banking collapse, that is, a chain reaction if Continental should fail" (Sprague 1986, 183).[6] Continental highlighted all the moral hazard issues associated with TBTF and excessive risk taking. Later, *The Wall Street Journal* (1994) wrote: "Continental's place in history may be as a warning against too-rapid growth and against placing too much emphasis on one sector of the banking business – in this case energy lending."

Sprague (1986, 249 and preface, xi) foretold the problems of 2007–2008:

The banking giants are getting a free ride on their insurance premiums and flaunting capital standards by moving liabilities off their balance sheets.... [T]he regulators ... should address the question of off-book liabilities.... Continental ... had 30 billion of off-book liabilities.

---

[4] William Isaac, chairman of the FDIC during the Continental bailout, later expressed regret, noting that most of the large banks about which the FDIC was concerned failed subsequently with greater losses to the FDIC than if they had been closed earlier (cited in Kaufman 1990, 12).

[5] With TBTF, banks and other financial market participants possess no incentive to diversify their exposure to other financial institutions thereby making TBTF a self-fulfilling need.

[6] Sprague (1986, 165) reported the concern that, if Continental failed, deposit withdrawals would spread to Manufacturers Hanover, a bank under duress because of its exposure to LDC debt.

I hope this book [*Bailout*] will help raise public awareness of the pitfalls ... of the exotic new financial world of the 1980s.

Sprague (1986, preface, x) also observed:

Continental was ... a link in a [bailout] chain that we had been forging since the 1971 rescue of Unity Bank.... Other bailouts [beyond Unity], of successively larger institutions, followed in ensuing years; there is no reason to think that the chain has been completed yet.

The policy of not allowing financial institutions to fail with losses to uninsured creditors also extended to nonbank financial institutions. The Fed's intervention in May 1982 into the bankruptcy of Drysdale Securities, a small dealer in government securities, is significant in that it established the precedent of not allowing creditors of nonbank financial institutions to incur losses (U.S. Congress 1982). Drysdale, which was capitalized at $20 million, became insolvent when an increase in interest rates lowered the value of its unhedged long position in long-term government securities. In a complicated transaction, Drysdale had funded its long position by borrowing high-yield government securities and then selling them in the RP (repurchase) market. However, it became unable to pay the coupon payments on the securities it had borrowed.

The banks Chase Manhattan and Manufacturers Hanover had brokered the RP transactions and claimed that as agents they had no liability for the coupon payments. After "Federal Reserve officials had discussions with senior officials of Chase and Manufacturers Hanover," the two banks agreed to assume responsibility for the payments due to the lenders of the securities (U.S. Congress 1982, 27). It is reasonable to conjecture that the New York Fed encouraged this outcome. Anthony M. Solomon, New York Fed president, testified (U.S. Congress 1982, 27, 36): "[T]here was nervousness in the market as to whether interest payments would be made ... you could have had the beginning of more of a ripple effect; you might say the beginnings of the seizing up of the market."

Similarly, the Fed's involvement in Long-Term Capital Management (LTCM) offered significant evidence of the reach of the financial safety net (Hetzel 2008b, ch. 17).[7] Greenspan (U.S. Congress 1998, 44, 45, 61) reviewed

---

[7] An interview with David Modest, former partner of LTCM, who complained about the inability of LTCM to raise capital after its creditors refused further funding, offered insight into the incentive that insolvent financial institutions have to take risk, "'It's really tough. They [LTCM] can't take enough risk' to make their money back" (*The Wall Street Journal* 2008h)

this involvement in a way that presaged the Fed's concern for AIG and the problems created by banks' off-balance-sheet activities after August 2007:

[T]he creditors of LTCM ... failed to stress test their counterparty exposures adequately and therefore underestimated the size of the uncollateralized exposure that they could face in volatile and illiquid markets. In part, this also reflected an under appreciation of the volume and nature of the risks LTCM had undertaken and its relative size in the overall market. By failing to make those determinations, its fellow market participants failed to put an adequate brake on LTCM's use of leverage.

[T]he [Basle] capital accord ... picks up what is on the balance sheet and essentially not much of anything of what is off the balance sheet, the famous derivatives. We have got to figure a way to do that.... Supervisors of banks and securities firms must assess whether current procedures regarding stress testing and counterparty assessment could have been improved to enable counterparties to take steps to insulate themselves better from LTCM's debacle.

Although phrased in an understated and convoluted manner, Greenspan argued that the failure of LTCM might have brought down the entire financial system.[8] What accounts for this fragility of the financial system? Greenspan's answer was that it results from a deliberate decision to provide a financial safety net, which undercuts market forces that would otherwise require financial institutions to hold large amounts of capital and limit their use of leverage. Greenspan (U.S. Congress 1998, 40, 84) testified:

Had the failure of LTCM triggered the seizing of markets, substantial damage could have been inflicted.... [T]he consequences of a fire sale triggered by cross-default clauses, should LTCM fail on some of its obligations, risked a severe drying up of market liquidity.... [A] fire sale may be sufficiently intense and widespread that it seriously distorts markets and elevates uncertainty enough to impair the overall functioning of the economy....

[T]he probability that in the event of a collapse of LTCM the whole system would necessarily unravel ... was significantly below 50 percent, but still large enough to be worrisome.... [T]he likelihood that nothing of systemic consequence would have occurred ... is better than 50–50.

[I]n the post-Civil War period, banks on average were required by the marketplace to hold 40 percent, 35 percent capital in order to hold their deposits. People wouldn't deposit in an institution with capital that was not significant. We have decided to create a system which, because of deposit insurance, because of the

---

[8] Commentators criticized Greenspan for supposedly allowing free-market views to blind him to the need for government regulation of bank risk taking. For example, Pearlstein (2010) wrote, "[W]e should have learned from Alan Greenspan's tenure as Fed chairman, economists who worship markets and distrust government don't make for great regulators." In fact, as shown by the quotations, when it came to the regulation of risk taking by financial institutions, Greenspan distrusted market discipline.

Federal Reserve's discount window and Fed wire, which creates riskless settlement, we have induced a fairly significant degree of leverage in the system.

Rep. Barney Frank (D-MA) (U.S. Congress 1998, 81, 83) commented:

Mr. Greenspan has said that this may happen again. So then the question is, if it was so important as to justify this intervention now, how do you persuade us to do absolutely nothing except wait again and trust entirely in your discretion to deal with it if it happens again?.... [Y]ou intervened in a way that left the mistake-makers better off.... [A] consequence ... was to leave some of the richest people in this country better off than they would have been if the Federal Government hadn't intervened; and that rankles a lot of us ... when we are told we can't do anything similar for people much needier.... I am disappointed that you tell us we can do nothing except allow for repetitions of this.

Goodfriend and Lacker (1999) addressed the contradiction of increasing stability through bailouts while decreasing it through the moral hazard arising from bailouts. The financial panic of 2008 fits the Goodfriend-Lacker hypothesis that the dialectic of excessive risk taking, financial losses triggered by a macroeconomic shock, and runs on insolvent institutions followed by further extension of the safety net will lead to ever larger crises. Lacker (2011) cited work by Malysheva and Walter (2010) documenting the expansion of the financial safety net during the 2008 recession:

According to a recent estimate by Richmond Fed staff, 40 percent of bank and savings institution liabilities were explicitly guaranteed at the end of 2009, while an additional 45 percent could reasonably be viewed, on the basis of official actions and statements, as implicitly guaranteed. Back in 1999, only 13 percent of bank and savings institution liabilities were implicitly guaranteed by this criterion, while 50 percent were explicitly guaranteed. Overall, government guarantees thus expanded from 63 percent of banking liabilities to 85 percent.

THE INTERACTION OF SHOCKS AND LACK
OF PORTFOLIO DIVERSIFICATION

Although the shock to the banking system from the decline nationwide in housing prices that began in 2006 was unprecedented, each of the crises recapitulated in this section also resulted from an unprecedented shock. The occurrence of aggregate shocks is not unprecedented. Each shock interacted with a lack of diversification in the asset portfolios of financial institutions to threaten the stability of the system.

The term "moral hazard" became common with the S&L (savings and loan) bailout incorporated into the Financial Institutions Reform, Recovery, and Enforcement Act (FIRREA) in 1989. The effort by government to subsidize housing off budget began seriously in 1966 with the extension of Reg Q to S&Ls, which by law had to specialize in housing finance. To assure S&Ls a *cheap* supply of credit, regulators kept Reg Q ceilings on their deposits at below-market interest rates. To assure S&Ls a *steady* supply of credit, regulators also maintained Reg Q ceilings on bank deposits at a lower level than on S&Ls. Starting with the increase in interest rates in 1969, these ceilings exacerbated cyclical instability in housing construction by causing disintermediation of deposits at S&Ls (Hetzel 2008b, ch. 12; Mertens 2008).

This policy of allocating cheap credit to S&Ls collapsed in the late 1970s. When market interest rates rose above the Reg Q ceiling rates on S&L deposits, holders of these deposits transferred their funds to the growing money-market mutual fund industry. By offering deposits payable on demand and issuing long-term mortgages, S&Ls had borrowed short and lent long. This maturity mismatch rendered them insolvent when short-term rates rose above the fixed rates on their mortgages. Regulatory forbearance then led the S&Ls to engage in risky lending in an attempt to regain solvency.[9]

In 1970, the government created Freddie Mac and expanded the activities of Fannie Mae in order to maintain the flow of funds to housing without having to raise Reg Q ceilings. Following a pattern of raising deposit insurance limits at times of interest rate peaks and S&L disintermediation, in 1980, in the Depository Institutions and Deregulation Act, Congress expanded the S&L subsidy by raising deposit insurance ceilings from $40,000 to $100,000 (Hetzel 1991, 9). Because CDs of $100,000 or more were not subject to interest-rate ceilings, S&Ls, regardless of their financial health, gained unlimited access to the national money market basically at government risk-free rates. Insolvent S&Ls then "gambled for resurrection" through risky lending. Deposit insurance for their liabilities encouraged this risk taking because the government bore the losses while the S&Ls reaped the gains. The cost of bailing out the S&Ls came to $130 billion (U.S. General Accounting Office 1996, 14). The proximate cause of the thrift industry insolvency, high peacetime inflation that raised market rates of interest and engendered deposit outflows from the S&Ls, was unprecedented.

In the 1970s, large money center banks exploited low, short-term real interest rates to buy illiquid, long-term debt of South American countries. When interest rates rose in the early 1980s, these countries threatened to default on their debt. The debts of the less-developed countries (LDCs) owed to the nine largest money center banks amounted to twice the size of

---

[9] On S&L failures, see Dotsey and Kuprianov 1990; Hetzel 2008b, ch. 12; Kane 1989; and Woodward 1990.

these banks' capital (Volcker 1983, 84). William Isaac (2008a), former chairman of the FDIC, commented, "Virtually every major bank in the country would have failed in 1984 had a couple of developing countries renounced their debts, which the FDIC considered a distinct possibility." The cause of the LDC debt crisis, the threat of widespread sovereign debt defaults, was unprecedented.

In the late 1980s, Texas banks concentrated their lending in oil and gas partnerships and in real estate development. When oil prices declined, all the big banks (Republic Bank, InterFirst Bank, First National City Bank, and Texas Commerce Bank) failed, with many being purchased by out-of-state banks. More generally, in the late 1980s, pushed by competition for the financing of business loans coming from the commercial paper market, large banks engaged in significant amounts of undiversified real estate lending (Hetzel 1991). Because of TBTF, they could do so with low capital ratios (Boyd and Gertler 1994).

In 1988, when the real estate market soured, assets at failed banks jumped to above \$150 billion (*The New York Times* 2008c), and by 1992, 863 banks with total assets of \$464 billion were on the FDIC's list of problem institutions (Boyd and Gertler 1994, 2). The aggregate shock, namely, declines in house prices in New England, Texas, and California, was unprecedented.[10] The Fed kept insolvent banks alive through its discount window.[11] In response, Congress passed the Federal Deposit Insurance Corporation Insurance Act (FDICIA) with the intent of forcing regulators to close banks before they became insolvent.

The next episode of financial instability occurred with the Asia and Russia crisis that began in the summer of 1997 (Hetzel 2008b, ch. 16). In early 1995, the Treasury with the Exchange Stabilization Fund, the Fed with swap accounts, and the IMF bailed out international investors holding Mexican Tesobonos (government debt denominated in dollars) who were fleeing a Mexico rendered unstable by political turmoil. That bailout created the assumption that the United States would intervene to prevent financial collapse in its strategic allies. Russia was included as "too nuclear" to fail.

Subsequently, large banks increased dramatically their short-term lending to Indonesia, Malaysia, Thailand, and South Korea. The Asia crisis emerged when the overvalued, pegged exchange rates of these countries

---

[10] In both California and Massachusetts, real house prices peaked toward the end of the 1980s and then fell 30% over the next seven years. Real house prices are measured by the OFHEO House Price Index deflated by the CPI less shelter (Wolman and Stilwell 2008).

[11] Of the 418 banks that borrowed from the discount window for an extended period, 90% ultimately failed (U.S. Congress 1991).

collapsed, revealing an insolvent banking system. Because of the size of the insolvencies as a fraction of the affected countries GDP, the prevailing TBTF assumption that Asian countries would bail out their banking systems suddenly disappeared. Western banks had not done due diligence in their lending under the assumption that in a financial crisis the combination of short-term maturities and IMF money would assure them a quick, safe exit. They abruptly ceased lending to Asian countries. The fundamental aggregate shock, the emergence of China as an export powerhouse that reduced the competitiveness of the Asian Tigers and rendered their pegged exchange rates overvalued, was unprecedented.

TO BAIL OR NOT TO BAIL? – THE CASE OF
THE MONEY-MARKET FUNDS

What are the trade-offs that society faces in creating a financial safety net to prevent bank runs? Or, as Senator Carter Glass put the issue during the Senate debate on the Banking Act of 1933 (the Glass-Steagall Act), "Is there any reason why the American people should be taxed to guarantee the debts of banks, any more than they should be taxed to guarantee the debts of other institutions, including the merchants, the industries, and the mills of the country?"[12]

There is a market demand for financial instruments redeemable at par or, in alternative terminology, with stable NAV (net-asset value). Many investors (depositors) want to be able to withdraw on demand a dollar for every dollar invested (deposited) in a financial institution. At the same time, investors also like to receive interest. Traditionally, banks have supplied such instruments. They have invested in interest-bearing assets while holding sufficient capital to guarantee against credit risk so that they can guarantee withdrawal of deposits at par. At the same time, the ability to withdraw bank deposits at par and on demand creates the possibility of bank runs.

In principle, regulators could draw a clear line demarcating the financial safety net. On the insured side, regulators would limit risk taking and require high capital ratios. On the uninsured side, creditors with their own money at risk would require limitations on risk taking and high capital ratios. The tension arises because regulators cannot draw a credible line separating the insured from the uninsured. Institutions on the uninsured

---

[12] Cited in Todd (2008) from Rixey Smith and Norman Beasley, *Carter Glass: A Biography* (1939).

side have an incentive to find ways to retain the cheap funds guaranteed by the perception that they are on the insured side while acquiring the risky asset portfolios with high returns of institutions on the uninsured side.

For example, some economists in the 1930s proposed a line with "narrow banks" on the safe side. These banks, which would hold 100 percent reserves against deposits and thus would be run-proof, would provide payment services. All other banks would be investment banks (Hart 1935). Friedman (1960, 73) pointed out "the existence of a strong incentive to evade the requirement of 100% reserve. Much ingenuity might thus be devoted to giving medium-of-exchange qualities to near-monies that did not qualify under the letter of the law as deposits requiring 100% reserves." The run on money-market funds following the Lehman bankruptcy illustrated these forces.

Because of the Lehman bankruptcy on September 15, 2008, a money fund, Reserve Primary Fund, "broke the buck." As a result of holding Lehman debt, the value of the fund's assets declined below the value of its liabilities.[13] Large institutional investors withdrew their funds from other prime money-market funds out of fear that these funds could also be holding paper from banks faced with the possibility of default. The Fed and the Treasury intervened to limit the run on prime money funds in two ways.

First, with the creation of the Asset-Backed Commercial Paper Money Market Fund Liquidity Facility (AMLF) announced September 19, 2008, money funds became eligible to borrow from the discount window at the Boston Fed using asset-backed commercial paper (ABCP) as collateral. Second, on September 29, 2008, the Treasury announced a program to guarantee the shares of money-market-fund investors held as of September 19, 2008, in participating funds. Prime money-market funds held significant amounts of short-term debt issued by banks. Especially given the uncertain financial situation of some large banks at the time, there was no ready alternative market for this debt.[14] By extending the financial safety net to prime money-market mutual funds, regulators avoided bank funding problems.

---

[13] As of March 2006, the Reserve Primary Fund invested only in government securities. It then began to invest in riskier commercial paper, which by 2008 comprised almost 60% of its portfolio. In that way, it could raise the yield it offered and attract more customers while exploiting the image of money-market mutual funds as risk free. *The Wall Street Journal* (2008n) wrote:

[B]y this September [2008], the Primary Fund's 12-month yield was the highest among more than 2,100 money funds tracked, according to Morningstar – 4.04%, versus an average of 2.75%. With this stellar yield, the fund's assets tripled in two years to $62.6 billion.

[14] Preventing a run on money-market funds worked as part of TBTF in that the prime funds held significant amounts of bank debt. "A large share of outstanding commercial

At the same time, regulators created moral hazard problems. Money-market mutual funds have competed with banks by offering redemption of their deposits at par (NAV stability). More precisely, they have used amortized cost accounting rather than mark-to-market accounting. As a result, when the value of their assets falls, they do not mark down the value of their shares. Shareholders then have an incentive to run in case the fund breaks the buck. With mark-to-market accounting, in contrast, there would be no incentive to run.

Effectively, prime money-market funds had been competing for funds as banks without the significant regulatory costs that come with being a bank. If, in September 2008, regulators had drawn the financial-safety-net line to exclude money-market mutual funds, these funds would have been subject to the market discipline of possible failure. They would then have had to make one of two hard choices to become run-proof. Prime money funds could have chosen some combination of high capital and extremely safe, but low-yielding, commercial paper and government debt. Alternatively, they could have accepted variable NAV as the price of holding risky assets. Either way, the money-market mutual fund industry would have had to shrink. At present, the incentive exists for money funds to exploit the government safety net by increasing the riskiness of their asset portfolios.[15]

TIME INCONSISTENCY AND EXPANSION OF THE FINANCIAL SAFETY NET

In testimony before the Financial Crisis Inquiry Commission, Ben Bernanke (*The New York Times* 2011a) stated, "As a scholar of the Great Depression, I honestly believe that September and October 2008 was the worst financial crisis in global history, including the Great Depression." As detailed in Chapter 4, given the magnitude of the monetary shock administered by the Federal Reserve, the banking system in the Depression was remarkably

---

paper is issued or sponsored by financial intermediaries" (Board of Governors 2008). This arrangement whereby banks raise funds indirectly rather than by issuing their own deposits arose as a way of circumventing the legal prohibition of payment of interest on demand deposits.

[15] The day after the Lehman bankruptcy, *The Washington Post* (2008d, A1) summarized the moral hazard arising from regulator bailouts:

Patricia McCoy, who served on the Fed's Consumer Advisory Council from 2002 to 2004, cautioned that ... "even though the Fed financing is temporary, it sends a huge message to the investment banking industry to continue to arrange your balance sheets to be dependent on short-term financing, because when you get into a liquidity crunch, you can turn to us and we'll help you out."

robust until the fears for the continuation of the gold standard and state-wide bank closures of early 1933. With the passage of time, what happened to create such fragility in the financial system in fall 2008?

The answer is that the moral hazard of the financial safety net has created a hair-trigger system. The subsidy to a financial institution from the financial safety net increases with the riskiness and illiquidity of the institution's asset portfolio, with leverage, and with reductions in capital. At the same time, the safety net skews financing toward short-term debt because it protects financial institutions from runs either through deposit insurance (explicit and implicit) or through short-term lending facilities. Financial institutions possess no incentive to develop more costly run-proof contracts with investors. The catalyst for runs in this hair-trigger system is a macroeconomic shock that causes the uninsured creditors of banks simultaneously to jump for the exit either to the too-big-to-fail institutions or to avail themselves of the exit money provided by central banks, especially through the Fed's discount window and since 2008 various other lending facilities such as TAF (Term Auction Facility).[16]

The working assumption of financial regulation has been that government does not need an explicit policy with credible commitment with respect to bank bailouts. Gerald Corrigan, former president of the New York Fed, used the term "constructive ambiguity." Although this characterization in principle admits of discretion not to bail out all bank creditors, the prevailing practice of regulators of preventing uninsured depositors and debt holders from incurring losses in the event of a bank failure restricts monitoring of risk taking by bank creditors. At least since the failure of the S&Ls in the 1980s, policy makers and the public have understood the resulting problem of moral hazard.[17] The assumption has been that government regulation can limit the resulting incentive to risk taking. However, the regular recurrence of financial crises that involve banks with portfolios rendered risky by the lack of diversification contradicts this assumption. In practice, government regulation of risk taking has not substituted for the market regulation that would occur if bank creditors had money at risk.[18]

---

[16] An analogy is the instability created by the Bretton Woods system of fixed exchange rates. Undervalued and overvalued exchange rates created one-way bets for speculators with central banks and the IMF taking the opposite side (Hetzel 2008b, ch. 9).

[17] The bailout of the government-sponsored enterprises (GSEs) in September 2008 reinforced the widespread understanding of the problems of the "GSE model" with its privatization of rewards and socialization of risk. However, with the financial turmoil following the Lehman bankruptcy in September 2008, governments explicitly extended that model to all financial institutions regardless of their too-big-to-fail status.

[18] *The Wall Street Journal* (2008a) wrote, "The recent financial blowups came largely not from hedge funds, whose lightly regulated status has preoccupied Washington for years,

FDICIA imposed the legal obligation on regulators for prompt corrective action (PCA). It set up guidelines in the form of successively lower capital ratios that required regulators to intervene to limit risk taking by troubled banks and to place them in conservatorship when their equity capital fell below 2 percent of assets. However, regulators have not applied these sanctions to large banks. The fact that FDIC losses in 2008 and 2009 from closing banks averaged more than 30 percent of assets is evidence of failure to apply PCA to small banks as well (Whalen 2010). The problem is not lack of authority. Bank regulators have the legal power to close banks.

Allowed discretion, regulators in practice have allowed insolvent banks time to work out their problems. They do not see themselves as the agents for the principals, who are taxpayers and healthy banks. Regulators have often posed the false alternative of immediate closure and liquidation of a bank with losses imposed on all its counterparties to the actual practice of using the Fed discount window to let out uninsured creditors while allowing the bank to continue to attempt to work out troubled loans. They do not discuss the obvious alternative of placing troubled banks in conservatorship with an immediate one-time haircut imposed on uninsured creditors (Kaufman 2010).

In conservatorship, guided by regulators on the bank's board, the bank continues to operate while awaiting a decision about whether to sell, restructure, or liquidate. Conservatorship with the threat of ultimate liquidation is admittedly difficult to make credible. Large banks operate in different countries with different rules for closure. However, the requirement in the Dodd-Frank Wall Street Reform and Consumer Protection Act that large banks have "living wills" outlining in detail how they deal with closure should mitigate the problems created by conservatorship with the possibility of ultimate liquidation. With a living will, creditors and counterparties should know how to protect themselves in such an event. For example, by holding appropriate collateral to back derivatives trades, they would plan for closure in a way that minimizes disruption.[19]

---

but from banks watched over by national governments.... 'I think it was surprising ... that where we had some of the biggest issues in capital markets were with the regulated financial institutions,' said Treasury Secretary Henry Paulson."

The amounts of money involved in the off-budget subsidies created by the financial safety net inevitably leave regulatory decisions open to challenge by the political system. Regulatory limitation of risky investments that are at least initially financially successful is likely limited to extreme cases where regulators have a black-and-white defense.

[19] As reported in *The New York Times* (2008l), after the Lehman bankruptcy, the counterparties in the derivatives trades of Lehman Brothers settled their accounts without significant problems. Counterparty risk can be handled by sophisticated market players.

The only way to solve the time-inconsistency problem that presently assures bailouts of troubled financial institutions and undercuts market discipline on risk taking is to eliminate the discretion of regulators to bail out such institutions.[20] Nothing in the Dodd-Frank Act mitigates the time-inconsistency problem. Consider an example subsequent to the 2008 interventions to bail out financial institutions (Torres 2011).[21]

Alerted by a new team of risk-hunters within the Fed that U.S. money market funds were dumping euro-region bank debt on fears of a Greek default, Bernanke and members of the Fed's Open Market Committee decided in a conference call that they had to take immediate action.... U.S. prime money market funds by the end of March [2010] had about $493 billion of certificates of deposit, commercial paper and asset-backed commercial paper from euro-region firms.... As the strains in Europe worsened, prime money funds shrank exposure at a pace of $54 billion a month.... On Sunday, May 9 [2010], European leaders in Brussels negotiated an unprecedented bailout plan to ease the crisis. Bernanke ... convened the FOMC meeting by teleconference. Armed with the staff's analysis, the Fed panel authorized Bernanke to make the swap lines available.... [T]he swap lines once again showed the Fed's willingness to step up as the world's lender of last resort for dollars.

WHO SHOULD REGULATE RISK TAKING?

There is recognition that financial institutions had excessively risky asset portfolios going into the 2008–2009 recession. In popular discourse, the desire to find culprits focused on the greed of Wall Street bankers and the inattention of regulators. Joe Nocera (2008), who writes *The New York Times* column "Talking Business," quoted Mr. Sinai, chief global economist at Decision Economics: "The system is broken. The animal spirits

---

[20] As explained by Kydland and Prescott (1977), government policies operated discretionarily cannot credibly shape expectations by promising to impose losses on private parties to limit risky behavior such as building in a flood plain because of the incentive to mitigate such losses on a one-time basis while promising pain in the future. Jürgen Stark (*Financial Times* 2009h), member of the Executive Board of the ECB, described time inconsistency more informally:

He [Stark] recalls working with the US during the late 1990s Asian financial crisis. The American approach, according to Stark, was: "We need the fire brigade! How to resolve the fundamental problem – this is an issue for tomorrow. First of all, we need to extinguish the fire, then we talk about the consequences."

[21] *The Wall Street Journal* (2011) reported on plans for the IMF to become a surrogate discount window for the Fed:

Under the plan, which has been encouraged by the U.S. and other members of the Group of 20 nations, the IMF would provide short-term foreign-exchange swaps to central banks in developing nations.... That would reduce political pressure on central banks to provide swap lines to countries that could be controversial domestically.

of the private sector, plus lax regulation, did it in." But why is "the system broken?" Should one base public policy on the emergence of a new generation of bankers who are not greedy and on regulators who have the ability and willingness to eliminate risky financial innovation? Alternatively, should one retract a financial safety net that subsidizes the making of risky bets by banks through the leveraging of low-cost, government guaranteed funds?

TEN

The Housing Crash

Subsidizing Housing and Bank Risk Taking

The severity of the boom-bust cycle in housing came from the cutting action of two blades of a scissors. The first blade was a government push to increase home ownership rates. Given the relatively inelastic supply of housing, the result was a sustained increase in house prices. The second blade was a financial safety net that encourages risk taking by banks. Given the increase in house prices and given the incentives to risk taking, banks concentrated their portfolios in housing mortgages (Hetzel 2009a).

USING THE GSES TO SUBSIDIZE HOUSING OFF BUDGET

Understanding the role of the subprime housing crisis in the 2008–2009 financial crisis requires understanding the role played by the government-sponsored enterprises (GSEs).[1] They increased the demand for the housing stock, helped to raise the homeownership rate to an unsustainable level, and, as a consequence of a relatively inelastic supply of housing due to land constraints, contributed to a sharp rise in housing prices.[2] That rapid rise in housing prices made the issuance of subprime and Alt-A loans appear relatively risk free.[3]

The homeownership rate was at about 64 percent in 1986, where it remained through 1995 (Figure 10.1). Starting in 1996 it began to rise.

---

[1] The GSEs are the Federal National Mortgage Association (FNMA) or Fannie Mae, the Federal Home Loan Mortgage Corporation (FHLMC) or Freddie Mac, the Federal Home Loan Banks or FHLBs, and the Federal Housing Administration (FHA). Subprime lending is to borrowers with a blemished credit history.

[2] Duca (2005, 5) provided citations showing that the rise in house prices was most pronounced in areas in which land supply was inelastic. Also, the swings in house prices were dominated by changes in land prices, not structure costs.

[3] Alt-A loans lack documentation for income and employment.

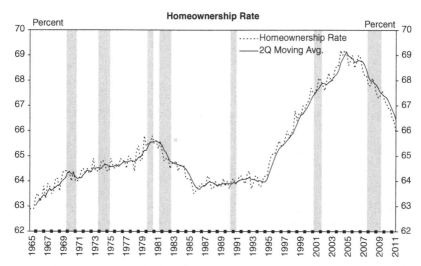

Figure 10.1. Homeownership rate.

Note: Homeownership rate is plotted with a two-quarter moving average. Homeownership rate is calculated as owner-occupied housing units divided by total occupied housing units. Data are from the U.S. Census Bureau via Haver Analytics. Shaded areas indicate NBER recessions. Heavy tick marks indicate the fourth quarter.

Homeownership rates peaked in 2005 at 69 percent.[4] In real terms, house prices remained steady over the period 1950 through 1997. Starting in 1999, they began to rise beyond their previous cyclical peaks (reached in the mid-1950s, late 1970s, and early 1990s) and then rose somewhat more than 50 percent above both their 1995 value and their long-run historical average.[5] Figure 10.2 shows the growth rate of house prices adjusted for inflation. The ratio of house prices to household incomes remained at its longer-run historical average of somewhat less than 1.9 until 2001. It then climbed sharply and reached 2.4 in 2006 (Corkery and Hagerty 2008).

The Clinton administration set ambitious goals to raise homeownership. A document called "The National Homeownership Strategy: Partners in

---

[4]   Tom Lawler pointed out to the author that a shift in the age mix of households contributed to the increase in the home ownership rate. From 1990 to 2000, the fraction of household heads under the age of thirty-five fell from 27.1% to 22.6% (U.S. Decennial Census). Household heads under the age of thirty-five have a lower homeownership rate than those over age thirty-five. Lawler estimated the increase in the home ownership rate from 1990 to 2000 due to this demographic effect as about 1.25 percentage points (correspondence with author).

[5]   Data on home ownership rates and real house prices are from Federal Reserve System (2008), "Mortgage Foreclosure Knowledge Snapshot" and "Synopses of Selected Research," respectively.

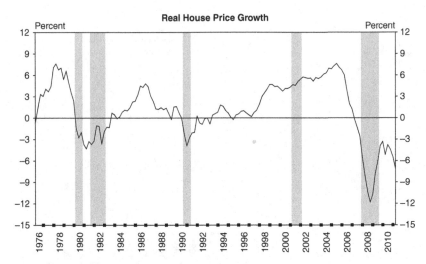

Figure 10.2. Real house price growth.

Note: Quarterly observations of four-quarter percentage changes in real house prices. Real house prices are constructed by deflating a nominal house price index by the price index for overall personal consumption expenditures. Observations from 1976Q1 to 1991Q4 use the all-transactions, not seasonally adjusted house price index from the Federal Housing Finance Agency (FHFA); 1992Q1 to 2009Q4 observations use the purchase-only, seasonally adjusted house price index from the FHFA. Data via Haver Analytics. Shaded areas indicated NBER recessions. Heavy tick marks indicate the fourth quarter.

the American Dream" began with a "Message from the President:" "This past year [1994], I [President Clinton] directed HUD [U.S. Department of Housing and Urban Development] Secretary Henry G. Cisneros to ... develop a plan to boost homeownership in America to an all-time high by the end of this century."[6] A key part of the strategy was to increase afford-ability by lowering down payments on mortgages. A HUD newsletter (U.S. Department of Housing and Urban Development 1998, 5) noted:

[T]he GSEs' lower income loans frequently do not appear to be addressing prob-lems of affordability, such as lack of cash for downpayment. A noticeable pattern among lower income loans purchased by the GSEs is the predominance of loans with high downpayments.

Chapter 4 of "The National Homeownership Strategy" noted, "For many potential homebuyers, the lack of cash available to accumulate the required

---

[6] The document, which was last revised on April 27, 2000, was available on the HUD Web site until 2007. See U.S. Department of Housing and Urban Development (2000). I am indebted to Joseph Mason for drawing it to my attention.

downpayment and closing costs is the major impediment to purchasing a home." The document outlined strategies to deal with this problem in Actions 35 ("Home Mortgage Loan-to-Value Flexibility") and 36 ("Subsidies to Reduce Downpayment and Mortgage Costs"):

> The partnership should support initiatives to reduce downpayment requirements.... Low- and moderate-income families often cannot become homeowners because they are unable to come up with the required downpayment and closing costs.... Nevertheless, great strides have been made by the lending community in recent years to reduce downpayment requirements, particularly for low- and moderate-income homebuyers.

> The New Jersey Housing and Mortgage Finance Agency administers its no-downpayment 100 Percent Mortgage Financing Program to encourage homeownership among lower income households. Many local lending institutions in recent years have developed innovative low-downpayment programs for first-time home-buyers.... Fannie Mae and Freddie Mac have instituted affordable loan products for home purchase that require only 3 percent from the purchaser when an additional 2 percent is available from other funding sources, including gifts, unsecured loans, and government aid.

Later, Lawler (2010a, 4) wrote:

> [H]ousing goals had been set by HUD, and those housing goals ... were hiked numerous times over the last decade [1990s], to the point where hitting them in all likelihood made the GSEs do some things that for safety and soundness reasons they shouldn't have done. The guy who pushed up the housing goals without any thought as to what the consequences or risks might be was Andrew Cuomo, Secretary of HUD from 1997 to 2001.

In 1990, Freddie Mac and Fannie Mae owned 4.7 percent of U.S. residential mortgage debt, and by 1997 they owned 11.4 percent. In 1998, that figure began to rise sharply, and in 2002 it reached 20.4 percent. (The figure is 46 percent including mortgage debt guaranteed for payment of principal and interest.)[7] After 2003, because of portfolio caps imposed on Fannie and Freddie by the Office of Federal Housing Enterprise Oversight (OFHEO) resulting from accounting irregularities, their market share declined. However, they continued to purchase subprime and Alt-A loans.[8]

---

[7]   Total residential mortgage debt outstanding is from Board of Governors Flow of Funds Accounts, table L. 218. Data on the holding of mortgages by Fannie and Freddie and on the total mortgage-backed securities they guaranteed are from Office of Federal Housing Enterprise Oversight (2008, 116).

[8]   *The Washington Post* (2008k) reported:

> In a memo to former Freddie chief executive officer Richard Syron and other top executives, former Freddie chief enterprise risk officer David Andrukonis wrote that the company was buying mortgages that appear "to target borrowers who would have trouble qualifying for

The Congressional Budget Office (U.S. Congress 2008) reported that as of 2008Q2 Fannie and Freddie held $780 billion or 15 percent of their portfolios in these assets.[9] The FHA also encouraged borrowers to take out high loan-to-value mortgages.[10]

From late 2005 through 2007, the GSEs (Fannie Mae and Freddie Mac) acquired and guaranteed loans with risky characteristics. The reason behind this decision remains controversial. The investment banks were securitizing subprime loans (the "private-label" mortgage-backed securities [MBSs]), and the GSEs wanted to maintain their market share. Also, the GSEs needed to reestablish their congressional support, which had eroded due to the accounting scandal. The purchase of subprime mortgages was "goal rich" because of the bipartisan support in Congress for the "affordable housing" goal of extending home ownership. Regardless of the motivation, the GSEs were a significant player among institutions that employed funding rendered cheap by implicit government guarantees to purchase the securities backed by risky mortgages.

a mortgage if their financial position were adequately disclosed." Andrukonis warned that these mortgages could be particularly harmful for Hispanic borrowers, and they could lead to loans being made to people who would be unlikely to pay them off.

Mudd [former Fannie Mae CEO] later reported that Fannie moved into this market "to maintain relevance" with big customers who wanted to do more business with Fannie, including Countrywide, Lehman Brothers, IndyMac and Washington Mutual. The documents suggest that Fannie and Freddie knew they were playing a role in shaping the market for some types of risky mortgages. An email to Mudd in September 2007 from a top deputy reported that banks were modeling their subprime mortgages to what Fannie was buying.... "I'm not convinced we aren't leading the market into this product," Andrukonis wrote.

9   The numbers could be larger. As reported in *The New York Times* (2008p):

The former executive, Edward J. Pinto, who was chief credit officer at Fannie Mae, told the House Oversight and Government Reform Committee that the mortgage giants now guarantee or hold 10.5 million nonprime loans worth $1.6 trillion – one in three of all subprime loans, and nearly two in three of all so-called Alt-A loans, often called "liar loans." Such loans now make up 34 percent of the total single-family mortgage portfolios at Fannie Mae and Freddie Mac.

Arnold Kling, an economist who once worked at Freddie Mac, testified that a high-risk loan could be "laundered," as he put it, by Wall Street and returned to the banking system as a triple-A-rated security.... Housing analysts say that the former heads of Fannie Mae and Freddie Mac increased their non-prime business because they felt pressure from the government and advocacy groups to meet goals for affordable housing.

10 The FHA insured no-down-payment loans through down-payment assistance programs. A homebuilder made a contribution to a "non-profit" organization, which cycled the money to the homebuyer. The homebuilder received his money back through an above-market price for the house. The buyer paid a fee to the "non-profit." The end result was a mortgage with no equity (*Wall Street Journal* 2008c). "The program ... now accounts for more than a third of the agency's portfolio" (*The New York Times* 2008b).

Table 10.1. *Fannie Mae conforming single-family loan characteristics,*
retained + guaranteed September 30, 2009

Loan characteristic	Unpaid principal balance, UPB ($billions)	% Total UPB	90+ day delinquency (%)
Total	2795.9	100.0%	4.72%
No special characteristics	1938.0	69.3%	1.78%
Special characteristic(s) present	857.9	30.7%	11.36%
Alt-A	258.8	9.3%	13.97%
FICO<620	112.3	4.0%	16.08%
FICO < 620 & OLTV > 90%	24.6	0.9%	25.32%
FICO 620–659	236.5	8.5%	11.32%
IO	189.3	6.8%	17.94%
Negative amortizing	14.6	0.5%	9.53%
OLTV > 90%	264.3	9.5%	11.56%
Subprime	7.6	0.3%	26.41%

Table 10.1 shows the composition of Fannie Mae's portfolio divided into
loans of different characteristics for 2009Q3 when Fannie Mae first began to
release such data. Freddie Mac does not release such detailed information,
but the fact that it also required a bailout from the government attested to
the riskiness of its portfolio. The table exhibits the fraction of single-family
(SF) mortgages held by Fannie Mae with at least one risky characteristic.[11]
This breakdown is useful because a loan need not be subprime to be risky.
For example, loans with high loan-to-value ratios or loans with borrower
discretion about when to make principal payments (option ARMs or negative amortizing loans) are risky but not necessarily subprime, that is, issued

[11] A FICO score is the numerical score given by credit agencies to a borrower based on the
individual's past credit history. There is no formal definition of what score renders a loan
"subprime," but a FICO score less than 620 is a common benchmark. OLTV is a measure
of the overall-loan-to-value ratio of a loan. For example, a loan with a 10% down payment
carries a loan-to-value of 90%. IO is interest only. That is, the borrower pays only interest
and is liable for the principal payment at a date in the future. "Negative amortizing" means
that the borrower possesses the option to make payments that fall short of the interest due
and thereby increase the principal owed.
   Sam Henly created the table. Data are from the 2009Q3 "Credit Supplement for
Investors" available at http://www.fanniemae.com/ir/pdf/sec/2009/q3credit_summary.
pdf. "Investor Update" information for Freddie Mac is available at http://www.freddiemac.
com/investors/pdffiles/investor-presentation.pdf.

to a borrower with a blemished credit record. As of 2009Q3, nearly a third (30.7 percent) of Fannie's single-family book was composed of loans that had at least one risky characteristic. Loans with at least one risky characteristic had a serious (90+ day) delinquency rate of 11.36 percent; loans without these specific characteristics had a serious delinquency rate of only 1.78 percent.

Early in the 2000s, the GSEs channeled increased foreign demand for riskless dollar-denominated debt into the housing market. When the interest rate on U.S. government securities fell to low levels, they encouraged foreign investors to shift from treasuries to agency debt (*The New York Times* 2008d). In doing so, investors could take advantage of somewhat higher yields on debt with an implicit government guarantee. In March 2000, foreigners owned 7.3 percent of the total outstanding of GSE debt ($261 billion) and, in June 2007, they owned 21.4 percent of the total ($1.3 trillion).[12] Foreign central banks and other official institutions owned somewhat more than $800 billion of GSE debt in 2008.[13]

Other government policies increasing the demand for the housing stock included Community Reinvestment Act (CRA) lending by banks. In 1996, lending under this program began to increase substantially because of a change in regulations that provided quantitative guidelines for bank lending to communities judged underserved by regulators (Johnsen and Myers 1996). Furthermore, in 1997, Congress increased the value of a house as an investment by eliminating capital gains taxes on profits of $500,000 or less on sales of homes (Taxpayer Relief Act of 1997). "Vernon L. Smith, a Nobel laureate and economics professor at George Mason University, said that the tax law was responsible for 'fueling the mother of all housing bubbles'" (*The New York Times* 2008q).

The Federal Home Loan Banks (FHLBs) also encouraged the increase in home mortgage lending. By law, the purpose of the FHLBs is to subsidize housing and community lending (12 U.S.C. § 1430(a)(2)). For example, as of December 31, 2007, the Federal Home Loan Bank system had advanced $102 billion to Citibank.[14] FHLB advances grew from $100 billion to $200 billion from 1997 through 2000 and then accelerated. As of 2008Q3, the

---

[12] "Report on Foreign Portfolio Holdings of U.S. Securities" from www.treas.gov/tic/sh/2007r.pdf.

[13] Board of Governors Statistical Release H.4.1 Memorandum Item.

[14] Data are from FDIC Statistics of Depository Institutions Report, Memoranda, FHLB advances (www2.fdic.gov/sdi/rpt_Financial.asp) and Federal Financial Institutions Examination Council (FFIEC) (https://cdr.ffiec.gov/public/SearchFacsimiles.aspx), (Schedule RC – Balance Sheet and RC-M–Memoranda, 5.a).

system had advanced $911 billion to banks and thrifts. In addition, the FHLBs subsidize housing directly by borrowing at their government-guaranteed interest rate and purchasing mortgage-backed securities for their own portfolio (typically 40 percent of their assets). As of 2007Q4, they held $132 billion of residential mortgage-backed securities.

Ashcraft, Bech, and Frame (2008) noted that FHLBs have become the lender of last resort for banks and thrifts, but without the supervisory authority constrained by FDICIA (the Federal Deposit Insurance Corporation Improvement Act of 1991). For example, advances to Countrywide Bank went from $51 billion in 2007Q3 to more than $121 billion in 2008Q1.[15] Between 2007Q2 and 2007Q4, advances to the Henderson, Nevada, bank of Washington Mutual, which failed in late September 2008, went from $21.4 billion to $63.9 billion. Because the FHLBs possess priority over all other creditors, they can lend to financial institutions without charging risk premia based on the riskiness of the institution's asset portfolio. Siems (2008, abstract) found the following about banks reliant on FHLB borrowing:

> [As] the liability side of the balance sheet has shifted away from core deposits and toward more borrowed money, the asset side of the balance sheet seems to have also shifted to fund riskier activities. Banks that have borrowed more from the Federal Home Loan Banks ... are generally deemed to be less safe and sound according to bank examiner ratings.

Just as had occurred in the 1980s with the S&Ls, funds provided by the FHLBs along with brokered deposits guaranteed by the FDIC allowed small banks and thrifts to grow rapidly and acquire risky asset portfolios concentrated in mortgages. For example, the Office of Thrift Supervision (OTS) closed IndyMac Bancorp in July 2008 at a cost estimated by the FDIC at $8.9 billion (*The Wall Street Journal* 2008d). From December 2001 through June 2008, its assets grew from $7.4 billion to $30.7 billion. As of the latter date, IndyMac financed 51 percent of its assets with FHLB advances and brokered deposits.[16] As of the first quarter of 2008, IndyMac was not on the FDIC's list of problem banks.

---

[15] Data are from the FFIEC (https://cdr.ffiec.gov/public/SearchFacsimiles.aspx). Shortly after the subprime crisis broke, *The Wall Street Journal* (2007a) reported about Countrywide, the largest independent mortgage lender in the United States, "Countrywide is counting on its savings bank, along with Fannie Mae and Freddie Mac, to fund nearly all of its future lending by drawing on deposits and borrowings from the Federal Home Loan Bank system." In January 2008, Bank of America agreed to a merger with Countrywide. MSNBC reported (2008), "Shares in Countrywide hit record lows in recent days on persistent rumors that a bankruptcy was imminent, a condition brought on by the widespread spike in mortgage defaults and foreclosures, especially in subprime loans."

[16] FDIC Call Reports (www2.fdic.gov/Call_TFR_Rpts/).

TBTF AND THE ABSENCE OF MONITORING

In response to the distress in financial markets that occurred after August 2007, popular commentary highlighted the private greed of bankers and the absence of control due to deregulation. It follows that there is a need for more regulation of risk taking. However, why was existing regulation deficient? Are not bank creditors (debt holders and depositors) also greedy? Do they not care about losing money? Why did they not monitor bank risk taking? As explained in Chapter 9, the major "deregulation" that has occurred has taken the form of an expanding financial safety net that has undercut the *market* regulation of risk taking by banks.

Because of the financial safety net provided by deposit insurance, by TBTF, by the FHLBs, and by the Fed's discount window, banks have access to funds whose cost does not increase with the riskiness of their asset portfolios. Bank asset portfolios became riskier, especially after 2003, through a significantly increased concentration in holdings of mortgages. Nevertheless, the cost of funds to banks did not rise in response. As measured by credit default swap spreads (senior debt, five-year maturity), the cost of issuing debt by the large banks did not increase until August 2007 when the subprime crisis appeared. As a result, banks had an incentive to increase returns by funding long-term, risky assets with short-term, government-guaranteed liabilities. For banks, this risk-maturity leveraging took the form of limited portfolio diversification due to concentration in real estate loans and also the creation of off-balance-sheet conduits holding mortgage-backed securities funded by short-term commercial paper.

The analysis of Jensen and Meckling (1976) explained how markets undistorted by government socialization of risk restrain risk taking. Equity holders in corporations have an incentive to take risks that are excessive from the perspective of bond holders because of the way that limited liability limits equity holders' downside losses without limiting their upside returns. As a result, debt holders demand a return that increases with leverage, covenants that limit risk taking, and accounting transparency. Because the financial safety net renders superfluous the need of creditors of banks to monitor, market mechanisms for limiting risk in banking are attenuated. There is no offset to the additional expected return that banks earn from holding riskier portfolios arising from a higher cost of funds. This incentive to risk taking in banking appeared in the 2000s when banks responded to the sustained increase in house prices by increased concentration in mortgages.

BANK EXPOSURE TO MORTGAGES AND SIVS

After 2000, the direct exposure of banks to the real estate market increased significantly. Measured as a percentage of total commercial bank credit, the amount of commercial bank assets held in real estate loans (residential and commercial) remained steady at 30 percent over the decade of the 1990s but then rose steadily after 2000 until reaching a little more than 40 percent in 2007 (Figure 10.3).[17] In 2002Q2, all real estate loans of FDIC-insured institutions (banks and thrifts) comprised 47.6 percent of loans and leases outstanding.[18] In 2008Q2, the figure had risen to 55.0 percent. The large banks of more than a billion dollars in assets accounted for the increase. They held $800 billion in residential loans in 2002 and $1.8 trillion in 2007 (Krainer 2008; Figure 10.4). However, bank exposure exceeded these numbers because of holdings of mortgages in off-balance-sheet (OBS) entities.[19]

In the 2000s, banks set up these OBS entities to hold securitized pools of mortgages.[20] Earlier, in the 1990s, securitization had evolved beyond that done by the GSEs with residential mortgages in order to tap the funds provided by cash investors (short-term investors who demand liquidity and the absence of risk of default and price fluctuation). Banks securitized consumer debt, credit card receivables, student loans, and auto loans. They financed pools of these assets by issuing asset-backed commercial paper (ABCP). Structured financing was the innovation that allowed for the financing of subprime and Alt-A mortgages through access to cash investors rather than relying on the smaller pool of specialized risk investors experienced in doing due diligence on residential mortgages.

Structured financing involved the division of these mortgage pools into classes (tranches), which possessed different priority for receipt of the income from the underlying mortgages. In particular, financial institutions divided pools of mortgages formed from residential subprime mortgages

---

[17] See Board of Governors statistical release H.8 (www.federalreserve.gov/releases/h8).

[18] See FDIC Call Report, Statistics on Depository Institutions (www2.fdic.gov/sdi/rpt_Financial.asp).

[19] Blasko and Sinkey (2006) pointed out that under Basel I, which set minimum capital requirements for banks starting in 1992, banks had an incentive to hold residential mortgages. Banks could engage in regulatory arbitrage under the Basel I capital standards because of the favorable treatment of residential real estate loans.

[20] The banks put RMBSs (retail mortgage-backed securities) and CDOs (collateralized debt obligations) into off-balance-sheet entities or conduits called qualified special purpose vehicles (QSPVs) or structured investment vehicles (SIVs). SIVs served two purposes. First, they created a profitable spread between the rates on these illiquid structured products and the rates on commercial paper used to leverage their financing. Second, by removing the assets from banks' books, they reduced capital charges.

Figure 10.3. Mortgage debt as a percent of total commercial bank credit.
Note: Data from Board of Governors, "Assets and Liabilities of Commercial Banks in the United States," Statistical Supplement to the Federal Reserve Bulletin, tables 1.54 and 1.26.

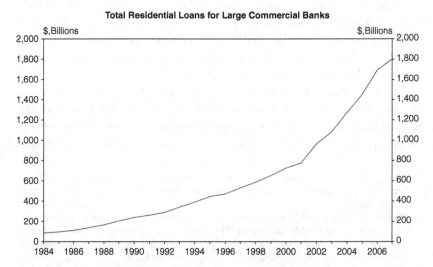

Figure 10.4. Total residential loans for large commercial banks.
Note: Total residential loans for banks with assets greater than $1 billion. Data from Krainer (2008).

into senior, mezzanine, and the "toxic-waste" or equity tranches, in that order of seniority, for the distribution (waterfall) of mortgage interest payments. These institutions worked with the mortgage-rating companies to ensure that just enough of the original pool included the lower tranches so that the senior tranches would receive AAA ratings.

The senior tranches could then go into an OBS SIV (structured investment vehicle) with bank-provided credit enhancements in the form of long-term, junior debt issued by the banks and in the form of backup lines of credit if the commercial paper used to leverage the SIV failed to roll over. The banks either retained the lower tranches on their balance sheets or sold them to hedge funds. Ratings agencies required these credit enhancements as a condition for rating the paper issued by the SIVs as AAA (A1/P1).[21] Banks incurred the risk by not using the alternative liquidity enhancement provided by issuing extendible commercial paper.

Despite the independent ("brain-dead") legal status of SIVs, commercial banks retained the credit risk through the credit enhancements required to make the SIVs eligible to issue high-quality commercial paper. The exposure of the commercial banking system to mortgages then included the mortgage debt held on their own books (the traditional banking system) plus the mortgage debt held in SIVs (the shadow banking system). As a result of this lack of diversification, commercial banks became vulnerable to an adverse shock affecting the mortgage market. That shock took the form of high rates of mortgage defaults beginning in 2006. When cash investors stopped buying the commercial paper issued by the SIVs in August 2007, regardless of the existence of formal credit enhancements, large banks supported their SIVs by taking their assets onto their own books. They did so to protect their future ability to remain in the securitization business.

The bank-sponsored SIVs created much of the demand for the securitized subprime and Alt-A loans. This OBS lending allowed the extension

---

[21] "[N]early every [ABCP] program is required by the rating agencies to maintain a back-up liquidity facility (usually provided by a large commercial bank) to ensure funds will be available to repay CP [commercial paper] investors at maturity.... CDO programs ... rely on bank liquidity support (usually in the form of a put to the bank) to back-stop 100% of a program CP in the event that the CP can not be rolled" (*J. P. Morgan Securities* 2007, 1 and 2). *The Wall Street Journal* (2007b) reported, "Globally, the amount of asset-backed commercial paper is about $1.3 trillion. Of this asset-backed paper, $1.1 trillion is backed by funding lines from banks, according to the Merrill report." Note that these "lines of credit" are not truly lines of credit. A line of credit is a contractual arrangement between a bank and a firm in which covenants protect the bank from lending in case of financial deterioration of the firm (Goodfriend and Lacker 1999). In reality, the off-balance-sheet entities simply had a put option on the bank.

of credit to previously ineligible borrowers through the funding of ARMs (adjustable-rate mortgages) and option ARMs (allowing for the initial ability to defer principal payments). In 2002–2003, ARMs constituted 16.5 percent of MBS issuance. From 2004 to 2006, that figure rose to 43 percent (*Mortgage Strategist* 2007, table 1.5). Until 2003, sophisticated investors specializing in mortgage credit risk had priced subprime MBSs. However, starting in 2004, that due diligence ceded place to a reliance on the prioritization of payment through the tranche structure of securitized debt (Adelson and Jacob 2008).

Indicative of the difficulty in monitoring the riskiness of bank portfolios was the lack of information on the amount of securitized mortgages held in bank conduits (OBS entities). Figures are available for the total direct holdings of banks in their portfolios. For the SIVs, however, one has only holdings of mortgages in both bank and nonbank sponsored SIVs (ABS issuers or issuers of commercial paper backed by mortgage securities). Between 1999Q4 and 2006Q4, the fraction of residential mortgages held directly by commercial banks and by bank and nonbank ABS issuers relative to total commercial bank credit grew from 28 percent to 53 percent. The fraction for total mortgage debt (residential plus commercial) grew 43 percent and 73 percent.[22] Although the numbers do not reveal the increase due exclusively to bank SIVs, much of the increase surely came from this source. For the three U.S. banks with the largest MBS holdings, in 2003Q3, the first quarter for which data are available, the amount of assets held in conduits financed by commercial paper and in which the banks retained explicit residual risk came to $94 billion. In 2007Q2, the amount came to $267 billion.[23]

In spring 2009, regulators conducting bank stress tests of the nineteen largest U.S. banks reported that "the institutions would record $900 billion in off-balance-sheet assets" (Katz 2009). The lack of knowledge by investors of the exposure of individual banks to these liabilities created much of the uncertainty about bank funding in the period starting August 2007. "Investors are wary of a company's unknown obligations as the world's

---

[22] The figure for mortgages held by banks does not include agency and GSE-backed securities. The data are from Board of Governors Flow of Funds Accounts, tables L.109 (Commercial Banking, total bank credit), L.218 (Home Mortgages, Commercial banking and ABS issuers) and L.220 (Commercial Mortgages, Commercial Banking and ABS issuers).

[23] The banks are Citibank, J. P. Morgan Chase, and Bank of America. See Federal Financial Institutions Examination Council, "Bank Holding Company's Credit Exposure and Liquidity Commitments to Asset-Backed Commercial Paper Conduits, FR Y-9C Call Reports, Schedule HC-S. A search of Form 10-Qs submitted by banks to the SEC revealed practically no information on the extent of liquidity commitments or credit enhancements to SIVs.

biggest banks and brokerages reported more than $1.3 trillion in write-downs and credit losses since the start of 2007, some stemming from losses at off-balance-sheet vehicles" (Katz 2009).

There are no available data for foreign banks. Based on the fact that U.S. financial institutions securitized subprime loans, the perception existed in 2007–2008 of a financial crisis made on Wall Street. However, government financial safety nets exacerbated the excessive risk taking by banks everywhere, not just in the United States. The International Monetary Fund (2008, table 1.6, 52) reported subprime-related losses for banks almost as large in Europe as in the United States.[24] As of March 2008, the IMF estimated that subprime losses for banks in Europe and the United States would amount, respectively, to $123 billion (with $80 billion already reported) and $144 billion (with $95 billion already reported). In June 2008, *The Financial Times* (2008b) reported, "Of the $387 billion in credit losses that global banks have reported since the start of 2007, $200 billion was suffered by European groups and $166 billion by US banks, according to data from the Institute of International Finance." For example, government-owned German banks lost significant amounts of money. *The New York Times* (2007) reported, "[I]n recent years, WestLB and others, like the Leipzig-based SachsenLB, have grown increasingly aggressive in their investment strategies, hoping to offset weak growth in areas like retail lending with high-yielding bets on asset-backed securities, including many with exposure to subprime mortgages."

Later, the Fed release of the identity of banks using its discount window in fall 2008 highlighted the importance of European banks. Reuters (2011) published a news account on two such banks:

European banks Dexia and Depfa made some of the worst possible business decisions, including forays into bond insurance, and were forced to repeatedly ask the Federal Reserve for emergency loans at the height of the financial crisis. According to Fed data released on Thursday [March 31, 2011], loans to the two foreign banks accounted for nearly half of all borrowing on Oct. 29, 2008, the day that the central bank's discount window lending peaked at $111 billion. Franco-Belgian Dexia and

---

[24] Not all countries had formal systems of deposit insurance. For example, Switzerland did not have an explicit TBTF policy, but the access of banks like UBS to the discount window of the Swiss National Bank without a policy precluding lending to insolvent banks made UBS appear to be part of a government financial safety net. Bloomberg Markets (July 2008, 48–9) wrote that the Swiss bank UBS reported losses totaling $38.2 billion between January 1, 2007, and May 9, 2008, and commented, "To buy the CDOs [collateralized debt obligations], the bank borrowed tens of billions of dollars at low rates.... From February 2006 to September '07, the CDO desk amassed a $50 billion inventory of super senior CDO tranches."

Dublin-based Depfa, a subsidiary of German-based Hypo Real Estate, continued to tap the Fed's emergency facilities for billions of dollars in short-term loans weeks after they were bailed out by the European governments in the fall of 2008. At the time, Dexia was the world's largest lender to municipalities and owned a U.S. bond insurance subsidiary, Financial Security Assurance, which guaranteed riskier securities linked to subprime mortgages. Short-term financing problems at Depfa, which also specialized in government and infrastructure lending, forced its parent, Hypo Real Estate, to seek help from the German government. Both Dexia and Depfa borrowed at short-term rates to finance long-term lending and ran into problems when credit markets froze.

During the 2008–2009 recession, attention focused on losses from large banks. However, the Jensen-Meckling incentive to risk taking reached across banks and thrifts of all sizes. The experience of community banks reproduced the 1980s experience of the S&Ls. Access to insured deposits and brokered CDs, which come without creditor monitoring of risk taking, allowed small community banks to grow rapidly and to take significant bets on the housing market, especially with option adjusted-rate mortgages. In an illustrative story, *The Wall Street Journal* (2009c) wrote:

> Founded a decade ago in a double-wide trailer, New Frontier hit $1 billion in assets in July of 2006 and, in a burst of growth, doubled in just 18 months.... The liquidation [of the bank] cost the FDIC an estimated $670 million.... New Frontier ... stood out for the high interest rates it paid on certificates of deposit. That attracted big investments from out-of-town brokerage houses.

Brokered certificates of deposit, which were around $50 billion in the mid-1990s, reached almost $800 billion in 2009 (*The New York Times* 2009d). At the same time, as illustrated by the access to cheap money offered by government-insured brokered CDs, it became apparent how difficult politically it would be to limit the subsidization to risk taking created by the financial safety net. For example, community banks, which lack the economies of scale to compete in offering residential mortgages, naturally concentrate in commercial real estate lending. However, that concentration made their portfolios risky in the 2008–2009 recession. *The New York Times* (2009d) wrote:

> William Isaac, chairman of the FDIC from 1981 to 1985, said he became wary [of brokered deposits] nearly three decades ago after watching the spectacular fall of Penn Square Bank of Oklahoma City, which had grown astronomically by gorging on brokered deposits. Alarmed by the practice, Mr. Isaac moved to eliminate FDIC insurance for most brokered deposits – a rule that provoked an industry revolt and was ultimately overturned.

> [In the 2008–2009 recession] the FDIC allowed many banks that lost their "well capitalized" status to keep taking brokered deposits.... Last year, the FDIC proposed

a new rule. Banks that rely too heavily on brokered deposits to accelerate their growth will have to pay a higher insurance premium.... Just as it did in the early 1980s, industry opposition emerged almost overnight. "'Brokered' is not a 4-letter word!" Dennis M. King, chief credit officer of North County Bank in Washington State, wrote in one of hundreds of letters the agency received condemning [FDIC Chairman] Ms. Bair's plan. "They are especially important to community banks in our present economic environment."

SHOULD GOVERNMENT SUBSIDIZE BANK RISK TAKING?

Significant leveraging exacerbated the fragility of the financial system during the 2008–2009 recession. Despite that fact, there has been little willingness to move away from the wide range of government policies that subsidize leverage by favoring debt over equity financing. The corporate income tax provides a strong incentive for corporations to finance themselves through the issuance of debt rather than equity. High debt levels make public corporations more susceptible to bankruptcy.

Significant leveraging also results from public policies to increase home ownership.[25] The result of using the tax code to advance home ownership through the deduction of home mortgage payments from income taxes is to skew the financing of the housing stock toward debt.[26] Just as the incentives to risk taking produced by the financial safety net encouraged leverage in the financial sector, affordable housing programs and increased riskiness of GSE portfolios starting in 2003 worked to make housing affordable by encouraging homeowners to leverage their home purchases with high loan-to-value ratios. Robert Shiller (2008) commented, "They [average homeowners] typically have all their assets locked up in real estate and are highly leveraged. And this is what they are encouraged to do."

Finally, the financial safety net subsidizes leverage in the financial system. Deposit insurance for depositors and TBTF for debt holders renders debt financing cheap relative to equity financing. The incentives for leveraging,

---

[25] Presumably, the justification for this policy is that homeowners are better citizens than renters, and subsidizing home ownership is more attractive politically than taxing renters. Alternatively, a market allocation of capital would on political grounds presumably result in too high a capital stock in the business sector of the economy (too high of a capital/labor ratio). By implication, the benefits of additional home ownership outweigh the costs in terms of the lower wages that result from a lower capital/labor ratio in the corporate sector.

[26] The benefit of the mortgage interest deduction goes disproportionately to the wealthy. For example, in 2008, 10.3% of households with income between $30,000 to $40,000 claimed the deduction, while 71.1% of households with income of $200,000 or more claimed it (*Congressional Quarterly Weekly* 2010, 550).

created both by government programs to increase home ownership and by the financial safety net, worked to create the fragility of the financial system revealed in the summer of 2007. One way to understand the political attractiveness of the systemic risk regulator incorporated into the Dodd-Frank Wall Street Reform and Consumer Protection Act passed in July 2010 was the desire to limit the risk taking and debt leverage of financial institutions directly without having to reduce the pervasive subsidies provided by government to banks that benefit from government guarantees of their debt issuance.

During the 2008–2009 crisis, the popular desire to personify the forces that produced the crisis in the form of villains became paramount.[27] However, in time, the country still must address whether the flaw that led to excessive risk taking by financial institutions came from a character defect in the form of excessive greed by Wall Street bankers and willfully ignorant regulators or came from a government-created system that subsidizes the use of leverage to make risky bets.

---

[27] Consider the criticism of former FOMC chairman Alan Greenspan by Paul Barrett (2009), assistant managing editor of *Business Week*, in a book review of *In Fed We Trust* by David Wessel:

If there's a villain looming over the Wessel version of why the government was so overwhelmed, it is Greenspan, who led the Federal Reserve from 1987 until 2006. As Wessel explains, Greenspan's strong libertarian leanings led him to scorn the ability of government employees to keep track of bonus-crazed bankers and traders.... Wessel makes a persuasive case that if our economic overseers do not renounce – clearly and openly – the lackadaisical deference to Wall Street that characterized the Greenspan era, they risk not anticipating the next crisis and determining how to avoid it.

ELEVEN

Bubble Trouble

Easy Money in 2003 and 2004?

The price system did not work to maintain real output at potential output in the 2008–2009 recession. Did the failure arise from the way in which the herd behavior of investors overwhelmed its stabilizing properties? Especially, did "easy" monetary policy in 2003–2004 allow investors to propel house prices to an unsustainable peak? Did the inevitable collapse of house prices then produce disruption to financial intermediation to an extent that overwhelmed the stabilizing macroeconomic properties of low interest rates in 2008? The issue is important for assessing what kind of stability the central bank should target – asset price stability or price stability.

In a review of Robert J. Samuelson's book, *The Great Inflation and Its Aftermath*, Scheiber (2008) wrote:

In 1998, after a global financial crisis threatened the expansion he'd so carefully cultivated, Greenspan flooded the economy with cash (not crazy), and kept interest rates low for more than a year (highly questionable). The extra money led to the tech frenzy that ended so badly in 2000. Beginning in 2001, Greenspan aggressively lowered interest rates and kept them low into 2004. Once again, all the excess cash resulted in a bubble – this one in real estate – the bursting of which we are now struggling through.... The prices of stocks and homes are every bit as vulnerable to inflation as the prices of toothpaste and sandwich bread, even if government statistics properly account only for the latter pair. And as we are discovering, the consequences of that inflation are every bit as damaging.

Are these criticisms of Greenspan for pursuing a policy of easy money in 2003–2004 correct?[1] Would a focus on asset prices in 2003–2004 have

---

[1] The other criticism of Greenspan is that he allowed financial market deregulation, which encouraged excess risk taking. For example, Paul Krugman (2009a) wrote, "The financial industry, in particular, ran wild under deregulation, eventually bringing on a crisis that has left 15 million American[s] unemployed, and required large-scale taxpayer-financed bailouts to avoid an even worse outcome."

produced a more restrictive monetary policy that would have forestalled the 2008–2009 recession? Did easy money create an asset price bubble in housing?

HOW TO THINK ABOUT EASY MONEY

There is an overlap between the credit-cycle and monetary-disorder views about the importance of the role of asset prices in *transmitting* the effects of monetary stimulus. According to the latter view, expansionary monetary policy in an environment of expected price stability provides economic stimulus through the way in which it raises asset prices. Higher asset prices are part of a portfolio rebalancing effect that, in the first instance, reconciles the public to holding higher cash balances.

Japan offers an example of the forcefulness of this effect (Hetzel 1999; 2003; 2004b). After the Louvre Accord in early 1987, as a result of a failure to raise the interbank rate as the economy grew strongly, the Bank of Japan (BoJ) allowed a significant monetary acceleration. Money growth (M2+CDs, four-quarter averages) increased from 7 percent in the mid-1980s to 12 percent at the end of the decade. Equity and real estate prices rose. However, the appropriate lesson is not that the central bank should target asset prices but rather that it should avoid inflationary monetary policies.

For the 2000–2001 recession, U.S. monetary policy offers an attenuated example of the destabilizing effects of the go-stop characteristic of procyclical monetary policy that arises through cyclical interest rate inertia (Hetzel 2008b, ch. 24). In early 1999, the FOMC was concerned that a funds rate increase would strengthen the dollar and undercut the IMF program to aid Brazil. Despite strong economic growth, the FOMC postponed raising the funds rate until its June 30, 1999, meeting.[2] Similarly, the FOMC

---

[2] At the February 2, 1999, FOMC meeting Alice Rivlin, Vice Chairman of the Board of Governors, commented (Board of Governors *FOMC Transcripts*, February 2–3, 1999, 62–64):

A couple of meetings ago I referred to the cheerful little elves who run the U.S. economy and get their kicks out of proving the cautious forecasters wrong. The only thing that can be said about the economic news since our last meeting is that the elves have scored again. When I heard that the estimate of the 1998 fourth-quarter GDP was likely to be about 5 percent, I said, "Wow!" ... The question now is: Have the elves run out of tricks or can they beat the game one more time? If it were not for the rest of the world, I would bet on the elves. However, I am not sure they speak Portuguese. I am not sure they can move the Brazilian political system into higher gear fast enough to reassure a nervous world market. I am not sure the elves, for all their ingenuity, can control the mood swings of international investors or control the contagion that might flow from a collapse in Brazil or from some other major negative event as yet unpredicted.

was hesitant to lower the funds rate when the cyclical expansion began to slow.[3] Plausibly, this cyclical inertia in the funds rate exacerbated the upward movement in equity prices in 1999 and early 2000 and the downward movement thereafter. Again, the inference is not that the central bank can and should control asset prices but rather that it should avoid cyclical inertia in the funds rate.

According to the credit-cycle view, a boom-bust cycle begins during economic recovery with low short-term interest rates that encourage renewed speculation. It is true that low short-term interest rates create the opportunity for the leveraged holding of long-term, risky assets. However, the issue is whether this leveraging could destabilize the financial system without the incentive to risk taking provided by the government's financial safety net (Chapters 9 and 10). From the monetary-disorder perspective, a low interest rate is appropriate if it arises as a result of the public's pessimism about the future.

The relevant test for whether monetary policy is stimulative is whether the real interest rate is low *relative* to the natural rate. The empirical proposition advanced here is that undesirably stimulative monetary policy arises only if the central bank fails to increase the funds rate in line with the LAW-with-credibility rule. That is, during economic recovery, the central bank should raise the funds rate promptly in response to sustained increases in rates of resource utilization. For monetary policy, the ultimate litmus test is not whether asset prices increase during recovery but whether inflation remains at the central bank's target.

EASY MONEY IN 2003–2004: WHAT IS THE EVIDENCE?

After June 25, 2003, when the FOMC lowered the funds rate to 1 percent, was monetary policy unduly easy? Proponents of the credit-cycle view, who reply affirmatively, point to an increase in house prices. However, as shown in Figure 10.2, the sustained increase in house prices began much earlier, namely, after 1997. The more plausible source of this sustained increase was government policy to increase the home ownership rate (Figure 10.1).

---

[3] Greenspan (2001b, 4) commented:

> By summer of last year [2000], it was finally becoming apparent that the growth of demand was slowing and its evident excess over the growth of potential supply, as proxied by a diminishing pool of available labor, was being contained.... Had we moved the funds rate lower at the first sign of economic slowing, we would have created distortions threatening an even greater economic adjustment at a later date.... [W]e took our first easing action on January 3 [2001].

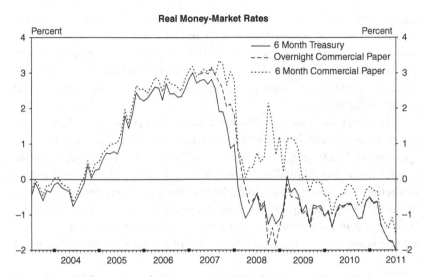

Figure 11.1. Real money-market rates.
Note: Real interest rate series is the nominal interest rate minus the two-quarter inflation forecasts from Macroeconomic Advisers. Nominal money-market rates are observed on the forecast posting date. Money-market rates are from the Board of Governors H.15 release via Haver Analytics. Heavy tick marks indicate December.

Leaving aside the housing sector, a review of macroeconomic variables reveals no evidence that monetary policy was expansionary during recovery from the 2000–2001 recession. Economic recovery was not strong by post-war standards. For the two-year period following the cyclical trough in 2001Q4, the cumulative growth rate of real GDP was 7.1 percent (almost equal to the cumulative growth rate of 7 percent after the 1991Q1 cyclical trough). This figure is half of the 14.5 percent number that characterized economic recoveries in the 1949–1982 period (omitting the 1980 expansion, which was shorter than two years). For this two-year period, payroll employment fell by 0.9 percent. The 1 percent level of the funds rate reached in June 2003, therefore, does not appear inappropriately low.

In coming out of the 2000–2001 recession, the Greenspan FOMC followed LAW procedures by initiating increases in the funds rate starting in June 2004 following evidence of sustained economic recovery in the form of sustained reductions in the unemployment rate (Hetzel 2008b, ch. 20).[4] The real,

---

[4] It is essential to distinguish between what Greenspan did and what he said. His pursuit of LAW with credibility procedures allowed the price system to work while providing a nominal anchor. In his rhetoric, Greenspan (2009) subscribed to the real-bills and Keynesian

short-term interest rate increased steadily beginning in mid-2004 (Figure 11.1). Most important, inflation of about 2 percent measured by the core PCE deflator remained close to the FOMC's implicit inflation target (Hetzel 2008b, ch. 20). The inflation numbers are impossible to reconcile with the assumption of an expansionary and ultimately inflationary monetary policy.

A focus on the short-term real interest rate also ignores the behavior of the term structure of interest rates that emerged given the credibility of the Greenspan Fed. In 2003–2004, financial markets realized that the funds rate was unsustainably low and long-term rates presaged the normalization of the term structure. Over the entire period, long-term rates (real and nominal) exhibited considerable stability and that stability was consistent with the actual moderate economic recovery, not an unsustainably rapid recovery consistent with overly stimulative monetary policy. From 2004 to 2006, the ten-year Treasury bond rate averaged about 4.25 percent. From 2006–2007, it averaged about 4.75 percent. This increase of half a percentage point is hardly an indication of the inflation scare that would have accompanied an inflationary monetary policy.[5]

Consider the recoveries from the two recessions prior to the 2008–2009 recession. Both exhibited a sustained interval of near zero short-term real interest rates (Figure 11.2). Both of these recoveries were times of significant pessimism about the future. In the first half of the 1990s, the feeling developed that low productivity growth would for the first time in history leave the younger generation worse off than the older one. As with the recovery from the 2001 recession, the recovery became known as the jobless recovery because of the slow growth in employment. Extreme pessimism also characterized the period after 2002 (Hetzel 2008b, ch. 20). A huge loss in

view that swings between investor optimism and pessimism overwhelm the operation of the price system:

[A] significant driver of stock prices is the innate human propensity to swing between euphoria and fear, which, while heavily influenced by economic events, has a life of its own. In my experience, such episodes are often not mere forecasts of future business activity, but major causes of it.

[5] Goldman Sachs (2009, 6) made these points:

Many commentators have attributed low bond yields, and therefore the credit boom, to excessively easy monetary policy.... [W]e see several problems with the idea that loose monetary policy was the principal cause of the boom (or the crisis that has followed). First ... the fall in real yields started too soon, has persisted for too long and has occurred too far out on the yield curve for monetary policy to be the primary cause. Second, the one thing that monetary policy can affect sustainably – inflation – didn't get out of control. Third ... the asset boom, to the extent there was one, was extremely localized, contradicting the view that overly-loose monetary policy drove a *generalized* bubble in risky assets. (italics in original)

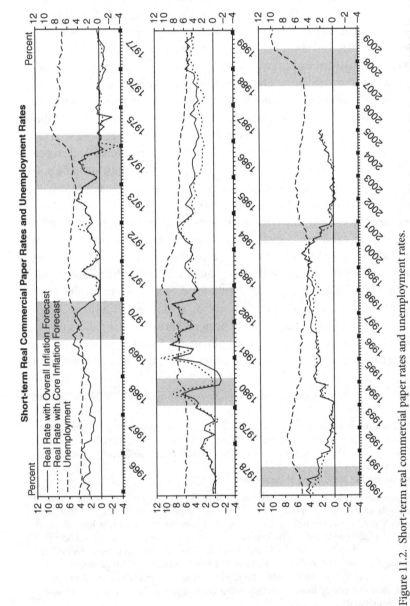

Figure 11.2. Short-term real commercial paper rates and unemployment rates.

Note: The real interest rate series is the commercial paper rate minus overall or core inflation forecasts made by the staff of the Board of Governors in the Greenbook. For a description of the series, see Chapter 11 "Appendix: Real Rate of Interest Shown in Figure 11.2." The unemployment series is the unemployment rate available to the FOMC at each meeting. Shaded areas indicate recessions. Heavy tick marks indicate December FOMC meeting.

wealth accompanied the decline in the stock market in 2000 and 2001; geo-political uncertainty centered on the Middle East rattled investors; and the governance scandals of companies like WorldCom and Enron made investors wary of investing in the stock market.

In addition, productivity growth soared in this latter period. If individuals extrapolate high productivity growth to the future and as a result anticipate being relatively better off in the future, they will attempt to smooth consumption by consuming more at present. The real interest rate must be higher to keep aggregate demand in line with potential output. In contrast, if individuals associate high productivity growth with the transitory substitution by firms of higher productivity for increased employment, uncertainty about future employment may exacerbate pessimism and require a lower real interest rate.

According to the LAW-with-credibility rule, the FOMC should begin to raise short-term interest rates when rates of resource utilization begin to increase in a sustained way. In the last two recessions, the FOMC used unemployment as the gauge of resource utilization rather than GDP (Figure 11.2). These two measures gave different signals because of the "jobless recovery" character of the two recessions. The use of the unemployment rate as the measure of resource utilization worked because optimism about the future did not revive (along with the need for an increase in real rates) until the public became optimistic again about job prospects.

WHAT ABOUT DEBT CYCLES?

Figure 11.3, which displays growth in real total private debt, shows that in the post-2003 period, the growth rate of private debt was in line with past recoveries. Figure 11.4 shows that the growth rate of debt did not lead to a high growth rate in consumption. It is true that, as shown in these figures, the growth of debt fell with the business cycle peak on December 2007. However, the magnitude of the decline was comparable to declines associated with the 1974–1975 and 1980 recessions and also with the 1990–1991 recession, although in the last one the decline stretched out over a longer interval. As shown in Figure 11.4, there was a sharp falloff in consumption in the 2008–2009 recession. The cessation of the growth in private debt between 2007Q3 and 2008Q3 only mirrors the falloff in consumption. Nothing in the graph allows one to disentangle causation from correlation.

The important point is that the reduction in debt in recession is not prima facie evidence that financial intermediation has broken down and that

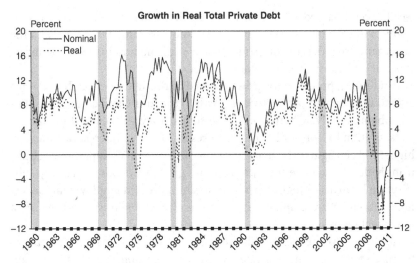

Figure 11.3. Growth in real total private debt.
Note: Quarterly annualized growth rate in credit-market debt liabilities of the household, nonfinancial business, and financial business sectors. Data are from the Board of Governors Flow of Funds. Real private debt series is the nominal series deflated by the overall price index for personal consumption expenditures from the Commerce Department. Data via Haver Analytics. Shaded areas indicate NBER recessions. Heavy tick marks indicate the fourth quarter.

banks are no longer transferring excess funds from savers to credit-worthy borrowers. Because of the increased uncertainty about future cash flows, individuals become more concerned about extended unemployment and personal bankruptcy and firms become more concerned about bankruptcy. As a result, both attempt to reduce their debt.

Apart from the easy-money criticism of monetary policy in 2003–2004, what about concerns over the longer-run accumulation of debt? As expressed by Martin Wolf (2010), "[A] series of bubbles helped keep the world economy driving forward over the past three decades. Behind these, however, lay a credit super-bubble, which burst in 2008. That is why private spending imploded." As shown in Figure 11.5, the steady growth in debt starting early on in the decade of the 1990s increased the ratio of private debt to GDP. Over the longer interval, from 1952 to 2009, this ratio rose from about 50 percent to almost 300 percent. But, what does one make of this fact? Was the economy six times more unstable in 2009 than in 1952? On the contrary, the increase in debt relative to GDP manifested increased economic stability.

Economists have never been able to turn credit-cycle views into a theory of cyclical fluctuations. An exchange of an IOU (debt) for an asset is

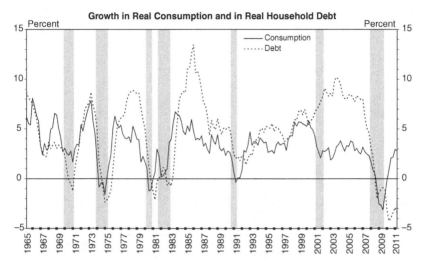

Figure 11.4. Growth in real consumption and in real household debt.
Note: Real consumption is personal consumption expenditures from the Commerce Department. Real debt is total credit-market liabilities for households from the Board of Governors Flow of Funds. Both series are deflated by the overall price index for personal consumption expenditures from the Commerce Department. Data via Haver Analytics. Shaded areas indicate NBER recessions. Heavy tick marks indicate the fourth quarter.

one way of effecting transactions. In periods of expansion, transactions of all sorts, including property transactions, increase. As a consequence, debt increases. However, the increase in debt arises endogenously as a concomitant of economic expansion.[6] In general, optimism about the future and debt increase together, but nothing in this correlation indicates anything about causation. As Willford King (U.S. Congress 1932b [March 21], 179), professor at New York University testified at the 1932 Goldsborough Hearings, "[W]hen people are optimistic they are inclined to go into debt; they buy things on time – radios, houses, and automobiles." Shifts between optimism and pessimism about the future do occur. However, the empirical issue is whether such shifts can produce cyclical fluctuations if the central bank allows the price system to operate.

WHAT GREENSPAN SAID AND WHAT HE DID

Greenspan rejected criticism that he should have identified the run-up in equity prices in the late 1990s as a bubble and deflated it with higher interest

[6] Debt also changes for many reasons unrelated to growth in real output. For example, if corporations change their financing by issuing debt to buy their equity, debt increases.

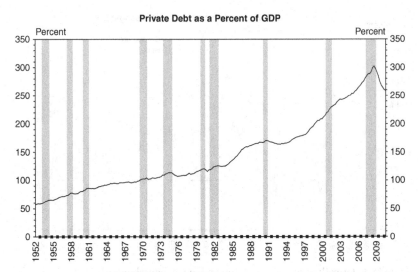

Figure 11.5. Private debt as a percent of GDP.
Note: Private credit as a percent of gross domestic product (GDP). Private credit is the sum of credit-market liabilities of the household, nonfinancial business, and financial business sectors from the Board of Governors Flow of Funds. GDP is from the Commerce Department. Data via Haver Analytics. Shaded areas indicate NBER recessions. Heavy tick marks indicate the fourth quarter.

rates. Greenspan's analytical framework harked back to his days as a student of Arthur Burns in the late 1940s. Burns' framework, in the Burns-Mitchell "measurement-without-theory" tradition, uses market psychology as the driving force of the business cycle (Burns 1954; Koopmans 1947; Friedman 1950). Like the credit-cycle analyses of the business cycle resuscitated in the 2008–2009 recession, this analysis is based on "descriptive realism," rather than on the maximizing behavior of individuals incorporated into a framework capable of yielding testable hypotheses. Supposedly, bust follows boom as "imbalances" develop that eventually tip the economy into recession. These "imbalances" derive from unjustifiable optimism about the future.

Consistent with the credit-cycle view, in his commentary on the 2001 recession, Greenspan (2001b) argued that bust follows boom when declines in risk premia reach their feasible limit:

[O]n occasion, asset prices can vary by more than can be attributed to underlying fundamentals. As risk premiums fall in an expansion, asset values in capital investment can be boosted, the economy experiences additional impetus, remembrances of recession fade, and risk premiums fall still further – sometimes to levels below any credible justification. There is, of course, a downside limit – somewhat above zero – where declines in risk premiums end. At that point, confidence ceases to expand.... Asset prices lose their upside potential and come under downward pressure as investors reevaluate risk and revise expectations for outsized gains.... A bursting speculative bubble has historically too often been the end result of this process.

Greenspan then defended the FOMC's performance by pointing out how difficult it is to move in advance of shifts of market psychology. What was important in Greenspan's commentary, however, was not his *understanding* of the dynamics of business cycles but rather his actual *practice* of monetary policy. In practice under Greenspan, apart from the departure in the last half of 1988 and first half of 1999 at the time of the Asia and Brazil crisis, policy remained focused on sustainable growth in real output, not on asset prices. Policy responded only indirectly to the behavior of asset prices as they affected growth in output (Hetzel 2008b, ch. 21). In the language used here, policy retained its LAW character. Greenspan (2001b) wrote:

Monetary policy, as we currently practice it, endeavors to lean against the propensities for economic overshooting.... [I]dentifying bubbles and their ultimate demise is exceptionally difficult.... Policy cannot fully anticipate the buildup or the ending of speculative excesses. Indeed, were we to lower overnight rates in advance of an expected break in asset prices, we would, presumably, only exacerbate the economic and financial imbalances. Our only realistic alternative is to lean against the economic pressures that may accompany a rise in asset prices, bubble or not, and address forcefully the consequences of a sharp deflation of asset prices.

In 2003–2004, the Greenspan FOMC did make a decision that would later have enormous implications. At this time, the FOMC backed off its long-run objective of returning to price stability and instead adopted an ill-defined objective of positive inflation, perhaps best characterized as 2 percent plus. As shown in Figure 11.6, starting in spring 2004, both core and headline PCE inflation moved persistently above 2 percent (dashed line). By summer 2008, that overshoot caused the FOMC to allow a growing negative output gap to persist by holding the funds rate unchanged at 2 percent. If the FOMC had maintained its target for price stability, which it had largely achieved in 2002, the sustained inflation shock that began in summer 2004 with the increase in energy prices would have yielded lower headline inflation numbers. The FOMC in summer 2008 might then have felt comfortable allowing the inflation shock to pass through to the price level while aggressively using monetary policy to deal with the worsening recession.

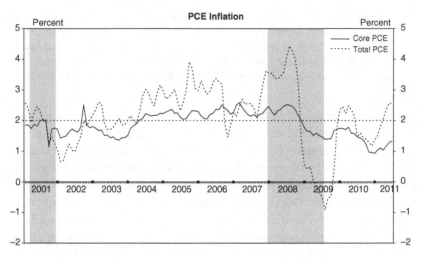

Figure 11.6. PCE inflation.

Note: Monthly observations of twelve-month percentage changes in the personal consumption expenditures (PCE) deflator. The dashed line is drawn at 2 percent. Data from
U.S. Dept. of Commerce, Bureau of Economic Analysis via Haver Analytics. Shaded
areas indicate NBER recessions. Heavy tick marks indicate December.

THE TAYLOR RULE AS A GUIDE TO POLICY
IN THE POST-2002 PERIOD

Using a forecast of the funds rate from an estimated Taylor rule showing
the forecasted funds rate in excess of the actual funds rate, Taylor (2009)
argued that monetary policy was overly stimulative in 2003 and 2004. Even
apart from the issue of whether estimated Taylor rules can serve as a normative benchmark for policy given the problems of inferring structural
from reduced-form relationships (Chapter 8, fourth section), in practice,
there are many different ways of measuring their right-hand variables:
inflation relative to target, the output gap, and the "equilibrium" real rate
that appears in the constant term. One can easily choose these variables to
arrive at contradictory assessments of the stance of monetary policy. For
example, Mehra and Minton (2007) and Mehra and Sawhney (2010) fitted
this period very well using a Taylor rule with core PCE (personal consumption expenditures) inflation and real-time estimates of an output gap based
on board staff (Greenbook) estimates of the output gap.

Taylor rules provide no uniform message about the appropriateness of
monetary policy in the post-2002 period. Weidner and Williams (2009)
pointed out the large discrepancy between output gaps estimated by the

Congressional Budget Office (CBO), which are based on estimates of worker productivity, and those inferred from the behavior of inflation. Among others, Laubach and Williams (2003) used the latter methodology. The difference between the estimates of the output gap for 2009Q1 by the CBO and those produced by Laubach and Williams is 4.2 percentage points (Weidner and Williams 2009). As measured by the CBO (Weidner and Williams 2009, figure 1), after 2001, the output gap remained consistently negative, apart from 2008 when it approached zero. With a persistently negative output gap, monetary policy could not have been significantly expansionary in the post-2002 period.

Macroeconomic Advisers regularly constructs a Taylor rule that uses a gap measured with the unemployment rate. Calculated using the forecasts from the *Blue Chip Economic Indicators* consensus forecast available in summer 2009, Macroeconomic Advisers' (2009, table 4) Taylor rule predicted a low for the funds rate of -7.1 percent, reached in early 2011. That is, a zero funds rate in summer 2009 was much too high. In contrast, using the same *Blue Chip* forecasts, Macroeconomic Advisers found that Taylor's Taylor rule predicted a low for the funds rate of only -0.8 percent, reached in early 2010. That is, a zero funds rate in summer 2009 was about right. Of course, the funds rate cannot be negative. What was at stake in the comparison was an estimate of the length of time for which the funds rate would remain near zero. The point here is that different plausible ways of estimating Taylor rules provide very different implications for the optimal funds-rate target.

In any event, for the period for which FOMC transcripts are available, there is no evidence that FOMC members in their policy go-around ever attempted to reach any consensus over the magnitude of an output gap (Hetzel 2008b, ch. 21, fn. 8). In real time, the required estimates of productivity growth make estimates of potential output too uncertain, and data revisions make estimates of contemporaneous output too uncertain for a Taylor rule to be of practical relevance.

The period after 2002 also illustrates the operational difficulties of implementing Taylor rules incurred because of their use of variables whose initially reported values are subject to significant revision. Starting in 2002, real-time estimates of inflation were later consistently revised upward. For 2004, the difference between the estimates of four-quarter core personal consumption expenditure (PCE) inflation available contemporaneously and those available later in 2009 reached almost two percentage points.

Finally, in understanding the behavior of the interest rate, ignoring expectations is problematic. In Taylor rule formulations, the real interest rate consistent with a zero output gap and with inflation equal to target is a constant. However, this "natural" interest rate should vary continually as shocks affect the public's estimate of its future welfare (the degree of optimism or pessimism about the future). In 2003–2004, the public was pessimistic about the future because of the decline in equity wealth after 2000, the 9/11 terrorist attack with the fear that more attacks were imminent, and the corporate governance scandals such as Enron and WorldCom. At the same time, productivity growth was soaring, perhaps because of the earlier investment in information technology. The economy needed a low real rate of interest (a low cost of consuming today in terms of foregone consumption tomorrow) to provide the contemporaneous consumption and investment demand necessary to absorb the supply of goods coming onto the market.

EMU AND ASSET PRICE VOLATILITY

Although asset prices are an inappropriate target for central banks, the monetary arrangements of a country do affect asset price volatility. Within a monetary union, the fact of a common currency exacerbates asset price volatility among regions, but the unique central bank is powerless to attenuate those fluctuations. Milton Friedman (Friedman and Mundell 2001, 11) argued against the formation of the European Monetary Union (EMU): "[The euro's] real Achilles heel will prove to be political; that a system under which the political and currency boundaries do not match is bound to prove unstable."[7] As in Friedman (1953), Friedman repeated his argument that floating exchange rates among countries obviate the need for fluctuations in their domestic price levels in response to changes in the real terms of trade because of changes in the desirability of the country as a place to invest. Consider the case of Ireland in the 2008–2009 recession.

After its accession to EMU, Ireland became an attractive destination for foreign investment. As a result, its terms of trade appreciated. Inflows of foreign capital translated into an increased demand by foreigners for titles of ownership on Irish assets, especially real estate. To induce the Irish owners

---

[7] In the 1990s, monetary regimes of pegged exchange rates collapsed in a number of spectacular crises. In 1992, the European Monetary System (the EMS) collapsed. In 1995, the Mexican devaluation not only threw Mexico into recession and inflation, but also destabilized countries throughout Latin America. In 1997, runs on the currencies of the Asian tigers, which were pegged to the dollar, precipitated the economic collapse of these countries (Hetzel 2008b, ch. 16). As a result, countries have moved away from pegged exchange rates toward the extremes of floating exchange rates and monetary union or dollarization. The countries of the European Monetary Union eliminated independent national central banks and adopted a single central bank with note issuing power (Hetzel 2002b). El Salvador and Ecuador adopted the dollar as their currency (dollarized).

of those titles to part with them, foreign investors had to offer them goods on attractive terms. For that to happen, the Irish had to find that the price of foreign goods had become cheaper in terms of their own goods. That appreciation in the terms of trade produced the required deficit on the trade or current account that mirrored the capital inflows.

The relative price of identical goods traded because of comparative advantage in production cannot change. Apart from costs of transportation, taxes, and so forth, the price of ballpoint pens must be the same in Ireland and abroad. The price of traded goods produced only in Ireland had to increase and also the price of capital assets such as land.[8]

There is a monetary counterpart to the terms-of-trade appreciation. As the price level in Ireland increases, Irish money holders import euros as well as foreign goods. With floating exchange rates, there is no necessary change in the Irish money stock and in the domestic price level. Friedman (Friedman and Mundell 2001, 19) argued, "Adjustment to the current rapid rise in productivity [in Ireland] and the inevitable subsequent tapering off would be easier if consumer prices were stabler and the punt was appreciating relative to other currencies."

With the appearance of the 2008–2009 recession, in a symmetric fashion, capital outflows from Ireland required a fall in the Irish price level and in the price of land.[9] The banking system amplified the boom-bust behavior of land prices by accumulating real estate loans during the boom phase. In the bust phase, the resulting fears about the solvency of Irish banks exacerbated cyclical outflows. In response, Ireland guaranteed all of the liabilities of its banks. Doubts then arose about the ability of the Irish government to cope with the deficit caused by the losses of its banks.[10]

---

[8] Measured by the S&P/Case-Shiller National HPI (home price index), in the United States, house prices increased by 140% over the ten-year interval from 1996 through 2006. Measured by the ESRI (Economic and Social Research Institute) Standardized Home Price index, in Ireland, house prices increased almost 320% over this interval (Lawler 2010b).

[9] The United States is a monetary union like EMU. A phenomenon similar to that of Ireland occurred in the United States. In the bust phase in real estate following the 2008–2009 recession, states with the most pronounced initial housing boom subsequently suffered the highest unemployment rates. In fall 2010, unemployment rates were 12.4% in California, 14.4% in Nevada, and 11.7% in Florida (*Financial Times* 2010c). In contrast to Ireland, Britain could adjust to capital outflows through a depreciation in its exchange rate. In 2008, relative to 2007, the change in capital inflows as a share of GDP in Britain amounted to -101% (McKinsey 2009, exhibit 9).

[10] In August 2010, the ten-year government bond spread of Irish over German yields was about 325 basis points. *The Wall Street Journal* (2010c) wrote:

As a result of its bank rescues, Ireland's budget deficit will rise to 32% of its economic output this year.... The ratio of Ireland's government debt to the size of its economy stood at 25% at the end of 2007. At the end of 2010, according to finance minister Brian Lenihan,

CONCLUDING COMMENT

Popular discourse has revived the credit-cycle view of the business cycle. As expressed by Daniel Yergin (*Financial Times* 2009):

> Too much leverage – wantonly made available with inadequate and misplaced regulation and inadequate credit ratings, reinforced by low interest rates – created an unstable and over-built edifice of debt that collapsed from its own enormous weight, ... The oscillating balance between "fear and greed" went to extremes in terms of greed; risk was underpriced.... Investor psychology, fed by easy credit, created Shilleresque bubbles in real estate ... that eventually burst.... Since every boom contains the seeds of the next bust, the best global growth in a generation created hubris, ensuring a major downturn.

According to this view, with the cheap credit made possible by an easy monetary policy, speculators pushed house prices to unsustainable heights. When house prices fell, homeowners who had bought at the peak found themselves "under water," that is, with mortgages greater in value than the value of the house. Defaults reduced the capital on bank balance sheets and as a result their willingness to lend. Restrictive lending practices limited credit availability and the ability of households and businesses to spend. Recession resulted when savers could no longer get funds to credit-worthy borrowers.

Martin Wolf (2008) explained "the origins of the crisis in the collapse of an asset price bubble and consequent disintegration of the credit mechanism." A Credit Suisse (2009) newsletter wrote:

> Every boom spawns its own shadow banking system sooner or later. Once the supply of shadow money starts to escalate, the bubble forms. When it breaks, panic sets in. If panic spreads, the supply of shadow money implodes. And the demand for "safe" money explodes. So "excess liquidity" can lead to depression and deflation, not inflation. It has just happened again on an epic scale. This is the Achilles heel of (democratic) capitalism. So governments and central banks put all hands to the pumps.

Such commentary considers monetary policy from the perspective of financial intermediation. From this perspective, the central bank influences financial intermediation through controlling the cost of funds to banks. By setting a low cost of funds through its interest-rate target, the central bank

---

it will be 98.6%. Most of that increase comes from the fact that the Irish government has chosen to pay the creditors of its decrepit, mostly state-owned banks in full....

Only one European government has chosen to impose significant losses on unsecured creditors in the latest crisis: Iceland.... But Reykjavik had something else going for it: A large proportion of its bank creditors were outside the country.

encourages banks to speculate by acquiring high-yielding, long-term, illiquid assets.

From the quantity-theory perspective offered here, the real interest rate is a price, which plays an essential role in the price system. In order to prevent the money creation that destabilizes prices, the central bank must follow a rule that allows market forces to set the real interest rate. When the public is pessimistic about the future, the short-term real interest rate must be low or even zero.

At such times, because of the subsidy to risk taking engendered by the financial safety net, banks have an incentive to leverage risky, illiquid portfolios using the cheap funding available from cash investors. However, central banks cannot allow monetary policy to be hostage to the pervasive moral hazard created by a financial safety net that removes market discipline from the financial sector.

APPENDIX: REAL RATE OF INTEREST SHOWN IN FIGURE 11.2

The short-term real interest rate is the difference between the commercial paper rate and Greenbook inflation forecasts made by the staff of the Board of Governors before FOMC meetings. The commercial paper rate is for prime nonfinancial paper placed through dealers (A1/P1). The dates for the interest rates match the publication dates of the Greenbooks. Because observations correspond to FOMC meetings, they occur irregularly within the year, and starting in 1979 the frequency is less than twelve times per year.

Predicted "overall" inflation is for changes in the implicit GNP (GDP from 1992 on) deflator until August 1992. Thereafter, the fixed-weight GDP deflator is used until March 1996. Thereafter, the GDP chain-weighted price index is used.

The board staff forecasts for "core" inflation become available only in January 1980. From 1966 through 1970, the "core" inflation forecast series also uses forecasts for the implicit GNP deflator. From 1971 through March 1976, the series labeled "core" is the GNP fixed-weight index. Thereafter, until January 1980, the series used is the gross business product fixed-weight index. From January 1980 until February 1986, the gross domestic business product fixed-weight index excluding food and energy is used. Thereafter, until January 2000, the CPI excluding food and energy is used. From January 2000 onward, the personal consumption expenditures chain-weighted index excluding food and energy is used.

For additional details, see Hetzel (2008b, ch. 4, appendix: Series on the Real Interest Rate, Real Rate of Interest, Greenbook Forecasts).

TWELVE

What Caused the Great Recession of 2008–2009?

The monetary-disorder explanation of the 2008–2009 recession proposed here discounts any role for expansionary monetary policy in 2003–2004 and instead points to contractionary monetary policy in 2008 (Hetzel 2009b; 2009c). The explanation starts with two shocks: correction of an excess in the housing stock and a sharp increase in energy prices. Taken together, they initiated the recession that began in December 2007. By themselves, these shocks would probably have led to only a moderate recession. A moderate recession became a major recession in summer 2008 when the FOMC ceased lowering the funds rate while the economy deteriorated. In 2008, concerned that persistent high headline inflation would raise expected inflation above its implicit 2 percent target, the FOMC imparted the kind of inertia to reductions in the funds rate characteristic of the stop phases in stop-go monetary policy (Chapter 8).

Monetary policy in 2008 prior to the September 15 bankruptcy of Lehman Brothers departed in two ways from the monetary policy procedures that had characterized the Volcker-Greenspan era. First, the FOMC went back to the stop-go practice of associating the level of the funds rate with the stance of monetary policy rather than following a rule to determine the appropriate level of the funds rate. In particular, perhaps because of the lack of recent experience with operating in an environment of near-price stability, FOMC members assumed that the 2 percent funds rate set at the April 30, 2008, FOMC meeting represented expansionary monetary policy.[1]

---

[1] In reference to Japan, Milton Friedman (1997) had commented on the common assumption that a low interest rate indicates easy monetary policy:

After the U.S. experience during the Great Depression, and after inflation and rising interest rates in the 1970s and disinflation and falling interest rates in the 1980s, I thought the fallacy of identifying tight money with high interest rates and easy money with low interest rates was dead. Apparently, old fallacies never die.

Second, the FOMC went back to the stop-go practice in the stop phases of attempting to manipulate a negative output gap to restrain inflation. Rather than letting an inflation shock pass through to the price level while using core inflation as its target, it reacted to the high headline inflation produced by a persistent energy price shock.

A BRIEF TAXONOMY

A taxonomy of the decline in real output in the 2008–2009 recession begins with the weakness in consumption. Figure 12.1 displays the behavior of real personal consumption expenditures (PCE) relative to a trend line fitted between business cycle peaks and extrapolated into the subsequent recession. By this measure, across the last three business cycles, trend growth in consumption fell from 4.1 percent to 3.8 percent and to 2.9 percent. From March 2001 to December 2007, monthly real PCE hugged the fitted trend line closely with maximum deviations of only -1.0 percent in February 2003 and 1.1 percent in July 2005 (Figure 12.1). Nothing in this behavior suggests excessive consumption made possible by excessive accumulation of debt. Beginning in May 2007, the shortfall of consumption from trend widened steadily until summer 2010 when it reached 9.8 percent (Figure 12.2).[2]

By summer 2008, this shortfall in aggregate demand caused businesses to accumulate unwanted inventories (Figure 12.3). An inventory cycle then set in. Figure 12.4 plots percentage changes in the inventory/sales ratio for the durable goods sector. As a cyclically sensitive measure of changes in output, it also plots percentage changes in the ISM (Institute of Supply Management) index for activity in the manufacturing sector (inverted scale). As shown in Figure 12.4, the dynamics of the inventory cycle greatly amplify cyclical fluctuations in output. As a result, large declines in real GDP and employment occurred in 2008Q4 and 2009Q1. However, those declines occurred as an endogenous response to the intensification of the recession in summer 2008.

In summer 2008, financial intermediation had already moved significantly away from the securitization markets and back to the banking system. However, there is no evidence of disruption to financial intermediation significant enough to have prevented businesses and consumers from obtaining credit. As with previous recessions, it is hard to find evidence of

---

[2] The fillip given to real personal disposable income (PDI) by the Bush tax cut in spring 2008 created a temporary plateau in real PCE interrupting the decline. Real PDI increased 5.2% in May 2008.

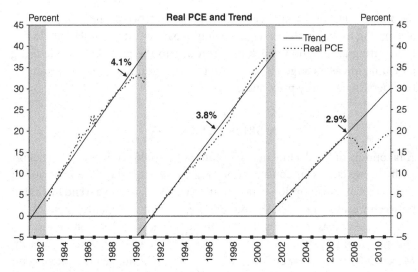

Figure 12.1. Real PCE and trend.

Note: Trend lines are fitted to the natural log of real personal consumption expenditures (PCE) between business cycle peaks with series normalized using the prior cycle peak value of real PCE and are extended into the subsequent recession. Observations on real PCE are the log of the index values of real PCE. Data from the Commerce Department via Haver Analytics. Shaded areas indicate NBER recessions. Heavy tick marks indicate December.

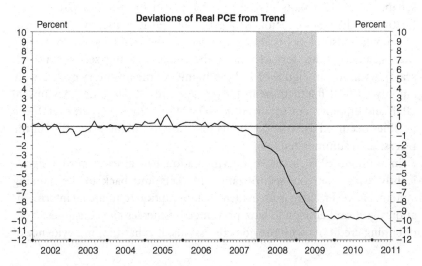

Figure 12.2. Deviations of real PCE from trend.

Note: Deviations are the difference between actual and trend real PCE shown in Figure 12.1. Shaded areas indicate NBER recessions. Heavy tick marks indicate December.

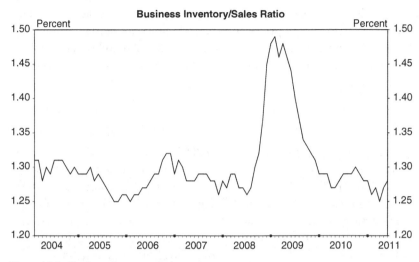

Figure 12.3. Business inventory/sales ratio.

Note: Monthly observations of inventories divided by sales for all businesses. Data from the Census Bureau via Haver Analytics. Heavy tick marks indicate December.

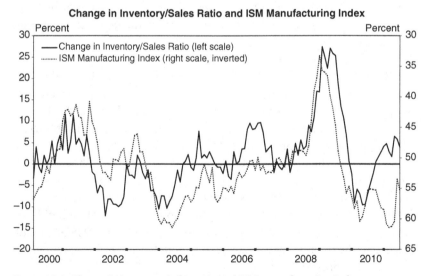

Figure 12.4 Change in inventory/sales ratio and ISM manufacturing index.

Note: Monthly observations of annualized percentage changes in the inventory/sales ratio for the durable goods sector and monthly observations of the Institute for Supply Management (ISM) index for the manufacturing sector (shown on an inverted scale). Data from the Census Bureau and Institute of Supply Management via Haver Analytics. Heavy tick marks indicate December.

a credit channel propagating an initial shock.[3] The thesis advanced here is that shocks to energy prices and the housing sector started a moderate recession with a cyclical peak in December 2007. An additional shock in the form of contractionary monetary policy then intensified the recession starting in summer 2008.

FROM MODERATE TO MAJOR RECESSION

One plausible explanation for the May 2007 starting date of the decline in consumption below trend is the depressing effect on real personal disposable income (PDI) of the sharp increase in energy and commodity prices, with prices peaking in summer 2008. Figure 12.5 displays the price of a barrel of oil measured in 2005 dollars. From $28.10 on November 1, 2002, the spot price of a barrel of oil rose to $72.20 on July 1, 2006, fell back to $52.20 on January 1, 2007, and climbed sharply to $122.20 on June 1, 2008.

Figure 12.6 displays three-month annualized growth rates in real PDI and real PCE. Both series declined over the course of 2007.[4] Figure 12.7 shows cycle relatives for real PDI for the 2008–2009 recession and for the combined prior postwar recessions. Unlike the prior recessions, the 2008–2009 recession displays almost no growth in real PDI for the year prior to the cycle peak. This lack of growth is evidence for the depressing effect of the inflation shock.

The decline in residential investment, which began to fall in 2005Q3, provided an additional shock. However, because residential investment is normally about 6 percent of GDP, even negative growth rates are not enough by themselves to cause a recession. For example, in 2007Q4, residential investment fell at an annualized rate of 29.3 percent but subtracted only 1.4 percentage points from GDP growth (Figure 12.8). The decline in residential investment was symptomatic of the excess stock of housing. The associated decline in housing wealth must also have depressed consumer spending. Figure 12.9 shows household net worth as a ratio to income along with the portion of wealth comprising the housing stock. Household net worth (relative to income) began to decline in 2007Q4. By 2008Q3, it had returned to the level reached in 2003Q2, although even that level remained well above the pre-1997 average.

---

[3] Examples of empirical studies finding minimal propagation of shocks from disruption to financial intermediation are Ashcraft (2003), Konishi et al. (1993), and Berrospide and Edge (2010).

[4] The three spikes in real PDI in the years 2008 and 2009 derived from the Bush tax rebate, augmented social security payments, and the Obama stimulus program, respectively.

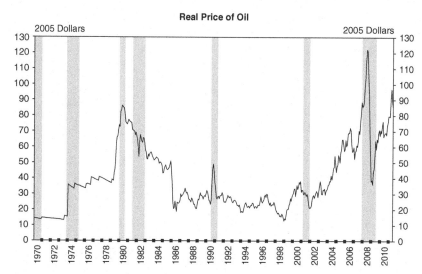

Figure 12.5. Real price of oil.

Note: Monthly observations of the West Texas intermediate crude oil spot price per barrel deflated by the personal consumption expenditures price index. Data from *The Wall Street Journal* and Commerce Department via Haver Analytics. Shaded areas indicate NBER recessions. Heavy tick marks indicate December.

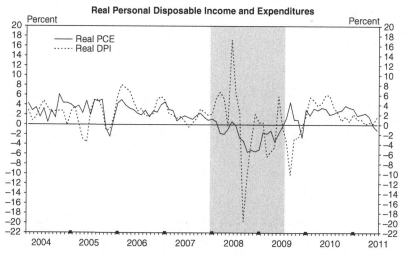

Figure 12.6. Real personal disposable income and expenditures.

Note: Three-month annualized percentage changes in real personal consumption expenditures (PCE) and real disposable personal income (DPI). December 2004 real DPI adjusted for the Microsoft dividend payment. Data from the Commerce Department via Haver Analytics. Heavy tick marks indicate December.

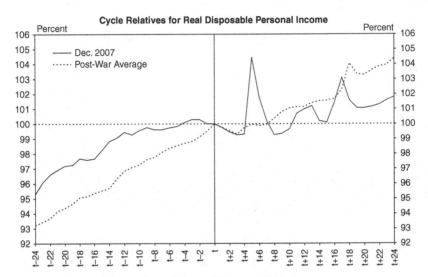

Figure 12.7. Cycle relatives for real disposable personal income.

Note: Monthly values of real disposable personal income calculated as a percent of cycle peak value. Postwar average is calculated using values for recessions between 1969–1970 and 2001 recessions. Data from the Commerce Department via Haver Analytics.

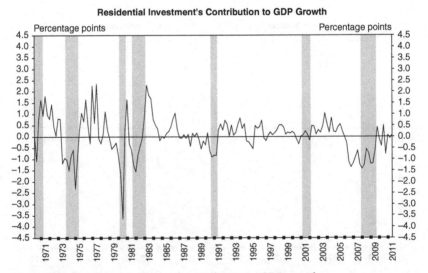

Figure 12.8. Residential investment's contribution to GDP growth.

Note: Quarterly observations of private residential investment's contribution to growth in real gross domestic product in seasonally adjusted annual growth rates. Data from the Commerce Department via Haver Analytics. Shaded areas indicate NBER recessions. Heavy tick marks indicate the fourth quarter.

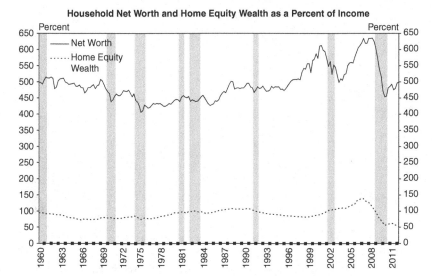

Figure 12.9. Household net worth and home equity wealth as a percent of income. *Note*: Series are household net worth and home equity wealth as a fraction of disposable personal income. Data are from the Board of Governors Flow of Funds via Haver Analytics. Shaded areas indicate NBER recessions. Heavy tick marks indicate the fourth quarter.

A critical clue to the reason that moderate recession turned into major recession is the timing of the intensification. Specifically, the recession intensified *before* the financial turmoil associated with the bankruptcy of Lehman on September 15, 2008. For the months January through March 2008, total nonfarm payroll employment declined on average by 47,000; for the months April through July, by 207,000; and for August and September, respectively, the declines increased to 267,000 and 434,000. Note that the payroll surveys are conducted in the second week of the month, which places the September decline chronologically before the Lehman bankruptcy.

Figures 12.10 and 12.11 document the fact that the intensification of the recession began in summer 2008. The former graph shows that the cyclical decline in payroll employment intensified in August 2008 (the t+8 observation). The latter graph makes the dating clearer. The moderate declines in employment that characterized the first half of the year intensified beginning in early August and in early September 2008.

The timing for the intensification of the decline in consumption tells the same story. For 2008Q1, 2008Q2, and 2008Q3, real PCE grew, respectively, by -1.0 percent, -0.1 percent and -3.9 percent (figures not shown). However,

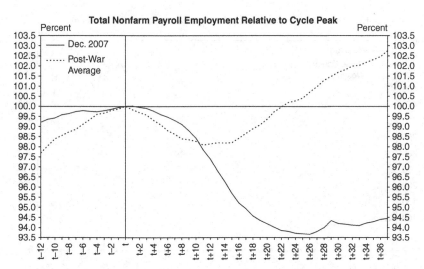

Figure 12.10. Total nonfarm payroll employment relative to cycle peak.
Note: Monthly values of total nonfarm payroll employment calculated as a percent of cycle peak value. Data from the Bureau of Labor Statistics via Haver Analytics.

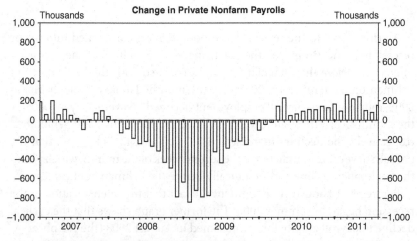

Figure 12.11. Change in private nonfarm payrolls.
Note: Monthly observations of the change in private nonfarm payroll employment in thousands. Data from Bureau of Labor Statistics via Haver Analytics. Heavy tick marks indicate December.

Table 12.1. *Contributions to percent changes in real GDP*

	2008				2009
	Q1	Q2	Q3	Q4	Q1
GDP	−1.8	1.3 (−1.0)	−3.7	−8.9	−6.7
PCE	−0.7	−0.1	−2.7	−3.5	−1.0
Nonres I	−0.1	−0.3	−1.2	−2.8	−3.9
Res I	−1.3	−0.6	−0.7	−1.2	−1.2

Note: Percentage changes at annual rates. GDP is gross domestic product; PCE is personal consumption expenditures; Nonres I is nonresidential fixed investment; Res I is residential investment. Data from Bureau of Economic Analysis (BEA).

the second-quarter figure is likely distorted upward by the boost to disposable income from the Bush tax rebate. Table 12.1 shows the *contributions* to real GDP made by real PCE, nonresidential investment, and residential investment in the critical period 2008Q1 to 2009Q1. The strength in real GDP growth in 2008Q2 of 1.3 percent was more than accounted for by the transitory additions to GDP growth from the strength in net exports, which added 2.0 percentage points, and government expenditures, which added 0.3 percentage points. Absent the impact of these transitory factors, annualized growth in 2008Q2 real GDP would have been −1.0 percent, which appears in parentheses in Table 12.1 for 2008Q2 real GDP growth.

The sustained weakness in consumption (real PCE) growth shown in Table 12.1 and in Figure 12.2 increased business inventories to unsustainable levels. Inventory/sales ratios (total business) climbed sharply from 1.27 in July 2008 to 1.48 by year-end (Figure 12.3). The reduction in output required to reduce excess inventories created much of the sharp annualized declines in real GDP for 2008Q4 and for 2009Q1 of -8.9 percent and -6.7 percent, respectively.

Just as the coincidence of the financial turmoil in fall 2008 with the deterioration in the headline GDP numbers created the impression of causation running from financial turmoil to a decline in output, the arrival of information in early October 2008 that the world economy had entered into recession produced a similar assumption imputing causation from correlation in financial and real instability. In fact, the world economy had already entered into recession in 2008Q2.[5] Until early October 2008 when figures began to arrive on the worsening economic situation abroad, the

---

[5] For 2008Q2 and 2008Q3, annualized real GDP growth was, respectively, −5.2% and −4.3% for Japan, −0.3% and −3.7% for Great Britain, and −1.2% and −1.6% for the Eurozone.

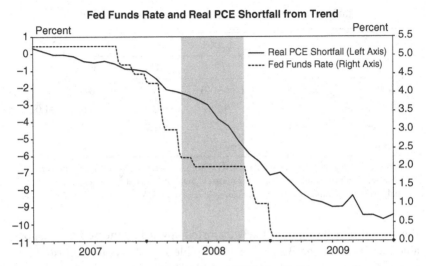

Figure 12.12. Fed funds rate and real PCE shortfall from trend.

Note: Deviations of real personal consumption expenditures from trend (from Figure 12.2). Data on the Fed funds-rate target are weekly averages. Apart from weeks that include a change in the target, the values are as follow: 1/1/07 to 9/10/07: 5.25%; 9/24/07 to 10/22/07: 4.75%; 11/5/07 to 12/3/07: 4.5%; 12/17/07 to 1/14/08: 4.25%; 2/4/08 to 3/10/08: 3.0%; 3/24/08 to 4/21/08: 2.25%; 5/5/08 to 9/29/08: 2.0%; 10/13/08 to 10/20/08: 1.5%; 11/3/08 to 12/8/08: 1%; 12/22/08 onward: 0.125%. Heavy tick marks indicate December.

expectation had existed that strength in the world economy would temper the U.S. recession. The realization that the world economy had entered into recession by 2008Q3 depressed equity markets in fall 2008. No doubt, the loss in wealth from the decline in equity markets depressed consumption independently of any disruption to financial intermediation.

The central empirical fact of the 2008–2009 recession is that the severe declines in output that appeared in the 2008Q4 and 2009Q1 real GDP numbers had already been locked in by summer 2008. The disruption in financial markets that occurred after the September 15, 2008, bankruptcy of Lehman Brothers coincided with but did not cause the sharp fall in output in the 2008–2009 recession.

MONETARY DISORDER?

The hypothesis here is that contractionary monetary policy turned a moderate recession into a severe recession during the summer of 2008.[6] In

---

[6]   Similarities exist especially between the 1973–1975 and 2008–2009 recessions. In both cases, mild recession accompanied inflation shocks and interest rate inertia accompanied

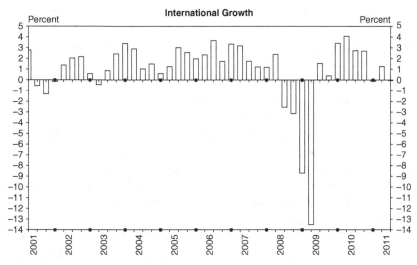

Figure 12.13. International growth.
Note: Annualized quarterly growth in real gross domestic product for G7 countries excluding the United States (Canada, France, Germany, Italy, Japan, and the United Kingdom). Data are from the OECD via OECD Stat. Heavy tick marks indicate the fourth quarter.

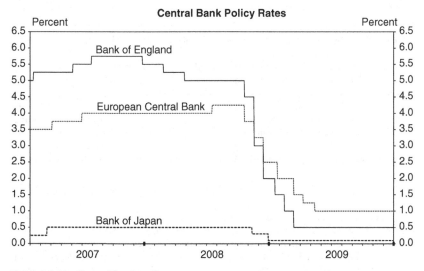

Figure 12.14. Central bank policy rates.
Note: Foreign central bank interest-rate targets. Data from Bloomberg. Heavy tick marks indicate December.

spring 2008, the FOMC departed from the lean-against-the-wind (LAW) procedures that had characterized the Volcker-Greenspan era by ceasing to lower the funds rate despite declining rates of resource utilization. Early in 2008, the FOMC did lower the funds rate in response to weakness in economic activity. In spring 2008, however, the FOMC became concerned that persistent headline inflation in excess of core inflation would destabilize expected inflation and would compromise its (implicit) inflation objective. As a result, the Fed, along with other central banks, recreated the stop phase of the stop-go monetary era by failing to lower the funds rate in response to sustained weakening in economic activity. In fall 2008, when the severity of the recession became apparent, central banks focused on financial intermediation and lowered their interest-rate targets only slowly.

Figure 12.12 displays the growing shortfall of consumption from trend that began in early summer 2007 (the percentage deviation from trend shown in Figure 12.2). The shaded area highlights the interval of time from March 18, 2008, until October 8, 2008, when the funds rate declined only one-quarter percentage point and real consumption declined steadily below trend. As measured by the LAW-with-credibility benchmark, monetary policy was contractionary over this interval. From this perspective, contractionary monetary policy turned a mild recession into a severe recession and created an extended need for low, negative short-term real interest rates.[7]

the transition from mild to severe recession. In early summer 1973, FOMC chairman Arthur Burns became concerned that the Watergate difficulties of President Nixon would prevent the Nixon administration from vigorously enforcing the price controls he desired to control wage growth and hence, he believed, inflation. As a result, the FOMC began to enforce rigorously money growth targets consistent with moderate growth in nominal expenditure. A double inflation shock occurred in the form of OPEC oil price increases beginning in fall 1973 and continuing into 1974 plus the spurt in prices accompanying the end to price controls in April 1974. In fall 1974 as the economy weakened further, the FOMC put inertia into funds rate decreases as a result of Burns' desire to use monetary policy as a bargaining chip with Congress to achieve restraint on the growth rate of government expenditure (Hetzel 2008b, ch. 10, section IV). Mild recession then turned into severe recession.

[7]   Macroeconomic Advisers (2008c) argued that monetary policy was restrictive:

Over the period that ended in April [2008], the FOMC strategy was to ease aggressively in order to offset the tightening of financial conditions arising from wider credit spreads, more stringent lending standards, and falling equity prices. We said that the FOMC was "running to stand still," in that those actions did not create accommodative financial conditions but were needed to keep them from becoming significantly tighter. Since the last easing [April 2008], however, the FOMC has abandoned that strategy. Financial conditions have arguably tightened more severely since April than during the earlier period, and yet there has been no policy offset. This pattern has contributed importantly to the severe weakening of the economic outlook in our forecast.

Despite declining rates of resource utilization, the FOMC limited downward movements in the funds rate out of concern that headline inflation persistently above 2 percent would raise inflationary expectations. As noted in the January 2008 FOMC *Minutes* (Board of Governors, January 29–30, 2008, 12), "[H]eadline inflation had been generally above 2 percent over the past four years, and participants noted that such persistently elevated readings could ultimately affect inflation expectations."[8]

Macroeconomic Advisers (2008a [February 29], 2) wrote, "[T]he FOMC is now facing … increased inflation concerns among investors. These concerns seem to have been sparked by the combination of the aggressive [easing] policy actions taken over January and the unfavorable news about inflation." Later, Macroeconomic Advisers (2008b [March 19], 1, 4) wrote:

One measure that the FOMC closely monitors is breakeven inflation rates derived from TIPS and nominal treasury securities.… The five-year five-year (5Y5Y) forward breakeven inflation rate has been on the rise in recent months, most notably since the FOMC became more aggressive in its easing actions in January.… [It has] become increasingly difficult for the Fed to describe inflation expectations as well anchored. Indeed, the Fed's own rhetoric on this had begun to fray, as "well anchored" inflation expectations were replaced by "reasonably well anchored" expectations in Chairman Bernanke's testimony last November and then by "fairly well anchored" expectations in the January minutes.

Within the shared FOMC consensus that persistent high headline inflation risked exacerbating inflationary expectations, one group of FOMC participants believed that the thrust of monetary policy was expansionary and on course to raise inflation whereas another group believed that monetary policy was appropriate because an increase in risk premia on risky borrowing offset the expansionary effect of a low funds rate. Under the LAW procedures that gave continuity to policy in the Volcker-Greenspan era, the FOMC had abandoned its stop-go practice of associating a restrictive level of monetary policy with a "high" interest rate and an expansionary policy with a "low" interest rate. It became willing to move the funds rate in response to sustained changes in rates of resource utilization without limits. In 2008, the FOMC reverted to its earlier practice of inferring the thrust of monetary policy from the level of interest rates and conditions in money markets.

---

[8] Starting after summer 2004 and lasting through summer 2008, twelve-month percentage changes in core PCE inflation fell consistently in a range of 2% to 2.5%. In summer 2008, headline PCE inflation almost reached 4.5%. The University of Michigan Survey of Consumers's measure for expected inflation over the next five to ten years reached almost 3.5%.

The June FOMC *Minutes* (Board of Governors, June 24–25, 2008, 6, 7, and 8) recorded sentiment within the FOMC over monetary policy:

[P]articipants continued to see significant downside risks to growth. At the same time, however, the outlook for inflation had deteriorated. Recent increases in energy and some other commodity prices would boost inflation sharply in coming months.... [P]articipants had become more concerned about upside risks to the inflation outlook – including the possibility that persistent advances in energy and food prices could spur increases in long-run inflation expectations.... Participants agreed that the possibilities of greater pass through of cost increases into prices, higher long-run inflation expectations feeding into labor costs and other prices, and further increases in energy prices all posed upside risks to inflation that had intensified since the time of the April FOMC meeting.

Some participants noted that certain measures of the real federal funds rate, especially those using actual or forecasted headline inflation, were now negative, and very low by historical standards. In the view of these participants, the current stance of monetary policy was providing considerable support to aggregate demand and, if the negative real federal funds rate was maintained, it could well lead to higher trend inflation.... However, other participants observed that the high level of risk spreads and the restricted availability of credit suggested that overall financial conditions were not especially accommodative; indeed, borrowing costs for many households and businesses were higher than they had been last summer.... With increased upside risks to inflation and inflation expectations, members believed that the next change in the stance of policy could well be an increase in the funds rate.

Concern for dollar depreciation also militated against lowering the funds rate. In early June 2008, Fed spokesmen made public statements expressing concern about a possible depreciation of the dollar. Because the foreign exchange value of the dollar is the province of the Treasury, the statements had to reflect Treasury views.[9] Chairman Bernanke (2008a) stated:

Another significant upside risk to inflation is that high headline inflation, if sustained, might lead the public to expect higher long-term inflation rates, an expectation that could ultimately become self-confirming.... We are attentive to the implications of changes in the value of the dollar for inflation and inflation expectations and will continue to formulate policy to guard against risks to both parts

---

[9] Newspaper accounts attributed official concern over the dollar to Chinese disquiet over the value of its U.S. Treasury debt. The *Financial Times* (2009b, 5) wrote:

The official total [in China's foreign exchange reserves] is $1,950bn.... Foreign investors now own about $3,000bn of US Treasuries, or more than half of the amount publicly available.... "We hope the US side will ... guarantee the safety of China's assets and investments in the US," Wang Qishan, a vice-premier, told Hank Paulson when the former US Treasury secretary visited Beijing in December.... One of the reasons the Bush administration was forced to recapitalize Fannie Mae and Freddie Mac last year, economists say, was because China had started to sell its bond holdings in the US agencies in favour of Treasuries.

of our dual mandate, including the risk of an erosion in longer-term inflation expectations.

Concern for the dollar continued into the fall. Later, Treasury Secretary Paulson told the *Financial Times* (2010b) that he "feared there would be a run on the dollar during the early phase of the financial crisis when global concerns were focused on the US.... 'It was a real concern,' Mr. Paulson said.... A dollar collapse 'would have been catastrophic.'" Presumably, this concern was a factor leading the Fed to keep the funds rate unchanged from its April 30, 2008, meeting until the reduction made on October 8, 2008 as part of a coordinated reduction in rates by major central banks.

In addition to the inertia in declines in the funds rate shown in the shaded area of Figure 12.12, the Fed's hawkish language about inflation and concern for a possible depreciation of the dollar tilted upward the market's expectation of the future funds-rate path rather than encouraging a decline. As of April 3, 2008, the six-month contract for federal funds futures implied a funds rate in September 2008 of somewhat below 2 percent. As of July 3, 2008, the six-month futures contract implied a funds rate above 2.25 percent in December 2008, and as of September 4, 2008, it implied a similar funds rate for February 2009.[10] Over the period from March through October 2008, long-term interest rates increased. The ten-year constant-maturity Treasury nominal bond yield was 3.3 percent on March 24, 2008, and 3.8 percent on August 29, 2008. Over the corresponding interval, the real (inflation-indexed) bond yields increased from 1.0 percent to 2.2 percent.[11]

The FOMC never succeeded in 2008 in arresting the below-trend growth that began in 2007. The FOMC *Minutes* contain a summary of the economic forecasts made by the Board of Governors staff for FOMC meetings and contained in a document then called the Greenbook. As indicated by the staff forecast for "a modest increase in unemployment," as of the September 2007 FOMC meeting, the economy had begun to grow below potential. By the March 18, 2008, FOMC meeting, "the staff projection showed a contraction of real GDP in the first half of 2008" (Board of Governors FOMC *Minutes*, September 18, 2007, 7, and March 18, 2008, 5). At its September 2007 meeting, the FOMC began to reduce the funds rate from its 5.25 percent value but then backed off from further reductions when the funds rate reached 2 percent with the April 30, 2008, meeting.[12]

---

[10] See Federal Reserve Bank of St. Louis *U.S. Financial Data*, various weekly issues.

[11] Figures are from Board of Governors statistical release H.15, "Selected Interest Rates."

[12] One difficulty raised in ex-post assessments of policy in this period is the downward revisions to a variety of real series (real PCE, real GDP, and payroll employment). These

As evident from the *Minutes* from the August and September 2008 FOMC meetings at which the FOMC did not lower the funds rate, reminiscent of the stop phases of stop-go monetary policy, in 2008 the FOMC allowed a negative output gap to persist in order to lower headline inflation and to restrain a possible increase in inflationary expectations. The *Minutes* (Board of Governors, August 5, 2008, 5–6, and September 16, 2008, 6) for these meetings record:

[R]etail sales had weakened during late spring and auto sales had dropped sharply in both June and July. The unemployment rate jumped during the intermeeting period. Participants expressed significant concerns about the upside risks to inflation, especially the risk that persistently high headline inflation could result in an unmooring of long-run inflation expectations.

[W]ith elevated inflation still a concern and growth expected to pick up next year if financial strains diminished, the Committee should also remain prepared to reverse the policy easing put in place over the past year in a timely fashion.

The severity of the 2008–2009 recession derived from the combined contractionary monetary policy of all the world's central banks. As shown in Figure 12.13, which displays real GDP growth for G7 countries excluding the United States, the world economy entered into recession in 2008Q2. Although their economies weakened in 2008, the central banks of these countries kept their policy rates basically unchanged

revisions showed the real economy deteriorating at a faster rate in 2008 than was apparent from contemporaneous data. For example, the contemporaneously available numbers on payroll employment showed reductions, respectively, of -84,000 and -159,000 for August and September 2008. Later benchmark revisions changed those numbers to -267,000 and -434,000, respectively. The post–August 2009 national income and product account (NIPA) revisions to real PCE lowered annualized growth from December 2007 through August 2008 to -1.9% from -0.7%. Although it was apparent in summer 2008 that the economy was growing below potential (Hetzel 2009b), with better data, the FOMC might have placed more emphasis on weakness in the real economy as opposed to a destabilization of inflationary expectations. In any event, the dating for the intensification of the recession, namely, summer 2008, requires use of the revised data.

These revisions highlight flaws in the use of Taylor rules as a guide to policy. As of July 2008, boosted by the dramatic increase in energy prices, the year-over-year percent change in the CPI was 5.6%, which was 3.6 percentage points more than the Taylor rule's 2% inflation target. With an inflation target of 2% and a benchmark interest rate of 2%, that fact implies a funds-rate target of 3.8%, lowered by half the value of the negative output gap. However, estimates of the output gap using contemporaneously available data would have been biased toward zero. It is likely that the Taylor rule would have prescribed an inappropriate increase in the funds rate in summer 2008. In contrast, the LAW-with-credibility rule, assuming FOMC credibility, prescribes that the FOMC allow the effect of the inflation shock on prices to dissipate. As measured by the consistently negative monthly numbers on contemporaneously available payroll employment starting in January 2008, this rule would have prescribed continued reduction in the funds rate in summer 2008.

until October 2008, with the ECB (European Central Bank) raising rates in July 2008 (Figure 12.14).[13]

In the Euro area, both headline and core CPI inflation were below 2 percent in mid-2007. Headline inflation rose to 4.0 percent in July 2008. The ECB focused on the possibility of higher wage settlements in Germany, Italy, and the Netherlands (*Financial Times* 2008c) and in July 2008 raised the interbank rate to 4.25 percent. "[ECB President] Trichet has been trying to signal to powerful German and French unions that inflation will remain low so they do not need to demand big raises in their contracts. For that reason, the bank raised rates as recently as this summer" (*The Washington Post* 2008h).

As late as the end of September 2008, the ECB continued to focus monetary policy directly on headline inflation. The *Financial Times* (2008f) wrote:

The economic crisis is proving the biggest test yet of the ECB's policy of strictly separating its efforts to calm financial markets, which have seen it greatly increasing the size of emergency liquidity injections this week, from its main interest rate policy aimed at combating inflation. Jean-Claude Trichet, the ECB president, last night reaffirmed the importance of "a clear separation."... The bank, which raised rates as recently as July, sees eurozone costs as less flexible than in the US, justifying a tougher monetary policy stance, especially with crucial wage negotiations looming in the German engineering sector.... Jacques Cailloux, a Royal Bank of Scotland economist, said, "a near-term cut would throw in the bin one year of careful communication on the ECB's crisis management strategy" as well as "confirm that the July rate rise was a mistake."

Consistent with contractionary monetary policy, core CPI inflation fell after summer 2008 in the major industrial countries. In both the United States and the eurozone, core CPI fell from 2.5 percent in summer 2008 to 1 percent in summer 2010. In Japan, core CPI inflation fell from 0 percent in summer 2008 to -2 percent in mid-2010.

Figure 11.1 shows measures of the short-term real interest rate measured using highly rated (A1/P1) six-month and overnight commercial paper as well as six-month Treasury bills. The decline in the Treasury bill rate that began in August 2007 shows the flight to safety that began at that time. The divergent behavior of the six-month commercial paper rate and of the overnight commercial paper rate shows the demand for liquidity that also began at this time and peaked after the Lehman default. If a low or negative level of the short-term real interest rate on Treasury bills is indicative of

[13] When the Fed, the Bank of England, and the ECB cut rates on October 8, 2008, the Bank of Japan did not. "The BOJ decided it was better to stand pat and guard against the potential risks of any rate cut, such as an asset bubble" (*Nikkei Weekly* 2008).

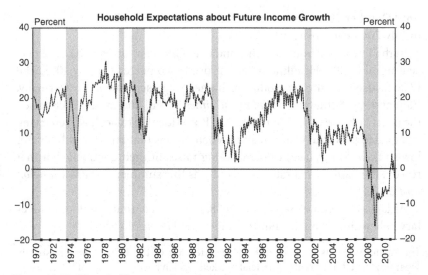

Figure 12.15. Household expectations about future income growth.
Note: The percentage of households expecting an increase in income over the next six months minus the percentage expecting a decrease. Data from the Conference Board Consumer Confidence Survey. Shaded areas indicate NBER recessions. Heavy tick marks indicate December.

expansionary monetary policy, then monetary policy was highly expansionary in 2008. If so, given the decline in inflation measured by the core PCE deflator to 1 percent in 2010, powerful nonmonetary forces overwhelmed the working of monetary policy. That implication is implausible in light of monetary experience over the longer historical record (Hetzel 2008b).

The hypothesis here is that the natural rate of interest (the real rate of interest consistent with maintaining real aggregate demand equal to potential output) lay below even the low real interest rates that prevailed in 2008–2009. The natural rate will be low or even negative if individuals are extremely pessimistic about the future. Figure 12.15 shows the pessimism that existed at this time. It is a diffusion index from the Conference Board constructed as the percentage of households expecting an increase in income over the coming six months minus the percentage expecting a decrease.[14]

[14] *Wall Street Journal* reporter Gerald Seib reported (2010):

The traditional American spirit of optimism about the future is fading. In two straight monthly Journal/NBC News polls, only a third of those surveyed have said the economy will get better in the next year. Notably, this level of pessimism cuts across all income lines.... [I]t represents a striking variation from the usual American impulse to think life will steadily improve.

Of course, the natural rate is an abstraction rather than an observable variable. The hypothesis in Hetzel (2008b) is that the lean-against-the-wind procedures (LAW with credibility) generally followed in the Volcker-Greenspan era moved real interest rates in line with the natural rate. In particular, sustained declines in rates of resource utilization (increases in the unemployment rate) indicate a real interest rate in excess of the natural rate. Implementation of these procedures in 2008 would have implied more vigorous reductions in the funds rate after the March 18, 2008, meeting when the funds rate reached 2.25 percent. With persistent reductions, the funds rate would have reached zero early in the fall.

At that point, monetary stimulus would have required sustained growth in the monetary base beyond the increased amount demanded by banks in the form of excess reserves after the Lehman bankruptcy. Monetary base growth would have had to be sufficient to maintain sustained growth in the monetary aggregates at whatever rate required to maintain growth in nominal expenditure consistent with targeted inflation and growth in potential output. Maintenance of growth in nominal expenditure would not in itself have assured continued growth in real output. However, it would have prevented disinflation, and it would have provided confidence that the price system would be allowed to work to return real output to potential. That confidence would have acted to sustain the confidence in the future necessary to encourage households to maintain their consumption and thus avoid a prolonged, deep recession.

Of course, this kind of counterfactual is contentious. Nevertheless, it is unfortunate that the Fed did not already have in place a policy of quantitative easing defined in terms of growth of the money stock, not bank reserves, in the event that the zero-lower-bound problem arose. The logical time to have formulated and advertised such a policy would have been in 2003 when the FOMC had become concerned about deflation. At that time, explicit enunciation of an inflation target would also have allowed the Fed to cope with a possible destabilization of inflationary expectations in summer 2008 associated with a policy of robust quantitative easing designed to maintain the rate of growth of the nominal expenditure of the public.[15]

---

[15] See the discussion in Goodfriend (2000 and 2001) and in Goodfriend (2011 forthcoming) of the proposals made by the Richmond Federal Reserve at the January 2002 FOMC meeting and the quotation from Richmond President J. Alfred Broaddus at the June 24–25, 2003, FOMC meeting cited in Chapter 16.

DISRUPTION TO FINANCIAL MARKETS

What about the alternative explanation for the intensification of the 2008–2009 recession, namely, a disruption to financial intermediation? In asking whether the disruption to financial markets produced by the subprime crisis caused the intensification of a moderate recession, the focus will be on the level of disruption to markets in the first three quarters of 2008, that is, prior to the Lehman bankruptcy on September 15, 2008. As measured by the decline in consumption, the recession intensified in 2008Q3 with an annualized decline in real personal consumption expenditures of -3.9 percent. Was the disruption in financial markets that followed the withdrawal of cash investors from structured financial products (especially subprime mortgages) that began in August 2007 sufficient in magnitude to have caused the intensification of the recession in summer 2008?

The story of the financial turmoil that began in August 2007 and revived in September 2008 is the story of the retreat of the cash investors who provided the short-term financing used by banks to leverage portfolios of long-term, illiquid assets, especially the structured financial products packaging subprime and Alt-A mortgages (Chapter 13). After August 2007, financial intermediation shifted away from securitization and back toward traditional bank lending (Figure 12.16). The cash investors who had provided the short-term financing for the securitized markets did not disappear. They put their funds into the insured deposits of banks and into government money-market funds. Certain financial transactions like leveraged buyouts ceased. However, none of these changes is evidence that creditworthy borrowers ceased obtaining credit. Banks continued to have access to funding either through the issuance of financial commercial paper, through increased Federal Home Loan Bank (FHLB) funding, or through traditional deposit taking.[16]

---

[16] Using panel data for banks and firms for Spain, Jimenez et al. (2010) found that supply-side effects due to curtailment of bank access to securitization markets did not affect aggregate credit use by firms. Jimenez et al. (2010, abstract, 2, and 4) wrote:

[W]hile the collapse of the private securitization market in 2008 contracted credit from more securitization-dependent banks, [the] aggregate firm-level impact of [a] securitization-driven credit crunch is close to zero.... While shocks to balance sheets of banks may have real effects via changes in bank credit supply (Bernanke 1983; Gertler and Kiyotaki 2010), how do we know that observed fluctuations in credit are driven by supply shifts, and not demand fundamentals? Most calls for policy makers to "lean against the wind" in the midst of a credit boom, or to subsidize banks in a credit crunch, are based on the premise that the primary failure lies o[n] the *supply* side.

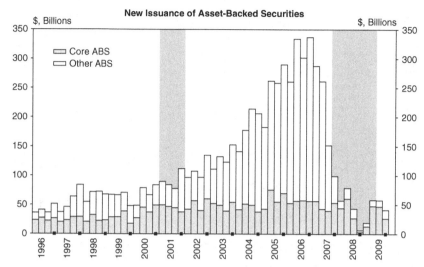

Figure 12.16. New issuance of asset-backed securities.
Note: Quarterly observations of new asset-backed security issuance. Core ABS consists of auto, credit card, and student loans. Other ABS primarily consists of home equity loans and ABS derivatives. Data from Bloomberg. Shaded areas indicate NBER recessions. Heavy tick marks indicate the fourth quarter.

In recession, risk premia rise and banks tighten lending standards, but for banks default risk increases. The issue is whether some market failure makes the increase in risk premia and decline in debt observed in recession into an independent factor that depresses economic activity. Alternatively, is the decline simply an inevitable concomitant of recession – a symptom rather than a cause? Because of the simultaneity problem, this issue is difficult to resolve empirically.[17] This section asks a simpler question. During the first three quarters of 2008, did measures of stringency in credit markets increase only to levels comparable to what existed in recent moderate recessions? If so, the intensification of the recession in 2008Q3 that turned

> [S]ome firms may not be credit constrained and may not want to increase their borrowing.... [E]ven for firms that are credit-constrained, banks may not be willing to go beyond the firms' total debt capacity.... For the set of firms with multiple borrowing banking relationships at the time of the securitization boom, the net impact of [the] credit channel for firm credit volume is zero, despite a large credit channel effect at the bank-firm level!

[17] However, as emphasized in Chapter 15, the promptness and magnitude of the intervention by governments and central banks into credit markets in the 2008–2009 recession turned this episode into an experiment into the effectiveness of credit policy as an instrument of economic stabilization.

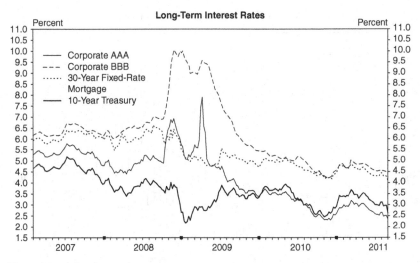

Figure 12.17. Long-term interest rates.

Note: Corporate AAA and BBB bond rates are from Merrill Lynch. Mortgage rate is from the Freddie Mac Primary Mortgage Market Survey. Treasury rate is the ten-year constant maturity rate from the Board of Governors H.15 Statistical Release. Data via Haver Analytics. Heavy tick marks indicate December.

a moderate recession into a major recession is unlikely to have stemmed significantly from financial market disruption.

Figure 12.17 shows long-term interest rates. Nothing in the series (Corporate AAA, Corporate BBB, thirty-year fixed-rate mortgage, and the ten-year Treasury) displayed indicates significant stress in financial markets before fall 2008. If credit markets were dysfunctional in summer 2008, Treasury yields would have declined more relative to the corporate and mortgage-market yields than occurred. Figure 12.18 shows credit default swap (CDS) spreads for two banks – Citibank and JPMorgan Chase.[18] The spreads became positive beyond a minimal amount in August 2007, widened in late 2007 when the banks' subprime losses became public, and widened again at the time of the Bear Stearns crisis in March 2008. By early September 2008, the CDS spreads are about 100 basis points for JPMorgan Chase and 150 for Citibank. Raising long-term senior debt became more expensive for the banks, but they still had available many other inexpensive funding sources such as insured deposits and FHLB borrowing.

Bank balance sheets were in good shape prior to the business cycle peak in December 2007 and as of 2008Q3 in significantly better shape than during

---

[18]   The CDS spread measures the amount of insurance paid to insure the debt of the banks against default.

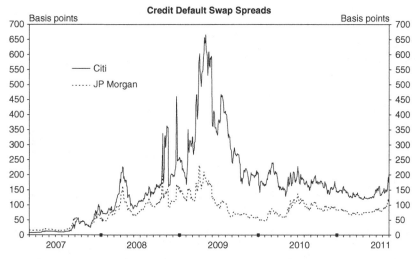

Figure 12.18. Credit default swap spreads.
Note: Credit default swap spreads are the insurance premium paid by a buyer for default protection on senior debt with five-year maturity. Data from Bloomberg. Heavy tick marks indicate December.

the period of stress around the start of the 1990s decade. Figure 12.19 shows for all U.S. commercial banks and for the top one hundred banks by total assets, nonperforming loans as a percentage of total loans. In 2007Q4, both series are still near their decade lows with nonperforming loans at 1.0 percent. Although in 2008Q3, nonperforming loans had risen to 2 percent, they were still well below the level that had prevailed over the earlier period of stress in real estate loans from 1987Q1 through 1992Q4. For this earlier period, nonperforming loans averaged 4.5 percent. Although the earlier period did include a recession, it was moderate. In 2008Q3, for the nation's large banks, loan loss reserves as a percentage of total loans (median values) were 1.5 percent. In contrast, three quarters into the recession beginning 1990Q3 (1991Q2), they were 2.6 percent.[19]

Net loan charge-offs (year-to-date) for all commercial banks did increase from $24.2 billion as of September 30, 2007, to $60.9 billion as of September 30, 2008. However, banks were also raising capital. On June 30, 2007, all commercial banks had $1.05 trillion in equity capital, and on September 30, 2008, they had somewhat more at $1.16 billion.[20] The point is not to deny

---

[19] Data from Federal Financial Institutions Examination Council, Call Reports, for various banks.
[20] Bank capital could be overstated through bank tardiness in loan loss provisioning. However, as of September 30, 2009, banks still reported $1.3 trillion in equity capital. Data

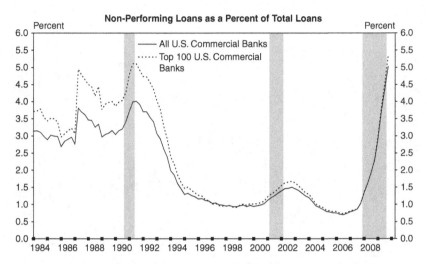

Figure 12.19. Nonperforming loans as a percent of total loans.
Note: Nonperforming loans include 90+ days past due loans and nonaccrual loans. Top 100 U.S. commercial banks based on total asset size. Data are from the Federal Financial Institutions Examination Council (FFIEC) Web site (https://cdr.ffiec.gov/public/ManageFacsimiles.aspx), Call Reports. Shaded areas indicate NBER recessions. Heavy tick marks indicate the fourth quarter.

that banks were under stress after August 2007. However, for the purpose of assessing the degree of stress prior to the initiation and the intensification of the recession, it is important not to confuse the heightened stress following the Lehman bankruptcy on September 15, 2008, with the prior level of stress.

As shown in Figure 12.20, consumer loan interest rates in 2008 either did not increase (auto loans) or declined (variable-rate credit cards). Figure 12.21 shows the two components of consumer credit: revolving (credit card) and nonrevolving. Annualized monthly changes in total consumer credit grew steadily at 4.3 percent from January 2008 through July 2008. The series falls in August, rises somewhat in September, and then falls steadily starting in October 2008.[21]

Figures 12.22, 12.23, 12.24, and 12.25 show survey data from small businesses gathered by the National Federation of Independent Businesses

are from the Federal Deposit Insurance Corporation, Statistics on Depository Institutions Report.
[21] The series "covers most short- and intermediate-term credit extended to individuals." Board of Governors, "Consumer Credit," Statistical Release G.19. The moderate growth of consumer credit in the first eight years of the 2000s does not indicate over-leveraging indicative of a "bubble" in consumer debt.

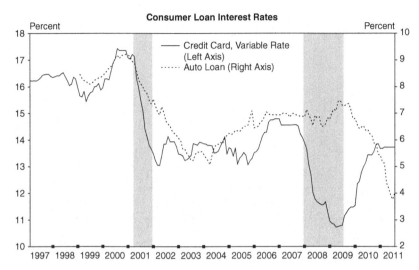

Figure 12.20. Consumer loan interest rates.
Note: Series are from a survey of financial institutions conducted by bankrate.com. Data via Bloomberg. Shaded areas indicate NBER recessions. Heavy tick marks indicate December.

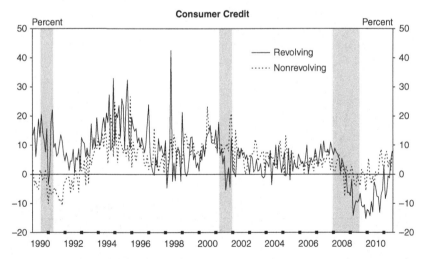

Figure 12.21. Consumer credit.
Note: Annualized monthly growth in consumer credit outstanding. Data are from the Board of Governors G.19 Release via Haver Analytics. Shaded areas indicate NBER recessions. Heavy tick marks indicate December.

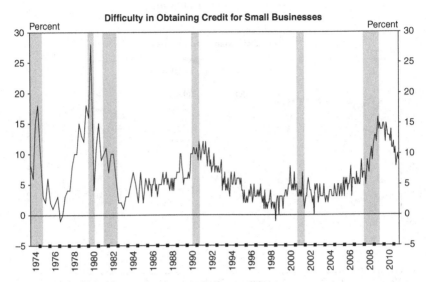

Figure 12.22. Difficulty in obtaining credit for small businesses.
Note: Net percent of small businesses reporting that credit was harder to get compared to the previous three months. Survey conducted by the National Federation of Independent Businesses, Small Business Economic Trends. Data via Haver Analytics. Shaded areas indicate NBER recessions. Heavy tick marks indicate December.

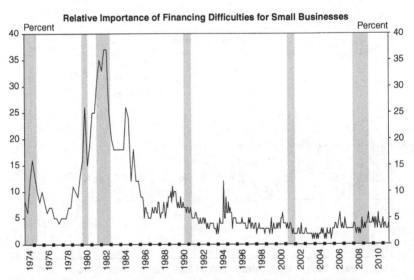

Figure 12.23. Relative importance of financing difficulties for small businesses.
Note: Percent of small businesses reporting "financial and interest rates" in response to the question, "What is the single most important problem facing your business today?" Survey conducted by the National Federation of Independent Businesses, Small Business Economic Trends. Data via Haver Analytics. Shaded areas indicate NBER recessions. Heavy tick marks indicate December.

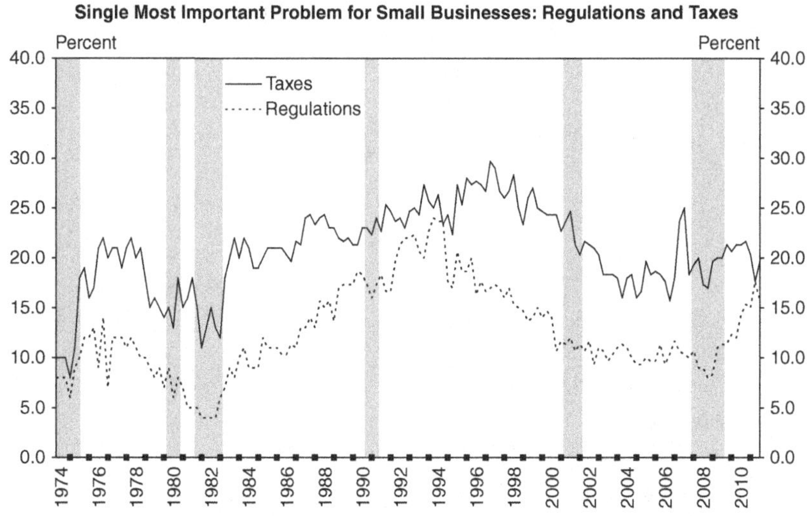

Single Most Important Problem for Small Businesses: Regulations and Taxes

Figure 12.24. Single most important problem for small businesses: regulations and taxes. *Note*: Percent of small businesses reporting either "government regulation" or "taxes" in response to the question, "What is the single most important problem facing your business today." Survey conducted by the National Federation of Independent Businesses, Small Business Economic Trends. Data via Haver Analytics. Shaded areas indicate NBER recessions. Heavy tick marks indicate December

(NFIB). As shown in Figure 12.22, prior to September 2008, as measured by the NFIB diffusion index, the net percent of businesses finding credit harder to obtain increased, but only to an extent comparable to the increase prior to the 1990 recession. The increase prior to the 1980 recession greatly exceeded both of these increases. Figure 12.23 shows the percentage of firms that reported obtaining credit as their primary problem. This series remained well below the levels reached in the early 1980s and peaks at only 6 percent. These measures of activity in credit markets prior to the Lehman bankruptcy on September 15, 2008, appear more consistent with the occurrence of a moderate recession rather than the occurrence of the severe world recession that emerged in summer 2008.

Figure 11.24 is of interest for evaluating statements made during the economic recovery from the 2008–2009 recession that attributed the slow pace of recovery to concern by business over government regulation and tax policies (Fisher 2010). It shows the percentage of firms that reported either taxes or government regulation as their primary problem. These issues were of concern to small business, but as shown in the figure, that concern was not elevated relative to the past.

Single Most Important Problem for Small Businesses: Labor Quality and Sales

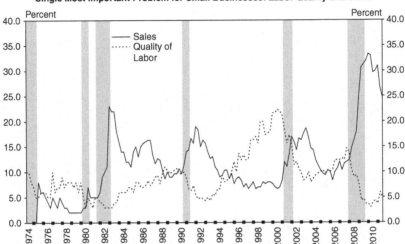

Figure 12.25. Single most important problem for small businesses: labor quality and sales.

Note: Percent of small businesses reporting either "sales" or "labor quality" in response to the question, "What is the single most important problem facing your business today?" Survey conducted by the National Federation of Independent Businesses, Small Business Economic Trends. Data via Haver Analytics. Shaded areas indicate NBER recessions. Heavy tick marks indicate December.

In addition, some policy makers attributed the persistently high unemployment in the recovery to skills mismatch in the labor market (Kocherlakota 2010).[22] According to this hypothesis, to a significant extent, job seekers lacked the skills sought for by employers. Figure 12.25 shows the percentage of firms that reported either quality of labor or sales as their primary problem. Contrary to the skills-mismatch hypothesis, quality of labor did not appear to be a major concern of small businesses. They were much more concerned about sales, that is, the lack of demand.[23] Hobijn

---

[22] The Beveridge curve plots the unemployment rate versus job openings. In 2010, the ratio of job openings to the unemployment rate rose. For a critical overview of the use of this fact as evidence for the skills-mismatch hypothesis, see Valletta and Kuang (2010).

[23] *The Washington Post* (2010b) wrote:

They [senior executives] blame their profound caution on their view that U.S. consumers are destined to disappoint for many years.... [W]hen [Jason] Speer and other executives were pressed on the role that tax and regulatory policies play in hiring, they drew only vague connections. Speer said his decision to hire is driven primarily by demand.... None of the executives interviewed linked a specific new government initiative with a specific decision to refrain from hiring.... [D]ecisions about hiring and expansion ... [David] Speer said are based on expectations for sales over years to come, not just the immediate future.

et al. (2011) noted that recent college graduates are not subject to structural unemployment issues such as skill obsolescence and the disincentive effects of extended unemployment benefits. Nevertheless, they experienced an increase in the rate of unemployment comparable to the general population.

THE FOCUS ON CREDIT MARKETS

The *Financial Times* (2008i) expressed the FOMC focus on credit markets in fall 2008:

Fed officials are not certain how effective further rate cuts would be in boosting growth.... [T]he main cause of high borrowing costs is the widening in risk spreads, not the risk free rate. Rate cuts would not change the fact that banks are capital constrained and raising credit standards.... They fear undermining the recent stability of the dollar and fueling the buying of commodities as an inflation hedge. Any resurgence in commodity prices would threaten an improving inflation situation.

The focus of the FOMC on the presumed dysfunction in credit markets appeared in the FOMC *Minutes* (Board of Governors, December 15–16, 2008, 8–9):

[P]articipants generally agreed that a continued focus on the quantity and the composition of Federal Reserve assets would be necessary and desirable. Specifically, participants discussed the merits of purchasing large quantities of longer-term securities such as agency debt, agency mortgage-backed securities, and Treasury securities. The available evidence indicated that such purchases would reduce yields on those instruments, and lower yields on those securities would tend to reduce borrowing costs for a range of private borrowers.

Several other participants ... noted that increases in excess reserves or the monetary base, by themselves, might not have a significant stimulative effect on the economy or prices because the normal bank intermediation mechanism appeared to be impaired.

In fall 2008, the FOMC focus on disruption to financial markets rather than on contractionary monetary policy as the source of the intensifying recession appeared in the failure of the FOMC to lower the funds rate at the September 16, 2008, FOMC meeting. Richard Fisher (2008, 1), president of the Dallas Fed, commented:

[T]he problem was clearly not the fed funds rate target. A rate cut was not, and is not, the cure for an economy where many banks cannot expand their balance sheets, or must shrink their balance sheets because of capital constraints.... Since the beginning of the year, I have been worried about the efficacy of reducing the fed funds rate given the problems of liquidity and capital constraints afflicting the financial system.... I was and I remain skeptical that lowering the fed funds rate is the most effective antidote for such a pathology, given that, in my book, rates held too low, too long during the previous Fed regime were an accomplice to that reckless behavior.

However, this diagnosis dismissed the possibility that the intensification of the recession that began earlier in the summer originated in contractionary monetary policy. Specifically, the level of real short-term interest rates maintained by the Fed was high relative to the natural rate of interest consistent with full employment. In this event, policy exacerbated the recession in two respects. First, the FOMC was tardy in lowering the funds rate to a near-zero value only at the December 16, 2008, meeting.[24] Second, statements by officials that the financial system and, as a consequence, the world economy were near collapse created pessimism and uncertainty. Those gloomy statements appeared to receive confirmation in October 2008 as news arrived that the rest of the world, not just the United States, had entered a severe recession in the previous summer. Moreover, output (GDP) fell sharply in 2008Q4 in response to the inventory correction that had begun in July 2008. This gloom must have lowered the natural rate of interest further relative to the existing level of short-term real interest rates.

The pessimism that developed in fall 2008 appeared in the following headlines. On September 30, *The Washington Post* (2008g) ran a number of stories under the large headline "House Rejects Financial Rescue, Sending Stocks Plummeting." The story "Opposition Crosses Party Lines; Dow Falls A Record 778 Points" reported, "A bipartisan rebellion in the House killed a $700 billion rescue plan for the nation's financial system.... [W]ith the Dow Jones industrial average down ... 7 percent, Treasury Secretary Henry Paulson Jr. tried to calm frazzled traders." Under the headline "As Contagion Spreads, Moods Abruptly Shift," *The Washington Post* reported "an abrupt end to the confident attitude displayed by European officials as recently as last week, when officials claimed that shareholders and investors there had less to fear than their American counterparts because European

---

[24] Two programs allowed the Fed to expand the size of its asset portfolio while preventing the resulting reserves creation from lowering the funds rate. First, on September 17, 2008, the Treasury announced the Supplementary Financing Program (SFP). The SFP absorbed reserves through the issuance of Treasury bills, the proceeds of which went into a special deposit at the New York Fed. Second, on October 6, 2008, the Board of Governors announced the payment of interest on the reserves that banks hold with the Federal Reserve banks. The board set the rate paid on required reserve balances at the average funds-rate target less 10 basis points. On October 22, 2008, it set the rate paid on excess reserves at the lowest funds-rate target in effect during the reserves maintenance period less 35 basis points.

banks weren't as heavily exposed to the troubled mortgage loans undermining the U.S. system."

Prompted by financial market turmoil, Congress passed the TARP (Troubled-Asset-Relief Program) $700 billion rescue package to buy distressed mortgage assets from banks on October 3, 2008. However, markets continued falling in October. On October 7, 2008, on page one, the headline for the *Financial Times* read, "Markets Routed in Global Sell-Off." On October 8, 2008, a front-page headline in *The Washington Post* read, "Retirement Savings Lose $2 Trillion in 15 Months."

Phillips Swagel (2009, 37), who as a member of the Treasury helped to craft TARP, wrote:

[T]he way in which the TARP was proposed and eventually enacted must have contributed to the lockup in spending.... Having long known that Treasury could not obtain the authorities to act until the Secretary and Chairman could honestly state that the (economic and financial) world seemed to be ending, they went up and said just that, first in a private meeting with Congressional leaders and then several days later in testifying on September 23 and 24. Americans ... could plainly see that the U.S. political system appeared insufficient to the task of a considered response to the crisis. Surely these circumstances contributed to the economic downturn.... A counterfactual to consider is that the Treasury and Fed could have acted incrementally, with backstops and a flood of liquidity on money markets and commercial paper – but not the TARP.

RELATING THE 2008–2009 RECESSION TO PAST RECESSIONS

The 2008–2009 recession possessed the hallmarks of other post–World War II recessions. In the post-Accord era, prior to cycle peaks, the Fed pushed the interest rate up to lower inflation (Hetzel 2008b; Romer and Romer 1989).[25] With the appearance of recession, the Fed lowered rates only reluctantly after the cyclical peak out of a concern that inflationary expectations were high relative to its implicit inflation objective. The experiences with the recessions of 1957, 1970, 1973, 1981, and 1990 all point to the failure of the Fed to manage a negative output gap to lower inflation in a controlled way that avoids recession. The 2008–2009 recession fit this general pattern.

The Fed entered into 2007 with the funds rate at a cyclical high. The occurrence of a shock to housing wealth and energy prices then rendered the real rate higher than was consistent with trend output growth. However, at the same time, the inflation shock pushed headline inflation well above

---

[25] The exceptions were the 1960 recession when the Fed raised rates to counter a balance of trade deficit and gold outflow and the 2001 recession.

the 2 percent inflation considered acceptable by the FOMC. Growth below trend, which emerged by early fall 2007, produced a negative output gap. Although the FOMC lowered the funds rate significantly in fall 2007 and early 2008, it backed off after April 2008. This inertia in funds rate reductions allowed a negative output gap to grow in magnitude to counter high headline inflation. The attempt to exploit a Phillips curve relationship to bend inflation down in a controlled fashion, however, was no more successful than in the past.

A SLOW RECOVERY AND SLOW MONEY GROWTH

A striking characteristic of the recovery from the 2008–2009 recession was its sluggishness. With previous deep recessions, real output recovered strongly following the cyclical trough. Over the five-quarter intervals following the cyclical troughs of 1975Q1 and 1982Q4, real GDP grew at the annualized rates of 5.5 percent and 7.8 percent, respectively. In contrast, the corresponding growth rate for real output over the five-quarter interval following the 2009Q2 trough was only 3.1 percent. The explanation offered here for the sluggish recovery is slow growth of the monetary aggregates in combination with declines in monetary velocity.

As noted in Chapter 8, after 1990, the monetary aggregate M2 became unreliable as an indicator of nominal spending by the public. Nevertheless, during the recovery from the 2008–2009 recession, its slow growth suggested a moderately restrictive monetary policy. After August 2007 when cash investors fled the off-balance-sheet entities created by banks, growth in M2 would have been boosted by the reintermediation through the banking system and disintermediation from the money markets. That reintermediation probably boosted the various components of M2 like small time deposits. Similarly M2 growth spurted starting in mid-September 2008 with the Lehman bankruptcy when businesses drew on their lines of credit at banks as a precautionary measure to build up liquidity. The interest sensitivity of M2 demand would also have augmented M2 growth after the FOMC started lowering the funds rate in September 2007.[26]

The monetary deceleration from early 2009 onward is striking.[27] As shown in Figure 12.26, starting in 2009, M2 grew only very slowly with

---

[26] Measured as the difference between the three-month Treasury bill rate and a weighted average of the own rates of return paid on the components of M2, the opportunity cost of holding M2 fell by almost three percentage points between early 2007 and early 2009. Data are from Federal Reserve Bank of St. Louis FRED database.

[27] The Fed could have controlled growth in M2 with the appropriate quantitative-easing strategy. Starting in mid-December 2008 when the FOMC lowered its funds-rate target

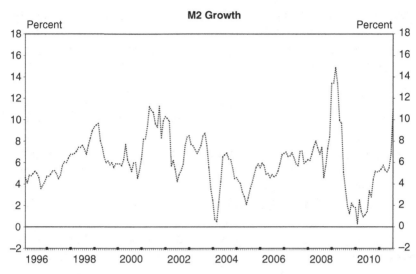

Figure 12.26. M2 growth.

Note: Monthly observations of six-month annualized growth rate of M2. Data from Federal Reserve Board via Haver Analytics.

six-month annualized growth rates less than 2 percent from mid-2009 through mid-2010.[28] Both the fall in market interest rates and the desire of corporations and households to increase liquid assets in an uncertain economic environment would have boosted real M2 demand. The low growth rate of M2 in combination with strong demand to hold purchasing power in the form of the liquid assets in M2 necessitated disinflation.

As measured by year-over-year percent changes in the core CPI (the CPI excluding food and energy), inflation fell from 2.5 percent in mid-2008 to less than 1 percent in fall 2010. In contrast to this disinflation, the expectation of inflation remained anchored. As measured by a variety of sources,

to near zero along with payment of interest on bank reserves, the textbook reserves-money-multiplier framework became relevant for the determination of the money stock. The reason is that the Fed's instrument then became its asset portfolio, the left side of its balance sheet, which determined the monetary base, the right side of its balance sheet. As a result, from December 2008 onward, the nominal (dollar) money stock was determined independently of the demand for real money. Although the reserves-money multiplier increased because of the increased demand by banks for excess reserves, the Fed retained control of M2 growth. Even if banks hold onto increases in excess reserves, the money stock increases one-for-one with open-market purchases.

[28] Growth in M1 was higher. Presumably, households took funds out of small time deposits and money-market fund shares, which are included in M2 but not M1, and redeposited them in the demand deposits and savings deposits included in the definitions of both M1 and M2, thereby boosting M1 growth while leaving M2 growth unaffected.

the expectation of inflation remained at 2 percent or higher.[29] Money growth consistent with an inflation rate of less than 2 percent limited real growth and the robustness of the recovery from the 2008–2009 recession.

A BANK PANIC OR A GARDEN-VARIETY RECESSION?

The 2008–2009 recession blindsided the economics profession. Given the accompanying switch back from financial intermediation through securitization to financial intermediation through the banking system and given the flight of the cash investors from financial institutions using leverage to increase returns by taking on interest rate and credit risk, it was natural to explain the recession as arising from a bank panic that propagated through the disruption to financial intermediation. However, on closer examination, the recession fits the historical pattern of past recessions. Going into the recession, interest rates were at unsustainably high levels. Contractionary monetary policy resulted from inertia imparted to reductions in the funds rate subsequent to the cyclical peak.

[29] These sources include the differences between the nominal and TIPS (inflation-adjusted) yields, the Survey of Professional Forecasters conducted by the Philadelphia Fed, and the Thomson Reuters/Michigan consumer survey.

THIRTEEN

What Caused the Great Leverage Collapse?

Two waves of deleveraging in financial markets occurred with one beginning in August 2007 and one in mid-September 2008. In each episode, in a discrete way, the unwillingness of cash investors to hold certain classes of short-term debt instruments increased. In the first episode, cash investors became unwilling to hold the asset-backed commercial paper (ABCP) used to finance the off-balance-sheet entities that commercial banks had set up to hold assets, especially mortgages. In the second episode, cash investors became unwilling to hold the shares of prime money-market funds that held the financial paper issued by banks and became unwilling to enter into the RP (repurchase) transactions that investment banks used to finance their inventories of securities.

The first wave of deleveraging caused banks to take onto their balance sheets mortgages with uncertain market value and, as a result, rendered problematic the solvency of one or more large banks. The second wave coincided with a shock that rendered uncertain the extent of the financial safety net protecting bank debt holders and, as a result, increased the uncertainty surrounding funding of banks. These funding problems and the uncertainty banks faced in predicting reserve outflows rendered them less able to provide a liquid market for debt instruments in general. There was then a general unwinding of funding through repurchase agreements as investors became uncertain of the liquidity of the pledged collateral. The most dramatic result was the sudden demise of the investment bank model that relied on very high leverage ratios achieved through RPs to finance inventories.

To what extent did the stress in financial markets caused by the two waves of deleveraging impact adversely the real economy? Essential to an answer is the behavior of cash investors.

THE CENTRAL ROLE OF THE CASH INVESTORS

Cash investors place their surplus funds for short periods of time in debt instruments that offer complete certainty of return. These investors include foreign governments and official institutions, pension funds, municipal governments, nonprofits, various entities with fiduciary responsibility, corporations, small businesses, and risk-averse individuals including those who hold shares in money-market mutual funds. Complete certainty of return requires both the absence of default risk and the characteristic of bank deposits of redemption at par. Various debt instruments in addition to Treasury bills have emerged to meet the needs of liquidity investors. Large negotiable CDs, commercial paper, and money-market mutual fund shares all grew significantly in the 1970s. The RP market grew in the 1980s (Cook and LaRoche 1993).

Gorton (2009, 36) used the term "informationally-insensitive" debt to describe the debt held by cash investors. He defined a panic as "an event where informationally-insensitive debt becomes informationally-sensitive." Central to the issue of whether the two waves of flight by cash investors played a role in depressing real economic activity is how these liquidity investors reacted to the adverse shocks concerning the safety of the instruments in which they invested. Did they abandon credit markets indiscriminately or selectively based on the adverse shocks? In the former case, these investors were an independent source of instability, and the markets in which they place their money should be protected by the financial safety net. In the latter case, these investors are capable of monitoring the risk taking of financial institutions and such monitoring should be encouraged by not extending the financial safety net to the markets in which they place their money.

The run in the commercial-paper market precipitated by the unexpected bankruptcy of Penn Central Railroad announced June 21, 1970, was a forerunner of the August 2007 and September 2008 runs. With SIVs taking the place of AAA corporations, this earlier episode illustrated the fundamentals of the 2007 and 2008 cash-investor runs. In the 1960s, companies with AAA ratings on their debt and with lines of credit to banks issued three-month to six-month commercial paper. They could bypass the banks because their debt did not require the monitoring that banks provide on the financial health of borrowers. By using the money market to raise funds, these companies lowered their funding costs.

Sherman Maisel (1973, 7), who was a member of the Board of Governors, wrote:

Borrowers [in the commercial-paper market] generally hold commitments from their bank for funds to pay off loans coming due if the lender decides not to renew, or roll over, the loan through commercial paper. The firms issuing commercial paper (the borrowers) have prime financial ratings.... Thousands of firms, individuals, trusts, foundations, and other lenders had purchased commercial paper on the assumption that it was a completely secure repository.... The Penn Central failure threatened the entire structure because it cast doubt on the basic assumption that the commercial paper of large, well-known companies was good security.

In response to the Penn Central bankruptcy, the Board of Governors and other regulators removed the Reg Q interest-rate ceiling on commercial bank certificates of deposit (CDs) in excess of $100,000. As the volume of commercial paper fell, corporations drew on their lines of credit with banks, and banks funded the loans with the issuance of large CDs.

THE DELEVERAGING SHOCK OF AUGUST 2007

Starting in the early 2000s, by creating AAA-rated debt out of lower-rated debt, structured financial products like CLOs (collateralized loan obligations), CDOs (collateralized debt obligations), and MBSs (mortgage-backed securities) allowed banks to tap into the supply of funds from cash investors to fund assets not previously funded by this class of investors. However, by summer 2007, rising default rates on subprime mortgages threatened to impact not only the bottom tranches but also the top AAA tranches of these structured-finance products. When in August 2007 cash investors came to believe that the top tranches of these MBS products were not AAA but instead were subject to default and would be illiquid in the event of a distressed sale, they ceased buying the commercial paper used to fund the structured investment vehicles or off-balance-sheet trusts holding them. Banks then took the MBSs onto their own balance sheets. From end-July 2007 through year-end 2007, asset-backed commercial paper, which funded bank SIVs, fell about $450 billion from a peak of $1.2 trillion, while bank credit increased about $500 billion.[1]

The shock to financial markets that produced the flight of cash investors from funding bank SIVs in August 2007 was the replacement of the housing boom with the housing bust. As shown in Figure 10.2, house prices began to fall in 2007. The resulting decline in housing equity created a problem for refinancing, which raised the delinquencies for subprime mortgages, especially those issued from late 2005 through 2006. With house prices

---

[1] See Federal Reserve Bank of St. Louis *U.S. Financial Data*, tables "Bank Loans" and "Commercial Paper Outstanding" (http://research.stlouisfed.org/publications/usfd/).

falling, borrowers who had financed practically the entire cost of a house by borrowing either found they could not refinance or became unwilling to refinance. With default rates rising on home mortgages, confidence disappeared in the AAA ratings given by the rating agencies to the senior tranches of the structured securities (MBS) held in bank SIVs.

The announcement on August 9, 2007, by the French bank BNP Paribas that it would not redeem shares from its money-market funds because it could no longer reliably value their holdings of U.S. subprime MBS precip-itated the sudden cessation by the commercial-paper market of funding for the SIVs holding structured securities.[2] Unlike the debt instruments securitized in the past, such as conforming mortgages and credit card receivables, it became apparent that these securities were hard to value, especially because the extent of the decline in house prices was impossi-ble to predict. Also, in the jargon of Wall Street, the "correlation" (diver-sification) assumptions used by the rating agencies to evaluate structured finance products became suspect. That is, defaults among assets like mort-gages from different parts of the country were more highly correlated than assumed.

As the commercial paper that financed SIVs failed to roll over, rather than having the SIVs draw down their lines of credit, banks took the mort-gages onto their own books. A similar retreat by cash investors occurred with the financing of the CDOs used by banks to fund leveraged buyouts. As banks took mortgages and leveraged loans onto their own balance sheets and dealt with difficult-to-predict continued balance sheet expansion, they became concerned about their ability for balance sheet expansion. Balance sheet stress then limited the willingness of banks to provide a liquid market for complicated securities.

FUNDING DIFFICULTIES OF EUROPEAN BANKS

The popular media blamed the financial crisis on the Wall Street investment banks that securitized the subprime mortgages. However, they responded to a demand for these products, and that demand came from banks desiring to profit from the spread between the returns on long-term, illiquid invest-ments and the cost of short-term funds. European banks were central to

---

[2] For a discussion of this episode, see Bernanke (2007b) and Covitz, Liang, and Suarez (2009). For a recounting of events, see Federal Reserve Bank of St. Louis, "The Financial Crisis: A Timeline of Events and Policy Actions" (http://timeline.stlouisfed.org/pdf/CrisisTimeline.pdf).

this demand.[3] In his testimony, Greenspan (2008) noted "the surge in global demand for U.S. subprime securities by banks":

Demand became so aggressive that too many securitizers and lenders believed they were able to create and sell mortgage backed securities so quickly that they would never put shareholders' capital at risk. ... Pressures on lenders to supply more "paper" collapsed subprime underwriting standards from 2005 forward.

In a bailout of UBS, the Swiss National Bank funded a "bad bank" intended "to hold up to $60 billion in mainly US mortgage assets" (*Financial Times* 2008k). The *Financial Times* (2009g) quoted "market insiders:"

If there was one group of investors who over-relied on rating and did relatively minimal credit work, it was SIVs and conduits, especially in Europe. Their investing strategy was a funding arbitrage [borrowing at low short-term rates and investing at higher ones].

The bank newsletter *The Institutional Risk Analyst* (2009) interviewed Hans-Joachim Dübel, CEO of Finpolconsult, about the use by German banks of SIVs to hold packages of MBSs with subprime securities:

[I]n early 2001, the EU decided to terminate the use of state guarantees [for the bank debt issued by the German Landesbanken] by 2002. However, the public bank lobby in Germany continued to fight the proposal. ... The result was a postponement of the end of issuance of state guaranteed debt for all banks from 2001 to 2005. ... [T]he German state banks started to issue massive amounts of state-guaranteed debt after 2001 ... especially during 2004 and early 2005. ... [Backed by these debt guarantees] they kept guaranteeing ABCP-conduits and other off-balance sheet vehicles such as SIVs that boomed precisely during the critical period. ... Those guarantees were called upon when the banks and investors funding ABCP and SIV called in their capital during 2007. ... They ["politicians"] knew that the typical loan portfolio for a Landesbank was only 20–25% of total assets, so the rest of the structure was typically securities.

The flight of cash investors from financing the off-balance-sheet entities of banks that began in August 2007 created a funding gap for the European banks that had borrowed dollars short-term in the commercial-paper market to fund their SIVs. Bernanke (2007b) emphasized the funding difficulties of European banks. McGuire and Peter (2009, 53) used "counterparty

---

[3] For example, *The New York Times* (2007) reported, "SachsenLB racked up more than 17 billion euros – nearly one-third of its total assets – in exposure to off-balance-sheet 'conduits' that had invested in subprime mortgages and other assets." *The New York Times* (2009e) wrote, "A document leaked recently from Bafin, the country's financial regulator, stated that German banks had 800 billion euros in bad debts on their books." Hau and Thum (2009) related the bad debt of the German state-owned banks to the political composition of their boards.

information to construct a measure of European banks' US dollar funding gap, or the amount of US dollars invested in longer-term assets which is not supported by longer-term US dollar liabilities." The uncertainty in their estimates comes from lack of public information about the maturity of borrowings by the banks from nonbanks. McGuire and Peter (2009, 54) reported:

If we assume that European banks' estimated liabilities to money market funds ... are also short-term liabilities, then the estimate [of "the major European banks' US dollar funding gap"] would be $2.1–2.3 trillion. Were all liabilities to non-banks treated as short-term funding, the upper-bound estimate of their US dollar funding gap would be roughly $6.5 trillion.

In response to the increased demand for dollars in August 2007 and September 2008, the Fed could have undertaken massive amounts of open-market purchases and allowed the marketplace to allocate the dollars to the banks in need through competitive bidding in the Fed funds market. In contrast, to forestall bank runs, the Fed channeled the dollars directly to banks with funding difficulties in ways designed to hide the identity of the banks.[4] The Term Auction Facility (TAF), established in December 2007, allowed foreign banks with offices in the United States as well as domestic banks to bid for funds, initially, for twenty-eight days. At its peak in March 2009, it lent about $500 billion. Swap lines with foreign central banks, which amounted to $620 billion by end-September 2008, allowed foreign central banks like the ECB to auction off U.S. dollars to their banks. The Fed's Commercial Paper Funding Facility (CPFF), which at its peak in December 2008 held $350 billion in commercial paper, purchased paper from foreign banks.[5] In contrast, the discount window (primary credit facility) lent only about $125 billion at its peak in October 2008.

---

[4] In its brief to stay a court order to release the names of the banks to whom the regional Reserve banks lent money, the Board of Governors (2009) wrote:

The Board has argued, and submitted declarations demonstrating, that public disclosure is likely to cause substantial competitive injury to these financial institutions including the loss of public confidence in the institution, runs on banks, and possible failure of some institutions. The Board's declarations also provided evidence that disclosure would impair the Board's ability to perform important statutory functions in a time of economic upheaval, including authorizing lending by the Reserve Banks to alleviate liquidity strains, achieving the desired level of short-term interest rates, maximum employment, and stable prices through monetary policy, and enabling Reserve Banks to provide liquidity to depository institutions and the banking system at the DW [discount window].

[5] The *Wall Street Journal* (2009d) reported, "The vast majority of commercial paper being purchased [from the CPFF] was issued by non-U.S. banks." Foreign governments with their vast holdings of dollar reserves could have bailed out their own banks. According to

The flight of cash investors from financing the off-balance-sheet entities of banks also revealed the weakness in the European system of bank supervision and resolution. Two factors caused the interbank loan market for European banks to become impaired. First, banks did not know which banks were solvent and which were insolvent. The "Landesbanken have continued to record the value of their credit assets at book, not market prices, even as banks in countries such as the US have marked these down" (Tett 2009). Heider, Hoerova, and Holthausen (2009, 6) wrote of European banks:

At that time [August 2007], subprime-mortgage backed securities were discovered in portfolios of banks and bank-sponsored conduits (SIVs) leading to a reassessment of risk. The extent of exposures was unknown and counterparties could not distinguish safe from risky banks.

Second, there was uncertainty within the EU over whether creditors of a branch bank located in one country with a parent in another country would be bailed out. Governments in the troubled banks' home countries did not want to bail out the depositors of another country. Most EU countries did not even possess laws allowing them to take over failing banks.[6] Giani (2009, 24) wrote:

In most countries the national insolvency law allows intra-group transactions to be retroactively ruled void if they were carried out during a "suspect period" preceding the insolvency.... The existence of limitations on cross-border transfers of assets and liquidity ... is ultimately based on a lack of international consensus regarding how the burdens should be shared in a crisis or insolvency resolution.

As a result of these uncertainties, European banks became unwilling to lend to one another. The spread of one-month Libor over OIS (OIS is a measure of term Fed funds) fluctuated around 50 basis points from August 2007 until mid-September 2008 when it rose sharply to 350 basis points. Like the Japanese banks in the early 2000s (Hetzel 2004b), banks (European and American) wanted to hold large amounts of excess reserves rather than having to borrow in the interbank market to offset reserve outflows and risk signaling funding difficulties. The ECB and the Fed accommodated the

the IMF table "Currency Composition of Official Foreign Exchange Reserves," at the end of 2008Q1, advanced economies held $1,438.2 billion in U.S. dollar reserves. Presumably, the use of the Fed's balance sheet to fund European banks' dollar needs allowed European governments to conserve their dollar holdings to deal with a possible depreciation of the euro or the pound.

6 For example, the conglomerate Fortis Holding operated in Belgium and Holland, but Belgium did not have authority to take over banks. When Fortis nearly collapsed, the Belgian shareholders blocked the sale of the bank to BNP Paribas as a way of bargaining over their compensation.

increased demand for reserves. The elevated level of Libor and the lack of trades in the interbank market reflected banks' reluctance to lend to one another. By itself, however, contrary to commentary in the financial press, these facts possessed no implications for the ability of banks to continue intermediating credit between savers and investors.

FROM BEAR STEARNS TO LEHMAN BROTHERS

On Sunday March 16, 2008, the Fed took two actions that significantly extended the financial safety net. First, under the 13(3) provision of the Federal Reserve Act allowing for lending to "any individual, partnership, or corporation" in "unusual and exigent circumstances," the Board of Governors approved a New York Fed lending facility of $30 billion for the investment bank Bear Stearns. The loans were "non-recourse" in that in the event of losses on the collateral the New York Fed would not have the ability to seek compensation from JPMorgan Chase, which acquired Bear Stearns that weekend.[7] Second, the board authorized the New York Fed to lend to primary dealers in government securities (the Primary Dealer Credit Facility or PDCF).

The Fed's extension of the financial safety net to facilitate the acquisition of the investment bank Bear Stearns by the commercial bank JPMorgan Chase reinforced the market's expectation that regulators would never allow a firm active in financial markets to fail with losses to debt holders.[8] Phillip Swagel (Swagel 2009, 26), Assistant Secretary for Economic Policy in the Bush Treasury from December 2006 to January 2009, wrote:

> The Fed's announcement of the Primary Dealer Credit Facility (PDCF) immediately after the collapse of Bear Stearns seemed to us and many Wall Street economists to remove the tail risk of another large financial institution suffering a sudden and catastrophic collapse.

The New York Fed lent to Bear Stearns under the authority of 13(3) of the Federal Reserve Act, which, subject to the approval of five members of the Board of Governors, authorizes a regional reserve bank, in this case, the New York Fed,

> to discount for any individual, partnership, or corporation, notes, drafts, and bills of exchange when such notes, drafts, and bills of exchange are indorsed or otherwise secured to the satisfaction of the Federal Reserve bank.

---

[7] JPMorgan Chase was liable for initial losses of $1.15 billion.

[8] "'For years, the investment banks have always assumed that in a systemic meltdown they would have access to the discount window. That has been demonstrated,' said Steve Crawford, former Morgan Stanley chief financial officer" (*Financial Times* 2008a, 2).

The language of 13(3) limits lending to liquidity rather than solvency problems. The fact that the loans have to be "secured" means that the collateral is sufficient to prevent losses in the event of a default. The reserve bank is then "perfecting" collateral that will become unavailable to other creditors. As a result, such a loan does not aid an insolvent institution unable to borrow from the markets. The institution gets a loan but loses marketable assets. By crossing this line to make possible the acquisition of Bear Stearns by JPMorgan Chase through taking risky assets off the books of Bear Stearns and putting them onto its own balance sheet with the SIV Maiden Lane LLC, the New York Fed sent the message that it would not allow any significant nonbank financial institution to fail.

Paul Volcker (2008) commented, "The Federal Reserve judged it necessary to take actions that extended it to the very edge of its lawful and implied power, transcending certain long embedded central banking principles and practices." Earlier, in explaining the refusal to lend to New York City, Arthur Burns (1975, 10) had stated, "The lending authority under paragraph 3 of Section 13 of the Federal Reserve Act [requires] that the borrower is basically creditworthy and possesses adequate collateral, and that the borrower's need is solely for short-term accommodation."

Bloomberg columnist Craig Torres (Torres et al. 2010) quoted two former Fed economists:

"The Fed absorbed that risk on its balance sheet and is now seen to be holding problematic, legacy assets," said Vincent Reinhart, a resident scholar at the American Enterprise Institute in Washington who was the central bank's monetary-affairs director from 2001 to 2007. "There is both an impairment to its balance sheet and its reputation." The Bear Stearns deal marked a turning point in the financial crisis for the Fed. By putting taxpayers at risk in financing the rescue, the central bank was engaging in fiscal policy, normally the domain of Congress and the U.S. Treasury, said Marvin Goodfriend, a former Richmond Fed policy adviser who is now an economist at Carnegie Mellon University in Pittsburgh. "Lack of clarity on the boundary between responsibilities of the Fed and of the Congress as much as anything created the panic in the fall of 2008," Goodfriend said.

What would have happened had the Fed allowed Bear Stearns to go into bankruptcy in March 2008? Other investment banks outside the Fed's too-big-to-fail (TBTF) safety net with significant real estate exposure included Lehman Brothers and Merrill Lynch. It is possible that at this time they could have recapitalized with the aid of outside investors. Later in September 2008, Bank of America bought Merrill Lynch. A headline in *The Wall Street Journal* (2008b) read: "Lehman Is Seeking Overseas Capital, As Its Stock Declines, Wall Street Firm Expands Search for Cash, May Tap Korea." Freeman (2009) reported, "In the months before the fall, Lehman rejected offers from Korea Development Bank to buy the entire firm and from China's Citic to buy half of it."

However, given the consensus that the Fed would not let Lehman fail, the chairman of Lehman, Richard Fuld, could bargain for a good price, perhaps with the kind of aid the Fed had provided to JPMorgan Chase in its takeover of Bear. For example, reporters from *The Washington Post* (2008b) wrote in July 2008, "We're not predicting that Lehman will fail – it won't, because of the Federal Reserve, which has let it be known that it will lend Lehman ... enough money to avoid collapsing, the way Bear Stearns did." *The Wall Street Journal* (2008o) wrote:

In the summer of 2008, Mr. Fuld remained confident, particularly given the security of the Fed's discount window. "We have access to Fed funds," Mr. Fuld told executives at the time. "We can't fail now."

In mid-September 2008, investors refused to fund Lehman Brothers and other Wall Street banks refused to save it. John Thain (*Financial Times* 2009e), then head of Merrill Lynch, commented on the balance sheet problems caused by the real estate lending of Lehman, "[T]he group looking at Lehman's balance sheet ... came back with the view that the size of the potential hole in their balance sheet was $20bn – a huge number." Various accounts agree that Treasury Secretary Henry Paulson decided to draw the line with Lehman and stop funding bailouts. Politically, his position had become untenable. As Harvard Professor Kenneth Rogoff (2008, 28) put it, "Society cannot let itself get blackmailed by the financial system." *The Wall Street Journal* (2008e) put Paulson's unwillingness to repeat a rescue like Bear Stearns in the form of a question, "Which other firms would take that [a Lehman rescue] as a cue to ask for U.S.-government help – and from which other industries? Detroit automakers were already knocking at the door."

Critics of Paulson argued that he should have bailed out Lehman. However, Lehman was only one insolvent financial institution. Before the market turmoil following Lehman, bailing them all out was not politically viable. In his book, *In Fed We Trust*, David Wessel, the economics editor of *The Wall Street Journal*, quoted Mr. Paulson as saying in a conference call, "I'm being called Mr. Bailout. I can't do it again" (*The New York Times* 2009g). In a meeting with Wall Street executives (*The Washington Post* 2008c):

Paulson, a former Goldman Sachs chairman, made an impassioned case: There would be no government money available for a Lehman Brothers buyout, he said. He had opened public coffers twice [for Bear and the GSEs] and was not prepared to do so again.... Several [executives] asked Paulson and Geithner [New York Fed president] whether there would be a broader government effort to address unfolding problems at Merrill Lynch, Washington Mutual and American International Group.... Paulson and Geithner stressed there would be no government money to help any firm that ran into trouble next.

THE FLIGHT OF THE CASH INVESTORS AFTER THE LEHMAN BANKRUPTCY

After Lehman Brothers filed for bankruptcy on September 15, 2008, cash investors became uncertain about the extent to which regulators had retracted the financial safety net, which had heretofore protected all creditors of important financial institutions. The hostile public reaction to the bailout of Fannie Mae and Freddie Mac earlier in September 2008 heightened the uncertainty over the newly defined coverage of the financial safety net.

The *Financial Times* (2008j) wrote:

"The impact of the investor pullback is borne most heavily by banks that are predominantly reliant on wholesale funding, a group that includes many European banks," says Alex Roever, analyst at JPMorgan.... "Prior to Lehman, there was an almost unshakable faith that the senior creditors and counterparties of large, systemically important financial institutions would not face the risk of outright default," notes Neil McLeish, analyst at Morgan Stanley. "This confidence was built up ever since the failure of Continental Illinois (at the time the seventh largest US bank) in 1984, a failure in which bondholders were [fully paid out]."

As a result, cash investors fled to the safety of government money funds and to a few large, too-big-to-fail banks. They fled from prime money-market funds that held the financial paper of large banks and from the RP market that financed the inventories of investment banks. Given the heightened demand for liquidity, financing in the commercial-paper market went from three or six months to overnight.

The *Financial Times* (2008g) provided a succinct summary of the shock wave in financial markets created by the unexpected retraction to uncertain boundaries of the financial safety net:

Even though the credit crisis has dragged on for more than a year, no senior bondholder in a large financial institution had lost money until Lehman Brothers collapsed into bankruptcy last month. The Wall Street bank's failure shocked debt investors who, until then, had mistakenly assumed that any large financial institution seen as an integral part of the financial system would not be allowed to fail.

Recognition of this risk was reinforced late last week when Washington Mutual, the embattled US mortgage lender, was seized by the authorities and its assets transferred to JPMorgan Chase. Though WaMu's depositors were protected, its senior bondholders faced the possibility that they would suffer losses on their investments.

"All the people who had assumed that senior debt obligations with banks were money good thought: 'Gosh, I can get caught up in the capital structure here,'" said a senior executive at a large European bank.

These two collapses triggered a rapid and widespread reassessment of the risk of lending money to financial institutions on both sides of the Atlantic. Banks that were considered by the market to be weak – or not sufficiently large to be rescued – quickly found their access to wholesale funding drying up. The result was that a series of large and medium-sized institutions found they were in effect cut off from the financial markets.... Wachovia, in the United States, Fortis and Dexia in Belgium, Germany's Hypo Real Estate and Bradford & Bingley in the UK were forced to go in search of a rescue from their national governments.

The treasuries and central banks of the United States and Europe spent the next year trying to undo the rearrangement of wholesale funding produced by the market's reassessment of the riskiness of different financial institutions caused by the suddenly ill-defined reach of the financial safety net. What was clear was that a financial system with a line that separated protected from unprotected institutions was untenable. Faced with a large financial shock, cash investors would jump to the protected side. In part through an effort to put out fires and in part through international competition to protect the funding base of national banks, after the failure of Washington Mutual, regulators extended the financial safety net to every financial institution. However, given the hostile populist reaction to large bank bailouts and given the initial uncertainty over the "stress testing" of large banks proposed in February 2009, financial institutions continued to operate in a highly volatile funding environment throughout the first half of 2009.

As a consequence of writing off $785 million in losses on Lehman Brothers debt, on Tuesday September 16, 2008, the money-market mutual fund Primary Reserve "broke the buck." That is, investors were unable to get back their entire principal. Institutional investors then withdrew funds from other prime institutional funds. Because these funds hold the commercial paper issued by banks, investors feared that other funds like Primary Reserve would be caught with debt from troubled financial institutions no longer covered by the financial safety net. On Tuesday, Wednesday, and Thursday of the week of September 14, 2008, investors withdrew $34.2 billion, $126.1 billion, and $85.5 billion from prime institutional funds. In the following week, outflows amounted to $66 billion.[9]

The disruption to the RP market appeared in the tri-party-repo market, in which institutional (cash) investors with short-term funds to invest

---

[9]   The numbers are from Money Fund Analyzer ™, a service of iMoneyNet.

arrange RP transactions using the brokerage services of one of two large New York City banks, the Bank of New York Mellon or JPMorgan Chase. These tri-party-repo banks hold the collateral of the investment banks used in the RPs and match the institutional investors with the investment banks wanting to finance their inventory of securities. During the day, the cash investors transfer funds from their accounts to the accounts of the investment banks in return for the collateral of an RP. The next morning, for one-day RPs, the transaction is unwound and the funds return to the account of the cash investors. After the Lehman failure, the cash investors simply left their funds in their accounts rather than engaging in an RP transaction.[10]

The demand deposits of banks rose sharply not only after the Lehman failure but also in late October after PNC Financial Service Group of Pittsburgh purchased National City Corporation of Cleveland. With the latter acquisition, it appeared that the Treasury would use the Troubled Asset Relief Program (TARP) to force the merger of weak banks with stronger banks. Regulators also imposed losses on the debt holders of Washington Mutual when they merged it with JPMorgan Chase on September 25, 2008. These actions added to the uncertainties over the reach of the financial safety net.

The turmoil caused by the Lehman bankruptcy made the remaining investment banks unviable. Because the prime brokerage operations of commercial banks were effectively included in the financial safety net whereas those of the investment banks were not, customers of the remaining investment banks shifted their accounts to commercial banks; the remaining investment banks then appeared uncompetitive.[11] Also, the hedge fund customers of Lehman's prime brokerage business in London had not realized that in bankruptcy, unlike in the United States, assets held in custodial account would be subject to a court stay. After the Lehman bankruptcy, hedge funds precipitately withdrew their assets from the prime brokerage operations of the London branches of investment banks like Goldman Sachs.

---

[10] This flight from the RP market appeared in the end-of-quarter balance sheet figures for the Bank of New York Mellon. Its end-2008Q2 assets were $130.1 billion, and its end-2008Q3 assets were $218.7 billion. Its end-2008Q2 demand deposits were $4.9 billion, and its end-2008Q3 demand deposits were $38.4 billion. Its end-2008Q2 reserves were $.13 billion, and its end-2008Q3 reserves were $38.0 billion. These numbers include also the impact of corporations drawing on their lines of credit and other forms of intermediation going through the banking system rather than through the money and capital markets like commercial-paper issuance. The figures are from the Federal Financial Institutions Examination Council (FFIEC) Web site (https://cdr.ffiec.gov/public/ManageFacsimiles.aspx), Call Reports.

[11] Prime brokers provide custodial accounts for the assets of hedge funds and assist them in making transactions like selling securities short.

The large investment banks had financed their inventories of securities with repurchase agreements (RPs). The flight by cash investors from financing securities with any risk of default and illiquidity appeared in the haircuts they required on RPs.[12] For example, the range of haircuts for RPs using asset-backed securities (ABS) went from around 5 percent in early 2007 to between 15 percent and 30 percent in October 2008. The range of haircuts for non-agency mortgage-backed securities (MBS) went from around 5 percent in early 2007 to between 30 percent and 50 percent in October 2008 (Credit Suisse 2009). Unable to finance their inventories cheaply, the remaining large investment banks were no longer viable.

The flight of the cash investors began an incipient rearrangement of intermediation through institutions judged less risky by the markets either because of their more conservative risk management or because of their undisputed TBTF status. In fall 2008, regulators and governments undertook massive efforts to preserve the funding status quo among financial institutions. How well did those efforts succeed? Did banks ration credit to borrowers with viable investment opportunities and, thereby, transmit a financial shock to the real economy?

The association of large declines in GDP with the financial turmoil created a public perception that banks were cutting off credit to credit-worthy investors, especially small business, and that the resulting tight credit exacerbated economic decline. However, the forces that created the declines in GDP emerged prior to the Lehman bankruptcy (Chapter 12). The issue of quantifying the extent to which a tightening of credit standards aggravated the decline in output after the Lehman bankruptcy founders on the problem of simultaneity (disentangling of causation from correlation). In recession, credit risk increases. For example, as of spring 2009, "credit card delinquency among small business [was] more than 12 percent" (*The New York Times* 2009c). Did banks limit credit to small businesses because they had become riskier *given* the recession or did banks limit credit to small business and thereby *exacerbate* the recession?

Although any progress on this issue will require detailed investigation such as Jimenez et al. (2010), one can characterize some aspects of how financial markets functioned after the Lehman bankruptcy. Although cash investors ceased funding illiquid assets with uncertain market value, there was no panicked general flight of investors from financial markets. Deposits in retail money funds rose slightly following the Lehman failure.

---

[12] A haircut is the discount from par value on a security purchased in an RP transaction. A large discount means that only a fraction of the face value of the security is lent.

The segment of the commercial-paper market that suffered was financial paper. The stock of asset-backed commercial paper held up, and nonfinancial companies continued to issue commercial paper. The declines in these categories began in spring 2009.[13]

Faced with increased uncertainty over withdrawals, money funds demanded short-term paper. As a result, one-to-four day issuance of commercial paper replaced longer-term issuance.[14] Rates on thirty-day nonfinancial commercial paper rated AA barely rose after the Lehman failure. The riskier A2/P2 paper rose about three percentage points. The increased demand for liquidity and increases in risk premia, however, do not provide evidence for market failure.

Rather than having a broker place their funds in RPs, cash investors left their funds in insured deposits or in large TBTF banks. Small time deposits at banks also began to increase sharply after the Lehman failure. At the same time, corporations drew on their lines of credit at banks as a precautionary measure to build liquidity given the deterioration in the economic outlook.

Whether having a resolution authority capable of placing financial institutions apart from commercial banks into conservatorship would have made a difference in fall 2008 is problematic. If regulators had placed Lehman into a bank-type conservatorship and imposed losses on its debt holders, they would have created the same shock to the wholesale funding of troubled financial institutions. The failure of Lehman created problems not because of its "interconnectedness," but rather because of the sudden increase in uncertainty over where regulators would draw the line between protected and unprotected institutions.[15] Suddenly, it appeared that troubled banks previously protected by the financial safety net might be exposed to market

---

[13] See the graphs in the weekly publication of the Federal Reserve Bank of St. Louis, "U.S. Financial Data" (http://research.stlouisfed.org/publications/usfd/).

[14] These numbers come from the Board of Governors statistical release "Commercial Paper Rates and Outstanding."

[15] Prior to the Lehman bankruptcy, concern existed that markets would have trouble unwinding all the derivative trades involving Lehman as counterparty. Those concerns proved unfounded. *The New York Times* (2008j) and the *Financial Times* (2008d) wrote:

Hundreds of traders who placed bets on Lehman Brothers' creditworthiness before it went bankrupt have settled their positions "without incident," according to a company that tracks derivatives contracts.... The overall system appears to have borne the shock successfully.

"We could have come to work today and had no trading, no one accepting anyone else's credit and the market going into total meltdown. The fact that [CDS] prices are available and that index moves have been relatively limited shows that we have liquidity and that the market is actually operating smoothly," he [a senior Credit Suisse banker] said.

discipline. The other side of TBTF is capital forbearance, and the losses on subprime and Alt-A mortgages had created widespread losses of unknown magnitude and location.

The FDIC reinforced the sudden, unforeseen retraction of the financial safety net that had occurred with the Lehman bankruptcy by not bailing out the debt holders of Washington Mutual (WaMu) at the time of its takeover by JPMorgan Chase on September 25, 2008. Washington Mutual was the largest thrift in the country and had aggressively marketed option ARMs (adjustable-rate mortgages that allowed the borrower flexibility to defer payments by adding to the principal of the loan). Large investors like Pimco and Blackrock providing unsecured wholesale funding for banks had already become nervous in July 2008 when the FDIC failed to make whole the uninsured depositors at the bank IndyMac.

Like WaMu and IndyMac, by summer 2008 Wachovia was in trouble because of its large holdings of mortgages acquired in the mid-2000s. Wachovia had been a conservatively managed bank before its merger with First Union in 2001. In 2006 with its purchase of GoldenWest, Wachovia became the most significant holder of option ARMs. GoldenWest had concentrated its mortgage lending in California and within California had concentrated in the suburbs. After September 25, 2008, Wachovia failed to obtain wholesale funding. On September 29, 2008, the FDIC forced the sale of Wachovia to Citigroup but later changed the buyer to Wells Fargo.

UNDOING THE POST-LEHMAN FUNDING FLIGHT TO SAFE BANKS

The retraction of the financial safety net to a narrower, ambiguous boundary caused by the Lehman bankruptcy and the losses imposed on Washington Mutual debt holders set off a flight of cash investors to safe institutions. Populist anger, which appeared in the initial rejection by the House of Representatives of the Treasury's request for TARP money, reinforced the possibility that regulators would no longer protect the debt holders of financial institutions from loss. To undo the rearrangement of funding flows arising from the flight to well-capitalized or indisputably TBTF banks, governments and regulators responded in an ad hoc way to expand the coverage of the financial safety net to *all* the liabilities of *all* financial institutions in *all* major countries.

On September 19, 2008, to counter the effects of the funds redemptions from the prime money-market funds, the Fed announced a program to use the discount window to make nonrecourse loans to banks using as collateral asset-backed commercial paper purchased from these funds (the Asset Backed Commercial Paper Money Market Mutual Fund Liquidity Facility, or AMLF). On the same day, the Treasury, using funds in the Exchange Stabilization Fund, announced guarantees for shareholders against losses in money-market mutual funds that participated by paying a fee (the Temporary Guarantee Loan Program, or TGLP). As a result of the TGLP, money funds offered unlimited protection whereas bank accounts offered protection only up to $100,000. To prevent the outflow of funds from banks to money funds, on October 3, 2008, the FDIC raised the limit on insured deposits for banks and credit unions to $250,000. Small businesses, however, often held deposits in excess of this amount.

Swagel (2009, 34) wrote, "There was incoming fire at the same time from banks, who (reasonably) complained that the Treasury guarantee put them at a competitive disadvantage against money-market mutual funds. After nearly every Treasury action, there was some side effect or consequence that we had not expected." On October 14, 2008, the FDIC announced that it would insure at banks, without any size limits on individual accounts, all of the $500 billion in non-interest-bearing deposits held chiefly by small businesses. Also on October 14, 2008, the FDIC created a Temporary Liquidity Guarantee Program (TLGP) to guarantee the issuance of new senior debt of all financial institutions with FDIC insurance for an amount up to $1.5 trillion. As of April 2009, the FDIC had guaranteed $340 billion in bank debt (Becker and Morgenson 2009).

On September 30, 2008, by guaranteeing the deposits and debt of its national banks, Ireland set off a competitive response by individual governments of Europe to protect the deposits of their national banks.[16] Acting to protect their domestic banks from a flight of depositors, foreign governments guaranteed the debt issued by their own banks.[17] Moreover, within countries, the incentive existed for depositors to flee to the troubled banks taken over by the government because of the government guarantees. *The Wall Street Journal* (2008k) reported, "As the U.K. has nationalized two troubled banks, and Ireland has taken the extraordinary measure of guaranteeing all deposits in its six largest financial institutions, other banks

---

[16] "The Irish guarantee ... covers an estimated €400bn of bank liabilities including deposits, covered bonds, senior debt and dated subordinated debt for two years" (*Financial Times* 2008h).

[17] Governments announced guarantees for the issuance of bank debt in the following amounts (in billions of U.S. dollars): Ireland ($641), Germany ($556), United Kingdom ($375), Netherlands ($254), Sweden ($169), Belgium ($114), and Austria ($108). See International Monetary Fund (2009) table 1.10, "Announced Sovereign Guaranteed Debt," 49.

have started complaining that the state-backed institutions are stealing their customers."

While not mentioning the pressure coming from the domestic bank sector, U.S. regulators referred to the competitive pressures coming from European deposit guarantees. *The New York Times* (2008j) and the *Congressional Quarterly Weekly* (2008, 2805) reported:

[Treasury Secretary Paulson] pointed in particular to the decision to guarantee all bank deposits and interbank loans, something the United States did to keep pace with similar decisions in Europe. "We had to," Mr. Paulson said, "Our banks would not have been able to compete."

FDIC Chairman Sheila Bair told reporters, "Their [foreign banks] guarantees for bank debt and increases in deposit insurance would put U.S. banks on an uneven playing field unless we acted as we are today" ["a blanket guarantee for business checking accounts"].

The Board of Governors announced special programs to purchase commercial paper. On October 7, 2008, the board announced creation of the Commercial Paper Funding Facility (CPFF) to purchase commercial paper from banks and corporations. On October 21, 2008, the board announced the Money Market Investor Funding Facility (MMIFF) to purchase commercial paper from money-market mutual funds. Both programs involved the creation of special purpose vehicles (SPVs) financed by the New York Fed.

CONCLUDING COMMENT

The unprecedented, vast expansion of government and central bank intervention into credit markets is captured by two comments in newspaper reports. *The Wall Street Journal* (2008l) wrote, "The Federal Reserve said it will bypass ailing banks and lend directly to American corporations." *The New York Times* (2008i) wrote, "It ought to make anyone nervous to have the government allocating capital, which in this environment could mean it is making the decision to let companies live or fail."

The magnitude of the long-run effects of the expansion in the financial safety net on risk taking by banks is unknown. However, for the economist, these actions have provided an experiment in the use of the allocation of credit by government and central banks as a countercyclical instrument for stimulating aggregate demand. The severity of the 2008–2009 recession and the slowness of the recovery suggest the inefficacy of such tools.

FOURTEEN

The Distinctions Between Credit, Monetary, and Liquidity Policy

In response to the turmoil in financial markets that followed the Lehman bankruptcy on September 15, 2008, policy makers implemented five different kinds of policies: liquidity, bailout, credit, monetary, and fiscal.[1] To evaluate the success or failure of these policies in this period, it is critical to distinguish among their differences.

AN OVERVIEW

Table 14.1, "Programs to Stimulate Financial Intermediation as of November 26, 2008," provides an overview of the liquidity, bailout, and credit programs implemented immediately after the Lehman bankruptcy. As noted in the subtitle to a table listing these programs in *The Washington Post* (2008j), the intention of these programs was to "unfreeze credit for home buyers, consumers and small business." In evaluating the effectiveness of the different policies, the key fact is the rapidity and magnitude of the liquidity, bailout, and credit policies compared to the slowness with which monetary policy responded. With respect to monetary policy, the FOMC did not begin to lower the funds rate until October 8, 2008, and did not push it down to near zero until its December 16, 2008, FOMC meeting. With the funds rate near zero, the Fed focused on programs to encourage credit flows rather than on money creation. This chapter explains the analytical distinction among different policies, whereas Chapter 16 assesses their ability to stimulate aggregate demand.

---

[1] For an elaboration of the differences in these policies, see Goodfriend (2011).

Table 14.1. *Programs to stimulate financial intermediation as of
November 26, 2008*

Use	Maximum Dollar Commitment	Funds Used as of Nov. 26, 2008
Federal Reserve Programs		
Commercial Paper Funding Facility	$1.8 Trillion	$271 Billion
Term Auction Facility	$900 Billion	$415 Billion
Term Securities Lending	$250 Billion	$190 Billion
Credit Extension to American International Group (AIG)	$123 Billion	$87 Billion
Money Market Investor Funding Facility	$540 Billion	$0 Billion
Citigroup Bailout	$291 Billion	$291 Billion
Discount Window Lending to Commercial Banks, Primary Credit		$92 Billion
Asset-Backed Commercial Paper Money Market Mutual Fund Liquidity Facility	$62 Billion	$62 Billion
Primary Dealer Credit Facility	$50 Billion	$50 Billion
Bear Stearns' Assets (Covered When Bought by J.P. Morgan Chase)	$29 Billion	$27 Billion
FDIC Programs		
Loan Guarantees	$1.4 Trillion	
Guarantee to GE Capital	$139 Billion	$139 Billion
Citigroup Bailout	$10 Billion	$10 Billion
Treasury Department Programs		
Troubled Asset Relief Program (TARP)	$700 Billion	$375 Billion
Stimulus Package	$168 Billion	$168 Billion
Exchange Stabilization Fund	$50 Billion	$50 Billion
Money Market Fund Share Guarantees		
Tax Breaks for Banks	$29 Billion	$29 Billion

Note: Data from "Parsing the Bailout," *Washington Post*, November 26, 2008.

THE ASSET AND LIABILITY SIDE OF THE FED'S BALANCE SHEET

In his discussion of commercial banks, Keynes also (1930 [1971c], 191) highlighted the distinct roles a central bank can play: controller of money creation and arbiter of financial intermediation:

A banker ... is acting both as provider of money for his depositors, and also as a provider of resources for his borrowing-customers. Thus the modern banker performs two distinct sets of services. He supplies a substitute for State Money by acting as a clearing-house and transferring current payments.... But he is also acting as a middleman in respect of a particular type of lending, receiving deposits from the public which he employs in purchasing securities, or in making loans.... This duality of function is the clue to many difficulties in the modern Theory of Money and Credit and the source of some serious confusions of thought.

Monetary policy (control of money creation) focuses on the size of the liability side of the central bank's balance sheet, and credit policy focuses on the composition of the asset side of its balance sheet. Monetary policy concerns the way in which the central bank uses asset purchases to control the liability side of its balance sheet: the monetary base (currency held by the public and commercial bank deposits held at the central bank). Credit policy involves the central bank's allocation of credit through changes in the composition of the asset side of its portfolio. Monetary policy focuses on the rule necessary to control money creation, and credit policy focuses on the influence of the central bank over financial intermediation.

Monetary policy encompasses the implications of how the central bank sets the funds rate for the monetary base in particular and money creation in general. To illustrate monetary policy, consider the central bank's open-market purchase of a long-term bond in a monetary regime in which the central bank does not have an interest-rate target. In exchange for the bond, through a bookkeeping operation, the bank of the seller of the bond creates a demand deposit for the seller. Also, through a bookkeeping operation, the central bank creates reserves (a deposit on itself) for the bank. Because the public's asset portfolio is more liquid after the exchange, the public rebalances its portfolio. Liquidity or portfolio rebalancing involves the purchase by the public of illiquid assets such as equity, real estate, or consumer durables (Hetzel 2004a).

In contrast to the Fed, in the 2008–2009 recession, the Bank of England (2009) explained its large-scale asset purchases in terms of money creation and portfolio rebalancing:

When a financial company sells an asset to the Bank [of England], its money holdings increase (i.e., it has additional deposits). If the company does not regard this extra money to be a perfect substitute for the assets it has sold, this would imply that it is now holding excess money balances. In order to rebalance the portfolio back to its desired composition, the company may use the money to purchase other assets. However, that just shifts the excess balances to the seller of those assets so that they look to purchase other assets as well. This process should bid up asset prices, in principle to the point where, in aggregate, the value of the overall asset portfolio has risen sufficiently to bring the share of money relative to all assets to its desired level. This is sometimes known as the portfolio balance effect.

Credit policy, distinct from monetary policy, focuses not on the control of money creation but rather on the influence of the central bank on conditions in credit markets. Commercial banks intermediate between savers, who temporarily forego consumption today in return for augmented consumption tomorrow, and investors, who obtain use today of the resources released as a result of the restraint on consumption exercised by savers. A central bank could also provide this intermediation service. That is, it could issue long-term debt and use the funds to provide financing to private enterprises. Until fall 2008, the monopoly on the issue of the money (the monetary base) that individuals use to effect finality in payment had defined a central bank. However, starting in 2009, with the funds rate basically at zero, Chairman Bernanke (2009a) emphasized the allocation of credit as the primary tool used by the Fed to influence the expenditure of the public.

To illustrate credit policy, consider a central bank open-market purchase of a private-sector risky asset, say, asset-backed commercial paper (ABCP). As before, in the first round, the central bank creates a demand deposit in exchange for the risky asset. However, another round follows in which it extinguishes the demand deposit by selling the public a Treasury bill. The focus of credit policy is on the exchange in the public's portfolio of the risky asset (the ABCP) for a riskless asset (the Treasury bill). The public's asset portfolio is now less risky and the public rebalances its portfolio to restore the original amount of portfolio risk. Risk rebalancing involves purchasing riskier assets, thereby lowering risk premia and increasing credit flows in riskier segments of the credit markets.

Credit policy involves taking risky private debt into the central bank's asset portfolio in an attempt to allocate the flow of credit among different segments of the financial market.[2] Similarly, credit policy can involve

---

[2] An analogy for understanding credit policy is sterilized foreign exchange intervention. In the context of an unchanged funds rate, consider Fed purchases of dollars with Eurodollars held in its own portfolio in the foreign exchange market to prevent dollar depreciation. To prevent an increase in the funds rate as the dollar reserves of banks fall, the Fed must buy Treasury securities to increase bank reserves. The result is to leave investors with more Eurodollar-denominated assets relative to dollar-denominated assets while interest rates and the monetary base remain unchanged. There is a portfolio-composition effect but no change in the monetary base.

central bank purchases of long-term assets and simultaneous sales of short-term sales to remove "duration" from the market. The idea is that the sellers of the long-term securities will purchase other long-term securities and raise their price (lower their yield). The Fed attempted to achieve this downward tilt in the yield curve in the early 1960s with Operation Twist (Hetzel 2008b, 69).

Until September 15, 2008, as a consequence of maintaining a funds-rate target, the Fed automatically sterilized credit-market interventions that added reserves. For example, lending under TAF (Term Auction Facility), which started in December 2007, left the size of the Fed's balance sheet unchanged. Because the addition of reserves through TAF lending would have lowered the funds rate, the New York Fed's Open Market Desk sold Treasury securities to absorb the addition to reserves. After September 15, 2008, the lack of available Treasuries in its portfolio (especially with the Treasury Securities Lending Facility or TSLF) restricted the ability of the desk to sterilize additions to reserves.[3] The Treasury then sterilized reserve additions through allowing the reserves received from the issuance of Treasury securities (via the Supplementary Financing Program) to remain in its deposits at the New York Fed.

LIQUIDITY POLICY MIXED WITH BAILOUT POLICY

Liquidity policy concerns increases in the demand for the liability side of the central bank's balance sheet (the monetary base) desired by banks (in the form of deposits with the central bank) and by the public (in the form of currency and demand deposits) during periods of height-ened uncertainty in financial markets. When the central bank sets a target for the funds rate, it automatically accommodates such demands as a consequence of preventing increases of the funds rate above tar-get. Classical central banking doctrine mandates that the central bank meet this increased demand through reserves and money creation, but without engaging in credit policy by allocating credit to insolvent banks (Humphrey 1975; 1989; 2010).

After the funding uncertainties created by the Lehman bankruptcy on September 15, 2008, large banks increased their demand for cash assets (reserves in the form of deposits with the Fed) by an amount sufficient to

---

[3]   With the TSLF, announced March 11, 2008, the New York Fed expanded from overnight to twenty-eight days its program of swapping Treasury securities temporarily for other less-liquid securities less in demand for RP (repurchase) agreements.

replace the run-off in reserves that would occur if the market ceased buying their short-term debt for a significant interval (up to one year). The cost of turning to regulators for a bailout in the event of a run was high given public hostility to bailouts. At the same time, the cost of holding excess reserves was minimal initially because of the payment of interest on reserves announced by the Board of Governors October 6, 2008, and later because of the near-zero funds rate. Furthermore, because the demand for loans was low, the opportunity cost to the banks of holding the reserves was low.

In fall 2008, initially, the Fed accommodated the increased reserve demand of banks primarily through short-term lending. Accommodation of this increased demand represented classical central bank policy in a financial crisis. The assumption that the Fed accommodated a significant increase in reserve demand by banks rather than forced the reserves on them is important for evaluating monetary policy. In the former case, there are no implications for the stance of monetary policy (the impact on the expenditure of the public), whereas in the latter case monetary policy is stimulative. The longer-run moderate growth of the monetary aggregate M2 provided evidence that the increase in bank reserves corresponded to an increased demand (Figure 12.26).

Additional evidence that the increase in bank reserves originated in bank demand came from the failure of the FOMC's large-scale asset purchase (LSAP) program to increase bank reserves. Figure 14.1 shows the steady increase in the Fed's holdings, starting in February 2009, of long-term treasuries ("Treasury portfolio") and GSE debt plus GSE mortgage-backed securities ("large-scale asset purchases"). Strikingly, these purchases, which in the first instance increased bank reserves, left the Fed's total liabilities and the amount of bank reserves basically unchanged. That is, there was a matching decline in the discretionary use of the Fed's discount window and facilities like the TAF, foreign central bank swap lines, and the Commercial Paper Funding Facility (CPFF).

For example, between the weeks ending March 19, 2009, and September 3, 2009, Federal Reserve credit (the assets in the Fed's portfolio) basic-ally remained unchanged at $2.04 trillion and $2.06 trillion, respectively. Between these two dates, however, securities held outright by the System Open Market Account (SOMA) increased from $747 billion to $1,491 billion. As is also evident from a comparison of the 12/31/2008 and 1/27/2010 bar charts in Figure 14.2, the LSAP open-market purchases left the total of Fed assets largely unchanged. When the Fed added reserves to the banking system through open-market purchases, the banks offset that increase through reduced use of the discretionary lending facilities offered

Federal Reserve System Assets

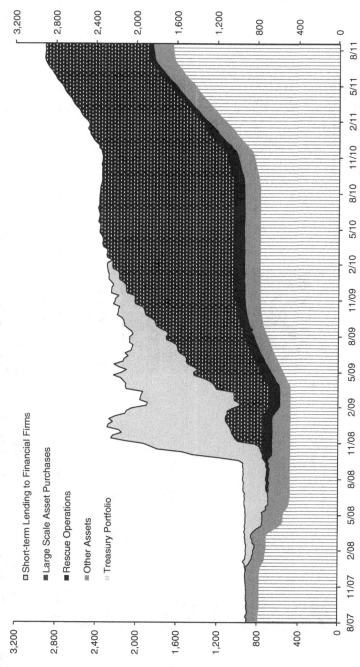

Figure 14.1. Federal Reserve System assets.

Note: Data from Board of Governors H.4.1 release, "Factors Affecting Reserve Balances." Short-term lending includes the Term Auction Facility, Foreign Currency Swaps, Asset-Backed Commercial Paper Liquidity Facility, Discount Window, Commercial Paper Funding Facility, Term Asset-Backed Securities Loan Facility, and the Primary Dealer Credit Facility. Large-scale asset purchases are open-market purchases of agency debt and agency mortgage-backed securities (MBS). Rescue operations include Maiden Lanes I, II, & III and other AIG-related credit.

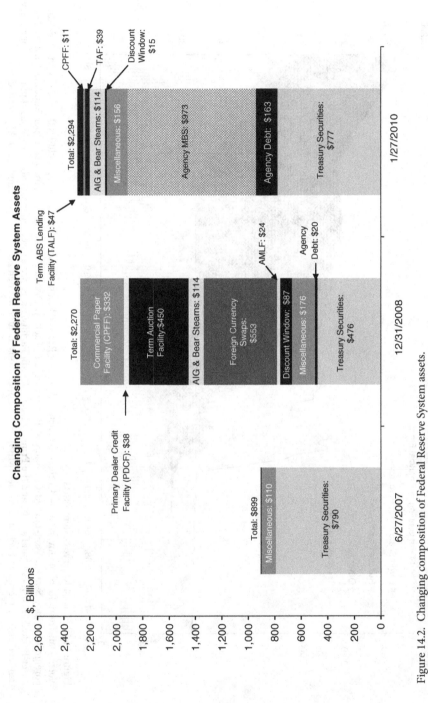

Figure 14.2. Changing composition of Federal Reserve System assets.
Note: Data from Board of Governors H.4.1 release, "Factors Affecting Reserve Balances." AMLF is the ABCP Money Fund Liquidity Facility.

by the Fed. The implication is that from the end of 2008 through early fall 2009, the Fed just accommodated the increased demand for bank excess reserves rather than forcing reserves out into the banking system. Stated alternatively, the dramatic increase in bank reserves (the monetary base) did not reflect a supply-side induced increase and thus did not reflect an expansionary monetary policy.

Newspapers misinterpreted the significance of the increase in the quantity of bank reserves. Consider the following examples from *The New York Times* (2009f; 2008g; 2008o):

[E]conomists say that Mr. Bernanke's most important accomplishment was to create staggering amounts of money out of thin air.

Banks continued to hoard cash, clogging crucial financial arteries that deliver money to businesses and consumers....

Fed officials have made it clear they are prepared to print as much money as needed to jump-start lending, consumer spending, home buying and investment. "They are using every tool at their disposal, and they will move from credit market to credit market to reduce disruptions," said Richard Berner, chief economist at Morgan Stanley.

Uncertain about the possibility of reserve outflows and reluctant to incur the stigma of being a distressed bank through recourse to borrowing in the funds market or use of the discount window, banks increased their demand for reserves. The Fed simply accommodated that increased demand. The high level of excess reserves possessed no evidence for or against a breakdown of financial intermediation. Contrary to the first sentence of the last quotation, the Fed did not conduct a policy with aggregate expenditure as the objective and with money creation as the instrument.

What was unusual about the actions of the Fed was the way in which the Fed allocated the additional reserves it created to distressed financial institutions and to markets like the commercial paper market considered dysfunctional. The Fed did so through special lending programs that disguised the identity of the banks receiving the reserves. It rejected both the alternative of engaging in massive open-market purchases of Treasuries and allowing the market to allocate the increased supply of reserves and the alternative of permitting banks desiring additional reserves simply to remain in the discount window. The goal was to get reserves to the distressed banks suffering reserves outflows without revealing the identity of those banks and thus advertising their distress.

Figure 14.3, which depicts the composition of the liabilities on the Fed's balance sheet, shows the sharp increase in bank reserve balances that occurred after September 15, 2008. As shown in Figure 14.4, which depicts

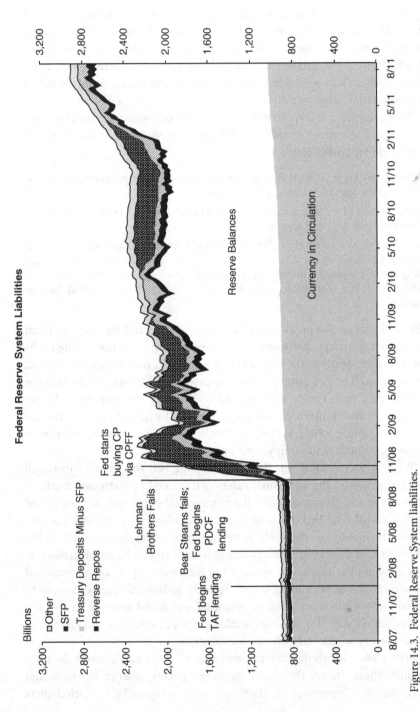

Figure 14.3. Federal Reserve System liabilities.

Note: Data from Board of Governors H.4.1 release, "Factors Affecting Reserve Balances." "Other" includes deposits from official institutions. SFP is Treasury deposits held at the Fed as a part of the Supplemental Financing Program.

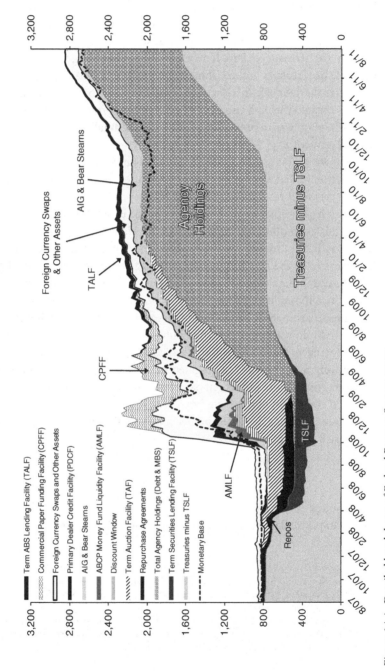

Figure 14.4. Detailed breakdown of Federal Reserve System assets.

Note: Data from Board of Governors H.4.1 release, "Factors Affecting Reserve Balances."

the composition of the assets on the Fed's balance sheet, the increase came through short-term lending programs like foreign currency swaps with other central banks. Figure 14.3 also shows how the Fed initially sterilized a significant amount of the increase in reserves arising from this lending through the Treasury's Supplementary Financing Program (SFP). With the SFP, the Treasury issued short-term securities and held the reserves received from their sale in an account with the New York Fed to soak up the reserves created through use of the Fed's lending programs. The reason for the sterilization was to prevent the funds rate from falling below its targeted rate of 2 percent as of September 15, 2008.

As shown in Figure 14.4, which presents more of a breakdown in the composition of Fed assets than Figure 14.1, after September 15, 2008, most of the increase in reserves came through two programs – TAF and the foreign currency swaps.[4] With TAF, the regional Federal Reserve banks auctioned dollars to domestic banks and to the New York agencies of foreign banks. With the foreign currency swaps, foreign central banks borrowed the dollars from the Fed and then auctioned them to their domestic banks. The U.S. and foreign central banks auctioned dollars for varying maturities, initially twenty-eight days under TAF, without revealing the identities of the banks. As shown in Figure 14.2, by year-end 2008, borrowing from the discount window accounted for very little of the increase in bank reserves that occurred in fall 2008. Although data on bank discount-window borrowing were available only aggregated by Federal Reserve district, market observers could figure out which banks were borrowing. Use of the auctions protected the anonymity of the borrowing banks and avoided the stigma that comes with it.[5] Distressed banks could obtain funds without paying a market risk premium.

CREDIT POLICY

Credit policy entails the use of the asset side of the Fed's portfolio to direct lending to particular sectors or borrowers. The ability of the Fed to conduct

---

[4] On October 29, 2008, the Fed announced swap lines with the central banks of Brazil, Mexico, Korea, and Singapore. It had previously authorized swap lines with Australia, Canada, Denmark, England, the European Central Bank, Japan, New Zealand, Norway, Sweden, and Switzerland.

[5] Armantier et al. (2011, abstract) found that after the Lehman bankruptcy in September 2008, banks were willing to pay a premium of 150 basis points "to borrow from the Term Auction Facility rather than from the discount window."

credit policy comes from its control over seigniorage. The increased holdings by large banks of excess reserves augmented the seigniorage revenue from money creation. In the past, because the Fed confined the assets in its portfolio to Treasuries, seigniorage became part of general government revenues and was subject to the constitutionally mandated congressional appropriations process (Hetzel 1997; Hetzel 2008b, ch. 16, appendix: Seigniorage and Credit Allocation). In the 2008–2009 recession, the Fed preempted the allocation of seigniorage revenues through its programs of intervening in credit markets. As shown in the bar charts of Figure 14.2 showing the composition of the Fed's asset portfolio on a date prior to the financial turmoil (June 27, 2007) and on two subsequent dates (December 31, 2008 and January 27, 2010), the Fed allocated funds to financial institutions and to markets it considered distressed.

To illustrate credit policy, consider the hypothetical alternative of matching the increase in excess reserves on the liability side of the Fed's balance sheet exclusively with Treasury securities on the asset side of the Fed's balance sheet. The increase in the Fed's holdings of Treasuries would correspond to a reduction in those securities in the asset portfolio of the public. The public would then decide on which assets to acquire to replace the Treasuries sold to the Fed. The Fed superseded this market allocation of credit. The success of the interventions of the Fed into credit markets then depended on its ability to identify externalities in the form of market failures whose correction lowered the costs of intermediating between savers and borrowers.

Credit policy possessed two components. The first component, complemented by bailout policy, endeavored to undo the flight of the cash investors after the Lehman bankruptcy to safe institutions and away from money funds and financial institutions suddenly considered susceptible to failure with losses imposed on their debt holders. A counterfactual is the response of the Fed in June 1970 to the disruptions in the commercial paper market produced by the Penn Central bankruptcy in which the Fed allowed banks to use the discount window freely without guiding reserves to individual institutions. The second component involved the attempt to revive the housing market through the purchase of GSE MBS and GSE debt. It also involved the attempt to revive the securitization markets through providing leverage to TALF (the Term Asset-Backed Securities Loan Facility). With respect to the first component, it is possible that the Fed avoided the example of Continental Illinois in 1984 of having to place a large bank into conservatorship. With respect to the second component, it is hard to point to tangible signs of success.

To aid housing, as shown in the 1/27/2010 bar chart of Figure 14.2, the Fed acquired significant amounts of agency (GSE) MBS ($1.1 trillion by April 2010) and GSE debt ($169 billion by April 2010). The magnitude of the intervention must have lowered the spread between the interest paid on agency (Fannie and Freddie) MBS and Treasury bonds of comparable maturity, although the amount remains in dispute because of the difficulty of adjusting for the prepayment risk present with the former and not the latter. This subsidy must have helped individuals who refinanced their mortgages. However, the benefit from any lowering of this yield spread for residential investment was overwhelmed by the large inventory of unsold houses. The months' supply of unsold new homes peaked at twelve months at the end of 2009, somewhat higher than in the previous recessions of 1990, 1982, 1980, and 1974. Single-family housing starts went from an annual rate of around 1.7 million in 2005 to 500,000 in early 2010.[6] The effort to revive the securitization market through TALF basically came to naught. As of early 2010, the Fed had outstanding only about $47 billion in loans made as part of the TALF program, and the ABS (asset-backed securitization) market remained depressed.[7]

The swap lines with foreign central banks illustrate the political economy issues involved in use of the composition of the Fed's balance sheet to allocate credit. Utilization of a swap line is credit policy. The way to explain this characterization is to start with a positive funds-rate target and no interest paid on reserves. When a foreign central bank draws on its swap line, the Fed receives an IOU for the dollars transferred to the foreign central bank, which lends them to its own banks or purchases foreign exchange. To prevent the addition of those dollars to the banking system from depressing the funds rate below target, the New York Open Market Desk sterilizes this reserves creation by selling a Treasury bill. Now, the amount of government debt owned by the public has risen. There is no money creation, just substitution of foreign government debt for U.S. Treasuries in the Fed's asset portfolio.

The Treasury could perform the same transaction with the Exchange Stabilization Fund. That is, the U.S. government could issue debt and use the

---

[6] Figures are from the Census Bureau and the National Association of Realtors.

[7] TALF entailed the creation of SIVs to hold ABS (commercial paper backed by issuance of student, car, and credit card loans). The Treasury would provide up to $20 billion of TARP money to serve as equity. The New York Fed would provide up to $200 billion in loans, with the ABS paper serving as collateral. The inability of TALF to revive securitization implied that intermediation had moved permanently back to the banking system and away from securitization because of the superior ability of banks to monitor risk.

dollars obtained to purchase foreign exchange from foreign central banks in return for dollars. The swap lines were not used in the spirit in which they were created, that is, for the purpose of sterilized foreign exchange intervention to prevent depreciation of the dollar under the Bretton Woods system of pegged exchange rates (Hetzel 1996). Instead, the Fed used the swap lines to provide the dollars used to bail out foreign banks that funded long-term risky assets with short-term dollar borrowing. If foreign central banks had wanted to bail out their own banks, they had the alternative of using their own dollar reserves.

BAILOUT POLICY

The Fed, the Treasury, and the FDIC provided support to individual institutions through a wide variety of programs. These programs involved lending facilities such as TAF, blanket guarantees on bank deposits and money-market fund shares, and special guarantees for large banks with losses related to mortgage lending. Bailout policy included support for nonbanks like AIG (American International Group) through direct lending. It also included conversion to bank holding company status for finance companies like GMAC (now Ally Bank) and for investment banks like Morgan Stanley and Goldman Sachs. Bailouts represented the extreme example of the attempt by governments and central banks to reverse the flow of wholesale funding to safe banks from financial institutions suddenly perceived as risky after the Lehman failure.

On Tuesday September 16, 2008, the day after the Lehman bankruptcy, the New York Fed lent AIG $85 billion in return for nearly 80 percent of its stock. The New York Fed later extended that aid. As reported in *The New York Times* (2008n):

The American International Group said Thursday that it had been given access to the Federal Reserve's new commercial paper program.... In addition to the $85 billion credit line and the $20.9 billion commercial paper program, AIG has a $38 billion facility from the Fed that provides liquidity for the company's securities.

Although most of the attention in the press focused on the payments in full that AIG Financial Products (AIGFP) made to its credit default swap (CDS) counterparties, which had purchased insurance on MBSs, AIG had made additional risky bets. AIG lent securities that it held and in return received cash collateral. It then sold this collateral to invest in residential mortgage-backed securities (RMBS). When those RMBS declined in value, AIG needed to post additional collateral, which it did not possess.

Chairman Bernanke (2009b) argued that "[T]he disorderly failure of AIG would have put at risk not only the company's own customers and creditors but the entire global financial system." Even though AIG is an insurance company rather than a bank, investors may have correctly considered it too big to fail. Its reputation came from its insurance business, which is highly regulated by state governments in the United States and by foreign governments abroad. It is conceivable that if regulators allowed a financial institution the size of AIG to go into bankruptcy with losses to creditors, markets could have run the largest troubled U.S. banks.

At the same time, forcing AIG to file for bankruptcy would still have left the policyholders of its insurance business protected. As explained in *The Wall Street Journal* (2008f):

AIG's millions of insurance policyholders appear to be considerably less at risk [than creditors of the parent company]. That's because of how the company is structured and regulated. Its insurance policies are issued by separate subsidiaries of AIG, highly regulated units that have assets available to pay claims. In the U.S., those assets cannot be shifted out of the subsidiaries without regulatory approval, and insurance is also regulated strictly abroad.... Where the company is feeling financial pain is at the corporate level, even while its insurance operations are healthy. If a bankruptcy filing did ensue, the insurance subsidiaries could continue to operate while in Chapter 11.

New York State Superintendent of Insurance Eric R. Dinallo testified before the House Financial Services Committee, "There would have been solvency" in AIG's insurance companies "with or without the Federal Reserve's intervention" (*American Banker*, 2009a). However, in the absence of a bankruptcy filing, New York insurance regulators allowed AIG to transfer $20 billion from its subsidiaries to the holding company (*The New York Times* 2008e).

Regulators had strong reasons for bailing out AIG to avoid explicit bailouts of troubled banks. AIGFP (AIG Financial Products) had offered CDS insurance to European banks, allowing them to take MBS off their balance sheets to avoid capital charges (regulatory arbitrage). Gros and Micossi (2008) wrote, "The K-10 annex of AIG's last annual report reveals that AIG had written coverage for over US $300 billion of credit insurance for European banks ... 'for the purpose of providing them with regulatory capital relief.'" *The Wall Street Journal* (2009b) reported:

The beneficiaries of the government's bailout of American International Group Inc. include at least two dozen U.S. and foreign financial institutions that have been paid roughly $50 billion.... The insurer generated a sizable business helping European banks lower the amount of regulatory capital required to cushion the losses on pools of assets such as mortgages and corporate debt. It did this by writing swaps that effectively insured those assets.... The concern has been that if AIG defaulted banks that made use of the insurer's business to reduce their regulatory capital, most of which were headquartered in Europe, would have been forced to bring $300 billion of assets back onto their balance sheets.

Also, as Phillip Swagel (2009, 33), Treasury undersecretary at the time, explained, "AIG provided credit guarantees to bank loans and thus a failure would have forced a capital raising by banks." Forcing banks to raise more capital would have worked against Treasury/Fed policy, which was to increase bank capital to increase bank lending as a way of jumpstarting the economy (Chapter 15). *New York Times* columnist Joe Nocera (2009) wrote:

At its peak, the A.I.G. credit-default business had a "notional value" of $450 billion.... [T]hat may be the single most important reason it [the Fed] can't let A.I.G. default. If the company defaulted, hundreds of billions of dollars' worth of credit-default swaps would "blow up," and all those European banks whose toxic assets are supposedly insured by A.I.G. would suddenly be sitting on immense losses. Their already shaky capital structures would be destroyed.

In November 2008, the New York Fed instructed AIG to pay the full amount it owed on the CDS contracts it had entered into with banks by buying the MBS underlying the CDS at face value. The New York Fed then placed the MBS into an off-balance-sheet entity (Maiden Lane III), which it financed.[8] *The Washington Post* (2009d) wrote:

The greatest beneficiaries were the French bank Societe Generale, which got more than $16 billion for assets valued in December at about $8 billion, and Wall Street giant Goldman Sachs, which got almost $14 billion for assets valued in December at about $6 billion. Other large beneficiaries included Deutsche Bank and Merrill Lynch.

The Fed took actions to help various financial institutions beyond AIG. Over the weekend prior to September 15, 2008, Ken Lewis, CEO of Bank of America (BofA), struck a deal with John Thain, CEO of Merrill Lynch, to purchase Merrill for $50 billion. On September 14, the Board of Governors had suspended Section 23A of the Federal Reserve Act, intended to prevent banks from bailing out their affiliates, in order to assure markets that BofA would be able to capitalize Merrill adequately. On September 21, 2008, the Fed approved applications by Goldman Sachs and Morgan Stanley to become bank holding companies and opened the discount window to their

---

[8] The banks purchasing the CDS insurance required that AIG post collateral. Even if AIG had gone into bankruptcy, the banks would have had the right to the collateral.

broker-dealer subsidiaries in New York and London. As a bank holding company, they could then issue debt guaranteed by the government with the FDIC's Temporary Liquidity Guarantee Program (TLGP).

On November 23, 2008, the Treasury, Fed, and FDIC announced a bailout for Citigroup. Citigroup, which had received $25 billion in the initial TARP allocation in return for preferred shares, received another $20 billion from TARP. Regulators also identified a pool of mortgage assets with book value of $306 billion. The Fed agreed to take losses on these assets beyond an initial amount allocated to Citigroup, the Treasury, and the FDIC.

Swagel (2009, 47) wrote:

[O]n November 25, 2008, Treasury, the Fed, and the FDIC jointly announced that Citigroup was being given another $20 billion of TARP capital ... and that the three federal agencies would provide guarantees against losses of a $306 billion pool of Citi assets. The Treasury had put up a modest amount of TARP money as a second loss position after Citi, the FDIC took the next set of losses, and the Fed then took the rest of the downside.... This position of the Treasury reflected the language of section 102 of the EESA [Emergency Economic Stabilization Act of 2008], which counted each dollar of gross assets insured by the TARP as a dollar against the $700 billion allotment. This meant it was most efficient ... for Treasury to take an early loss position.... [T]he Fed then uses its balance sheet to take the tail risk. The crucial new development in the use of TARP resources was the use of the Fed's balance sheet to effectively extend the TARP beyond $700 billion.

On January 16, 2009, regulators announced a similar package to "ring fence" $118 billion of the real estate loans that Bank of America had acquired mainly through its acquisition of Merrill Lynch. By January 2009, the market capitalization of Citigroup had fallen to $17.2 billion from $250.4 billion in March 2007, while that of Bank of America had fallen to $36.7 billion from $225.3 billion over this period (*Financial Times* 2009a).

MONETARY POLICY

With a positive funds rate, monetary policy involves the behavior of the funds rate and its implications for the control of the liability side of the Fed's balance sheet (the monetary base). With a zero funds rate, monetary policy involves the implications for the liability side of the Fed's balance sheet of open-market purchases and sales of assets. With attention focused on credit policy, the FOMC lowered the funds rate only cautiously after September 15, 2008. After establishment of the near-zero value for the funds rate on December 16, 2008, monetary policy involved market guidance over the likely duration of this near-zero value as a way of influencing the term structure of interest rates. The FOMC statement issued at the January 27,

2010, FOMC meeting included language that "The Committee ... continues to anticipate that economic conditions ... are likely to warrant exceptionally low levels of the federal funds rate for an extended period."

WILL THE FED PLAY A PERMANENT ROLE
IN ALLOCATING CREDIT?

In the period following the Lehman bankruptcy, the credit policy (credit allocation) of the Fed went through two phases, as evidenced in Figures 14.1 and 14.2. In the first phase, the Fed accommodated the increased demand of banks (foreign and domestic) for dollar reserves. It did so in a way that got reserves to banks no longer able to rely on wholesale funding markets (cash investors) and in a way that concealed the identity of the troubled banks. In the second phase, the Fed intervened directly in credit markets to revive intermediation in specific sectors. Through the purchase of GSE debt and MBS, it attempted to revive the housing market. With TALF, it attempted to revive the securitization market. When TALF failed to achieve this objective, the Fed began purchasing Treasury securities in addition to GSE securities and debt.

To understand the potential for the Fed to become permanently involved in the allocation of credit, it is necessary to understand the innovation of the payment of interest on reserves (IOR), which began on October 10, 2008.[9] With IOR, banks effectively sterilize additions to reserves by voluntarily holding them in order to receive interest from the Fed. Open-market operations with the public, which add reserves, then do not exert downward pressure on the funds rate. Because IOR endows the Fed with the ability to expand the size of its asset portfolio without the associated reserve creation depressing the funds rate below target, it can expand the size of its asset portfolio to allow it to intervene more aggressively to allocate credit.

As economic recovery from the 2008–2009 recession proceeds, the Fed will eventually raise the funds rate. It could simply sell assets to reduce the size of its asset portfolio and the monetary base by whatever amount required to validate its increased funds-rate target. Bank reserves would automatically fall in line with the decrease in the precautionary demand of banks for reserves. In practice, there may be a limit to the amount of assets the Fed is willing to sell. Politically, it may be difficult for the Fed to sell agency (GSE) securities and debt because of the precedent of using its balance sheet to support the housing market. In this situation, the Open Market Desk can

[9] The original idea of using IOR came from Goodfriend (2002).

The Market for Reserves without IOR

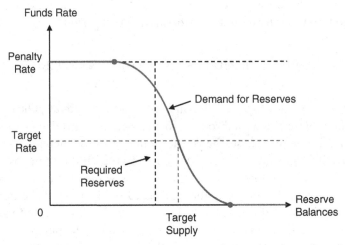

Figure 14.5. The market for reserves without IOR.
Note: Diagram from Keister et al. (2008).

use reverse RPs to sterilize reserves or it can rely on Treasury issuance of short-term debt (SFP bills). Explicit authority from Congress for the Fed to issue its own debt to sterilize reserves is unlikely. No doubt IOR will also come into play. Effectively, with IOR, the Fed can act like a GSE issuing debt to finance the purchase of housing assets.

To understand how IOR allows the Fed to expand the size of its asset portfolio independently of its funds-rate target, consider the bank reserves market depicted schematically using three graphs adapted from Keister et al. (2008). Figure 14.5 shows the market for bank reserves with a positive funds rate and no IOR. There is a penalty rate at which banks can borrow freely from the discount window. This rate imposes a ceiling on interest rates. The FOMC sets a lower target rate for the funds rate. The New York Open Market Desk then supplies an amount of reserves (target supply) that accommodates the amount of reserves banks demand at that target rate. The demand for reserves includes required reserves, which is predetermined in the reserves-accounting period given lagged-reserves accounting. The remainder of reserves supplied (the difference between the target supply and required reserves) constitutes banks' demand for excess reserves.

Figure 14.6 shows a market for bank reserves similar to the corridor (tunnel) system run by the Bundesbank before the creation of the ECB.

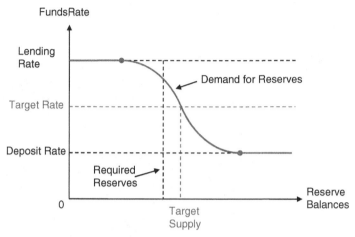

Figure 14.6. The market for reserves with IOR as a floor in a tunnel.
Note: Diagram from Keister et al. (2008).

There is a ceiling and a floor to the interest rate and an interbank rate that lies between the two. Under IOR, the interest rate paid by the Fed on the bank reserves deposited with it constitutes the floor – the deposit rate. Because banks will not lend in the interbank market for reserves at a rate less than the IOR rate they receive from deposits at the Fed, the IOR constitutes a floor on the interest rate.

In Figure 14.7, the Fed uses the IOR rate as its target rate. Now, the New York Open Market Desk can undertake open-market purchases of any magnitude without having the associated reserves creation depress the funds rate below the FOMC's target. The banks deposit the additional reserves with the Fed.[10] When the FOMC raises the funds rate from the 2010 target of between 0 percent and 0.25 percent, it can maintain the size of its asset portfolio (retain its GSE debt and MBS) by using the IOR rate as its funds-rate target. In principle, Congress can permanently change the character of the Fed by requiring it to hold large amounts of housing assets as a way of subsidizing the housing sector. The alacrity with which the Fed divests itself of its GSE assets as it raises the funds rate above the 2010 near-zero value will signal the extent of its determination to return to the traditional role of

[10] With open-market purchases, there remains a one-for-one addition to the money stock through increased demand deposits. At the given funds-rate target, monetary policy therefore becomes more stimulative with increases in the size of the Fed's asset portfolio.

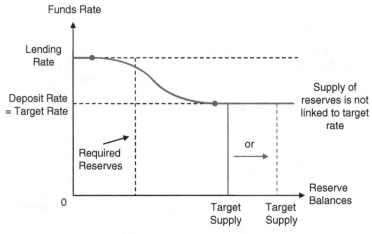

Figure 14.7. The market for reserves with IOR as the policy instrument.
Note: Diagram from Keister et al. (2008).

a central bank focused on monetary policy as opposed to credit policy and the allocation of credit.

LSAP VERSUS QE2: CREDIT VERSUS MONETARY POLICY IN NOVEMBER 2010

Chairman Bernanke (2010c) characterized the decision of the FOMC in November 2010 to expand its System Open Market Account (SOMA) portfolio in regular increments by $600 billion dollars as a policy of large-scale asset purchases (LSAP), not quantitative easing (QE). (The press, however, named the program QE2.) The distinction highlighted the underlying assumption that the stimulative effect of the expansion of the Fed's asset portfolio would work entirely through the way in which the concentration of those purchases in Treasury securities of long-term maturities increases the price of those securities. As a concomitant of those purchases, bank reserves increase; however, that increase was presumed irrelevant. It induces no incentive on the part of banks to purchase assets, and the resulting money creation creates no portfolio rebalancing by the public through which individuals attempt to make their asset portfolios less liquid by purchasing illiquid assets. This characterization emphasized the way in which the Fed thought about its policies starting in fall 2008 as influencing financial intermediation rather than money creation.

A hallmark of Fed procedures is the absence of any explicit framework specifying what macroeconomic variables the Fed controls and how it exercises that control. How the Fed uses its policy instrument to control macroeconomic variables like the nominal expenditure of the public is left unstated. With QE2 and the inevitable ambiguity about the extent to which the program increased the prices of long-term bonds, the public used the level of bank reserves as a measure of the stance of monetary policy. Because bank reserves were at historically high levels, monetary policy had to be "accommodative." Unfortunately, such judgments ignore the demand by banks for reserves.

Consider QE2. As of the end of April 2011, the time of writing this chapter, QE2 had produced an increase in Fed securities holdings of $416 billion. However, European banks increased their holdings of dollar excess reserves by more than that amount.[11] They had good reason to accumulate excess reserves in 2011. First, the possibility was real that the troubled peripheral countries in Europe like Greece would at least partially default on their external debt and impose losses on the European banks holding that debt. Second, the European Banking Authority was under pressure to make national regulatory authorities subject their banks to rigorous "stress tests."[12]

The alternative to the quantitative easing programs would have been a clear target for the growth rate of dollar GDP (expenditure) with bank reserves as the policy instrument. The amount of bank reserves required to maintain the necessary growth rate of money would have been a technical detail. In practice, the popular press simply assumed that large amounts of excess reserves implied an expansionary monetary policy and ignored the demand for those excess reserves.

[11] The Board of Governors statistical release "Assets and Liabilities of Commercial Banks in the United States (Weekly), SA – H.8" contains a table "Assets and Liabilities of Foreign-Related Institutions in the United States." The table lists "cash assets," which is a good proxy for dollar reserves. From November 2010 through April 20, 2011, this entry increased by $453.2 billion (from $301.7 billion to $754.9 billion. The entry "net due to related foreign offices" changed by a comparable magnitude. Foreign banks increased their holding of dollar reserves through their agency banks in the United States.

[12] *The New York Times* (2011b) wrote:

[I]t was "absolutely crucial" that the [stress] tests were "tough and transparent" and formed part of a longer-term process of bank rehabilitation involving recapitalization, closing or merging weak institutions and then restructuring the debts of some countries and banks by requiring senior bondholders to accept losses.... Germany has a specific problem with bad debts among its regional lenders, or Landesbanks, while large French, British and German banks are hobbled by their large holdings of Greek and Irish sovereign debt, creating the potential for a domino effect in the event of a sovereign default.

DOES MACROECONOMIC STABILITY REQUIRE
CENTRAL BANK CREDIT ALLOCATION?

Is the role of the central bank to control speculative excess or to control money creation by allowing the price system to function? After the Fed regained its independence with the 1951 Treasury-Fed Accord, Allan Sproul, president of the New York Fed, debated William McChesney Martin, chairman of the FOMC, over the role of a central bank (Bremner 2004). Martin advocated "bills only," that is, the New York Open Market Desk should buy and sell only Treasury bills. Sproul wanted the desk to buy and sell Treasury securities at all maturities. Martin won, but the New York Fed remained attached to the view that monetary policy worked through the way in which the Fed influences the "cost and availability of credit." For Martin, financial markets should allocate credit. For Sproul, the Fed should not only influence the cost of credit but also the supply of credit at all maturities of the Treasury market wherever market stresses appear.[13]

Despite this disagreement, beyond using the discount window to aid troubled banks, there was never any significant allocation of credit by the Fed before fall 2008.[14] To understand how radical was this departure from Fed and traditional central bank practice, note that during the one time that Fed policy makers decided that government should intervene to facilitate intermediation in financial markets, the Fed led the move for a completely independent organization to supply the credit. In the Hoover administration during the Depression, "Governor Eugene Meyer became the Hoover administration's principal advocate of the RFC [Reconstruction Finance Corporation] bill.... [T]his legislation was drafted and promoted mostly by the Board and its staff" (Todd 1996, 106, 108). The RFC recapitalized banks by purchasing preferred stock from them. The important point is that the

---

[13] The best long-run historical overview of the evolution of the understanding of monetary policy within the Fed and the resulting manifestation of that understanding in the procedures for implementing policy is Meulendyke (1998).

[14] In 1932, the Reconstruction Finance Corporation (RFC) lent Central Republic Bank $90 million. Because the bank's chairman, Charles "General" Dawes, had been Calvin Coolidge's vice president, the bank was known as a Republican bank. House Speaker John Nance Garner, Roosevelt's choice for vice-presidential running mate and Texas Democrat, declared in congressional debate, "I plead with you to let all the people have some drippings.... How can you say that it is more important in this nation that the New York Central Railroad should meet the interest on its bonds ... than it is to prevent the forced sale of 500,000 farms and homes?" Garner persuaded Congress to insert language in the Federal Reserve Act that allowed the Fed to lend money to small business (see Reynolds 2008). As detailed in Fettig (2002) and Schwartz (1992), this 13(b) language was the basis for a small number of loans by the Fed to small businesses in the 1930s.

RFC purchased this stock through the proceeds from issuing debt. In that way, the activities of the RFC remained completely separate from those of the Fed.

Before the Lehman bankruptcy, William McChesney Martin had defined modern central banking. According to his view, the central bank uses a short-term interest rate as its policy variable and allows markets to set long-term rates and to allocate credit. The central bank also eschews all kinds of direct controls, whether they are price controls or margin requirements intended to control stock market speculation. The message is "markets work," whether it is the price system or financial markets. Because of the extensive intervention of the Fed in credit markets during the 2008–2009 recession, the appropriate role of a central bank in economic stabilization is now an open question.

FIFTEEN

Fed Market Interventions

The Experiment with Credit Policy

For Chairman Bernanke (1983), monetary shocks caused the Great Recession. Frictions in financial markets (the credit channel) were important as a propagation mechanism. Later, as FOMC chairman and in the context of the 2001 and 2008–2009 recessions, he adopted the view that the initial shocks originated as the bursting of bubbles in asset markets. In response to a question from Henry Kaufman asking "[H]ow will the Federal Reserve respond to further financial speculative activities," Bernanke (2009d) responded:

You just introduced perhaps the most difficult problem in monetary policy of the decade, which is how to deal with asset bubbles. We've had two big asset bubbles in this decade, and both have resulted in severe downturns, particularly the credit bubble.

Based on the assumption that the 2008–2009 recession originated in a disruption in financial markets, Bernanke (2008b) provided the rationale for the unprecedented intervention into credit markets by central banks and governments in fall 2008:

History teaches us that government engagement in times of severe financial crisis often arrives late, usually at a point at which most financial institutions are insolvent or nearly so. Waiting too long to act has usually led to much greater direct costs of the intervention itself and, more importantly, magnified the painful effects of financial turmoil on households and businesses.

Policies to stimulate aggregate demand by augmenting financial intermediation provided an extraordinary experiment with credit policy as opposed to monetary policy. The vast extent, magnitude, and prompt implementation of these policies meant that they should have exercised a notable impact on public expenditure. Counterfactuals are inherently controversial, and in the absence of these programs the recession could have been worse. Nevertheless, it is hard to reconcile the actual occurrence of severe recession with the presumption that the intervention into credit markets that began in fall 2008 was effective in stimulating aggregate demand.

THE RATIONALE FOR CREDIT-MARKET INTERVENTIONS

After economic recovery began in 2009, policy makers defended their actions in the fall 2008 crisis with the contention that bailing out troubled financial institutions saved the financial system from collapse and prevented the recurrence of another Great Depression. However, addressing the stresses created by the flight of the cash investors could have been done without the detailed, specific interventions into credit markets that actually occurred. An appraisal of actual policy after the Lehman bankruptcy requires examination of the validity of the rationale for these interventions. The rationale for policy in the post-September 15, 2008, period was that a breakdown in financial intermediation had pushed the economy into recession and that intervention into individual credit markets and the rescue of troubled financial institutions would revive intermediation and the economy. Did that rationale offer a good guide to policy?

Policy makers believed that the 2008–2009 recession originated in a breakdown in financial intermediation. As Bernanke (2009b) explained, this belief motivated the vast intervention into credit markets that began after the Lehman failure in September 2008:

The credit boom began to unravel in early 2007 when problems surfaced with subprime mortgages.... [F]inancial institutions – reeling from severe losses on mortgages and other loans – cut back their lending.... [G]iven the ongoing problems in credit markets, conventional monetary policy alone is not adequate to provide all the support that the economy needs. The Fed has therefore taken a number of steps to help the economy by unclogging the flow of credit to households and businesses. In doing so, we have demonstrated that the Fed's toolkit remains potent, even though the federal funds rate is close to zero and thus cannot be reduced further.

This policy of countercyclical aggregate demand management by reinforcing the health of bank balance sheets reflected conventional beliefs in 2008. Those beliefs derived from a comparison of the presumed unsuccessful experience in Japan and the presumed successful experience in the 1990s of Scandinavian countries in dealing with bank crises. In Japan, land prices peaked in 1991 and fell steadily thereafter. This decline produced losses on bank real estate lending. Given public opposition to using public monies to recapitalize banks, the Japanese government temporized.[1] Japan suffered a "lost decade" of growth.[2]

After banking crises in the early 1990s in Scandinavia, governments cleaned up bank balance sheets quickly and output growth resumed promptly.[3] Honkapohja (2009, 25–6) wrote:

> Several lessons can be drawn from the Nordic crises.... A key starting point is that maintaining confidence in the banking system is crucial.... Political guarantees for obligations of banks were a major step in maintaining confidence.... [T]he impacts of banking collapses in the three Nordic countries were short-lived and the economies recovered fairly quickly from the crisis and economic growth resumed.

Bernanke (2009a, 1, 2, and 4) rejected a policy based on money creation, which he termed "quantitative easing," given his interpretation of the Japanese experience, in which a high level of excess reserves failed to stimulate economic activity, and given his understanding of the Depression. Instead, he favored "credit easing" – the use of the asset side of the Fed's

---

[1] Bernanke (2007a) wrote:

> A weak banking system grappling with nonperforming loans and insufficient capital ... [provides an example] of financial conditions that could undermine growth. Japan faced just this kind of challenge when the financial problems of banks and corporations contributed substantially to sub-par growth during the so-called "lost decade."

[2] Counter to this view, Japan began large-scale capital infusions into banks in 1999 but did not experience sustained real GDP growth until 2002. For a history of Japan from a monetary perspective, see Hetzel (1999; 2003; 2004b).

[3] Any attempt to draw lessons from these episodes without reference to monetary policy is problematic. Hetzel (2002b) explained how the Louvre Accord produced easy monetary policies in countries in the last part of the 1980s and how German reunification then produced tight monetary policies in the early 1990s. The Nordic banking crisis was related to this swing in monetary policy and did not arise as an independent factor. The Finnish experience described by Honkapohja (2009) was typical of the experience of Scandinavian countries:

> [A]fter German unification, interest rates rose in Europe and also in Finland, as a result of a more expansive fiscal policy combined with tighter monetary policy in Germany.... [M]onetary conditions became very restrictive due to an increase in real interest rates and appreciation of the Finnish markka. Real interest rates rose dramatically from the start of 1990 until the end of 1992 as a result of the defense of the Finnish markka against speculative attacks.

> Jonung (2008, 31) properly accounted for the effect of changes in capital flows in a system of pegged exchange rates on the real terms of trade and on domestic price levels:

> [G]iven a framework of a pegged exchange rate, financial liberalization and credit expansion have proven to be major driving forces behind boom-bust cycles across the globe.... Once the crisis developed, the introduction of a floating exchange rate and the ensuing depreciation marked the end of the crisis and signaled recovery.

balance sheet to allocate credit to segments of the credit markets deemed dysfunctional:

[A]lthough the subprime debacle triggered the crisis, the developments in the U.S. mortgage market were only one aspect of a much larger and more encompassing credit boom.... The abrupt end of the credit boom has had widespread financial and economic ramifications. Financial institutions have seen their capital depleted by losses and writedowns and their balance sheets clogged.... [T]he Federal Reserve has ... a range of policy tools to provide direct support to credit markets.... [T]hey have one aspect in common: They all make use of the asset side of the Federal Reserve's balance sheet.

[I]n a pure QE [quantitative easing] regime, the focus of policy is the quantity of bank reserves, which are the liabilities of the central bank; the composition of loans and securities on the asset side of the central bank's balance sheet is incidental.... [T]he Bank of Japan's policy approach during the QE period was ... gauged primarily in terms of its target for bank reserves. In contrast, the Federal Reserve's credit easing approach focuses on the mix of loans and securities that it holds and how this composition of assets affects credit conditions for households and businesses.... [T]o stimulate aggregate demand in the current environment, the Federal Reserve must focus its policies on reducing those [credit] spreads and improving the functioning of private credit markets....

When markets are illiquid and private arbitrage is impaired by balance sheet constraints ..., one dollar of longer-term securities purchases is unlikely to have the same impact on financial markets and the economy as a dollar of lending to banks.... Because various types of lending have heterogeneous effects, the stance of Fed policy in the current regime – in contrast to a QE regime – is not easily summarized by a single number.... [T]he usage of Federal Reserve credit is determined in large part by borrower needs.

As indicated by Bernanke's reference to Japan, policy makers attributed Japanese economic stagnation in the 1990s to a banking system rendered dysfunctional by a weakened balance sheet arising from loan losses incurred with the collapse of housing prices early in the decade. In his appeal for funds to congressional leaders after the failure of Lehman, Bernanke (*The Washington Post* 2008f) explained the rationale for removing troubled mortgage assets from the books of banks:

The situation is severe, he [Bernanke] said, and the Fed is out of tools. If the problem isn't corrected, the United States could enter a deep multi-year recession akin to Sweden or Japan in the early 1990s.

In a summary of the consensus about the macroeconomic consequences of failure to maintain a solvent banking system, Posen (2000, 5–6) wrote:

The contractionary process [banks calling in loans] is frequently ... touched off by the collapse of an asset price bubble.... This begins a cycle of credit contraction ...

and once this cycle starts, the size of the bad loan problem is likely to expand.... Banks cut back new lending to low-risk, low-return projects because of the absence of potentially capital-rebuilding large gains.... [T]he banks actually work against macroeconomic recovery with their inefficient lending behavior.

Posen (1998, 127–8) also summarized the consensus about appropriate policy:

There is no issue in the current Japanese economic situation about which there is as much intellectual agreement as the need to recapitalize the viable Japanese banks and close the ones that are not.... [P]ublic injection of trillions of yen into the banking system and public supervision of the disposal of distressed loans, real estate, and other assets are required to restore the Japanese financial system. Government use of the Resolution and Collection Bank to create a liquid market in the disposal of foreclosed real estate ... will be needed.

Sheila Bair, chairman of the FDIC, reiterated this credit view in an interview in *The Washington Post* (2009a) in which she defended the creation of the Public-Private Investment Program (PPIP) to take the bad assets off the books of banks through sales to SIVs. The SIV funding would come in part by private investors but with government equity to absorb losses beyond an initial amount and with significant leveraging coming from funds provided by the Fed:

The government's plan to strip the banks of troubled assets could force some firms to record large losses, but the painful purge would help restore confidence in the banking system.... She said the greatest challenge was persuading banks and taxpayers to accept the necessity of the costly program. "This takes courage to do, but if we don't do it, history shows that this kind of mechanism – recognize the losses, get at the root of it and move on – this is how you jump-start the economy.

INTERVENTION INTO CREDIT MARKETS
ON A MASSIVE SCALE

In the 2008–2009 crisis, policy to stimulate aggregate demand focused on maintaining financial intermediation by promoting healthy bank balance sheets. Treasury Assistant Secretary for Economic Policy Phillip Swagel explained the rationale for policy: Government would buy the bad mortgage assets of banks, credit would flow again from savers to investors, and the economy would revive. This rationale guided planning in the Treasury in 2008 before the Lehman bankruptcy. Political reality, however, kept these plans on hold until the financial turmoil precipitated by the Lehman Brothers bankruptcy on September 15, 2008. Swagel (2009, 40, 48–9, 2, and 26) laid out the "playbook" for stimulating aggregate demand:

From the vantage point of early September, it still looked like buying $700 billion of assets would be enough to settle markets – there were about $1 trillion each of whole loans and structured products such as MBS and CDOs on American firms' balance sheets.... Winnow the banking system by putting out of business insolvent institutions (including through nationalization where a buyer is not at hand). Avoid supporting zombie firms that could squander resources and clog credit channels.... Recapitalize the surviving banks to ensure that they have a buffer against further losses. Resolve uncertainty about the viability of surviving banks by either taking away or "disinfecting" their toxic assets such as through ring fence insurance. The near term goal is ... to give them [banks] the confidence to put capital to work.

[P]olitical constraints were an important factor in the reluctance at the Treasury to put forward proposals to address the credit crisis early in 2008. The options that turned into TARP [Troubled Asset Relief Program] and subsequent actions were written down in March of 2008 – to buy assets, insure them, inject capital into financial institutions, or to massively expand federally guaranteed mortgage refinance programs in order to improve asset performance from the bottom up.... But there was no prospect of getting any of this.... Such a massive intervention in financial markets could only be proposed if Secretary Paulson and Chairman Bernanke went up to Congress and told them that the financial system and the economy were on the verge of collapse.

After the Lehman bankruptcy, Paulson and Bernanke went to Congress with just that message. *The Washington Post* (2008f) reported, "We are headed for the worst financial crisis in the nation's history, Bernanke said, according to three people present. 'We're talking about a matter of days.'" Congress passed TARP, which provided funding to purchase the bad mortgage debt of banks. As the *Financial Times* (2008e) put it:

When Hank Paulson first laid out the logic of the $700bn rescue plan he put it in the following terms: Illiquid mortgage-related securities were "clogging up our financial system" and choking off the flow of credit to the economy.

The original program envisioned "reverse auctions" in which banks would sell their bad mortgage assets to the government through market-determined prices. Immediately, practical mechanics and the politics of openly subsidizing large Wall Street banks interfered. The nonstandard mortgages packaged into the MBS held by banks made determination of a market price difficult if not impossible. Given the lack of a market for these structured products, a market price would have been only a fraction of the original par value. At such low prices, banks preferred to hold onto the MBS and hope for a return of the housing market. On the one hand, the recapitalization of the banks would occur only if Treasury bought the MBS at prices in excess of the realistic, low market prices. On the other hand, buying the MBS at inflated prices that subsidized the banks was politically untenable. Swagel (2009, 44) noted:

A concern of many at Treasury was that the reverse auctions would indicate prices for MBS that were so low they would make other companies appear to be insolvent if their balance sheets were revalued to the auction results.... [T]o some at Treasury the whole auction setup looked like a big science project.

In the week ending October 11, 2008, the world's major stock markets declined by about 20 percent. This severe decline meant that the Treasury had to do something quickly. As a result, the Treasury changed the objective of the TARP program from buying the troubled assets of banks to injecting capital into banks – an objective that Congress never would have approved. Swagel (2009, 39–40) wrote:

The problem with the criticism on capital injections vs. asset purchases is that Secretary Paulson never would have gotten legislative authority if he had proposed from the start to inject capital into banks.... Secretary Paulson would have gotten zero votes from Republican members of the House of Representatives for a proposal that immediately would have been portrayed as having the government control 20 percent of the banking system. And Democratic House members would not have voted for it without the bipartisan cover of votes from Republicans.

On October 14, 2008, regulators called the nine largest banks to Washington to inform them that the government was going to purchase preferred stock in them. Although the press release described participation as voluntary, the presence of all the banks' regulators conveyed the message that participation was mandatory. "[T]he Treasury says [the program] is voluntary.... Reports, however, indicate that some of the companies had to be strongarmed into the deal" (National Public Radio 2008). As conceived by the Treasury, TARP would stimulate the economy through increased bank lending coming from strengthened bank balance sheets.

However, in the heat of the financial crisis, TARP became a cover for bailing out at least one large, troubled bank. *American Banker* (2009c) wrote later:

Paulson began by inviting the nine largest commercial and investment banks to the Treasury on Oct. 14 and effectively forced them to take $125 billion from the government in return for stock and warrants.... It wasn't just that the government was investing in banks.... [I]t was that the banks had no choice.... Looking back, many observers agree that it was a mistake. The argument at the time was that having all of them take the money would ensure no stigma was attached to the funds. The troubled institutions would be able to use the capital to prop themselves up, while the healthy ones would essentially serve as cover for the others. But that's not how it worked out.

The healthy banks soon announced they did not need the funds, fueling speculation about the firms that said nothing. What's more, with the nine banks receiving half of the original $250 billion allotted to the Capital Purchase Plan, questions quickly arose about whether the Treasury needed even more money to prop up the system.... After Paulson assured the public the TARP money would be used by the banks to make more loans, lawmakers demanded proof.... TARP money quickly became tainted.... Jamie Dimon, the chief executive of JPMorgan Chase & Co., branded TARP money a "scarlet letter," and began declaring his intention to repay it.... TARP also stirred public outrage at bankers, who were blamed for starting the housing crisis.

TARP revived neither bank lending nor the economy. It did bail out two too-big-to-fail (TBTF) banks and politically sensitive smaller financial institutions as well as General Motors and Chrysler. *The Wall Street Journal* (2009a) wrote:

> More than 200 publicly traded banks have collected a total of $191.5 billion from ... TARP.... Nearly half – $90 billion – has gone to two companies, Citigroup and Bank of America.... Since mid-October, when Treasury announced plans to directly inject capital into healthy banks, the Dow Jones Wilshire bank index has skidded 56%.

The premise of policy that policy makers could close insolvent banks to "unclog" the financial system proved politically unrealistic. Keeping a bank alive through too big to fail is no problem, but closing a bank is quite another. The Treasury refused TARP funds to a Cleveland bank (National City) that had gone heavily into subprime mortgages but extended TARP money to a Pittsburgh bank (PNC) that then acquired the Cleveland bank.[4] Swagel (2009, 48) wrote:

> The denial of funds to NatCity Bank and its acquisition by PNC ... set off a firestorm of criticism that banks were using their TARP funds for mergers rather than to support lending.... [T]he furor revealed that there was no prospect for putting out of business a large number of banks.

As a mechanism for jump-starting the economy through increased bank lending, TARP foundered. By late October, "the tide of public opinion had begun to turn against the TARP, so much that there began to be doubts as to whether Congress would release the second stage of the TARP funds at all" (Swagel 2009, 45). Treasury had recognized the fiscal character of bank rescues through its initial request for funding from Congress. With the failures of TARP evident, however, the Treasury turned to the Fed's balance sheet

---

[4] *The Washington Post* (2008i) wrote:

The government's power to choose winners and losers in the crisis was illustrated yesterday when the Cleveland-based bank National City was forced to sell itself when regulators turned down its request for a Treasury investment after deciding the firm was too weak to save.... Instead, the Treasury gave $7.7 billion to PNC Financial Services Group to help buy National City. It did not require that the money be used for new lending, the stated purpose of the government plan.... Treasury officials yesterday backed away from plans to publicize a new round of investments in about 20 large regional banks over concerns that firms not on the list would be perceived as unhealthy and punished by investors.

to finance the fiscal transfers required to aid banks. Although presaged by the Bear Stearns and AIG bailouts, the wholesale movement by the Fed into fiscal policy changed the character of the central bank in a fundamental way. The Fed took on the character of a GSE set up by Congress to allocate credit to particular sectors of the economy, especially troubled banks and housing. Swagel (2009, 44) wrote:

What we did not fully see in late October and early November was that the Federal Reserve's balance sheet could be used to extend the TARP, as was done in late 2008 and early 2009 with ring fence insurance applied to the assets held by Citi and Bank of America and then in larger scale with the TALF and Public-Private Investment Funds later in 2009.

On November 25, 2008, the Board of Governors announced the creation of the Term Asset-Backed Securities Lending Facility (TALF). This program set up special purpose vehicles (SPVs or SIVs) to buy $200 billion in asset-backed securities and consumer and small business loans. The Treasury provided $20 billion in equity while the New York Fed provided nonrecourse financing, which meant that the Fed would incur any losses beyond the equity cushion. On February 10, 2009, the board announced a willingness to expand the size of the program to $1 trillion and expanded the collateral to include commercial and private-label residential mortgage-backed securities. The February 10 announcement came as part of a larger attempt by regulators to revive the original TARP objective of strengthening bank balance sheets as a way of reviving lending.

Having committed to credit policy to stimulate the economy, the Treasury and the Fed gave up completely on the constitutional stricture to reserve fiscal policy to the Congress. Swagel (2009, 48) wrote of the Citi bailout:

As had been the case with the Bear Stearns transaction, the precise mechanics of the arrangement were not widely understood in Washington. A key insight, however, is that under pricing insurance coverage is economically similar to overpaying for assets – but it turns out to be far less transparent. This insight underpins both the TALF and the bank rescue programs announced by the Obama administration in March 2009. The federal government is effectively providing potential buyers of assets in either program with a two-part subsidy of both low-cost financing and low-cost insurance. This federal contribution then helps to close the bid-ask spread and restore functioning in illiquid markets.

Likewise, the Treasury and Fed gave up on any attempt to limit the moral hazard created by bailouts. Swagel (2009, 48) wrote:

From the perspective at Treasury in November, however, the second Citi transaction meant that we had slipped behind the market and were back into reactive mode rather than having a pro-active approach to stabilize the financial system broadly.

Moreover, the downside insurance appeared to give rise to moral hazard.... A feeling of resignation likewise marked the work by Treasury staff on a similar ring fence insurance scheme and additional TARP capital promised to Bank of America late in 2008 and formalized on January 16, 2009, the last business day of the Bush administration. Everyone understood why it was necessary, but it was the final indication that the formation of well-considered policy was past.

Finally, in reference to the use of TARP funds to bail out General Motors and Chrysler, Swagel (2009, 48) recognized the difficulty of limiting bailouts to banks once the necessary funds no longer have to pass through the congressional appropriations process:

[T]he use of TARP to support the automobile companies was straightforwardly political: Congress did not want the burden of writing this check, and President Bush did not want his administration to end with their bankruptcy. TARP support is akin to burning public money while waiting and hoping that industry stakeholders arrive at a sustainable long-term arrangement. This thus appears to be the American approach to systemically significant "zombie" firms.

William Isaac (2009), former chairman of the FDIC, wrote:

[Treasury Secretary Henry Paulson] sold the TARP Troubled Asset Relief Program on the basis of purchasing "toxic assets" from financial institutions. Instead, Paulson invested it in the stock of banks, most of which did not need or want the money.... Paulson went beyond the banks, including GM, Chrysler and GMAC. I cannot imagine a basis for declaring GMAC a systemically important institution.

On February 10, 2009, Treasury Secretary Timothy Geithner announced a number of initiatives related to the objective of strengthening bank capital. The absence of details, however, disquieted markets and the Dow, which had started at 8,271, fell to 7,889 by day's end. The program involved a "stress test" (the Supervisory Capital Assessment Program or SCAP) under which bank examiners would evaluate banks' capital adequacy based on the worst-case-scenario assumption that the recession would worsen. Banks undercapitalized by this criterion would have to sell nonperforming loans, take the resulting losses, and raise new capital. Failure to raise the required new capital would lead to an infusion of capital by the government. "[T]he central premise of the Capital Assistance Program was that participating banks would receive government funds to ensure they remained amply capitalized" (Lacker 2011, 3). Financial markets associated that forced infusion of capital with nationalization. As a result, SCAP created enormous uncertainty about the commercial viability of banks.[5]

---

[5] From September 2008 through the end of the year, the S&P 500 stock index and the KBW stock index of bank shares fell by about the same amount, around 30%. By early March 2009, the S&P had fallen almost 50% while the index of bank shares had fallen just more

The financial press ran stories about the nationalization of large banks.[6] *The New York Times* (2009a, B1) wrote:

If policy makers were even remotely honest, analysts said, they would force banks to take huge write-downs and insist on a high price in return for taking bailout money. For practical purposes, that could mean nationalization.

Similarly, Cassidy (2010, 29) wrote:

Larry Summers [President Obama's National Economic Council director] was confronted by a number of economists who believed that the financial crisis would not end unless the government took over stricken banks. Summers told the critics that if they proved right in the following months the Administration would move toward nationalization.

In March 2009, outrage at the bonuses paid to AIG employees increased investor fears of government involvement in running banks. President Obama said, "How do they justify this outrage to the taxpayers who are keeping the company afloat" (*The Washington Post* 2009b, A1)? In an example of how heated the rhetoric became, Sen. Charles Grassley (R-IA) said that the executives of AIG should "follow the Japanese model ... resign, or go commit suicide" (*The Washington Post* 2009c, A1).

As measured by credit default swap spreads (the cost of insuring bank debt against default), the uncertainty created by SCAP peaked in spring 2009. The CDS spread for Citibank exceeded 650 basis points in early April (Figure 12.18) while that for Bank of America reached 400. Bank equity holders feared the dilution of their stocks through forced recapitalization. Concern was also acute about the fate of the regional banks not identified as TBTF through the initial allocation of TARP funds. Lacker (2011, 4) commented, "U.S. banking institutions raised substantial amounts of equity in public markets or through direct placements between the beginning of the crisis in 2007 and the fall of 2008 when events raised uncertainty about government dilution and made such investments problematic."[7]

---

that 70%. The exaggerated decline in the value of bank stocks in the latter period reflected the uncertainty created by the SCAP program.

6   "Rumors circulated that the administration was considering the outright nationalization of many large financial institutions" (Lacker 2011, 2).

7   After the Lehman bankruptcy, the uncertainty created by the unexpected retraction of the financial safety net and the confusion about the extent of its new, more limited reach also made banks reluctant to recapitalize themselves by issuing equity. Specifically, bank equity holders had to deal with "debt overhang." As a consequence of a provision in FDICIA, banks must maintain an adequate leverage ratio, which is the ratio of a bank's capital to its assets. Capital comprises tangible common equity and debt. For U.S. banks on average

On May 7, 2009, the Fed announced the results of the stress test. Even under the worst-case outcome of a worsening recession assumed by the exercise, the banking system was well capitalized. Nine of the original nineteen recipients of TARP money in October 2008 possessed adequate capital (Tier 1 capital in excess of 6 percent of total assets). The remaining ten firms needed to raise only an additional $75 billion. That result suggests that the original forced TARP injection of capital into banks in fall 2008 served the purpose of recapitalizing at most a couple large TBTF banks while attempting to avoid the stigma associated with singling out an individual bank as troubled.

Apart from the GSEs, loan securitization ceased in the 2008–2009 recession. The attempts by the Treasury and the Fed to revive this market manifested the belief that the recession originated in a breakdown in financial intermediation. The Financial Stability Plan announced by Geithner on February 10, 2009, revived the original purpose of TARP to remove troubled assets from banks' balance sheets, albeit financed in this instance to a significant degree outside of the congressional appropriations process by the Fed rather than through issuance of Treasury debt. The Public-Private Investment Program (PPIP) would acquire bad mortgage assets from banks. The intention was to create a "bad bank" to remove the impaired assets from banks' balance sheets. Sheila Bair, chairman of the FDIC, used the term "aggregator bank" to avoid the opprobrium of the term "bad bank." The belief was that subsidized loans from the Fed would bridge the gap between the unwillingness of banks to sell mortgage assets at their low market values and the desire of investors to buy such assets cheaply (see *The Washington Post* 2009a).

---

in 2008, the leverage ratio amounted to about 7%, which broke down into about 3% for equity and 4% for debt.

Prior to the losses incurred by debt holders of Washington Mutual (WaMu), the market perception had been that regulators would protect all debt holders from loss in the event of a bank failure. However, after the WaMu resolution, debt holders appeared to be at risk. If, based on market valuation of its assets, a bank's losses reached beyond the equity cushion, debt holders were subject to losses. As a result, the initial beneficiaries from the issuance of new equity would be the existing debt holders through an increase in the value of their debt rather than the bank's existing equity holders. That fact made it difficult for banks to recapitalize by issuing equity.

Finally, because government policy limited the ability of banks to declare fully expected losses, bank balance sheets were suspect. Lacker (2011, 2) commented:

Securities and Exchange Commission (SEC) regulations prevented reserving for expected future loan losses more than four quarters ahead, even if they were reasonably forecastable. So uncertainty about future loan losses and government rescue policy, combined with limitations in financial reporting, made new equity issuance nearly impossible.

The TALF and PPIP programs to revive securitization and to remove bad assets from the books of banks basically came to nothing. As a result, the credit-market initiatives of the Fed turned to large-scale asset purchases (LSAP). The Fed eventually purchased $1.25 trillion of agency (GSE) MBS, $200 billion of agency debt, and $300 billion of longer-term treasuries. There are no clear measures of the extent to which the Fed's intervention in the housing market lowered the cost of mortgage financing. However, the intervention itself did not revive the housing market. More generally, the failure of the attempts to revive securitization indicated that financial intermediation had shifted back to the banking sector because of the recognition of the need for due diligence of many of the loans that had been carelessly packaged into structured securities.

LEARNING FROM THE CREDIT EXPERIMENT

Initially to avert and later to mitigate a serious recession, the government and the Fed undertook on a massive scale both fiscal stimulus and credit-market interventions. Bernanke (2009c) expressed the promptness with which these government interventions occurred:

History is full of examples in which the policy responses to financial crises have been slow and inadequate, often resulting ultimately in greater economic damage and increased fiscal costs. In this episode, by contrast, policymakers in the United States and around the globe responded with speed and force to arrest a rapidly deteriorating and dangerous situation.

Based on the assumption that government could make up for the shortfall in private spending from full-employment spending, government enacted two fiscal stimulus programs. The first stimulus program – the Bush tax cuts enacted February 13, 2008 – entailed the issuance of $124.4 billion in debt. The second stimulus program – the Obama initiative – entailed the issuance of $787.2 billion in debt (*Congressional Quarterly Weekly* 2009). The *Economic Report of the President* (2010, 51–2) emphasized the magnitude of the "fiscal stimulus ... designed to fill part of the shortfall in aggregate demand caused by the collapse of private demand."

At an estimated cost of $787 billion, the Act [American Recovery and Reinvestment Act of 2009] is the largest countercyclical fiscal action in American history. It provides tax cuts and increases in government spending equivalent to roughly 2 percent of GDP in 2009 and 2¼ percent of GDP in 2010. To put these figures in perspective, the largest expansionary swing in the budget during Franklin Roosevelt's New Deal was an increase in the deficit of about 1½ percent of GDP in fiscal 1936.

Based on the assumption that the government and the central bank could make up for the shortfall in private lending from full-employment lending, government, regulators, and the Fed intervened massively in private credit markets. Congress appropriated $700 billion in TARP money. In explaining the rationale for the Treasury's purchase of preferred stock in banks through the TARP program, *The New York Times* (2008h) explained the prevalent credit-multiplier view of how regulators could jump-start the economy:

Another advantage of the recapitalization plan is ... the Treasury would get more bang for the buck. Because banks have debt-to-equity ratios of 10-to-one or higher, a dollar spent buying an equity stake would support 10 times as many assets as a dollar spent buying up individual securities [from banks].

At the end of 2009, government had distributed the following amounts of TARP funds (*The Washington Post* 2009e):

$208 billion for the Capital Purchase Program to inject capital into banks in return for preferred stock. $87 billion for the Auto Industry Financing Program providing loans to General Motors, Chrysler, and their finance companies. $70 billion to bail out AIG. $50 billion for the Home Affordable Modification Program (HAMP) to avoid home foreclosures by encouraging a reduction in monthly mortgage payments. $40 billion to bail out Citigroup and Bank of America. $30 billion for the Public-Private Investment Program (PPIP) to take the toxic assets off the books of financial institutions. $5 billion to guarantee Citigroup and Bank of America against losses on their mortgages.

As is evident in the interventions portrayed in Table 14.1, "Programs to Stimulate Financial Intermediation as of November 26, 2008," regulators, government, and the Fed undertook multiple initiatives to subsidize financial intermediation. In addition, through numerous programs, the government subsidized the housing market. A tax credit passed by Congress created an $8,000 credit for first-time homebuyers and a $6,500 credit for repeat homebuyers. Through its LSAP programs, the Fed purchased enormous amounts of GSE debt and MBS. The Treasury and the FDIC pushed programs to prevent homeowners from losing their homes through foreclosure. The Treasury used the GSEs to support the housing market. "[T]he U.S. government directly or indirectly, underwrites nine of every 10 new residential mortgages [and the Treasury covers] an unlimited amount of losses at mortgage giants Fannie Mae and Freddie Mac" (*The Wall Street Journal* 2009g).

Motivated by the belief that the 2008–2009 recession originated with losses imposed on banks by their exposure to real estate loans and propagated through a consequent breakdown in the ability of banks to get loans to credit-worthy borrowers, governments and regulators intervened massively in credit markets to spur lending. In addition to specific interventions into credit markets, regulators and the Fed basically extended too big to fail to all financial institutions. They did so to arrest the flight of the cash investors from troubled financial institutions reliant on wholesale funding set off by the retraction of the financial safety net implied by the willingness to allow Lehman to go into bankruptcy. The empirical investigation of Afonso, Kovner, and Schoar (2010, abstract) demonstrated the success of this latter effort:

In the two days after Lehman Brothers' bankruptcy, loan amounts and spreads become much more sensitive to borrower characteristics. In particular, poorly performing large banks see an increase in spreads of 24 basis points, while borrowing 1% less, on average. Once the bailout of American International Group (AIG) is announced, these spreads return to pre-crisis levels likely as a response to the government's implicit support.

If the problem was the failure of banks to lend to credit-worthy borrowers willing to spend, the scale of Fed and government intervention should have revived both lending and the economy. In the event, the loans and leases of all U.S. commercial banks declined steadily from around $7,250 billion in fall 2008 to around $6,500 billion in March 2009.[8] That fact is consistent with a recession like the others in the post–World War II period caused by restrictive monetary policy (Chapter 8). Despite the vast intervention to assure the flow of credit, the country suffered a recession as severe as any in the post-War period. In the 2008–2009 recession, employment in the non-farm business sector fell 7 percent (2007Q4 to 2009Q2). By comparison, in the severe 1981–1982 recession, it fell only 3 percent (1981Q3 to 1982Q4).

MARKET OR GOVERNMENT FAILURE?

The credit-cycle view and its Keynesian cousin, termed here the market-disorder view, place the blame for cyclical fluctuations on violent shifts in the expectations of investors and businesspeople – shifts that occur independently of whether the central bank follows a rule that allows the price system to work. These alternations in optimism and pessimism about the

---

[8] After the passage of the immediate crisis, Bernanke (2010b) testified:

Despite their stronger financial positions, banks' lending to both households and businesses has continued to fall. The decline in large part reflects sluggish loan demand and the fact that many potential borrowers no longer qualify for credit, both results of a weak economy.

future overwhelm the stabilizing properties of the price system. At the same time, the failure of the price system to stabilize economic activity provides an opening for government intervention into the economy to make up for the shortfalls in private spending and in private lending relative to their full-employment levels.

According to the credit-cycle view, in recession, a financial system rendered dysfunctional by the collapse of a bubble in asset prices prevents the transfer of control over resources from savers to credit-worthy borrowers. The incentive furnished by a low real interest rate to transfer consumption from the future to the present is overwhelmed by pessimism about the future. Accordingly, central banks can make up the shortfall in lending from the full-employment level through taking private debt onto their balance sheets. Analogously, according to the Keynesian view, governments can make up the shortfall in spending from the full-employment level through deficit spending.

In the 2008–2009 recession, policy makers responded based both on a credit-cycle and Keynesian view of the world. According to the 2010 *Economic Report of the President*, the 2008–2009 recession was an example of good play but an even worse hand.[9] In a section titled "The Unprecedented Policy Response" in chapter 2 ("Rescuing the Economy from the Great Recession"), *The Economic Report of the President* (2010, 46) stated:

Given the magnitude of the shocks that hit the economy in the fall of 2008 and the winter of 2009, the downturn could have turned into a second Great Depression. That it has not is a tribute to the aggressive and effective policy response.

The *Economic Report* (2010, 47, 49) characterized monetary policy (as opposed to credit policy) as contractionary:

Conventional interest rate policy ... could do little to deal with the enormous disruptions to credit markets.... Statistical estimates suggest that based on the Federal Reserve's usual response to inflation and unemployment, the subdued level of inflation and the weak state of the economy would have led the central bank to reduce its target for the funds rate by about an additional 5 percentage points [below zero] if it could have (Rudebusch 2009).... As a result, monetary policy is in fact unusually tight given the state of the economy.

The absence of any mention of money creation as an effective means of providing monetary stimulus at the zero lower bound on the short-term interest rate highlighted the presumed impotence of monetary policy. Accordingly, "efforts to stabilize the financial system have been a central

---

[9] The terminology is from Velde (2004).

part of the policy response" (*Economic Report* 2010, 49). Through its enumeration of the numerous programs designed to "increase credit flows," the
Economic Report highlighted the focus of policy on programs designed to
increase the flow of credit (see *Economic Report* 2010, 49–50).

The purpose of the government interventions into credit markets and
the economy that began with TAF in December 2007 and with the Bush
fiscal stimulus in February 2008 was to prevent a serious recession. Despite
the scale of these interventions, the economy went into a prolonged, deep
recession. Later, policy makers would redefine their mission from preventing a recession to preventing the recurrence of the Great Depression. It is
certainly possible that in fall 2008 if regulators had forced large banks like
Citibank and Bank of America into immediate liquidation, the recession
would have been significantly more severe. However, the issue remains of
why the economy experienced a severe recession despite prompt, vigorous intervention of the government and the Fed to stimulate spending and
credit flows.

The answer given here is that policy makers misdiagnosed the cause of
the recession. The fact that lending declined despite massive government
intervention into credit markets indicated that the decline in bank lending
arose not as a cause but as a response to the recession, which produced both
a decline in the demand for loans and an increase in the riskiness of lending. In their efforts to stimulate the economy, policy makers would have
been better served by concentrating on maintaining significant growth in
money as an instrument for maintaining growth in the dollar expenditure
of the public rather than on reviving financial intermediation.

HOW EXTENSIVELY SHOULD THE CENTRAL BANK
INTERVENE IN THE ECONOMY?

Prior to fall 2008, a central bank chose one of two objectives. It could target
either the exchange rate or domestic economic conditions, including the
inflation rate. In either case, the central bank was the unique institution
charged with controlling the chosen objective. The central bank did not rely
on government intervention in specific markets to achieve either exchange-
rate or price-level objectives. If the central bank targeted the exchange rate,
it did not rely on exchange controls, multiple exchange rates, tariffs, quotas, or other administrative measures. If the central bank targeted the inflation rate, it did not rely on wage and price controls, guideposts, anti-trust
actions, or special intervention into the wage- and price-setting decisions
of firms. The central bank did not allocate credit either through subsidized

lending at the discount window or quotas on the credit that individual banks can extend.

Given the extensive intervention by central banks starting in fall 2008 into financial markets both in terms of bailing out insolvent financial institutions and in terms of allocating credit, the appropriate role of a central bank is now unsettled. The former consensus that a modern central bank could achieve its objectives while allowing the market to allocate credit has disappeared. Understanding the 2008–2009 recession will shape the future nature of central banking. The question remains of whether central banks will return to a role consistent with the market allocation of resources or whether they will remain heavily involved in the operation of credit markets.

SIXTEEN

Evaluating Policy

What Are the Relevant Counterfactuals?

Popular discourse explains the 2008–2009 recession by reference to the Depression. In the Depression, supposedly, the failure of speculative investments undertaken by banks threatened bank solvency. Panicked depositors ran the banks; the Fed did nothing; the financial system collapsed; and the economy crashed. The story then shifts to the present in which again risky investments wounded banks, which restricted credit and supposedly pushed the economy into recession. This time, however, governments and central banks saved the banks from a panicked run and prevented the recurrence of the Great Depression.[1]

A *New York Times* (2010a) editorial, which concerned the Obama administration's proposed tax on large banks to generate revenue in an amount equal to the $120 billion of TARP money invested in banks, expressed this view of the 2008–2009 recession:

> [T]he crisis spawned by banks' recklessness cost the country a lot more than $120 billion. Any calculation must also include the deepest recession since the 1930s and the loss of more than seven million jobs.... The crisis occurred because banks that had grown too big to fail came too close to failure – driven by a reckless pursuit of risk and profit. Credit froze, and the government was forced to put enormous public resources at their disposal to keep them afloat.

Likewise, in the Depression, a consensus existed that the risk taking of greedy bankers led to economic decline. Later, Friedman and Schwartz (1963a) produced a reappraisal that emphasized monetary contraction. In the Great Inflation that lasted from 1965 until the Volcker disinflation in

---

[1] Chairman Bernanke (2010a, 1) wrote:

> [I]n contrast to the 1930s, policymakers around the world worked assiduously to stabilize the financial system. As a result, although the consequences of the financial crisis have been painfully severe, the world was spared an even worse cataclysm that could have rivaled or surpassed the Great Depression.

1983, a consensus that blamed the market power of corporations and unions for inflation led to the wage and price controls imposed in 1971 (Hetzel 2008b). Only after the Volcker disinflation and the control of inflation by central banks without periodic recourse to bouts of high unemployment did a consensus develop that emphasized monetary factors as the determinants of trend inflation. Just as subsequent scholarship changed the popular understanding of the Depression and the Great Inflation, it is likely that subsequent scholarship will change the understanding of the 2008–2009 recession.

MONEY CREATION VERSUS CREDIT-MARKET INTERVENTION

A policy counterfactual for the 2008–2009 recession would be for the Fed to have focused on money creation rather credit allocation. Such a policy would have emphasized the liability side of the Fed's balance sheet rather than manipulation of the asset side. It would have entailed a quantitative easing strategy with stable nominal expenditure as the objective, money growth as an informational variable, and reserves creation as an instrument varied without extraneous constraints. Such a policy would have required a clearly articulated set of systematic procedures (a rule).

Earlier, in 2003, when the issue of disinflation and the zero lower bound (ZLB) arose, the Richmond Fed had urged such a strategy on the FOMC. If the FOMC had articulated this strategy to the public in 2003 and then had taken it off the shelf in September 2008, the financial markets and the public would have been reassured that the Fed was in control. Implementation of policy as a rule would have stabilized expectations and at least mitigated the gloom that characterized late 2008 and 2009. Instead, actual policy, based as it was on the conjectured collapse of the financial system with an ensuing Great Depression and implemented as it was in a chaotic and fitful way, created fear and confusion.

In 2003, Al Broaddus (Board of Governors, *Transcripts of the Federal Open Market Committee*, June 24–25, 2003, 33–5), president of the Richmond Fed, urged the FOMC to adopt a strategy for operating at the ZLB:[2]

[C]onfronting deflation just like confronting inflation involves a credibility problem.... Moreover, unlike inflation, the credibility problem in dealing with deflation is compounded by the zero bound on nominal interest rates.... [D]eflation has the potential to create deflation expectations and actual deflation simply because people may doubt that we can and will use monetary policy to combat

---

[2]   Marvin Goodfriend was the senior policy adviser at the Richmond Fed.

deflation effectively at the zero bound. My concern is that waiting to say or think about how we would deliver further monetary stimulus if rates were to fall to zero could in some circumstances lead the public to conclude that we can't do it.... [T]hat's why I think it's essential that we begin to talk about this.... [C]ommon sense tells us ... that at some point a determined expansion of the monetary base has to be effective against deflation at the zero bound. If that were not the case, we could eliminate all taxes, and the government could permanently finance its operations with money creation alone.... [T]he bang for the buck of quantitative policy at the zero bound at this point is anybody's guess.... [T]here is at least the possibility that we might have to expand our balance sheet enormously – well beyond its normal steady-state size – to be effective.

Further, since short-term government securities are perfect substitutes for the base at the zero bound, we probably would have to accomplish any such expansion through purchases of longer-term securities, first government securities and then private securities. But that ... would require us to have an exit strategy for draining large quantities of the monetary base once the deflation has been broken – if in fact earlier we had to increase the base substantially. Since we would be selling long-term bonds back to the public in volume at more normal 3 or 4 percent rates, after having purchased them at rates near zero, we could face a substantial capital loss. Conceivably, in a really unusual situation, we could have insufficient assets in our portfolio to bring the base back down. In that latter situation, we would presumably have to have some arrangement with the Treasury to recapitalize us with short-term government debt to allow us to complete the draining operations.... [U]ntil we work through this "what next" scenario and communicate a credible strategy, addressing it to the public at some point, I think our contingency plans for confronting deflation will be incomplete. In my view, that would be a serious omission.... We don't have a stash of credibility as deflation fighters yet. If we delay thinking about and developing a strategy for dealing with further disinflation and it continues – and especially if it accelerates – we could wind up with a sizable credibility deficit.

For the FOMC to have acted on the Richmond proposal to develop a publicly articulated contingency for the implementation of monetary policy in the event that the ZLB constraint became binding, the chairman would have had to depart from the policy of discretion to allow the FOMC to discuss monetary policy as a strategy. Such a departure has never been countenanced, either because FOMC chairmen see it as diminishing their control of FOMC decision making or because they believe that discretion is superior to policy with rule-like characteristics. However, if the FOMC had been willing to take up the Richmond proposal to formulate policy in the event that the ZLB constraint became binding, the FOMC would not have been placed in the situation described by Wessel (2009): "In a fast-breaking crisis that demands a prompt, decisive response, waiting for a committee to reach a consensus can be a mistake." Under the Richmond proposal, the Fed would have retained its federal structure in that decision making in fall 2008 would not have been given over under the 13(3) provisions of the Federal Reserve Act basically to two individuals – Ben Bernanke as chairman of the Board of Governors and Timothy Geithner as president of the New York Fed, with the board approving their actions.

As shown by the Bernanke and James citation in Chapter 6 ascribing the contrasting economic fortunes of countries in the Depression to their adherence to or early departure from the gold standard, as an academic, Bernanke had accepted the professional near-consensus about the monetary causes of the Great Recession. He had argued for a credit channel, that is, dysfunction in financial intermediation, as a force propagating the declines in nominal expenditure produced by deflationary monetary policy to declines in the real sector. In 2008, Bernanke's academic work suggested that he would have found it reasonable to pursue the quantitative-easing policy outlined in the Broaddus citation earlier in this chapter, albeit with an explicit inflation target to discipline inflationary expectations. In criticizing the Bank of Japan (BoJ) for not using money creation to stimulate aggregate demand, Bernanke (2000, 158–9) had written about the need for the BoJ "to stimulate the economy":

First – despite the apparent liquidity trap – monetary policymakers retain the power to increase nominal aggregate demand and the price level. Second, increased nominal spending and rising prices will lead to increases in real economic activity.

The general argument that the monetary authorities can increase aggregate demand and prices, even if the nominal interest rate is zero, is as follows: Money, unlike other forms of government debt, pays zero interest and has infinite maturity. The monetary authorities can issue as much money as they like. Hence, if the price level was truly independent of money issuance, then the monetary authorities could use the money they create to acquire indefinite quantities of goods and assets. This is manifestly impossible in equilibrium.... This is an elementary argument, but ... it is quite corrosive of claims of monetary impotence.

[A]n inflation target ... would give private decision makers more information about the objectives of monetary policy.... [A] quantitative inflation target ... would have avoided many of the current troubles, I believe, if it had been in place earlier.

As long as the Fed stabilizes expected inflation, with the funds rate at the zero lower bound, the price system will still work in that changes in the degree of optimism or pessimism about the future will cause markets to forecast a shorter or longer period of a zero funds rate and, correspondingly, a relatively higher or lower real bond rate. There is then a positive "long-term" natural interest rate consistent with full employment. However, the "short-term" natural rate could be negative. That is, a return to full employment within, say, four quarters, could require a negative real interest rate. The central bank can then stimulate expenditure (raise the short-term natural rate) by increasing the real money balances held by the public. There will be some "high" level of real money balances (some very aggressive expansion of the money stock) that makes this short-term natural rate positive.

INSTILLING FEAR OR CONFIDENCE?

Paul Volcker, who became FOMC chairman in August 1979, based the post–October 6, 1979, operating procedures on the quantity-theory premise that through its control over money creation the central bank controls the dollar expenditure of the public (Hetzel 2008b). A sustained, low rate of money growth would produce a low rate of growth of dollar expenditure and, ultimately, low inflation. That premise rested not on the stability of money demand but rather on the assumption that the price level serves to endow the nominal stock of money with the real purchasing power desired by the public. Because of its monopoly control over the monetary base and, as a result, its control over the nominal money stock, the central bank is the unique institution responsible for control of nominal (dollar) expenditure and inflation.

In the spirit of the Volcker disinflation, in fall 2008, the Fed could have announced a policy of monetary stimulus. In the past, all severe recessions have been succeeded by robust recoveries. The Fed could have announced a path for nominal expenditure growth consistent in the short run with the historic pattern of V-shaped recoveries. The long-run path would be consistent with an estimate of trend real growth plus an announced inflation target.[3] Of course, there is no assurance of hitting a path for nominal expenditure growth over a short period of time like a quarter. However, in the stop-go period, nominal output growth followed monetary accelerations and decelerations with an approximate lag of two quarters (Hetzel 2008b, figure 23.2). To have made the procedures credible, the Fed would have had to commit to large changes in the monetary base. The monetary base or bank reserves simply would have been an instrument with nominal expenditure as the relevant target. To contain inflationary expectations, the Fed also would have needed to announce an explicit inflation target.

Figure 16.1 shows the behavior of nominal and real GDP growth. In the first part of the decade, the FOMC maintained the growth rate of nominal GDP at a level that produced the near price stability of almost 1 percent

[3]   The historical precedent for such a policy is the vigorous recovery from the March 1933 business cycle trough with exogenous monetary base growth provided by gold inflows (Chapter 5).

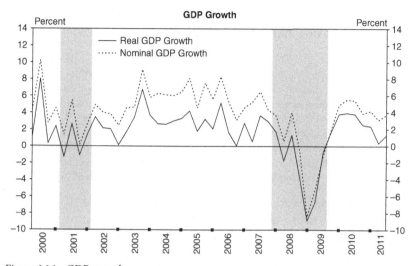

Figure 16.1. GDP growth.

Note: GDP growth is quarter-over-quarter change at annualized rate. Data from Bureau of Economic Analysis via Haver Analytics. Shaded areas indicate NBER recessions. Heavy tick marks indicate the fourth quarter.

in 2003 and early 2004. Starting in 2004, in response to the decision to abandon price stability in favor of 2 percent or 2 percent plus inflation, the FOMC maintained a correspondingly higher growth rate of nominal GDP (Hetzel 2008b, ch. 20). In mid-2006, nominal GDP growth declined moderately, and then in mid-2007 it began a steep descent.

A fundamental hypothesis of the quantity theory is that the central bank can sustain nominal output growth at business cycle frequencies. That hypothesis follows from a Phillips curve in which the relationship between inflation and output is not hard-wired. A focus on monetary policy as opposed to credit policy during the 2008–2009 recession would have led the FOMC to a policy of money creation sufficient to prevent the actual significant decline in nominal expenditure. The counterfactual of what would have happened to real GDP raises the controversial issue of the nature of the Phillips curve. At a minimum, a policy of money creation to sustain the growth rate of nominal expenditure when the funds rate reaches the floor of zero would work to prevent the Fed from implementing a contractionary monetary policy.

The actual policy followed instilled disquiet and fear rather than confidence. On Thursday, September 18, 2008, FOMC Chairman Bernanke and Treasury Secretary Paulson briefed congressional leaders (*The Wall Street*

Journal 2008h) and asked for "a new facility to hold auctions and buy up distressed assets from financial institutions:"

> Mr. Bernanke gave a "chilling" description of current conditions.... He described the frozen credit markets, busted commercial paper markets and attacks on investment banks. The financial condition of some major institutions was "uncertain," he said. "If we don't do this, we risk an uncertain fate," Mr. Bernanke added. He said if the problem wasn't corrected the U.S. economy could enter a deep, multi-year recession akin to Japan's lost decade of the 1990s or what Sweden endured in the early 1990s when a surge in bad loans plagued the economy and sent unemployment to 12%.... Friday, Messrs. Bernanke and Paulson instilled fear into lawmakers' hearts during a round of briefings with their dire warnings about the cost of inaction.

According to another account (*International Herald Tribune* 2008), "'If we don't do this,' Bernanke said... 'we may not have an economy on Monday.'" According to a later account by *The Wall Street Journal* reporter David Wessel (2009):

> "No economy has ever faced the financial meltdown we're facing without undergoing a major recession," he [Bernanke] told the stunned leadership behind closed doors. "Without congressional action, it would be deep and prolonged." Looking back, he [Bernanke] said soberly, "We came very close in October to Depression 2.0."

Dominique Strauss-Kahn (*Financial Times* 2009f), managing director of the International Monetary Fund, said shortly after September 15, 2008, "Intensifying solvency concerns about a number of the largest US-based and European financial institutions have pushed the global financial system to the brink of systemic meltdown." The metaphor of a fireman putting out a fire captures the idea of regulators preventing an exogenously arising bank run from causing the collapse of the financial system. In an article titled "Fireman Hank," the editor of the *Financial Times* Lionel Barber (2010) wrote that the book written by Henry Paulson, Treasury secretary at the time of the Lehman collapse, "[R]eminds us not merely of the failure of markets but of government's decisive role in rescuing the system from itself."

FOLLOWING THE PENN CENTRAL EXAMPLE

The Fed's defense of policy after the Lehman bankruptcy September 15, 2008, was that it rescued the financial system from collapse and thereby rescued the economy. The Fed's counterfactual was that of allowing the collapse of the financial system and thus of the economy. However, allowing a collapse of the financial system was a straw man. A more relevant counterfactual is that of using the discount window to allow banks to borrow to

avoid failures through runs but for a limited duration before regulator intervention. This policy would not have compromised to the same extent the
basic principle articulated by Bagehot that the central bank should restrict
lending to liquidity support rather than solvency support.

A counterfactual to the detailed intervention by the Fed into credit
markets after the Lehman bankruptcy is its response to the Penn Central
bankruptcy in June 1970 when cash investors suddenly became uncertain
over whether AAA-rated commercial paper issued by blue chip corporations was default free. In response to the disruption in the commercial
paper market, corporations drew on their lines of credit at banks and the
Fed accommodated the increased demand for reserves through lending
freely at the discount window.

Swagel (2009, 32) pointed out that such a result would have run counter
to the desire in fall 2008 to encourage financial intermediation by strengthening bank balance sheets:

What we did not realize would occur were two things: the breaking of the buck by
the Reserve Fund, and the reaction of foreign investors.... We could have known
better ... that foreign investors were not prepared for Lehman to collapse.... The
events together led to a run on money market mutual funds, and this in turn caused
commercial paper markets to freeze. If left unstopped, this would have forced issuers of commercial paper to turn to their backup lines of credit – meaning that banks
would have been forced to massively fund these lines simultaneously under circumstances that were never contemplated and then hoard capital against those lines.

Simultaneously with lending freely at the discount window, the Fed could
have let the funds rate go to zero as a consequence of undertaking massive open-market purchases to satisfy the increased collective demand for
the dollar reserves of the banking system. The discount window would
have been available to counter the stresses placed on individual banks by
the flight to safe institutions set off with the Lehman bankruptcy and the
abrupt retraction of the financial safety net. A contemporaneous headline
in *The Wall Street Journal* (2008m) captured the resulting flight of deposits from weak to strong financial institutions: "Deposits Are Flowing to
Healthier Banks: Customers Put Cash in Institutions That Avoided Worst of
Credit Mess – and Yank It From Those That Didn't." The article started, "As
the U.S. government wrestles with deciding which battered banks are worth
helping and which aren't, bank customers are voting with their deposits."

Individual banks threatened by the withdrawal of wholesale funding by
cash investors would have borrowed at the discount window. Regulators
could then have effectively performed in fall 2008 the (SCAP) stress test

they performed in spring 2009 (Chapter 15).[4] They could have given banks a fixed amount of time to raise funds to repay discount-window borrowing. That is, they would have initially granted banks access to primary credit, but after a month of borrowing they would have changed the status of that borrowing from primary to secondary credit.[5]

Failure to replace lending classified as secondary credit with market funding would have resulted in regulators placing a bank in conservatorship. Under conservatorship, the bank continues to operate but with a majority of regulators on its board who supervise either the reorganization or eventual liquidation of the bank.[6] The results of the SCAP exercise performed in spring 2009, which assumed a worse economy than existed in fall 2008, indicated that almost all large banks were healthy enough to have survived market discipline.

What then could the regulators have done with the problem institutions? There were alternatives that would have at least limited the moral hazard

---

[4] Even earlier, after August 2007, U.S. banks turned to the Federal Home Loan Banks (FHLBs) to replace funding lost from the flight of the cash investors. Without the FHLBs, U.S. banks would have been forced into the discount window where their borrowing would have been monitored by bank regulators.

Similarly, in December 2007, the Fed established swap lines with the European Central Bank, the Swiss National Bank, and a number of other central banks. These central banks then lent the dollars to their domestic banks suffering dollar outflows due to the flight of the cash investors. In December 2007, the Fed also opened the Term Auction Facility (TAF), which lent dollars to the New York offices of foreign banks.

[5] Primary credit is available to banks experiencing liquidity problems and is available for short periods of time. The Board of Governor's Web site offers the following explanation of secondary credit available from the discount window (http://www.federalreserve.gov/monetarypolicy/bst_lendingdepository.htm):

Secondary credit ... is extended on a very short-term basis, typically overnight, at a rate 50 basis points above the primary credit rate. In contrast to primary credit, there are restrictions on the uses of secondary credit extensions. Secondary credit is available to meet backup liquidity needs when its use is consistent with a timely return by the borrower to a reliance on market sources of funding or the orderly resolution of a troubled institution. Secondary credit may not be used to fund an expansion of the borrower's assets. Moreover, the secondary credit program entails a higher level of Reserve Bank administration and oversight than the primary credit program. Reserve Banks typically apply higher haircuts on collateral pledged to secure secondary credit. In addition, the liquidity position of secondary credit borrowers is monitored closely, and the Federal Reserve typically is in close contact with the borrower's primary federal regulator.

[6] *The New York Times* (2009a) wrote that

William Seidman, a former chairman of the Federal Deposit Insurance Corporation ... said that the government should simply take control of the banks it tries to rescue. "When we did things like this, we took the banks over," Mr. Seidman said. "This is a huge, undeserved gift to the present shareholders."

incentives of outright bailouts of financial institutions and their debtors. With AIG, the regulator of AIG Financial Products (the Office of Thrift Supervision) could have taken over the London unit issuing the credit default swaps (CDS) and put the insurance part into bankruptcy. The solvency of AIG's insurance subsidiaries was never in question (Chapter 14). That action would have wiped out AIG's stockholders while preserving value for reimbursing the Fed for possible losses on AIG's credit default swap portfolio.[7]

The investment banks like Goldman that experienced runs by the cash investors engaging in the RPs (repurchase agreements) that financed their collateral but were solvent could, as they did, become bank holding companies with access to the Fed's discount window. Lehman would still have had to go into bankruptcy. If a large bank like Citibank had not been able to extricate itself from the discount window by raising additional capital, the Fed could have continued to lend long-term through the window but could have enforced draconian asset sales to reduce the size of the bank. These actions would not have prevented the shift in funds by the cash investors from financially weak institutions to the clearly too-big-to-fail institutions, but they would have prevented the wholesale expansion of the financial safety net that did occur through blanket guarantees on all liabilities of all financial institutions.

KEEPING FISCAL POLICY AT THE TREASURY AND MONETARY POLICY AT THE FED

In 2008, the quantum leap in the involvement of the Fed in bailouts and credit allocation pushed it heavily into fiscal as opposed to monetary policy. The sea change in what the Fed considered to constitute standard monetary policy is evident from the prior skepticism of Bernanke (2000, 164) toward placing assets other than government securities into the portfolio of a central bank. With short-term interest rates at zero, to stimulate spending, Bernanke had urged the Bank of Japan (BoJ) to acquire long-term government bonds as a way of exchanging illiquid assets for money, but he had

---

[7] The problem with the swap portfolio was the need for additional cash collateral. Even though AIG had taken the same side on all its credit default swap bets, basically insuring against a sharp decline in house prices, none of the insured MBS had defaulted with the need for cash payments. AIG insured only AAA-rated MBS, and as of fall 2010 none had yet defaulted. Still, given the collateral requirements behind the CDS, the Fed lacked leverage to make the counterparty financial institutions like Goldman and Credit Agricole take haircuts.

dismissed the possibility of acquiring private debt for reasons of political economy:

In thinking about nonstandard open-market operations, it is useful to separate those that have some fiscal component from those that do not. By a fiscal component I mean some implicit subsidy, such as would arise, for example, if the BOJ purchased nonperforming bank loans at face value (this is of course equivalent to a fiscal bailout of the banks, financed by the central bank). This sort of money-financed "gift" to the private sector would expand aggregate demand for the same reasons that any money-financed transfer does. Although such operations are perfectly sensible from the standpoint of economic theory, I doubt very much that we will see anything like this in Japan, if only because it is more straightforward for the Diet to vote subsidies or tax cuts directly. Nonstandard open-market operations with a fiscal component, even if legal, would be correctly viewed as an end run around the authority of the legislature, and so are better left in the realm of theoretical curiosities.

Swagel (2009, 26) also made the point that bailouts are fiscal, not monetary, policy.[8] As such, they are properly the province of the political system, not the central bank:

[W]ork [on "break the glass options"] evolved from a recurring theme of the input we received from market participants over the prior year [prior to the September 15, 2008, Lehman bankruptcy], which was that the solution to the financial crisis was for Treasury to simply buy up and hold the "toxic" assets on bank balance sheets.... All of these options [for dealing "with a financial sector crisis arising from an undercapitalized system"], however, would require Congressional action – this would move the focus of financial markets policy back from the Fed to the Treasury, which would be appropriate in what was a problem reflecting inadequate capital rather than insufficient liquidity. But there was no prospect for getting any of this [from Congress].

After the Lehman bankruptcy, regulators complained about the absence of a conservatorship for financial institutions not chartered as a bank. However, if bankruptcy is an undesirable way of dealing with the failure of a nonbank financial institution, why had not Congress, encouraged by a Fed sensitive to the constitutional prerogative of Congress to control fiscal policy, already created such an alternative? Perhaps part of the answer is that congressmen assumed that the Fed would handle such bankruptcies off-budget so as to spare them constituent criticism.

Swagel (2009, 25) commented on the Bear Stearns bailout:

[T]he Fed acted to provide JP Morgan with financing to purchase Bear Stearns.... [M]any people (at least in Washington, DC) did not understand the implications of

---

[8] See Goodfriend (1994; 2011); Hetzel (1997); and Hetzel 2008b, ch. 16 "Appendix: Seigniorage and Credit Allocation."

non-recourse lending from the Fed.... [I]t took some time before the political class realized that the Fed had not just lent JP Morgan money to buy Bear Stearns, but in effect now owned the downside of a portfolio of $29 billion of dodgy assets.

Having decided to bail out Bear Stearns, the Fed could have used that event to clarify the issues arising from its involvement in fiscal policy to force Congress to deal with the failure of a nonbank financial institution (Goodfriend 2011). *The Washington Post* (2008a) wrote shortly after the collapse of Bear Stearns:

With its March 14 decision to make a special loan to Bear Stearns and a decision two days later to become an emergency lender to all of the major investment firms, the central bank abandoned 75 years of precedent under which it offered direct backing only to traditional banks. Inside the Fed and out, there is a realization that those moves amounted to crossing the Rubicon, setting the stage for a deeper involvement in the little-regulated markets for capital that have come to dominate the financial world. Leaders of the central bank had no master plan when they took those actions, no long-term strategy for taking a more assertive role regulating Wall Street. They were focused on the immediate crisis.... Fed leaders knew that they were setting a precedent that would indelibly affect perceptions of how the central bank would act in a crisis. Now that the central bank has intervened in the workings of Wall Street, all sorts of players in the financial markets will assume that it could happen again. Major investment banks might be willing to take on more risk, assuming that the Fed will be there to bail them out if the bets go wrong.... The parties that do business with investment banks might be less careful about monitoring whether the bank will be able to honor obscure financial contracts. That would eliminate a key form of self-regulation for investment banks.

RETHINKING THE FED'S REJECTION OF RULES FOR DISCRETION

Any proposal for severely restricting the financial safety net and eliminating too-big-to-fail (TBTF) depends on the ability of government to commit credibly to such a policy. Credible commitment would require removing the bail-out decision from the hands of bank regulators including the Fed. If credible, such commitment would avoid the worst of all outcomes – nonintervention when the market expects intervention as occurred in summer and fall 1998 when markets were surprised by the failure of the IMF to bail out Russia (Hetzel 2008b, ch. 16) and when the Fed failed to bail out Lehman Brothers as it had done with Bear Stearns.

The Treasury should make the decision whether to bail out a financial institution. Placing responsibility for the rescue of troubled financial institutions with the Treasury, under strictures approved by Congress, would bring policy into conformity with the Constitution, which gives Congress responsibility for fiscal policy.[9] A decision by the Secretary of the Treasury to bail out a large bank would make clear the fiscal nature of the decision. Just as in the Depression, the United States could set up a Reconstruction Finance Corporation that would issue debt and purchase equity in troubled banks (Todd 1996). Although the political system has bailed out private corporations, such bailouts are the exception. Because they are controversial, government bailouts generate the public discussion that provides for accountability.[10]

Evaluation of the feasibility of such a proposal requires a counterfactual of what a financial system would look like with a severely limited safety net. The large amount of funds in government and prime money-market mutual funds holding short-term government securities and prime commercial paper is evidence of the extensive demand by investors for debt instruments that are both liquid and safe. In the absence of the safety net, these investors would constitute a huge market for financial institutions marketing themselves as safe because of high capital ratios and a diversified asset portfolio of high-grade loans and securities. Effectively, the market would create a parallel narrow banking system.

These institutions would constitute a large enough core of run-proof institutions so that in the event of a financial panic creditors could withdraw funds from risky institutions and deposit them in the safe institutions.[11] The risky institutions would then have to create contracts that did not allow withdrawal on demand. For example, they could issue extendible six-month commercial paper. Hedge funds, which are not covered by the financial safety net, have powers to restrict investors from

---

[9] Barney Frank [D-MA] stated in *The Washington Post* (2008e):

   No one in this democracy – unelected – should have $800 billion to dispense as he sees fit.... It may be that there is so much bad debt out there clogging our system that we may have to have some intervention. But it shouldn't be the unilateral decision of the chairman of the Federal Reserve with the backing of the secretary of the Treasury.

[10] Sprague (1986, 5) wrote:

   The four congressionally approved bailouts were for Chrysler Corporation, Lockheed Corporation, New York City, and Conrail.... Each was preceded by extensive public debate.... The contrast between the publicly discussed congressional bailouts and the behind-the-scenes bank rescues by FDIC has generated a debate that seems destined to continue so long as we have megabanks in the nation that might fail.

[11] Because the safe banks would have an incentive to hold only assets for which they had done due diligence rather than complicated, opaque financial products, their accounting would be more persuasive to creditors. "'When investors don't have full and honest information, they tend to sell everything, both the good and bad assets,'" said Janet Tavakoli, president of Tavakoli Structured Finance (*The New York Times* 2008m).

making redemptions on demand. Depositors at the safe banks would earn a low rate of return, but they, not the taxpayer, would be the ones paying for the financial safety.

To credibly restrict the financial safety net, the regulators must place into conservatorship any bank that experiences a run (Hetzel 2009a). If there is an immediate need for the equivalent of debtor-in-possession financing after a bank enters conservatorship, the Treasury would supply funds from the Exchange Stabilization Fund or transfer Treasury tax and loan accounts to the bank.[12] Under conservatorship, regulators would assume a majority of seats on the bank's board of directors. The directors would then decide whether to sell, liquidate, break up, or rehabilitate the bank. By law, this conservatorship would have to eliminate the value of equity and impose an immediate haircut on all holders of debt and uninsured deposits. Thereafter, as long as the bank remained in conservatorship, its existing deposits and debt would be fully insured.

After being placed into conservatorship and after the haircuts imposed on holders of the bank's debt, the bank could still be insolvent as indicated by a lack of bidders for the bank without government financial assistance. In this event, regulators would levy a special assessment on banks to recapitalize the failed institution. The specific mechanism would involve an elaboration of the ideas of Calomiris (1989), who examined the criteria that led to successful state bank insurance programs in the nineteenth century. The FDIC would divide banks into groups of, say, ten, with the ten largest in one group, the next ten largest in another group, and so on. The individual banks would pay deposit premia into their own fund and would be subject to an assessment to replenish the fund if a bank in their group required FDIC funds.

Each group would have an advisory board that would make recommendations to the FDIC for its group about regulating risk, setting the level of insurance premia, and designing risk-based insurance premia. The FDIC,

---

[12] *The New York Times* (1991) noted how the Treasury used its tax and loan accounts to bail out the Bank of New England. Through the contrast with a small Harlem bank (Freedom National) in which uninsured depositors incurred losses with its closure by regulators, the same article drew attention to the practice of too big to fail:

After the Bank of New England and two sister banks were seized by Federal regulators on Jan. 6 [1991], the Federal Deposit Insurance Corporation guaranteed all deposits, even those exceeding the $100,000 legal limit for insured deposits. The agency said that failing to repay completely all depositors of the third-largest banking company in New England would have been catastrophic for the region's economy. Treasury's balance at the Boston bank [Bank of New England] soared to $1.8 billion, helping the bank drastically reduce its dependence on higher-cost loans from the Federal Reserve.

subject to Basel standard minimums, would set individual group capital standards and other regulations to limit risk taking. The incentive would then be for banks in a group to lobby the FDIC to prevent excessive risk taking by the other banks in their group.[13] As a check, the public would see the cost of subordinated debt of each group relative to that of the others.

Under this arrangement, because of the relatively small number of banks in the group, banks could feasibly monitor one another for excessive risk taking, and they would have an incentive to do so. At the same time, there would be too many banks to collude. In the event of a run on a solvent bank, the other banks in the group would possess the information needed to lend to the threatened bank to limit the run just as they did in the pre-Fed clearinghouse era. A demonstrated willingness of banks to support one another would inspire depositor confidence.

Essential to eliminating the ability of government to bail out the creditors of banks would be elimination of the legal authority of the Fed to make discount-window loans.[14] In the event of a financial panic, the Fed

---

[13] In this way, FDIC deposit insurance would become consistent with the common understanding of insurance in which a fund accumulates assets and the directors of the fund impose constraints on risk taking to mitigate moral hazard. The FDIC is in reality the combination of a tax on bank deposits and a government program to pay losses on deposits incurred by bank closings. As explained by William Isaac (2008b), former chairman of the FDIC:

[T]here is no FDIC fund. Anything the FDIC lays out to handle a bank failure must be borrowed by the Treasury.... [P]remiums paid by the banks to the FDIC are a tax to compensate the government for putting its full faith and credit behind bank deposits.

[14] Goodfriend and King (1988) and Schwartz (1992) advocated closing the discount window. One can make the classic argument for the discretion to allow use of the discount window for other than extremely short-lived liquidity needs. In principle, with superior information that comes from its supervisory authority, the Fed can do better with discretion because it can distinguish between desirable intervention to offset nonfundamental runs and undesirable intervention to offset fundamental runs. (The distinction comes from Diamond and Dybvig 1983.) However, in practice, identifying the difference between such runs is problematic. The assumption that the Fed will not bail out a troubled institution is historically counterfactual.

Historically, bank insolvencies have come at difficult times for monetary policy, especially times of high interest rates, for example, the failures of Franklin National in 1974 and Continental Illinois in 1984. The Fed may be reluctant to use its limited political capital with Congress to close a large bank, instead preferring to conserve that capital for situations in which raising the funds rate is politically painful.

A second-best solution to abolition of the discount window to enforce market discipline on banks would be to have real-time disclosure of the identities of banks using the window. Use of the window would then be a last resort for a troubled bank and would signal the need for immediate closure by regulators. Under The Dodd-Frank Wall Street Reform and Consumer Protection Act, the Fed can wait for two years before it must reveal the identity of discount-window borrowers.

would not be passive. It would flood the market with liquidity by undertaking massive purchases of securities in the open market. It would use its payment of interest on bank reserves to maintain its funds-rate target (Goodfriend 2002; Keister et al. 2008).[15]

White (2010, abstract) noted that, under the National Banking System, "inducing more disclosure, marking assets to market, and ensuring prompt closure of insolvent national banks, the Comptroller of the Currency reinforced market discipline." That changed with the creation of a central bank capable of creating bank reserves through a discount window. In the 1920s, the Fed used discount-window lending to keep alive troubled banks. White (2010, 36) reported that as of 1925, "the Fed estimated that 80 percent of the 259 national member banks that had failed since 1920 had been 'habitual borrowers.' This problem was confirmed in later years." After the traumatic experience with the bank failures of the Depression, the Fed used discount-window lending to troubled banks to fulfill its mandate for financial stability. In doing so, it departed from the policy of the Comptroller of the Currency in the National Banking era of using market discipline to limit bank risk taking. The moral hazard problems created by the Fed's financial safety net appeared in force after August 2007.

In addition to closing the discount window, the Fed would have to limit bank daylight overdrafts to a maximum amount given by prearranged collateral posted with it. Because the Federal Home Loan Bank (FHLB) system has assumed the lender-of-last-resort function, legislation should abolish it (Chapter 10). To limit deposit insurance to include only individuals who are neither wealthy nor financially sophisticated, the FDIC would limit payouts on insured deposits at failed banks to a maximum amount per year for an individual Social Security number.[16] Such a payout limitation would

---

[15] Goodfriend and Lacker (1999) explained the role of the Fed's discount window in the safety net and highlighted reasons for the Fed's inability to commit not to lending to insolvent banks. They predicted increased financial market instability and an extension of discount-window lending to nonbank financial intermediaries. As they explained, in principle, the Fed could make use of its discount window contingent on meeting loan covenants that limit excessive risk taking of the sort imposed by at-risk debt holders of private corporations and that banks themselves impose on commercial businesses. In reality, government regulators lack this ability. They must design an objectively verifiable set of criteria to limit risk that works for all banks and in all situations that exist or could exist. The reason is that they must defend their regulations in the political system and must guard against international regulatory competition in which foreign regulators favor their own banks over the banks of other countries. In general, regulators are understandably reluctant to allow a bank to fail and eliminate individuals' livelihoods. Inevitably, they will emphasize the possibility of a bank rectifying its problems given a little more time.

[16] With the Internet, it has become easy to check on the financial health of a bank. See, for example, the Web site of Institutional Risk Analytics. With the disappearance of the

also eliminate the current insurance coverage of brokered CD deposits.[17] Finally, the Fed should eliminate the swap lines, which other central banks use to replace the dollar outflows of their troubled banks.

CREDIT POLICY AND THE FINANCIAL SAFETY NET VERSUS THE CONSTITUTION AND FREE MARKETS

Especially starting in mid-September 2008, when the Fed moved to credit policy as a tool of macroeconomic demand management, Fed policy and the extension of the financial safety net became intertwined. Credit policy focused on undoing the withdrawal of wholesale, uninsured funding from highly leveraged banks with portfolios of problematic mortgage assets. Credit policy also emphasized superseding the market allocation of credit through use of the Fed's portfolio to buy MBS (mortgage-backed securities) and debt from the GSEs (Fannie Mae and Freddie Mac). Given the failure of the aggressive use of credit policy to prevent a prolonged, deep recession, policy makers should examine critically its use.

The current extensive financial safety net, which protects bank creditors from loss, and credit policy, which undoes the market allocation of credit, are incompatible with a system of free enterprise. The last, vast interference with the operation of the market economy, namely, the Nixon price controls, occurred with the encouragement of FOMC Chairman Arthur Burns (Hetzel 2008b, ch. 8). Ironically, the expansionary monetary policy followed by Burns to exploit the existence of price controls caused their breakdown. Shortages of hamburger on store shelves were obvious to shoppers, and pictures of farmers drowning baby chicks appeared in newspapers. The graphs of money growth and inflation featured by Milton Friedman in his *Newsweek* columns made the point that high rates of money growth, not greedy corporations, were responsible for inflation.

Unfortunately for the political economy of free markets, the way in which the financial safety net subverts the market monitoring of risk essential to a capitalist economy is hidden. The misallocation of resources and the excessive risk taking promoted by the financial safety net appear only periodically in financial crises. Inevitably, the popular press scapegoats bankers.

---

financial safety net, banks would compete for depositors by providing accurate information on their financial health to such Web sites.

[17] At present, depositors can receive up to $50 million in deposit insurance by using a broker who divides deposits among many insured banks under a program called Certificate of Deposit Account Registry Service (Mincer 2008).

No doubt bankers are greedy, but they respond rationally to the way in which the safety net skews incentives toward risk taking.

Moreover, both community bankers and Wall Street bankers understand the subsidy offered by the government guarantees of their debt. However, the off-budget provision of that subsidy makes it invisible to taxpayers. Bankers can use the rhetoric of protecting the depositor of modest means to defend deposit insurance. Unlike price controls, which ended up creating opposition from businesses irritated by government intrusion into their price setting, the interference with the operation of a market economy by the financial safety net is invisible to the public but lobbied for by bankers.

What the public does understand is the perverse wealth transfers created by the financial safety net. Those wealth transfers create the impression that the market system is biased in favor of the wealthy. Government bailouts of financial firms appear as bailouts of the wealthy unaccompanied by assistance for the average citizen. Bailouts of banks are primarily bailouts of the uninsured debt holders of banks, and these debt holders are sophisticated investors.[18]

The financial safety net, by sparing the debtors of troubled financial institutions from losses, involves a perverse wealth transfer to those debtors from the general public either as taxpayers or as depositors of healthy banks paying the premiums for FDIC insurance. Wealth transfers are fiscal, not monetary, policy. Wessel (2009) wrote:

In the Great Panic, the Fed emerged as almost a fourth branch of government ..., deciding which financial firms would live and which would die and lending hundreds of billions of dollars and putting taxpayers at risk without having to get congressional approval.... "It's been inappropriate in a democracy," said Barney Frank, the Massachusetts Democrat.

CONCLUDING COMMENT

In the *Time* (2009) "Person of the Year" article devoted to Ben Bernanke, Bernanke stated:

Virtually every large financial firm in the world was in significant danger of going bankrupt. And we knew – and I knew – based on my experience as a policymaker, I knew that if the global financial system were to collapse, in the sense that many of

[18] One blogger tracked down the major bond holders of Citigroup and Bank of America, which received government bailouts in late 2008. Koppenheffer (2009) identified them as Pimco, Vanguard, MetLife, Fidelity (life insurance subsidiary of AIG), Prudential, Dodge & Cox, and TIAA-CREF.

the largest firms were to fail, and the financial sector essentially stopped functioning, I knew that the implications for the global economy would be catastrophic. We would be facing, potentially, another depression of the severity and length of the Depression in the 1930s. And that this was not at all hypothetical.

What would have happened on September 15, 2008, if regulators had allowed the investment banks and a large bank like Citibank to fail catastrophically? Given the reliance of Fed policy makers on discretion in policy making, such a counterfactual seems natural. However, for others, it is also fair to ask how robust the financial system would have been if the Fed had consistently followed a rule allowing market discipline to regulate the risk taking of banks. What if the Fed had followed a rule in the post–World War II period of forcing troubled banks into conservatorship and imposing losses on debt holders by refusing insolvent banks access to the discount window? Moreover, would there have been a serious recession if the Fed had in place a rule for stabilizing the growth of dollar expenditure through the required money creation?

SEVENTEEN

The Business Cycle

Market Instability or Monetary Instability?

The business cycle with its alternation of cyclical expansion and contraction is a recurrent feature of the economy. The human misery associated with contractions or recessions manifests a failure of the price system. But what kind of failure? There are two schools of thought. One school, the market-disorder view, which includes the credit-cycle and Keynesian traditions, takes the failure as endemic to a free market system of economic organization. The opposing school, the monetary-disorder (quantity-theory) view, attributes major cyclical instability to interference by central banks with the operation of the price system.

THE ISSUES THAT DIVIDE ECONOMISTS
INTO DIFFERENT SCHOOLS

There are two fundamental issues in monetary economics. One issue concerns whether the price level is a real or a monetary phenomenon. Does the price level emerge as an aggregation of dollar prices in individual markets in which those dollar prices are determined by real factors affecting supply and demand particular to those markets? Alternatively, does the price level depend on the monetary arrangements of a country, that is, the way in which the central bank controls money creation?

An alternative formulation of this issue is whether there is a clear distinction between the determination of equilibrium values of nominal and of real variables. How does one give empirical content to the rationality postulate, which states that welfare depends only on real, not nominal, variables? In the quantity-theory tradition, the central bank possesses the power to control nominal variables independently of the behavior of real variables. In particular, it can control the nominal expenditure of the public as the sum of trend growth in real output and a targeted value of inflation.

In the Keynesian tradition, there is a hard-wired relationship between nominal and real variables measured by the empirical correlations of the Phillips curve. In the early version of the Phillips curve, that relationship held between trend inflation and the unemployment rate. Later versions posited a structural relationship between fluctuations in inflation and deviations of unemployment from a benchmark value (the NAIRU). These more recent versions reflect the assumption that the central bank can control trend inflation without unemployment trade-offs, but there remain trade-offs between the variability of inflation and unemployment.

The second issue concerns how well the price system works to clear markets. In recession, there are two relevant margins along which individuals substitute. One is intertemporal. Do variations in the real interest rate serve as an adequate flywheel to counter fluctuations in optimism and pessimism about the future so as to maintain aggregate real demand equal to potential output? The real business cycle (RBC) tradition answers with an unequivocal yes (Kydland and Prescott 1982). The quantity-theory tradition provides a contingent yes. Changes in the contemporaneous price of resources in terms of future resources foregone (the real interest rate) can redistribute aggregate demand across time to offset the effect of real shocks provided that the central bank does not interfere with the market determination of the real interest rate through money creation and destruction. The credit-cycle and Keynesian traditions answer this question with an unequivocal no. The real interest rate is a weak reed for moderation of fluctuations in aggregate demand that occur in response to sudden shifts between optimism and pessimism about the future.

The other margin of substitution is between labor and leisure. Do variations in the real wage, which measures the relative price of these variables, work adequately to clear labor markets? The RBC tradition answers affirmatively. In a recession, unemployment increases because workers want to take additional leisure at present and work harder in the future. Advocates of the other traditions argue for stickiness in nominal wages that keeps real wages at an undesirably high level. However, there is no agreement among these latter groups over whether declines in real wages reduce unemployment. The quantity-theory tradition, which attributes major recessions to monetary contraction, argues for wage stickiness as a component of price stickiness that generates monetary nonneutrality. The credit-cycle tradition, which emphasizes "imbalances," argues for the need for real wages to decline. The Keynesian tradition, which dismisses the ability of the price system to equilibrate macroeconomic activity, argues for wage stickiness; but, at least in early formulations, it dismissed wage flexibility as an important equilibrating force.

Disagreement among views comes to a head during recessions with the occurrence of low or, perhaps, zero short-term nominal interest rates. The issue becomes, "How can a recession occur with the presumption of expansionary monetary policy evidenced by low short-term interest rates?" The quantity-theory tradition highlights a precipitating monetary shock that reduces the short-term real interest rate consistent with full employment (the natural rate), perhaps, to a negative value. Monetary policy can be contractionary even with low nominal short-term interest rates.

The debate over the self-equilibrating power of the price system to prevent cyclical fluctuations appears in the rules-versus-discretion debate.[1] In the credit-cycle and Keynesian traditions, unpredictable swings between optimism and pessimism that overwhelm the stabilizing behavior of the real interest rate render desirable policy maker flexibility to respond period by period without any constraints imposed on that response. In the quantity-theory tradition, a rule that allows the price system to work will cause the public to anticipate that shocks that depress output below potential will be transitory. Sustained optimism about the future will then mitigate the impact of adverse shocks by smoothing consumption (Friedman 1957).[2]

---

[1] The term comes from Simons (1948), "Rules Versus Authorities in Monetary Policy." Lucas (1976; 1980) used the term in the sense of Simons to argue for the conduct of policy as a systematic procedure. In monetary policy, such a systematic procedure allows the policy maker to respond to incoming information about the economy, but in a constrained way that renders the inflationary expectations of the public predictable. Lucas challenged the prevailing Keynesian view of optimal policy as proceeding each period while taking variables like the capital stock and expected inflation as fixed over the relevant policy horizon. Unfortunately for the clarity of debate, Barro and Gordon (1983) used the terms "rule" and "discretion" differently. In their usage, the policy maker always conducts policy with a rule. The difference is whether the policy maker must reoptimize each period or can commit to a course of action that ties his hands in the future in a way that avoids the time-inconsistency issue highlighted by Kydland and Prescott (1977).

[2] Low and negative real interest rates arise from the way in which sustained monetary shocks create pessimism about the future. The quantity-theorist Irving Fisher believed that even in the midst of the Depression the potential productivity of capital remained high. If the Fed stopped deflation, investment would resume. Fisher (U.S. Congress, 1932b, 348–9) testified before Congress:

[T]he airplane business ... was regarded by many as something quite equivalent to the railroad development in the seventies; and there were the radio and sound pictures, the chemical industries, the development of the automobile, the Patent Office was choked with inventions. ... To-day the greatest laboratories in this country are not the university laboratories ... but the laboratories of industrial concerns, like the American Telephone & Telegraph Co. ... Now inventions have become almost a matter of mass production. ... [I]t is my opinion that what we called the new era then, and which now is laughed at as absurd, was nearer normal than the present era. ... The normal ... is much nearer 1929.

IS THE ECONOMY INHERENTLY UNSTABLE BECAUSE
MARKETS ARE NOT COMPETITIVE?

In a conjectural world of optimizing households and profit-maximizing firms, a Walrasian auctioneer who calls out prices can find a set of prices that are optimal in that they leave no room for further gains from trade. No trades are left that would make someone better off without making somebody else worse off. Provided that the actors in this world take that set of prices as given and believe that they can buy and sell whatever amount they desire at those prices, the amount that households want to consume will equal what firms want to produce. In the *Wealth of Nations*, Adam Smith advanced the hypothesis that the self-interested behavior of individuals would produce this constellation of prices provided that government provided protection for property rights.

This protection required that government erect no barriers hindering the free entry and free exit of firms from markets. Internally, such barriers included the creation of monopolies, and externally they included protectionist measures. Given free markets, the self-interest of individuals in using their labor and capital resources in the most remunerative employment, when coordinated through prices determined by these competitive markets, directed resources to their most socially productive use.

At the level of the individual market, the evidence favors Smith's hypothesis.[3] The order underlying the decentralized allocation of resources coordinated by the price system that Smith perceived predominates over economic chaos and disorganization. Neither shortages nor surpluses are characteristic of individual markets, but they do appear when governments fix prices. Price dispersion is limited in that individuals are quick to arbitrage differences in prices. Smith's basic hypothesis that the self-interested behavior of individuals results in an allocation of resources such that particular resources yield the same return in all uses and, as a result, align the self-interest of the individual with the collective interest in a prosperous economy appears validated by the evidence that free market economies exhibit a level of wealth vastly superior to state-controlled economies. There is a professional consensus that competitive markets have produced the rising secular trend in per capita income observed in countries like the United States (Figure 7.1).

The consensus among economists about the desirability of organizing production and exchange around competitive markets is summarized in

---

[3] Humphrey (1999) documented the fact that quantity theorists also believed in the efficacy of the price system in allocating resources.

the First Fundamental Theorem of Welfare Economics. Despite the ignorance of individual actors about the aggregate economy and about its other actors, their self-interested behavior mediated by the price system produces an allocation of resources that reconciles the diverse plans of these actors, makes their plans consistent with the scarcity of resources, and allows the execution of all trades that would improve an individual's welfare without harming someone else. These assumptions give power to economists' concepts of opportunity cost and its application in the form of cost-benefit analysis and of the welfare-improving benefits of free trade.

However, a professional consensus has never existed over the Smithian hypothesis that the absence of government restraints on market entry and exit will ensure competitive markets. Moreover, there is no consensus over whether the organization of economic activity that results from free entry into markets is consistent with macroeconomic stability. Various strands of the market-disorder school have argued that free markets lead to market power in the form of monopolies that prevent the self-equilibrating properties of the price system from operating on an aggregate level. A perennial variant is that even with competitive markets shifts in popular psychology overwhelm the working of the price system. Proponents of the market-disorder school deduce from the existence of macroeconomic instability in the form of inflation and cyclical fluctuations in output that some form of market power vitiates the stabilizing properties of the price system on the aggregate level. That market power can take the form of powerful monopolies or the herd behavior of individuals in financial markets.

In the event of a prolonged recession accompanied by individual suffering, indisputably, some combination of shocks and frictions in the operation of the price system produces a sustained shortfall of output from potential. What combination of shocks and frictions can explain the paradox of a world of unlimited wants coexisting with a shortfall of aggregate demand that leaves productive resources, especially labor, idle? The explanations offered by the market-disorder view and the monetary-disorder view differ with regard to their empirical judgment about the nature of the relevant shocks and frictions. The market-disorder school works back from the obvious market failure presented by recession to cast doubt on the prerequisite for the existence of Walrasian prices, namely, that individual actors are small enough to take prices as given.

Accordingly, the absence of atomistic markets that hinders the ability of the price system to adjust to shocks appears in two ways: monopolists with market power and investors displaying herd behavior. As evidenced by large corporations and labor unions, product markets display monopoly power. As evidenced by the manipulation of markets through the use of inside information, financial markets display monopoly power. Moreover, businessmen and financiers display herd behavior that overwhelms the self-equilibrating characteristic of the price system. The power of the monopolist or the herd turns individual self-interest into an exploitive and destructive force that injures the weak.

Until the Volcker disinflation, most economists and policy makers interpreted inflation as prima facie evidence that some economic actors are large enough to exploit monopoly market power. In the 1960s and 1970s, the utilization of incomes policies and, in the extreme, wage and price controls arose in response to the popular perception that the greed of large corporations and powerful labor unions powered general increases in prices. However, the failure of controls to suppress inflation and the associated appearance of shortages caused a consensus to emerge that central banks should assume responsibility for the control of inflation (Hetzel 2008b).

Unlike the case of inflation, there has been almost no progress toward consensus over the causes of the business cycle. Currently, the market-disorder view has reappeared in the form of the credit-cycle view. Its reappearance influenced the Dodd-Frank legislation, which created a systemic-risk regulator – the Financial Stability Oversight Council (FSOC). Based on the assumption that the 2008–2009 recession originated in excessive risk taking by large financial institutions, this umbrella regulator has been tasked with limiting risk taking in financial markets.

MONETARY NONNEUTRALITY

According to the quantity-theory tradition, in the absence of monetary disorder, the price system works well enough to prevent prolonged cyclical fluctuations in economic activity. Recessions originate in central bank behavior that causes the price level to evolve in an unpredictable fashion. The resulting absence of a common set of expectations to coordinate the necessary changes in dollar prices set by individual firms in a way that separates fluctuations in the price level from the behavior of relative prices causes the price system to fail in its ability to coordinate economic activity.[4]

---

[4] The following quotations provide this flavor of the quantity-theory tradition about the neutrality of money interrupted by episodes of monetary nonneutrality.
John Stuart Mill (1848 [1987], 488) wrote:

There cannot ... be intrinsically a more insignificant thing, in the economy of society, than money; except in the character of a contrivance for sparing time and labor ...; like many

The basic cause of monetary nonneutrality lies in the dual role of money as a medium of exchange and as a numeraire. Because individuals use money to settle transactions, money becomes the natural collective choice of individuals for a numeraire. The use of dollar prices as the measure of value (the numeraire) is an informationally economical way to keep track of relative prices – the exchange rates between goods about which individuals really care. However, money creation by the central bank unrelated to the change in demand for real money balances (purchasing power) forces the price level to change to maintain the real money balances desired to make transactions. When the central bank conducts monetary policy in a way that causes the money stock to vary unpredictably (relative to real money demand), the price level evolves in an unpredictable manner. Unpredictability of the price level undercuts the ability of money prices to serve as numeraire.

Wicksell (1935 [1978], 7) wrote:

A remedy for fluctuations in the value of money proposed in more recent times is that in agreements extending into a more or less remote period of time the measure of value (unit of value) should be something other than money, for example the average price of a number of commodities (the so-called multiple standard).[5] It is clear, however, that a commodity which serves as a medium of exchange naturally comes to be used also as a measure of value for transactions in goods and services which are near or simultaneous in time; and since it then becomes difficult or undesirable to prescribe any fixed limit, money has gradually been transformed into a general measure of value.

If firms sold their products in a central market and set their dollar prices every period, then market forces would always produce dollar prices in a way that determined both market-clearing relative prices and a price level that renders nominal money creation by the central bank consistent with the public's desired amount of purchasing power. Why then do firms set dollar prices for multiple periods? Alternatively, why do not all markets

---

other kinds of machinery, it only exerts a distinct and independent influence of its own when it gets out of order.

Knut Wicksell (1935 [1978], 6) took up again the machinery metaphor to explain how one can understand the working of the real economy (a machine) without discussing the medium of exchange role of money (the lubricating function of oil). However, he adds, "By means of money (for example by State paper money) it is possible – and indeed this has frequently happened – to destroy large amounts of real capital and to bring the whole economic life of society into hopeless confusion." Finally, D. H. Robertson (1928 [1948], 2) wrote:[A] monetary system is like a liver: it does not take up very much of our thoughts when it goes right, but it attracts a deal of attention when it goes wrong.

[5] Wicksell could be referring to Marshall's (1925 [1956]) tabular standard. For a history of proposals for indexation, see Humphrey (1974).

clear with continuous price changes like the market for a standardized commodity such as wheat? Note first that for a homogeneous product widely sold with standard properties, futures markets develop to serve the function of allowing users of the product to make plans without worrying about unexpected relative price variability.

Firms selling heterogeneous products sell the service of nominal price stability along with their product. Firms planning production must invest effort in selecting inputs from among a vast array of alternatives. They lack the resources to alter continually their production plans, and changing an individual input can disrupt production. Stability in the dollar prices firms pay (adjusted for the common expectation of inflation) for these goods reduces the cost of planning. Firms then provide the service provided by futures markets for standardized commodities by changing their dollar prices only infrequently when the relative price of their product gets significantly out of line with marginal cost. Nothing in this practice of setting dollar prices for multiple periods, however, allows the central bank to reduce the variability of real output by increasing the variability of inflation.

Consider the decision that firms make when setting a dollar price for multiple periods. When such firms (assumed to possess some short-lived monopoly power) set dollar prices, they intend only to set relative prices. As a result, they change their dollar prices for two reasons: first, to *change* the relative price of their product; second, to *preserve* its relative price. The latter changes offset expected inflation (the average change in dollar prices that firms expect all other firms to make). Assume now that the central bank makes the price level evolve unpredictably. Monetary nonneutrality arises from the absence of a coordinating mechanism for preserving relative prices in the face of this unpredictability.

In the event of monetary contraction, the price level consistent with maintaining real money at the level demanded for transactions at full employment falls. Without a reduction in the price level, aggregate nominal demand falls and firms' markups (product price over the marginal cost of production) widen. However, the individual firm does not know how all other firms will change their dollar prices and, consequently, how aggregate demand and the price of factor inputs like labor will evolve. As a result, the firm does not know how a reduction in the dollar price for its product will affect its markup and demand for its product.

In the absence of a reduction in the price level, an individual firm might lower its price with little increase in demand. Alternatively, without comparable price reductions by its competitors, it could sell too much and sell at a loss. The first firm to change its dollar price in a way that gropes after the price level consistent with central bank actions incurs a cost from a misaligned relative price. Because firms do not capture the externality from moving the price level to its flexible-price value (the price level that leaves firms' markups at optimal values), they initially reduce the quantity produced of their product.

Imagine now a Walrasian nominal price auctioneer who calls out changes in the price level whenever firms' markups on average differ from their profit-maximizing levels. (The auctioneer operates only in response to monetary shocks. He knows the real business cycle core of the economy and knows when the central bank has set the funds rate so as to create an incipient difference between the real interest rate and the natural rate.) All firms change their dollar prices in line with the announced changes, and trades are executed when markups return to their profit-maximizing levels. There is then monetary neutrality. Rational expectation is the assumption that the self-interest that firms have in getting their relative prices right causes them to coordinate price-preserving changes in dollar prices based on the predictable behavior of inflation. With a credible rule that coordinates expectations on an inflation target, the central bank makes the auctioneer unnecessary.[6]

PROPAGATION OF A MONETARY SHOCK

One way to ask how monetary nonneutrality arises is to ask what makes the price system efficient in dealing with real but not monetary shocks. For a large, diversified economy, real shocks arrive continually and mainly affect a limited number of markets. In a world characterized by the absence of monetary shocks, the price system works well to maintain trend real growth. Individuals remain optimistic about prospects for their future income and consequently their wealth, and, as a result, the real interest rate remains above zero. Optimism about the future limits the uncertainty associated with decisions that require a forecast of the future. In contrast, unpredictability in the evolution of the price level affects all markets because of the universal use of dollar-denominated prices as a device for economizing on the information needed to communicate relative prices. An aggregate monetary shock that disrupts production and causes individuals to become more pessimistic about the future in a discrete way requires a pervasive change in resource allocation.

---

[6] Friedman (1968 [1969b]) and Lucas (1972 [1980]) argued for nonneutrality arising from unanticipated/anticipated effects rather than short-run/long-run effects. From the former perspective, nonneutrality reflects a coordination failure (Cooper and John 1988).

In a discrete way, firms and individuals become concerned about the "tail risk" of bankruptcy or prolonged unemployment. A firm considering an investment becomes less certain of future demand. When the fear of job loss and extended unemployment become a reality, a consumer's estimate of his permanent income (wealth) today becomes less certain. One can infer this increased concern over unemployment from comparing the likelihood of unemployment and the duration of unemployment for boom and recession years. In 1982, which included the November trough of a severe business cycle, 22 percent of individuals in the labor market experienced unemployment.[7] In contrast, in the boom year 2000, only 8.6 percent of workers experienced unemployment some time during the year. In the 2008–2009 recession, the unemployment rate rose sharply, from about 4.5 percent in fall 2007 to a peak of 10 percent in mid-2009. Moreover, in the recession year of May 2010, the long-term unemployed as a percent of total unemployed (unemployed twenty-seven weeks or longer as a percent of total unemployed) reached 46 percent. In contrast, in 2000, the number was about 10 percent.[8] In the 2008–2009 recession, the increased fear of an adverse economic outcome appeared in the steady increase in personal saving as a percentage of disposable personal income from around 2.1 percent in 2007 to 5.9 percent in 2010Q2.

A Pew Research Center poll (*The Wall Street Journal* 2010a) found that between the onset of the recession in December 2007 and May 2010 the percentage of employed workers who experienced reduced work hours was 28 percent. The percentage who experienced a pay cut was 23 percent. The percentage of employed workers who had to take unpaid leave and the percentage forced to switch to part-time work were, respectively, 12 percent and 11 percent. The survey also documented a change in consumption patterns: 71 percent bought less expensive brands and 57 percent cut back on or canceled vacations. The percentage who borrowed money from friends or family was 24 percent.[9]

As noted previously, The First Fundamental Theorem of Welfare Economics concerns the conditions required for the existence of a set of prices that permits all trades that increase the welfare of individuals without

---

[7] "Work Experience Supplements," Current Population Survey, Bureau of Labor Statistics.
[8] Household data, table A-12. "Unemployed Persons by Duration of Unemployment," Bureau of Labor Statistics.
[9] Increased uncertainty appears in the desire of firms to hold additional liquid assets. *The Wall Street Journal* (2009f) reported:

Stung by the financial crisis, companies are holding more cash – and a greater percentage of assets in cash – than at any time in the past 40 years. In the second quarter [2009], the

decreasing the welfare of others. However, microeconomics has nothing to say about how markets discover this set of market-clearing relative prices. The discovery of a new set of relative prices consistent with a world in which everyone becomes at a discrete time more uncertain and more fearful about the future requires time. Hayek (1945) noted the ability of the price system to coordinate specialized production because of the efficient way in which prices convey information. However, sharp changes from optimism to pessimism about the future temporarily overwhelm the ability of the price system to provide this coordination in the specialization of production.

Once monetary disorder has shocked the economy and produced a discrete increase in pessimism and uncertainty about the future, there is little that fiscal and credit policy can do to hasten the required discovery process of the new set of relative prices. The shortfalls in lending and spending from their full-employment levels are symptoms of the extended price-discovery process. Treating the symptoms will not cure the underlying problem of uncertainty introduced by monetary disorder into the evolution of the price level and the resulting discrete increase in uncertainty about the future.

CONCLUDING COMMENT

Sustained monetary shocks that necessitate reductions in the price level of uncertain magnitude initiate recessions because of the informational problems involved in moving to a lower price level consistent with full employment (L'Huillier 2010). Monetary policy that renders the evolution of the price level unpredictable undercuts the ability of firms setting dollar prices to coordinate changes in their dollar prices so as both to set predictable relative prices and to achieve an average of dollar prices that offsets the effect on purchasing power of the monetary absorptions engineered by the central bank. Propagation of such shocks occurs through the discrete increase in uncertainty produced about the future.[10] In response to the resulting desire by households and firms to become less indebted and more liquid and of households to reduce their consumption to save more, the relative prices that allocate resources must change in a pervasive way. Demand shifts from luxury to basic items. That reallocation of resources and the required reconfiguration of relative prices require time.

---

500 largest nonfinancial U.S. firms, by total assets, held about $994 billion in cash and short-term investments, or about 9.8% of their assets, according to a *Wall Street Journal* analysis of corporate filings. That is up from $846 billion, or 7.9% of assets, a year earlier.

[10] For a general discussion of how an increase in uncertainty affects macroeconomic variables, see Fernandez-Villaverde et al. (2009).

EIGHTEEN

Why Is Learning So Hard?

Learning the lessons of the experience with regimes of fiat money has been slow in part because of the lack of a dialogue between the academic community of economists and the policy makers of central banks. The major impediment to such a dialogue is the unwillingness of the Fed to advance as the starting point for dialogue a conceptual framework explaining what variables it controls and how it exercises that control. Economics imposes the discipline required to learn about the structure of the economy and the way in which monetary policy affects economic activity. Policy makers should initiate an ongoing dialogue with the academic community using the language of economics. In such a dialogue, the Fed should be willing to discuss the conceptualization of a central bank as a creator of money and should be willing to reconsider its adherence to discretionary as opposed to rule-based policy making.

CONCEPTUALIZATION OF A CENTRAL BANK WITHOUT REFERENCE TO MONEY CREATION

At the conclusion of its November 3, 2010, meeting, the FOMC announced:

Currently, the unemployment rate is elevated, and measures of underlying inflation are somewhat low, relative to levels that the Committee judges to be consistent, over the longer run, with its dual mandate. Although the Committee anticipates a gradual return to higher levels of resource utilization in a context of price stability, progress toward its objectives has been disappointingly slow. To promote a stronger pace of economic recovery and to help ensure that inflation, over time, is at levels consistent with its mandate, the Committee decided today to expand its holdings of securities. ... [T]he Committee intends to purchase a further $600 billion of longer-term Treasury securities by the end of the second quarter of 2011, a pace of about $75 billion per month.

Nowhere did the FOMC characterize the $600 billion of additional purchases of Treasury securities in terms of additional money creation. Chairman Bernanke characterized the decision as one of large-scale asset purchases (LSAPs) intended to influence conditions in financial markets rather than monetary base creation (quantitative easing or QE). Bernanke (2010d, 2) commented, "[T]he use of the term 'quantitative easing' ... is inappropriate. Quantitative easing typically refers to ... changing the quantity of bank reserves, a channel that seems relatively weak."

Larry Meyer, head of Macroeconomic Advisers and a former member of the Board of Governors, characterized the decision to purchase additional Treasury securities in a CNBC interview:[1]

ERIN: This unemployment issue is the big issue. And now you have the Fed going about it by printing money and I know you said there is a risk it won't work, but what are the calculations they are running to get some sort of link, even if it is a derivative link between, "we print X amount of dollars in quantitative easing and Y happens to the unemployment rate" or is it really true that they have no clue?

Laurence Meyer: First of all, here is how they would answer the question that you asked. It has nothing to do with printed money. It has nothing to do with the size of the balance sheet. It has nothing to do with the level of reserves. The only thing you need to focus on is, "what happens to equity prices, what happens to the dollar, and what happens to borrowing costs?" That's what they're trying to do. Now we know in normal times, and today too, that higher equity prices are good for aggregate demand. We know that the dollar falling increases our trade competitiveness. That's good for U.S. aggregate demand and lower borrowing costs should be as well. So take your mind off printing dollars and take your mind off the size of the balance sheet and reserves and just focus on the purpose of this. The purpose of this is to improve financial conditions. If it doesn't, it won't work.

The LSAP language of credit policy as opposed to the QE language of monetary policy allowed the Fed to sidestep politically charged debates. With the former language, the FOMC focused on the asset side of its balance sheet and disregarded the liability side (the monetary base) as irrelevant. In that way, the Fed avoided formulation of an explicit objective such as the growth rate of nominal expenditure of the public. Also, it never had to mention seigniorage or money creation.

Seigniorage is the inevitable concomitant of the increase over time in the monetary base: currency and the reserves held by commercial banks with the Fed. As an accounting matter, open-market purchases of government securities create this base money by extinguishing government debt. The

---

[1] See http://macroadvisers.blogspot.com/2010/11/mas-meyer-discusses-fed-fomc-meeting.html.

government then issues new debt to maintain the existing stock of debt held by the public; it deposits the money received for that issue of debt into its account at the New York Fed; and it then spends down that account to purchase goods and services. Seigniorage, which allows this purchase of goods and services, is a tax paid by those who hold the base money created by the Fed.

The political economy problem for the Fed is the misleading associations made by the loose language used to describe the seigniorage tax. "The Fed is monetizing government debt" becomes "The Fed is abetting the deficit spending of the government." Reference to "money creation" becomes "The Fed is running the printing presses." The latter expression suggests that the Fed is an "out of control" government agency. The association of money creation and inflation, which is the depreciation of the internal value of the dollar, also suggests depreciation of the foreign exchange value of the dollar. Not only is the foreign exchange value of the dollar the province of the Treasury, but also foreign central banks come under domestic political pressure when their currencies appreciate relative to the dollar.

Unfortunately, the steadfast avoidance by spokesmen for the Fed of the conceptualization of a central bank as a "creator of money" limits the Fed's ability to clarify public discussion of monetary policy. That limitation is especially evident when the funds rate is pushed against the lower bound of zero. Confusion in public discourse begins with the careless use of the term "liquidity trap" to characterize a situation of impotence on the part of the central bank.

This confusion arises because of the faulty generalization from the particular case of an open-market purchase of a short-term Treasury bill. With short-term interest rates at zero, such an exchange would leave unchanged the degree of liquidity in investors' portfolios. However, a true liquidity trap, which has never existed, would only arise if all the assets subject to purchase by the Fed were as liquid as these short-term Treasury bills. In fact, there are always illiquid assets available for purchase. Moreover, in principle, the Fed could purchase newly created long-term Treasuries or consols (bonds with a perpetual promise to pay a regular coupon) from the Treasury – the so-called helicopter drop of money made famous by Milton Friedman. Even with zero short-term interest rates, a sufficiently large open-market purchase by the Fed of illiquid assets would cause the public to increase its spending to return its asset portfolio to its original degree of liquidity.

The zero lower bound (ZLB) problem is different from a liquidity trap. With the funds rate at zero, the Fed encounters the ZLB. Expansionary monetary policy must then take the form of purchases by the Fed of illiquid assets rather than further reductions in the funds rate. It is wrong to infer from the existence of a zero funds rate, however, that the Fed has lost the ability to control the nominal expenditure of the public.

In the 2008–2009 recession, the combination of a near-zero short-term interest rate and elevated levels of excess reserves created the false impression that the existence of the ZLB (mislabeled as a "liquidity trap") had rendered monetary policy impotent. Banks had an incentive to hold large amounts of excess reserves because of the significant cost of dealing with a large outflow of reserves. No evidence existed of an unusually large demand for monetary aggregates like M2 – the hallmark of a liquidity trap. Nothing occurred to suggest that sustained money creation would have failed to stimulate the dollar expenditure of the public.

After September 2008 when banks increased their demand for excess reserves in response to funding volatility and the apparent retraction of the financial safety net, the failure of the Fed to distinguish between the creation of excess reserves and the creation of money led to the unfortunate impression of the impotence of monetary policy. That impression confused debate over the Fed's decision in fall 2010 to purchase an additional $600 billion in Treasury securities. Newspapers labeled the purchase of securities by the Fed as QE2, or the second round of quantitative easing. The first round of purchases of Treasury and GSE securities began in spring 2009. In the summary offered by *The New York Times* (2010b), "[I]t is increasingly plain to see that the Fed has all but played its hand, and the economy is still in deep trouble."

Consider the more detailed comments made in a *Washington Post* (2010b) editorial:

"Central bankers alone cannot solve the world's problems," he [Chairman Bernanke] admonished. It's especially hard to solve them after you have already taken interest rates to near zero and bought a trillion dollars worth of mortgage-backed securities and other bonds. These extraordinary steps – known as quantitative easing – have left the Fed with few cards to play. ... The Fed's inability this time to magically produce a wave of growth, even when abetted by fiscal stimulus, suggests that the United States faces a crisis that is structural.

Most generally, the impression of the impotence of monetary policy in recession derives from the conceptualization of a central bank as a large financial intermediary, which exercises its influence through the encouragement it gives to financial intermediation. In deep recession, the absence of loan demand by business supposedly breaks the financial transmission mechanism. The central bank "cannot push on a string." From this perspective, in a deep recession, low (nominal and real) interest rates evince the powerlessness of monetary policy. Given the prevailing pessimism about the future, even very low interest rates can fail to stimulate expenditure.

Consider the commentary by Peter Eavis (2010) in "Heard on the Street" in *The Wall Street Journal*:

The problem is that the Fed already has spent more than $1.7 trillion buying bonds in the first round of quantitative easing, which ended in March. The central question is why wasn't that enough to prevent the economy's slowdown? [B]anks have $1 trillion just idling on their books that isn't being used to fuel higher amounts of lending. And that lack of loan growth requires little explanation: Borrowers are reluctant to take on more credit, as banks are to extend it.

This can be dealt with in two ways. The Fed can remain cautiously accommodative while household balance sheets repair and real-estate markets truly bottom. Once those have occurred, people will want to borrow more and banks will be more likely to lend. … [T]he only way QE2 is going to "repair" household balance sheets is if it is big enough to drive up the value of assets like real estate to the point that they are better aligned with liabilities. But the amounts of money that need to be printed to lift, say, U.S. house prices substantially is likely to be huge and potentially destabilizing. QE2 could end up a ship steered by drunken sailors.

One reason for the absence of a satisfactory discussion of the ability of the Fed to control the dollar expenditure of the public is discussion of money creation as a one-time exchange of money for a liquid asset in the portfolio of the public. The argument for the ability of the central bank to control nominal variables like dollar expenditure comes from its ability to maintain a sustained exchange of money for illiquid assets in the portfolio of the public.[2] With such a policy, one can work back from a long-run result in which the public holds only money and no interest-bearing assets in its asset portfolio. Because that outcome is not a tenable equilibrium, one can deduce that a portfolio rebalancing effect would cause the public to attempt to run down its money balances by increasing its expenditure. That outcome holds even when short-term interest rates are zero (Sims 1994).

Which conceptualization of a central bank is the more useful: the central bank as a large financial intermediary or the central bank as a creator of money? Experience across countries and across time has demonstrated that the behavior of inflation and, consequently, the dollar expenditure of the public depend on the way in which the central bank controls money creation, not financial intermediation. From the quantity-theory (money-creation) perspective, in a deep recession, the real interest rate is

---

[2]   Consider the criticism in this spirit in the 1932 hearings on the Goldsborough Bill made by Representative Goldsborough of Governor Harrison's claims of the Fed's impotence to control the price level reproduced in Chapter 3.

low because of pervasive pessimism about the future. However, because of its unlimited power to create money, perhaps by buying long-term debt created expressly by the Treasury, the central bank retains the power to compel the public to increase its expenditures in an attempt to run down its money balances.

The empirical implications of the quantity theory come from the dual hypothesis that there is a well-defined demand for a real quantity of money by the public and that the central bank controls the nominal quantity of money. In the contemporaneous world of unstable, interest-sensitive money demand, it is impossible to measure this real demand accurately. It nevertheless follows that a feedback rule from the rate of growth of the public's dollar expenditure to money growth will produce sustained changes in money that give the central bank the power to force portfolio rebalancing by the public and thereby control the public's dollar expenditure.

Of course, control over the dollar expenditure of the public does not translate into predictable control over real expenditure. It is important to keep in mind what monetary policy can and cannot do. Beyond providing a nominal anchor, an optimal monetary policy allows for the consistent operation of the price system. In that way, monetary policy has the ability to provide for macroeconomic stability and, in the language of the Federal Reserve Act, "maximum employment." However, once having shocked the economy with contractionary monetary policy, there is no monetary panacea for inducing a quick recovery. A contractionary monetary shock produces a discrete increase in uncertainty about the future created by the fear of extended unemployment and bankruptcy. Only with the passage of time can individuals and corporations reduce leverage in response to this uncertainty. Only with the passage of time can the price system discover a new set of relative prices and resource allocations consistent with a world in which fear has replaced optimism about the future (Chapter 17).[3]

Given the real nature of the way in which a monetary shock propagates, there is no quick way in recession to restore output to potential beyond advertisement by the central bank that it can and will sustain the dollar expenditure of the public. Given steady growth in dollar expenditure, the price system will in time restore output to the level made possible by the economy's physical and human resources. Especially in the event of the occurrence of the ZLB problem, the power to maintain the dollar

---

[3]   In the deep recessions of 1974–1975 and 1981–1982, the public may have associated recession with the attempt to lower inflation so that when inflation fell it regained confidence about the future and recovery ensued. In the 2008–2009 recession, nothing comparable existed to create the belief that recession would end soon.

expenditure of the public derives from the ability of the central bank to create unlimited amounts of money. However, to provide the public with the required confidence that recession will end, the Fed would have to make the transition to a conceptualization of a central bank as a creator of money.

At the same time, the Fed would have to assure the public that it will control money creation to prevent the emergence of inflation. To do that, it would have to formulate monetary policy as a consistent strategy – a rule. To make that transition, the Fed would have to abandon the language of discretion. Not only would the Fed have to announce an explicit inflation target, but also it would have to announce a rule for achieving that target based on an explicit conceptual framework explaining what monetary policy controls and how it exercises that control. Just as with avoidance of the idea of a central bank as the creator of money, abandonment of the language of discretion would require a radical change in central bank culture.

CENTRAL BANK OPACITY AND THE LANGUAGE OF DISCRETION

The Fed uses the language of discretion to communicate the rationale for its actions to the public. In the spirit of discretion, each period, the FOMC makes a decision about whether to move the funds rate away from its prevailing value based on the contemporaneous behavior of the economy. In the *Minutes*, it defends its decision through a commonsensical appeal to the behavior of the economy rather than through an analytical framework relating its policy instrument (the funds rate) to explicit, quantitative objectives (employment and inflation). In the context of discretion, transparency entails a description of FOMC members' reading of the state of the economy. In the spirit of discretion, in which the FOMC considers each policy action as an independent event given the contemporaneous state of the economy, individual policy actions are always optimal and shocks always arise independently of the choice of policy actions.

This view of central banking corresponds to the Keynesian tradition in which the desirability of discretion comes from intrinsic (hard-wired) inflation persistence. Each period, the central bank observes macroeconomic shocks and then expands or contracts aggregate nominal demand to move aggregate real demand appropriately. The inertial character of the expectations of the public prevents those expectations from countering the aggregate demand management of the central bank.

Central bank silence about objectives and strategy possesses a long tradition. Viner (1937, 391–2) wrote:

If the controlling agency [central bank] were operating on the basis of a clearly formulated and simple policy or rule of action, which was made known to the public, it would be possible to describe the international mechanism [of the gold standard] as it would operate under such a policy. But central banks do not ordinarily disclose their policy to the public, and the evidence seems to point strongly to a disinclination on the part of central bankers as a class to accept as their guide the simple formulae which are urged upon them by economists and others, or to follow simple rules of their own invention. All central banks find themselves at times facing situations which appear to demand a choice between conflicting objectives, long-run versus short-run, internal stability versus exchange stability ... and they seem universally to prefer meeting such situations *ad hoc* rather than in accordance with the dictates of some simple formula. Whatever may be the merits of this attitude, it results in practice in behavior by central banks which fails to reveal to the outsider any well-defined pattern upon which can be based predictions as to their future behavior. ... [D]iscretionary power suffices to give some phases of the international mechanism ... [an] unpredictable relationship to other phases of the mechanism.

Schumpeter (1954, 696) explained the lack of policy explicitness by central banks as an effort to limit criticism:

One of the difficulties we experience in finding out what it was the Bank [of England] meant to do at any given time, or even what its practice actually was, is the reticence of its official spokesmen who, even when they were forced to say something, did their best to confine themselves to innocuous trivialities that would give as little scope to hostile criticism as possible. ... [T]he Bank had few friends. ... [A]nnouncement of policy would have brought down upon directors hosts of unbidden advisers, every one of them convinced that he knew much better what the Bank ought to do – and there would have been the danger of public outcries for legislation to force the Bank to take, or to refrain from taking, particular courses of action.

By packaging each change in the funds rate as optimal in a common sense way in the context of the contemporaneous behavior of the economy, the Fed can ex post rationalize each policy action as "good play." When a bad outcome occurs, the "poor hand" of exogenous real shocks trumps good play. Friedman (1960, 86) wrote:

An amusing dividend from reading *Annual Reports* of the Federal Reserve System *seriatim* is the sharp cyclical pattern that emerges in the potency attributed to monetary forces and policy. In years of prosperity, monetary policy is a potent instrument, the skillful handling of which deserves credit for the favorable course of events; in years of adversity, other forces are the important sources of economic change, monetary policy has little leeway, and only the skillful handling of the excessively limited powers available prevented conditions from being even worse.

Friedman (1960, ch. 4, fn. 5) then cited the 1933 Board *Annual Report* on the banking crisis in early winter 1933:

The ability of the Federal Reserve banks to meet enormous demands for currency during the crisis demonstrated the effectiveness of the country's currency system under the Federal Reserve Act. ... The crisis of February and March 1933, therefore was not a currency crisis but a banking crisis, and was occasioned not by a shortage of currency but by a loss of confidence in the solvency of banks and by a depreciation in bank assets consequent upon the drop in prices of all classes of property caused by the depression. ... It is difficult to say what the course of the depression would have been had the Federal Reserve not pursued a policy of liberal open-market purchases.

Traditionally, Fed spokesmen have emphasized the powerlessness of monetary policy in recession. Friedman and Schwartz (1963a, 372) cited a June 16, 1930, letter from John U. Calkins, governor of the San Francisco Fed, to Governor Young. "[W]ith credit cheap and redundant we do not believe that business recovery will be accelerated by making credit cheaper and more redundant." Governor Miller (U.S. Congress 1928, 183) argued earlier:

In a time of recession you can not stop the recession by the lowering of the discount rate, the cheapening of the cost of credit, or by making credit more abundant. ... You have got to have a demand for something before you can either stimulate that demand or restrain it. And at a time when the business community does not want to make any business commitments, when it is hesitant about the business outlook, you can not do very much with your rate.

Central bankers never accept responsibility for recessions. Instead, they blame imbalances in the private sector. During the recovery from the 2008–2009 recession, why did not the Fed act to dissipate uncertainty by accepting responsibility for nominal expenditure, set a target path for nominal expenditure based on a vigorous recovery and long-run price stability, and then create the requisite amount of money? Possibly, setting a target for nominal expenditure would have suggested that policy makers could solve a problem they believed originated elsewhere, either by uncertainty over fiscal policy or banker speculative excess. Perhaps this belief was correct; however, without an analytical framework within which to debate academic economists, there is no way to have a dispassionate debate over the causes of recession.

For the Fed, the political economy problem with an explicit analytical framework is the attractiveness of the language of discretion, which allows communication with the political system that avoids the language of trade-offs. The language of discretion facilitates the message that monetary policy never deviates from the simultaneous pursuit of price stability and maximum employment. In contrast to the language of discretion, which portrays monetary policy as the period-by-period response to exogenous shocks, the language of rules assumes that the operation of the price system imposes continuity on optimal procedures. There is an optimal rule that provides a nominal anchor and that allows the price system (the real interest rate) to work to stabilize economic activity. By implication, the Fed can learn from its past history which procedures have worked successfully and which have worked unsuccessfully.

Beyond the language of discretion, the FOMC chairman and, since 2004, increasingly regional Fed bank presidents communicate with financial markets about their assessment of the state of the economy. Markets understand the underlying consistency in policy and use this assessment in their forecasts of the path of the funds rate and the term structure of interest rates. The group left out of this communication is academic economists with models that require rules because of the models' forward-looking agents who use information efficiently. As discussed in the next section, the absence of communication by the Fed in terms of the consistency of its policy procedures renders dialogue with the academic community difficult and limits the ability to learn from historical experience.[4]

WHY IS LEARNING SO HARD?

Economists as microeconomists support the allocation of resources by the price system. The way in which market-determined prices clear markets becomes obvious with the shortages and surpluses produced by government price controls. However, the self-regulating character of the price system is not as readily demonstrable for macroeconomic fluctuations. For the macro economy, market clearing entails fluctuations in the real interest rate that influence how individuals collectively distribute their demand over time for resources. The price system is self-regulating if market-determined fluctuations in the real interest rate are allowed to work to maintain real aggregate demand close to potential output. The counterpart to price controls is interference by the central bank in the market determination of the real interest rate made possible by its ability to create and destroy money.

---

[4] With the language of discretion, monetary policy is the responsibility of the individual judgment of policy makers. Given human nature and the costs involved in monetary mistakes, a dialogue of policy makers with academics over what has worked and what has *not* worked is impractical. With a publicly articulated rule discussed extensively with the economics profession, dialogue would be less charged in that policy makers would be implementing as much as possible a broad-based consensus about how to conduct policy.

The counterpart to the absence of price controls is a rule that allows market forces to determine the real interest rate.

The language of discretion facilitates the periodic departure from these procedures without raising a red flag that would engender controversy. In the Volcker-Greenspan era, the Fed departed twice – once after the Louvre Accord and once during the Asia crisis. Each time, a concern for the foreign exchange value of the dollar initiated the departure. The departures produced monetary expansion and created inflationary pressures – mini go-stop cycles. In the Bernanke era, the Fed departed from its lean-against-the-wind (LAW) procedures in spring and summer 2008 when it maintained the funds rate unchanged despite significant deterioration in the real economy. The departure represented a combination of concern for inflationary expectations and for depreciation of the dollar on the foreign exchanges. These departures were the macroeconomic equivalent of the microeconomic equivalent of price fixing.

Constitutionally, the Fed is a creation of Congress and accountable to it. Members of the House and Senate Banking committees possess a self-interest in reelection and accordingly possess their own agendas. Most often, this agenda involves "affordable housing," that is, programs to subsidize home ownership that appeal to the housing lobby. However, an agenda can also directly concern the Fed, for example, by requiring the Fed to pursue consumer protection through regulation of mortgage and consumer lending. Hearings with the FOMC chairman allow members of the banking committees to express support for a variety of constituent concerns, including job creation and economic issues in general such as income inequality. An amorphous focus by the Fed on the state of the economy allows the chairman to convey general support for the concerns of congressmen while retaining control over the setting of the funds rate. By focusing communication on a "look-at-everything" response to the economy rather than articulation of a reaction function (a rule), the FOMC chairman also transfers debate over policy to the Fed's home turf of following the evolution of economic activity.

The result is a system that relies above all on the judgment of the particular FOMC chairman rather than on rules. Whether this system is a source of continuing periodic monetary instability depends on the fundamental source of economic instability. Does instability arise from market disorder such as a credit cycle in which an unpredictable, manic-depressive alternation in the herd behavior of investors periodically renders the system of financial intermediation dysfunctional? Alternatively, does instability arise from monetary disorder produced by the ability of the central bank to create and destroy money in a way that interferes with the market determination of the real interest rate?

From the perspective of the former, market-disorder view, with its emphasis on the inherent instability of the economy, the ability to learn useful lessons from the past is limited. From the perspective of the latter, monetary-disorder view, with its emphasis on the continuity provided by the working of the price system, the ability to learn useful lessons from the past is genuine. That ability to learn, however, is impeded by the Fed's language of discretion, which obscures from economists the evolution in the consistent component of monetary policy.

NINETEEN

How Should Society Regulate Capitalism?

Rules versus Discretion

Are competitive markets self-regulating or are they overwhelmed by market power? In the case of corporations, market power takes the form of monopolies. In the case of financial markets, it takes the form of the herd behavior of investors. As illustrated by the following quotation from the *Financial Times* (2009c), the 2008–2009 recession prompted a change in the intellectual climate in favor the latter market-disorder view:

The onset of the worst global recession since the 1930s has led many to suppose the era of liberal economics and light-touch financial regulation ushered in by Thatcher and Ronald Reagan is over. Failures of untrammeled capitalism are blamed for the crisis. Discredited "socialist" solutions are back: banks are nationalized or rescued with taxpayers' funds; borrowed money is pumped into economies in a Keynesian effort to boost demand.

How should society regulate capitalism, and, as a by-product, what role should the central bank play? During the 2008–2009 recession, the United States returned to the popular ethos that existed in the Great Depression and in the Great Inflation. Namely, popular discourse held that private markets failed to discipline the self-interest of individuals in a way that causes that self-interest to redound to the public interest. Belief in the self-interest of individuals coordinated by the price system ceded before a belief in the greed of powerful players.

Once again, with the 2008–2009 recession, attitudes have shifted in favor of the discretion that allows direct intervention into markets to deal with the presumed arbitrary, unpredictable exercise of the market power embodied in the herd behavior of investors. "Animal spirits offer an explanation for why we get into recessions. ... [T]rust is replaced by deep mistrust" (Shiller 2009a). Robert Skidelsky (2008) commented on Keynes' analysis of the Depression:

His [Keynes] basic question was: How do rational people behave under conditions of uncertainty? The answer he gave was profound and extends far beyond economics. People fall back on "conventions." ... Above all, we run with the crowd.

In comments on the book *Animal Spirits* by George Akerlof and Robert Shiller, Louis Uchitelle (2009) continued this idea:

There was nothing rational, well informed or unemotional about the behavior that has all but collapsed the economy. That leaves most of America's economists without a believable framework for explaining how we got into this mess. Akerlof and Shiller are the first to rework economic theory for our times.

As a result, attitudes have shifted against rules that discipline expectations while allowing markets to work freely. The belief is that the undisciplined animal spirits of investors would overrun any central bank rule that permitted market forces to determine the real interest rate. Similarly, any rule to encourage market monitoring of risk taking through allowing the creditors of banks to incur losses in the event of a run would founder through panics that close solvent and insolvent banks alike.[1]

Is the only constant the inconstancy arising from the unpredictability of shifts in investor psychology from irrationally optimistic to irrationally pessimistic? Alternatively, does the logic of the price system impose continuity in the behavior of the economy? In the former world, there is a need for policy-maker discretion. In the latter world, there is a need for rules that impose consistency.

There is a monumental need to understand how well the price system works to provide macroeconomic stability. Learning requires an understanding of the monetary experiments given to the world in the painful, slow process of the learning by central banks of how to manage a regime of pure fiat money. Learning from the last century of experience requires a conversation between central bankers and academic economists, not just between the FOMC chairman and members of the congressional banking committees. For this dialogue to occur, the Fed will have to abandon the language of discretion for the language of rules and for the analytical framework of economics. Accountability imposes the desirability of

---

[1] A *Wall Street Journal* (2008g) blog wrote:

The way Congressman Barney Frank put it ... was that we should celebrate, Monday, September 15, as "Free Market Day" – Lehman Brothers was allowed to fail and the free market to work on that day. Now, the next day, Chairman Frank continued, AIG had been bailed out so "the national commitment to the free market lasted one day."

In a similar spirit, *The New York Times* (2008f) reported: "'There are no atheists in foxholes and no ideologues in financial crises,' Mr. Bernanke told colleagues last week."

"an economist standard" constituting an informed academic community capable of commenting on monetary policy in an ongoing fashion. Both central bankers and academics will then have to take responsibility for putting that conversation into a form that is accessible to an informed public.

Chapter 1 reproduced President Kocherlakota's (2009) criticism that "macroeconomists let policymakers down ... because they did not provide policymakers with rules to avoid the circumstances that led to the global financial meltdown." Friedman and Schwartz (1963a, 371) criticized the disarray among policy makers in the Depression: "Lack of a common universe of discourse and inability to reduce differences of opinion to quantitative terms were probably important factors enabling differences to persist for so long with no approach to a meeting of minds." Even after eighty years since the onset of the Depression, there is no agreement over how to design policy and institutions to prevent financial and monetary instability from destabilizing real economic activity. What is needed is a dialogue among academics and policy makers, and that dialogue is possible only if monetary policy makers engage academic economists in debate using the language and models of economics.

The 2008–2009 recession once again highlighted the recurring relationship between economic, financial, and monetary instability. The imperative of understanding the causal relationship between these phenomena and of using that understanding to design policy to prevent future recurrences of world recession is transcendentally important. A person (*Financial Times* 2009d) speaking for Angela Merkel, Germany's chancellor, said, "Another crisis like this one and the west will be wiped out."

Knut Wicksell (1935 [1978], 3 and 7) said in his *Lectures on Political Economy*:

[W]ith regard to money, everything is determined by human beings themselves, i.e. the statesmen, and (so far as they are consulted) the economists; the choice of a measure of value, of a monetary system, of currency and credit legislation – all are in the hands of society.

Wicksell followed up by noting:

The establishment of a greater, and if possible absolute, stability in the value of money has thus become one of the most important practical objectives of political economy. But, unfortunately, little progress towards the solution of this problem has, so far, been made.

Why is progress so slow? Is learning difficult because of the random character of the operation of the economy? Alternatively, is learning difficult because of the opacity of central bank communication caused by unwilling-ness to articulate what is systematic about policy and by an unwillingness to announce the periodic departures that occur from the underlying system-atic character of policy?

Postscript

In the summer of 2011, financial turmoil returned and the economic recovery faltered. Many elements of the fall 2008 flight to quality by short-term investors repeated. These cash investors switched out of uninsured money market funds and into insured bank deposits. Two sources of uncertainty caused this switch.[1] First, investors became concerned about the political impasse over raising the U.S. debt ceiling (*Wall Street Journal*, June 13, 2011). As a result, funds normally parked in Treasuries were placed in bank deposits. Second, investors became fearful of defaults on Greek debt. They became aware of a flight of depositors from Greek banks (Bloomberg, June 9, 2011). Efforts of the Greek government to enact austerity measures provoked street demonstrations and threats of resignation by members of Parliament (*Financial Times*, June 7, 2011). Germany began arguing publicly with the European Central Bank (ECB) over the extent to which the holders of Greek debt would be forced to share in the cost of a bailout (*Financial* Times, June 10, 2011).

The blanket deposit insurance offered during the fall 2008 crisis by the FDIC for non-interest-bearing demand deposits exacerbated this flight. The *American Banker* (2011) wrote:

The program was most useful to community banks which could use the coverage to prevent business customers with transactions accounts above the standard insurance limit from going to large banks that were presumed "too big to fail."

Three years after being launched at the height of the financial crisis, the Federal Deposit Insurance Corp.'s blanket coverage of no-interest deposits is still in effect .... An idea originally meant to help community banks has become a double-edged

---

[1] Between the weeks ending September 10, 2008 and October 1, 2008, the deposits of domestically chartered commercial banks jumped by $475 billion. Between the weeks of June 15, 2011 and August 3, 2011, these deposits jumped by $396 billion (Board of Governors, Statistical Release H8, "Assets and Liabilities of Commercial Banks in the United States").

sword at the largest institutions, whose large-deposit inflows have swelled as investors nervous about recent economic shocks rush to safety.

Nervous investors withdrew cash from prime money market funds with exposure to European banks and placed it in money center banks like JPMorgan Chase. The money funds in turn reduced their holdings of the dollar-denominated deposits like certificates of deposit (CDs) of European banks.[2] In response, central banks bailed out the European banks and their debt holders. Through swap lines, the Fed loaned dollars to the ECB and the ECB loaned dollars to the banks with dollar-funding problems. Moral hazard arises because the creditors of European banks – that is, the money market mutual funds – have been taken out of their positions through lending by the central bank. As a result, they possess no incentive to monitor the risk taking of banks.

This reintermediation into the banking system distorts the information in money useful for predicting the nominal (dollar) expenditure of the public. From May 2010 to May 2011, M2 grew at 5.3 percent.[3] From May 2011 through August 2011, M2 grew at an annualized rate of 25 percent. The former figure of 5.3 percent is a more accurate measure of money growth related to nominal expenditure.

In 2011, the recovery from the 2008–2009 recession slowed. According to the advance release of the Bureau of Economic Analysis, real GDP grew only about 0.9 percent in the first two quarters of the year. According to *Blue Chip Financial Forecasts* (2011) made in September 2011, professional forecasters expected real growth over the second half of 2011 of slightly less than 2 percent. What kind of shock, real or monetary, can account for this slowdown in the recovery from the 2008–2009 recession?

The identification of macroeconomic shocks in real time is always problematic. At least within the business community, popular discourse favored the argument that uncertainty over government regulation and taxes had limited job creation. Although ultimately that contention may prove to be correct, its validity is not obvious. Consider Figure 7.1, which shows

[2] "As of month-end August [2011], the MMFs [money market mutual funds] sampled reduced their total exposure to European banks by … 27% relative to month-end May 2011 … the lowest level in percentage terms within Fitch's historical time series (*Fitch Ratings* 2011).

[3] Although this interval preceded the flight to insured deposits that began in June 2011, it is still biased upward by a change in the way in which the FDIC calculated insurance premiums on bank deposits. Prior to April 2011, it had imposed the assessment on domestic deposits. Afterward, as a result of Dodd-Frank, it imposed the assessment on all bank liabilities. Consequently, U.S. banks repatriated deposits formerly swept off their balance sheets into offshore banks. Such sweeps no longer lowered their FDIC assessments.

a secular increase in real output per capita. There is no empirical work demonstrating that either the trend rate of increase or the deviations from trend correlate with such real factors as marginal tax rates and changes in the degree of government regulation. Perhaps there has been an increase in concern among businesses about future tax rates and regulation, but it seems unlikely that the magnitude is such as to have overwhelmed for the first time the forces leading to sustained real growth.[4] Historically, only prolonged monetary disorder has been associated with sustained shortfalls of output from trend.

How can a monetary shock account for the slow recovery in output and employment from the 2008–2009 recession? As background, consider the premise of the quantity theory, namely that because individuals use money to make transactions, they desire to proportion their money holdings to their nominal expenditures. Control over money creation by the central bank then endows it with control over nominal expenditure growth.[5] In the last half of 2010 and first half of 2011, money creation was consistent with nominal GDP growth of near 4 percent (Figure 16.1). At the same time, as a carryover from the Greenspan era, the Fed had stabilized expected inflation at 2 percent (or somewhat more) and, as a result, created a gravitational pull of inflation toward 2 percent.[6] However, money has failed to grow sufficiently to create the nominal expenditure growth required to accommodate both the 2 percent inflation and a normal recovery of output following a deep recession.[7]

Until the fall of 2010, excess unemployment depressed inflation below the expected 2 percent base. However, beginning in late 2010, a strong

---

[4] A problem with the hypothesis that uncertainty over tax and regulatory policy is discouraging firms from hiring workers is that firms have maintained their equipment and software expenditures. As of 2011Q2, these capital expenditures were near their pre-recession peak. Because capital investment involves a long-term commitment, if firms are willing to invest, they should be willing to hire.

[5] The additional assumption that real forces determine potential output growth then gives a central bank the ability to control trend inflation as the difference between trend nominal and real expenditure growth.

[6] The five-year, five-years-ahead measure of expected inflation yielded by the difference between the interest rate on nominal Treasury securities and the interest rate on Treasury Inflation Protected Securities (TIPS) has remained steady at around 2.75 percent since 2005. The corresponding five-year measure of expected inflation has been much more volatile and was artificially depressed in 2008 by the liquidity premium paid for the holding of nominal Treasury securities.

[7] Despite the high level of bank reserves of about $1.6 trillion in September 2011, banks have found it more prudent to keep their excess reserves invested with the Fed at an interest rate of .25% than to attempt to run them down by extending loans and buying securities and, as a by-product, spur money growth.

inflation shock pushed inflation higher than this 2 percent base.[8] The slow growth of real GDP in 2011 resulted from the way in which the resulting surge in overall inflation crowded out real growth given the relatively fixed level for nominal expenditure growth.[9]

In September 2011, the long-term real interest rate, measured by the yield on ten-year inflation-protected Treasury securities (TIPS), fell basically to zero. Many market observers inferred that monetary policy retained little ability to stimulate economic activity. However, such low real rates of interest merely reflected the pessimism about the future produced by low real growth. The problem was not the inability of the Fed to depress real interest rates further. The problem was the mismatch between low nominal expenditure growth and relatively high expected inflation.

Again, the identification of shocks in real time is inevitably contentious. One would like to have the additional perspective of time. With respect to the contention that uncertainty from government regulatory and tax polices limited the economic recovery, one would like to know whether output returns to its long-run trend value shown in Figure 7.1 without a markedly pro-business change in the political environment. With respect to the monetary-mismatch contention, one would like to know whether real output growth revives as the inflation shock subsides given continued growth in nominal GDP of 4 percent.

In the fall of 2008, the FOMC concluded that the recession derived from shocks to financial intermediation. As a result, it focused on the size and composition of the Fed's asset portfolio. Despite massive intervention into credit markets, the economy went through a serious recession and then a prolonged slow recovery. In the fall of 2011, the FOMC continued its focus on credit markets through operation twist, which lengthened the maturity of the Fed's holding of government securities.

Perhaps the decline in growth from its secular trend starting in 2008 possessed real causes. If with the benefit of time and study the prolonged economic decline that began in 2008 can be attributed at least in part to monetary policy, however, then it is time to reconsider the arguments Friedman (1970) made for a rule. A rule that would maintain the growth of nominal expenditure in recession would limit the ability of monetary policy makers to act on the belief that recessions arise from real shocks.

---

[8] Crude oil prices (measured by dollars paid per barrel for Brent crude oil) rose from around $70 per barrel in the fall of 2009 to as high as $130 per barrel in 2011.

[9] From 2010Q3 through 2011Q2, nominal GDP growth was fairly steady at 3.8%. However, from the four quarters of 2010 to the first two quarters of 2011, the fixed-weight GDP deflator rose from an average of 1.6% to 2.5%.

Because real-time identification of shocks is problematic, such a rule would "play the historical odds" that recessions are due primarily to contractionary monetary policy. It would prevent policy makers from compounding initial mistakes through the inevitable human desire to attribute recessions to real shocks beyond their control rather than to contractionary monetary policy.

Bibliography

Adelson, Mark H. and David P. Jacob. "The Subprime Problem." *The Journal of Structured Finance*, Spring 2008.

Afonso, Gara, Anna Kovner, and Antoinette Schoar. "Stressed, Not Frozen: The Federal Funds Market in the Financial Crisis." Federal Reserve Bank of New York Staff Reports, no. 437, March 2010 .

Aldrich, Wilbur. *Money and Credit*. New York: The Grafton Press, 1903.

Allen, Frederick L. *Since Yesterday: The 1930s in America*. New York: Harper & Row. Reprinted First Perennial Library, 1972.

American Banker. "Senators Doubt Fed Could Regulate Systemic Risk." March 6, 2009a, 2.

"FDIC Premium Rule Targets Banks' More Costly Funding." March 9, 2009b, 3.

"Tarp's Toll Expected To Be Felt For Years." September 22, 2009c, 1.

"Small Bank Program Is Big Banks' Headache." September 13, 2011.

Anderson, Benjamin M., Jr. "Equilibrium Creates Purchasing Power." *The Chase Economic Bulletin* 11 (June 12, 1931), 3–16.

"The Goldsborough Bill and the Government Security Purchases of the Federal Reserve Banks." *The Chase Economic Bulletin* 12 (May 16, 1932), 3–15.

Anderson, Richard G. "Retail Sweep Programs and Money Demand," Federal Reserve Bank of St. Louis *Monetary Trends*, November 2002.

Armantier, Olivier, Eric Ghysels, Asani Sarkar, and Jeffrey Shrader. "Stigma in Financial Markets: Evidence from Liquidity Auctions and Discount Window Borrowing During the Crisis." Federal Reserve Bank of New York *Staff Reports*, no. 483, January 2011.

Ashcraft, Adam B. "New Evidence on the Lending Channel." Federal Reserve Bank of New York, Banking Studies working paper, November 20, 2003.

Ashcraft, Adam, Morten L. Bech, and W. Scott Frame. "The Federal Home Loan Bank System: The Lender of Next to Last Resort." *Journal of Money, Credit and Banking* 42 (June 2010), 551–83.

Axilrod, Stephen H. "The FOMC Directive as Structured in the Late 1960s: Theory and Appraisal." in Board of Governors of the Federal Reserve System, *Open Market Policies and Operating Procedures - Staff Studies*, July 1971, 3–36.

Balderston, Theo. "The Banks and the Gold Standard in the German Financial Crisis of 1931." *Financial History Review* 1 (April 1994), 43–68.

Balke, Nathan S. and Robert J. Gordon. "Appendix B: Historical Data." in Robert J. Gordon, ed., *The American Business Cycle: Continuity and Change*. Chicago: The University of Chicago Press, 1986, 781–810.

Bank of England. "Quantitative Easing." *Quarterly Bulletin*, 2009Q2, 90–100.

Barber, Lionel. "Fireman Hank." *Financial Times*, February 6–7, 2010, 16 (Life and Arts).

Barrett, Paul M. "While Regulators Slept: What Leaders at the Fed, the Treasury and the S.E.C. Said and Did After They Woke Up to the Panic of 2008." *The New York Times Book Review*, August 9, 2009, 10.

Barro, Robert J. and Gordon, David B. "A Positive Theory of Monetary Policy in a Natural Rate Model." *Journal of Political Economy* 91 (August 1983), 589–610.

Becker, Jo and Gretchen Morgenson. "Geithner, Member and Overseer of Finance Club." *The New York Times*, April 26, 2009, 1.

Bell, Elliott V. "The Bankers Sign a Truce." *Current History*, December 1934, 257–63.

Bennett, Barbara A. "'Shift Adjustments' to the Monetary Aggregates." Federal Reserve Bank of San Francisco *Economic Review* (Spring 1982), 6–18.

Benston, George J., Robert A. Eisenbeis, Paul M. Horvitz, Edward J. Kane, and George G. Kaufman. *Perspectives on Safe & Sound Banking*. Cambridge, MA: MIT Press, 1986.

Benston, George J. and George G. Kaufman. "Is the Banking and Payments System Fragile?" *Journal of Financial Services Research* 9 (1995), 209–40.

Berg, Claes and Lars Jonung. "Pioneering Price Level Targeting: The Swedish Experience 1931–1937." *Journal of Monetary Economics* 43 (1999), 525–51.

Bernanke, Ben S. "Nonmonetary Effects of the Financial Crisis in the Propagation of the Great Depression." *American Economic Review* 73 (June 1983), 257–76.

"The Macroeconomics of the Great Depression: A Comparative Approach." *Journal of Money, Credit and Banking* 27 (February 1995), 1–28.

"Japanese Monetary Policy: A Case of Self-Induced Paralysis?" in Ryoichi Mikitani and Adam S. Posen, eds., *Japan's Financial Crisis and its Parallels to U.S. Experience*. Washington DC: Institute for International Economics, 2000, 149–66.

"On Milton Friedman's Ninetieth Birthday." Remarks at the Conference to Honor Milton Friedman, University of Chicago, November 8, 2002.

Remarks at the meetings of the Eastern Economic Association, Washington DC, February 20, 2004. Available at the Board of Governors Web site (http://www.federalreserve.gov/newsevents/speech/2004speech.htm).

"The Financial Accelerator and the Credit Channel." Speech at The Credit Channel of Monetary Policy in the Twenty-first Century Conference, Federal Reserve Bank of Atlanta, June 15, 2007a.

"The Recent Financial Turmoil and its Economic and Policy Consequences." Remarks at the Economic Club of New York, October 15, 2007b.

"Remarks on the Economic Outlook," International Monetary Conference, Barcelona, Spain, June 3, 2008a.

Remarks on the President's Working Group Market Stability Initiative, October 14, 2008b.

"The Crisis and the Policy Response." Speech delivered at the Stamp Lecture, London School of Economics, January 13, 2009a.

"Four Questions about the Financial Crisis." Speech at Morehouse College, Atlanta, GA, April 14, 2009b.

"Reflections on a Year of Crisis." Speech at the Federal Reserve Bank of Kansas City's Annual Economic Symposium, Jackson Hole, Wyoming, August 21, 2009c.

"On the Outlook for the Economy and Policy." Speech given at the Economic Club of New York, November 16, 2009d.

"Economic Policy: Lessons from History." Speech at the 43rd Annual Alexander Hamilton Awards Dinner, Center for the Study of the Presidency and Congress, Washington, DC, April 8, 2010a.

"Economic Outlook." Testimony before the Joint Economic Committee, U.S. Congress, April 14, 2010b.

"Aiding the Economy: What the Fed Did and Why." *Washington Post*, November 4, 2010c.

"Rebalancing the Global Economy." Speech given at the Sixth European Central Banking Conference, Frankfurt, Germany, November 19, 2010d.

Bernanke, Ben and Harold James. "The Gold Standard, Deflation, and Financial Crisis in the Great Depression: An International Comparison." in R. Glenn Hubbard, *Financial Markets and Financial Crises*. Chicago: The University of Chicago Press, 1991, 33–68.

Berrospide, Jose M. and Rochelle M. Edge. "The Effects of Bank Capital on Lending: What Do We Know, and What Does It Mean?" Board of Governors of the Federal Reserve System, working paper, August 17, 2010.

Blasko, Matej and Joseph F. Sinkey. "Bank Asset Structure, Real-Estate Lending, and Risk-Taking." *Quarterly Review of Economics and Finance* 46 (2006), 53–81.

Blinder, Alan S. "The Fed Is Running Low on Ammo." *The Wall Street Journal*, August 26, 2010, A15.

Bloomberg Markets. "The Mess at UBS." July 2008, 36–50.

Bloomberg. "Greece Faces 'Bank Crisis' as Depositors Flee," June 9, 2011.

Blue Chip Financial Forecasts, Aspen Publishers.

Board of Governors of the Federal Reserve System. "Review of the Month." *Federal Reserve Bulletin* 16 (November 1930), 655–8.

Annual Reports, 1932 and 1933.

"Statistics of Bank Suspensions." *Federal Reserve Bulletin*, September 1937.

Federal Open Market Committee *Minutes of Actions*, 1936–March 1976.

Banking and Monetary Statistics: 1914–1941. Washington, DC: Board of Governors of the Federal Reserve System, November 1943.

Transcripts of the Federal Open Market Committee, April 1976–present.

Banking and Monetary Statistics: 1941–1970. Washington, DC: Board of Governors of the Federal Reserve System, November 1976.

Minutes of Federal Open Market Committee Meetings, Annual Report, various issues, 1993–present.

Federal Reserve Press Release, October 7, 2008.

"Defendant Board of Governors of the Federal Reserve System's Memorandum of Law in Support of Motion for a Stay Pending Appeal." *Bloomberg L.P., Plaintiff, v. Board of Governors of the Federal Reserve System, Defendant*, Civ. No. 08 CV 9595 (LAP), United States District Court for the Southern District of New York, August 26, 2009.

"Assets and Liabilities of Commercial Banks in the United States (Weekly), SA – H.8" (http://www.federalreserve.gov/releases/h8).

Commercial Paper Rates and Outstanding Summary (http://www.federalreserve.gov/releases/cp).

Consumer Credit, Statistical Release G.19 (http://www.federalreserve.gov/releases/g19).

Factors Affecting Reserve Balances of Depository Institutions, Statistical Release H.4.1 (http://www.federalreserve.gov/releases/h41/).

Flow of Funds, Statistical Release Z.1 (http://www.federalreserve.gov/releases/z1).

FOMC *Minutes*, various issues (http://www.federalreserve.gov/monetarypolicy/fomc_historical.htm).

Selected Interest Rates, Statistical Release H.15 (http://www.federalreserve.gov/releases/h15).

Bordo, Michael D. "The Impact and International Transmission of Financial Crises: Some Historical Evidence, 1870–1933. *Revista di Storia Economica*, 2nd ser., 2 (1985), 41–78.

"Some Historical Evidence 1870–1933 on the Impact and International Transmission of Financial Crises." NBER Working Paper Series, No. 1606, April 1985.

"An Historical Perspective on the Crisis of 2007–2008." Rutgers University and NBER, paper presented at the Central Bank of Chile Twelfth Annual Conference on "Financial Stability, Monetary Policy, and Central Banking," Santiago, Chile, November 6–7, 2008.

Bordo, Michael D., Michael Edelstein, and Hugh Rockoff. "Was Adherence to the Gold Standard a Good Housekeeping Seal of Approval During the Interwar Period?" NBER Working Paper No. 7186, 1999.

Bordo, Michael D. and Joseph G. Haubrich. "Credit Crises, Money and Contractions: An Historical View." *Journal of Monetary Economics* 57 (January 2010), 1–18.

Bordo, Michael D. and John Landon-Lane. "Exits from Recessions: The U.S. Experience 1920–2007. NBER Working Paper Series, Working Paper 15731, February 2010a.

"The Banking Panics in the United States in the 1930s: Some Lessons for Today." Paper prepared for the Conference "Lessons from the 1930s Great Depression for the Making of Economic Policy." The British Academy. London, April 16–17, 2010b.

Bordo, Michael D., Angela Redish, and Hugh Rockoff. "The U. S. Banking System from a Northern Exposure: Stability versus Efficiency." *Journal of Economic History* 54 (1994), 325–41.

Bordo, Michael D. and David C. Wheelock. "Price Stability and Financial Stability: The Historical Record." Federal Reserve Bank of St. Louis *Review* 80 (September/October 1998), 41–62.

"The Promise and Performance of the Federal Reserve as Lender of Last Resort 1914–1933." Federal Reserve Bank of Atlanta Conference Commemorating the 100th Anniversary of the Jekyll Island Conference, Jekyll Island, Georgia, November 5–6, 2010.

Boyd, John H. and Mark Gertler. "The Role of Large Banks in the Recent U.S. Banking Crisis." Federal Reserve Bank of Minneapolis *Quarterly Review* 18 (Winter 1994), 2–21.

Bratter, Herbert J. The Committee for the Nation: A Case History in Monetary Propaganda. *The Journal of Political Economy* 49 (August 1941), 531–53.

Bremner, Robert P. *Chairman of the Fed: William McChesney Martin, Jr. and the Creation of the American Financial System*. New Haven, CT: Yale University Press, 2004.

Bresciani-Turroni, Constantino. *The Economics of Inflation. A Study of Currency Depreciation in Post-War Germany.* London: G. Allen & Unwin Ltd., 1937.

Brimmer, Andrew F. "International Finance and the Management of Bank Failures: Herstatt vs. Franklin National." Paper presented at the American Economic Association, Atlantic City, New Jersey, September 16, 1976.

British Labor Statistics, Historical Abstract 1886–1968. Department of Employment and Productivity. London: Her Majesty's Stationery Office, 1971 .

Bundesministerium für Arbeit und Sozialordnung und eigene Berechnungen. Bundesarbeitsblatt 7–8/1997, Bevölkerung und Erwerbstätigkeit im Deutschen Reich und in der Bundesrepublic Deutschland, 1928–1997, 1997 .

Bureau of the Census, U.S. Department of Commerce. *Historical Statistics of the United States, Colonial Times to 1970,* Part 2, 1975.

Bureau of Labor Statistics. "Unemployed Persons by Duration of Unemployment." Household Data (http://www.bls.gov/news.release/empsit.t12.htm).

"Work Experience of the Population (Annual)" (http://www.bls.gov/news.release/work.htm).

Burgess, W. Randolph. "Reflections on the Early Development of Open Market Policy." Federal Reserve Bank of New York *Monthly Review* 46 (November 1964), 219–26.

Burns, Arthur F. "Economic Research and the Keynesian Thinking of Our Times"; "Keynesian *Economics* Once Again"; "Mitchell on What Happens During Business Cycles"; "New Facts on Business Cycles"; "Wesley Mitchell and the National Bureau." in Arthur F. Burns, ed., *The Frontiers of Economic Knowledge.* Princeton: Princeton University Press, 1954.

Statement before the House Subcommittee on International Finance, Committee on Banking and Currency, April 4, 1974.

Statement before the Joint Economic Committee, October 8, 1975.

Reflections of an Economic Policy Maker, Speeches and Congressional Statements: 1969–1978. "Monetary Targets and Credit Allocation," Washington DC: American Enterprise Institute, 1978, 367–71.

Butkiewicz, James L. "Governor Eugene Meyer and the Great Contraction." *Research in Economic History* 26 (2008), 273–307.

Cagan, Phillip. "The Monetary Dynamics of Hyperinflation." in Milton Friedman, ed., *Studies in the Quantity Theory of Money.* Chicago: The University of Chicago Press, 1956.

Cairncross, Alec and Barry Eichengreen. *Sterling in Decline: The Devaluations of 1931, 1949 and 1967.* Oxford: Basil Blackwell, 1983.

Calomiris, Charles W. "Deposit Insurance: Lessons from the Record." Federal Reserve Bank of Chicago *Economic Perspectives* 13 (1989), 10–30.

"Greenback Resumption and Silver Risk: The Economics and Politics of Monetary Regime Change in the United States, 1862–1900." NBER Working Paper No. 4166, September 1992.

Calomiris, Charles W. and Gary Gorton. "The Origins of Banking Panics: Models, Facts, and Bank Regulation." in Charles W. Calomiris, ed., *U.S. Bank Deregulation in Historical Perspective.* Cambridge: Cambridge University Press, 2000, 93–163.

Calomiris, Charles W. and Joseph R. Mason. "Contagion and Bank Failures During the Great Depression: The June 1932 Chicago Banking Panic." *The American Economic Review* 87 (December 1997), 863–83.

"Fundamentals, Panics, and Bank Distress During the Depression." *The American Economic Review* 93 (December 2003), 1615–47.

Calomiris, Charles W. and Eugene N. White. "The Origins of Federal Deposit Insurance." in Charles W. Calomiris, ed., *U.S. Bank Deregulation in Historical Perspective.* Cambridge: Cambridge University Press, 2000, 164–211.

Campa, Jose Manuel. "Exchange Rates and Economic Recovery in the 1930s: An Extension to Latin America." *The Journal of Economic History* 50 (September 1990), 677–82.

Capie, Forrest and Alan Webber. *A Monetary History of the United Kingdom, 1870–1982.* London: George Allen & Unwin, 1985.

Cassel, Gustav. *Postwar Monetary Stabilization.* New York: Columbia University Press, 1928.

"Memorandum of Dissent." League of Nations, 1932, 74–5.

Cassidy, John. "No Credit." *The New Yorker,* March 15, 2010.

Chandler, Lester. *Benjamin Strong, Central Banker.* Washington DC: The Brookings Institution, 1958.

Choudhri, Ehsan U. and Levis A. Kochin. "The Exchange Rate and the International Transmission of Business Cycle Disturbances: Some Evidence from the Great Depression." *Journal of Money, Credit, and Banking* 12 (November 1980), 565–74.

Churchill, Winston. in United Kingdom, *Parliamentary Debates* (Commons), 5th ser., vol. 187, col. 1466–7. London: Hansard (1924–1925).

Clarida, Richard, Jordi Gali, and Mark Gertler. "The Science of Monetary Policy: A New Keynesian Perspective." *Journal of Economic Literature* 37 (December 1999), 1661–1707.

Cogley, Timothy. "Monetary Policy and the Great Crash of 1929: A Bursting Bubble or Collapsing Fundamentals." Federal Reserve Bank of San Francisco *Economic Letter,* March 26, 1999.

Cole, Harold L. and Lee E. Ohanian. "New Deal Policies and the Persistence of the Great Depression: A General Equilibrium Analysis." *Journal of Political Economy* 112 (August 2004), 779–816.

Congressional Quarterly Weekly. "Rescue Takes On A New Purpose." October 20, 2008, 2804–5.

"Sorting Out the Bailouts." February 23, 2009, 394–409.

"A Housebound Economy." March 8, 2010, 544–52.

Cook, Timothy Q. and Robert K. LaRoche. *Instruments of the Money Market.* Richmond, VA: Federal Reserve Bank of Richmond, 1993.

Cooper, Russell and Andrew John. "Coordinating Coordination Failures." *The Quarterly Journal of Economics* 103 (August 1988), 441–63.

Corkery, Michael and James R. Hagerty. "Continuing Vicious Cycle of Pain in Housing and Finance Ensnares Market." *The Wall Street Journal,* July 13, 2008, A2.

Covitz, Daniel, Nellie Liang, and Gustavo Suarez. "The Evolution of a Financial Crisis: Panic in the Asset-Backed Commercial Paper Market." Board of Governors of the Federal Reserve System, August 20, 2009.

Credit Suisse. "Long Shadows: Collateral Money, Asset Bubbles, and Inflation." Fixed Income Research, *Market Focus,* May 5, 2009.

Croushore, Dean and Tom Stark. "A Real-Time Data Set for Macroeconomists." Federal Reserve Bank of Philadelphia Working Paper No. 99-XX, May 1999.

Currie, Lauchlin. "The Failure of Monetary Policy to Prevent the Depression of 1929–1932." *Journal of Political Economy* 42 (April 1934), 145–77.

Daiger, J. M. "Bank Failures: The Problem and the Remedy." *Harpers Magazine* 162 (April 1931), 513–27.

Darin, Robert and Robert L. Hetzel. "A Shift-Adjusted M2 Indicator for Monetary Policy." Federal Reserve Bank of Richmond *Economic Review* 80 (Summer 1994), 25–47.

Deutsche Bundesbank. *Geld und Bankwesen 1876–1975.* 1976.

Diamond, Douglas W. and Phillip H. Dybvig. "Bank Runs, Deposit Insurance, and Liquidity." *Journal of Political Economy* 91 (June 1983), 401–19.

Dotsey, Michael and Anatoli Kuprianov. "Reforming Deposit Insurance: Lessons from the Savings and Loan Crisis." Federal Reserve Bank of Richmond *Economic Review* 76 (March/April 1990), 3–28.

Duca, John V. "Making Sense of Elevated Housing Prices." Federal Reserve Bank of Dallas *Southwest Economy* 5 (September/October 2005), 1–12. http://www.dallas-fed.org/research/swe/2005/swe0505b.html.

Dwyer, Gerald P., Jr. "Wildcat Banking, Banking Panics, and Free Banking in the United States." Federal Reserve Bank of Atlanta *Economic Review* (December 1996), 1–20.

Eavis, Peter. "How the Fed's QE2 Could Drift Off Course." *The Wall Street Journal*, August 12, 2010, C10.

Eccles, Marriner S. Summary of statements by Marriner S. Eccles, Governor of the Federal Reserve Board, in reply to questions by Members of the Committee on Banking and Currency of the House of Representatives at hearings on the Banking bill of 1935, March 4–20, 1935 (pamphlet file Federal Reserve Bank of St. Louis).

Economic Report of the President. Washington DC: U.S. Govt. Printing Office, various issues.

Eggertsson, Gauti B. "Great Expectations and the End of the Depression." *American Economic Review* 98 (September 2008), 1476–516.

Eichengreen, Barry. "The Bank of France and the Sterilization of Gold, 1926–1932." *Explorations in Economic History* 23 (1986), 56–84.

  Golden Fetters: The Gold Standard and the Great Depression, 1919–1939. Oxford: Oxford University Press, 1995.

Eichengreen, Barry and Richard Portes. "The Anatomy of Financial Crises." in Richard Portes and Alexander K. Swoboda, *Threats to International Stability.* Cambridge: Cambridge University Press, 1987.

Eichengreen, Barry and Jeffrey Sachs. "Exchange Rates and Economic Recovery in the 1930s." *Journal of Economic History* 45 (December 1985), 925–46.

Eichengreen, Barry and Peter Temin. "The Gold Standard and the Great Depression." NBER Working Paper 6060, June 1997.

Epstein, Gerald and Thomas Ferguson. "Monetary Policy, Loan Liquidation, and Industrial Conflict: The Federal Reserve and the Open Market Operations of 1932." *Journal of Economic History* 44 (December 1984), 957–83.

Esbitt, Milton. "Bank Portfolios and Bank Failures During the Great Depression: Chicago." *Journal of European History* 54 (June 1986), 455–62.

Federal Deposit Insurance Corporation. Statistics on Depository Institutions Report. (http://www2.fdic.gov?sdi/rpt_Financial.asp).

Federal Financial Institutions Examination Council. Call Reports for various banks. (https://cdr.ffiec.gov/public/ManageFacsimiles.aspx).

Federal Reserve Bank of St. Louis. "The Financial Crisis: A Timeline of Events and Policy
    Actions." (http://timeline.stlouisfed.org/pdf/CrisisTimeline.pdf).
    U.S. Financial Data, various issues. (http://research.stlouisfed.org/publications/
    usfd/).
Federal Reserve Bank of Minneapolis. "Kenneth Rogoff." *The Region* December 2008,
    19–29.
Federal Reserve System. *Federal Reserve's Homeownership and Mortgage Initiatives*. 2008.
    http://www.richmondfed.org/community_development/foreclosure_resource_
    center/research_and_pubs/index.cfm.
Feldman, Gerald D. *The Great Disorder: Politics, Economics, and Society in the German
    Inflation, 1914–1924*. Oxford: Oxford University Press, 1997.
Ferguson, Albert Thomas, Jr. Critical Realignment: The Fall of the House of Morgan and
    the Origins of the New Deal. Ph.D. thesis, Princeton University, June 1981.
Ferguson, Niall and Brigitte Granville. "Weimar on the Volga: Causes and Consequences
    of Inflation in 1990s Russia Compared with 1920s Germany." *The Journal of
    Economic History* 60 (December 2000), 1061–87.
Ferguson, Thomas and Peter Temin. "Made in Germany: The German Currency Crisis of
    July 1931." Alexander J. Field, ed., *Research in Economic History* 21 (2003), 1–53.
    "Comment on 'The German Twin Crisis of 1931.'" *The Journal of Economic History* 64
    (September 2004), 872–6.
Fernandez-Villaverde, Jesus, Pablo Guerron-Quintana, Juan F. Rubio-Ramirez, and
    Martin Uribe. "Risk Matters: The Real Effects of Volatility Shocks." April 14,
    2009.
Fettig, David. "Lender of More Than Last Resort." Federal Reserve Bank of Minneapolis,
    The Region, December 2002, 1–12 (http://www.minneapolisfed.org/pubs/region).
Financial Times. "Regulation of Investment Banks Set for Scrutiny." March 20,
    2008a, 2.
    "European Banks Harder Squeezed by Credit Crunch than US Rivals." June 6,
    2008b, 1.
    "Wages Raise Fears of Euro Zone Inflation." June 14–15, 2008c, 3.
    "Foundations of the CDS Industry Shaken by Bank Collapse." September 16,
    2008d, 25.
    "Rationale Behind Strategy Fails to Win Widespread Agreement." September 26,
    2008e, 2.
    "Inflation Falls but ECB Looks Set to Hold Rates." October 1, 2008f, 4.
    "Monolith's Failure Redraws Risk Landscape." October 1, 2008g, 18.
    "Irish Bank Guarantee Raises Issue of State Aid." October 1, 2008h, 1.
    "Watchful Fed Keeps an Open Mind." October 3, 2008i, 2.
    "The Lehman Legacy." October 13, 2008j, 11.
    "Swiss to Fund $60bn 'Bad Bank' for UBS." October 17, 2008k, 1.
    "Market Jitters Reduce Time to Get It Right." January 22, 2009a, 3.
    "China's Dollar Dilemma." February 23, 2009b, 5.
    "The Iron Age." May 2–3, 2009c, 14.
    "Merkel Makes a Mark." June 6–7, 2009d, 8.
    "Thain: The Inside Story." September 14, 2009e, 14.
    "Scramble to Avoid Collapse." October 13, 2009f, 1.
    "Bankers Seek to Detoxify the Alphabet Soup." October 13, 2009g, 27.

"Strong Stuff." Life and Arts, October 17–18, 2009h, 1.

"Wall Street's Titans Grilled in Tense Exchanges." January 14, 2010a, 4.

"Paulson Feared Run on the Dollar." February 1, 2010b.

"Sun-Belt Workers See No Sign of Recovery." October 7, 2010c, 6.

(European edition). "Greek Rift Widens." June 7, 2011, p. 3.

"Trichet Escalates Row with Germany." June 10, 2011, p. 1.

Fischer, Gerald C. and Carter Golembe. "Compendium of Issues Relating to Branching by Financial Institutions." Prepared by the Subcommittee on Financial Institutions of the Committee on Banking, Housing and Urban Affairs. U.S. Senate, 94th Congress, 2nd sess., Committee Print, October 1976.

Fisher, Irving. Address of Professor Irving Fisher delivered at a Meeting of the District of Columbia Bankers Association, October 23, 1929. in William J. Barber, ed., *The Works of Irving Fisher.* Vol. 10, *Booms and Depressions.* London: Picering & Chatto, 1997.

Fisher, Richard. "Responding to Turbulence." Remarks before the Money Marketeers of New York University, September 25, 2008.

"Monetary Policy Going Forward (Citing Bagehot, Bernanke and Babe Laufenberg)," Remarks before the Greater Houston Partnership, Houston, Texas, September 1, 2010.

Fitch Ratings. Macro Credit Research. "U.S. Money Funds and European Banks: Exposures and Maturities Decline Further." September 23, 2011.

Flandreau, Marc. "New Deal Financial Acts and the Business of Foreign Debt Underwriting: Autopsy of a Regime Change." Graduate Institute of International Studies and Development, Geneva, February 3–4, 2011.

Flood, Mark D. "The Great Deposit Insurance Debate." Federal Reserve Bank of St. Louis *Review* 74 (July/August 1992), 51–77.

Fortune Magazine. "Federal Reserve." May 1934, 65–9, 115, 6, 120–6.

Freeman, James. "Banking on a Rescue." *Business Bookshelf. The Wall Street Journal,* August 12, 2009, A13.

Friedman, Milton. "Wesley C. Mitchell as an Economic Theorist." *Journal of Political Economy* 58 (December 1950), 465–93.

"The Case for Flexible Exchange Rates (1953)." in Milton Friedman, ed., *Essays in Positive Economics.* Chicago: The University of Chicago Press, 1953.

A Theory of the Consumption Function. Princeton: Princeton University Press for the National Bureau of Economic Research, 1957.

A Program for Monetary Stability. New York: Fordham University Press, 1960.

"Inflation: Causes and Consequences (1964)" in Milton Friedman, ed., *Dollars and Deficits.* Englewood Cliffs, NJ: Prentice-Hall, Inc., 1968.

"The Monetary Studies of the National Bureau" (1964). in Milton Friedman, ed., *The Optimum Quantity of Money and Other Essays.* Chicago: Aldine Publishing Company, 1969a, 261–84.

"The Role of Monetary Policy (1968)" in Milton Friedman, ed., *The Optimum Quantity of Money.* Chicago: Aldine, 1969b, 95–110.

The Counter-Revolution in Monetary Theory. London: The Institute of Economic Affairs, 1970.

"The Fed Has No Clothes." *The Wall Street Journal,* April 15, 1988.

"The Quantity Theory of Money" in John Eatwell, Murray Milgate, and Peter Newman, eds., *The New Palgrave Money.* New York: W. W. Norton, 1989, 1–40.

Money Mischief: Episodes in Monetary History. Orlando, FL: Harcourt, Brace, Jovanovich, 1992.

"Rx for Japan: Back to the Future." *Wall Street Journal*, December 17, 1997.

Friedman, Milton and Robert Mundell. "One World, One Money?" *Options Politiques*, May 2001, 10–30.

Friedman, Milton and Anna J. Schwartz. *A Monetary History of the United States, 1867–1960.* Princeton: Princeton University Press, 1963a.

"Money and Business Cycles." *Review of Economics and Statistics* 45 (February 1963b), 32–64.

Monetary Statistics of the United States. New York: National Bureau of Economic Research, 1970.

Gali, Jordi. Monetary Policy, Inflation, and the Business Cycle: An Introduction to the New Keynesian Framework. Princeton and Oxford: Princeton University Press, 2008.

Garrett, Garet. "A Story of Banking." *The Saturday Evening Post*, August 8, 1931.

Gertler, Mark and Nobuhiro Kiyotaki. "Financial Intermediation and Credit Policy in Business Cycle Analysis." *Handbook of Monetary Economics*, 2010.

Giani, Leonardo. "The Complementarity between Financial Supervision and Crisis Intervention: A Lack in the EU Framework at the Time of the Crisis." University of Siena, Italy, September 29, 2009.

Giersch, Herbert, Karl-Heinz Paquu, and Holger Schmieding. *The Fading Miracle: Four Decades of Market Economy in Germany.* Cambridge: Cambridge University Press, 1992.

Gjerstad, Steven and Vernon L. Smith. "From Bubble to Depression?" *The Wall Street Journal*, April 6, 2009, A15.

Goldman Sachs. "The Savings Glut, the Return on Capital and the Rise in Risk Aversion." *Global Economics Paper No: 185*, May 27, 2009.

Goodfriend, Marvin. "Discount Window Borrowing, Monetary Policy, and the Post-October 6, 1979 Federal Reserve Operating Procedure." *Journal of Monetary Economics* 12 (September 1983), 343–56.

"Interest Rate Policy and the Inflation Scare Problem." Federal Reserve Bank of Richmond *Economic Quarterly* 79 (Winter 1993), 1–24.

"Why We Need An 'Accord' for Federal Reserve Credit Policy." *Journal of Money, Credit, and Banking* 26 (August 1994), 572–84.

"Overcoming the Zero Bound on Interest Rate Policy." *Journal of Money, Credit, and Banking* 32 (November 2000, Part 2), 1007–35.

"Financial Stability, Deflation, and Monetary Policy." Bank of Japan Institute for Monetary and Economic Studies. *Monetary and Economic Studies* 19, No. S-1 (February 2001), 143–67.

"Interest on Reserves and Monetary Policy." Federal Reserve Bank of New York *Economic Policy Review* 8 (May 2002), 13–29.

"The Monetary Policy Debate Since October 1979: Lessons for Theory and Practice." Paper for "Reflections on Monetary Policy: 25 Years after October 1979." Conference at Federal Reserve Bank of St. Louis, October 7–8, 2004.

"Policy Debates at the FOMC: 1993–2002." Federal Reserve Bank of Atlanta and Rutgers University Conference, "A Return to Jekyll Island: The Origins, History, and Future of the Federal Reserve." November 5–6, 2010, Cambridge University Press (forthcoming).

"Central Banking in the Credit Turmoil: An Assessment of Federal Reserve Practice." *Journal of Monetary Economics*, January 2011.

Goodfriend, Marvin and Robert G. King. "Financial Deregulation, Monetary Policy and Central Banking." Federal Reserve Bank of Richmond *Economic Review* (May/June 1988), 3–22.

"The New Neoclassical Synthesis." NBER *Macroeconomics Annual*, eds. Ben S. Bernanke and Julio Rotemberg, 1997.

"The Incredible Volcker Disinflation." *Journal of Monetary Economics* 52 (July 2005), 981–1015.

Goodfriend, Marvin and Jeffrey M. Lacker. "Limited Commitment and Central Bank Lending." Federal Reserve Bank of Richmond *Economic Quarterly* 85 (Fall 1999), 1–27.

Gorton, Gary. "Slapped in the Face by the Invisible Hand: Banking and the Panic of 2007." Paper prepared for the Federal Reserve Bank of Atlanta 2009 Financial Markets Conference: Financial Innovation and Crisis, May 11–13, 2009 and May 9, 2009.

Grant, James. *Money of the Mind: Borrowing and Lending in America from the Civil War to Michael Milken*. New York: Farrar Straus Giroux, 1992.

Greenspan, Alan. "The Financial Safety Net." Remarks at the 37th Annual Conference on Bank Structure and Competition of the Federal Reserve Bank of Chicago, May 10, 2001a.

"Economic Developments." Speech to the Economic Club of New York, May 24, 2001b.

"Alan Greenspan's Congressional Testimony–Prepared Statement." *Business News*, October 24, 2008 (http://news.hereisthecity.com/news/business_news/8386.cntns).

"Inflation is the Big Threat to a Sustained Recovery." *Financial Times*, June 26, 2009, 9.

Greer, Guy. "Wanted: Real Banking Reform." *Harpers Magazine*, October 1933, 533–46.

Gros, Daniel and Stefano Micossi. "The Beginning of the End Game." *Vox*, September 20, 2008 (http://www.voxeu.org/index.php?q=node/1669).

Grossman, Richard S. "The Shoe That Didn't Drop: Explaining Banking Stability During the Great Depression." *The Journal of Economic History* 54 (September 1994), 654–82.

Hamilton, James D. "Monetary Factors in the Great Depression." *Journal of Monetary Economics* 19 (1987), 145–69.

"The Role of the International Gold Standard in Propagating the Great Depression." *Contemporary Policy Issues*, April 1988.

"Was the Deflation During the Great Depression Anticipated? Evidence from the Commodity Futures Market." *The American Economic Review* 82 (March 1992), 157–78.

Hansen, Alvin H. *Fiscal Policy and Business Cycles*. New York: W.W. Norton & Co., 1941.

Harris, Seymour E. *Twenty Years of Federal Reserve Policy*. 2 vols. Cambridge: Harvard University Press, 1933.

Hart, Albert G. "The 'Chicago Plan' of Banking Reform." *Review of Economic Studies* 2 (1935), 104–16.

Hau, Harald and Marcel Thum. "Subprime Crisis and Board (In-)Competence: Private vs. Public Banks in Germany." Paper prepared for the 49th Panel Meeting of Economic Policy in Prague, March 13, 2009.

Haubrich, Joseph G. "Non-Monetary Effects of Financial Crises: Lessons from the Great Depression in Canada. *Journal of Monetary Economics* 25 (March 1990), 223–52.

Hayek, Friedrich A. "The Use of Knowledge in Society." *The American Economic Review* 35 (September 1945), 519–30.

"The Fate of the Gold Standard (1932)" in R. McCloughy, ed., *Money, Capital and Fluctuations, Early Essays of F. A. Hayek*. London: Routledge and Kegan Paul, 1984.

Haywood, Charles F. and Charles M. Linke. *The Regulation of Deposit Interest Rates*. A Study Prepared for the Association of Reserve City Bankers, 1968.

Heider, Florian, Marie Hoerova, and Cornelius Holthausen. "Liquidity Hoarding and Interbank Market Spreads: The Role of Counterparty Risk." Working Paper Series No. 1126, European Central Bank, December 2009.

Hetzel, Robert L. "The October 1979 Regime of Monetary Control and the Behavior of the Money Supply in 1980." *Journal of Money, Credit, and Banking* 14 (May 1982), 234–51.

"The Rules versus Discretion Debate over Monetary Policy in the 1920s." Federal Reserve Bank of Richmond *Economic Review* 71 (November/December 1985), 3–14.

"Too Big to Fail: Origins, Consequences, and Outlook." Federal Reserve Bank of Richmond *Economic Review* 77 (November/December 1991), 3–15.

"Sterilized Foreign Exchange Intervention: The Fed Debate in the 1960s," Federal Reserve Bank of Richmond *Economic Quarterly*, (Spring 1996), 21–46.

"The Case for a Monetary Rule in a Constitutional Democracy." *Economic Quarterly*, 83 (Spring 1997), 45–65.

"Arthur Burns and Inflation." Federal Reserve Bank of Richmond *Economic Quarterly* 84 (Winter 1998), 21–44.

"Japanese Monetary Policy: A Quantity Theory Perspective." Federal Reserve Bank of Richmond *Economic Quarterly* 85 (Winter 1999), 1–25.

"German Monetary History in the First Half of the Twentieth Century." Federal Reserve Bank of Richmond *Economic Quarterly* 88 (Winter 2002a), 1–35.

"German Monetary History in the Second Half of the Twentieth Century: From the Deutsche Mark to the Euro." Federal Reserve Bank of Richmond *Economic Quarterly* 88 (Spring 2002b), 29–64.

"Japanese Monetary Policy and Deflation." Federal Reserve Bank of Richmond *Economic Quarterly* 89 (Summer 2003), 21–52.

"How Do Central Banks Control Inflation?" Federal Reserve Bank of Richmond *Economic Quarterly* 90 (Summer 2004a), 47–63.

"Price Stability and Japanese Monetary Policy." Bank of Japan *Monetary and Economic Studies* 22 (October 2004b), 1–23.

"What Is the Monetary Standard, Or, How Did the Volcker-Greenspan FOMC's Tame Inflation?" Federal Reserve Bank of Richmond *Economic Quarterly* 94 (Spring 2008a), 147–71.

The Monetary Policy of the Federal Reserve: A History. Cambridge: Cambridge University Press, 2008b.

"Should Increased Regulation of Bank Risk-Taking Come from Regulators or from the Market?" Federal Reserve Bank of Richmond *Economic Quarterly* 95 (Spring 2009a), 161–200.

"Monetary Policy in the 2008–2009 Recession." Federal Reserve Bank of Richmond *Economic Quarterly* 95, (Spring 2009b), 201–33.

"World Recession: What Went Wrong?" *Economic Affairs* 29 (August 2009c), 17–21.

Hetzel, Robert L. and Yash Mehra. "The Behavior of Money Demand in the 1980s." *Journal of Money, Credit, and Banking* 21 (November 1989), 455–63.

Historical Statistics of the United States, *Earliest Times to the Present, Millennial Edition*, vol. 3, part C, "Economic Structure and Performance." New York: Cambridge University Press, 2006.

vol. 5, part E, "Federal Government Finances." New York: Cambridge University Press, 2006.

Hobijn, Bart, Colin Gardiner, and Theodore Wiles. "Recent College Graduates and the Labor Market." Federal Reserve Bank of San Francisco *Economic Letter*, March 21, 2011.

Hoenig, Thomas M. "Too Big Has Failed." Speech delivered in Omaha, Nebraska, March 6, 2009 (http://www.kansascityfed.org/home/).

Holtfrerich, Carl-Ludwig. *The German Inflation 1914–1923: Causes and Effects in International Perspective*. New York: Walter de Gruyter, 1986.

"Monetary Policy under Fixed Exchange Rates (1948–70)." in Deutsche Bundesbank, ed., *Fifty Years of the Deutsche Mark*. 1999, 307–401.

Honkapohja, Seppo. "The 1990s Financial Crises in Nordic Countries." Bank of Finland Research Discussion Papers 5, 2009 (http://ssrn.com/abstract=1427260).

Hori, Masahiro. 1996. New Evidence on the Causes and Propagation of the Great Depression. Ph.D. Dissertation, University of California, Berkeley.

Humphrey, Thomas M. "The Concept of Indexation in the History of Economic Thought." Federal Reserve Bank of Richmond *Economic Review* 60 (November/December 1974), 3–16.

"The Classical Concept of the Lender of Last Resort." Federal Reserve Bank of Richmond *Economic Review* 61 (January/February 1975), 2–9.

"Lender of Last Resort: The Concept in History." Federal Reserve Bank of Richmond *Economic Review* 75 (March/April 1989), 8–16.

"Mercantilists and Classicals: Insights from Doctrinal History." Federal Reserve Bank of Richmond *Economic Quarterly* 85 (Spring 1999), 55–82.

"Lender of Last Resort: What It Is, Whence It Came, and Why the Fed Isn't It." *Cato Journal* 30 (Spring/Summer 2010), 333–64.

Institutional Risk Analyst. "Germany's Subprime Crisis: Interview with Achim Dübel." May 27, 2009.

International Currency Review. "Inter-Agency Feuding and the Penn Square Fiasco." 14 (October 1982), 31–35.

International Herald Tribune. "36 Critical Hours." October 3, 2008, 1.

International Monetary Fund. "Global Financial Stability Report: Containing Systemic Risks and Restoring Financial Soundness." Washington, DC, April 2008.

"Global Financial Stability Report." April 2009.

Irving, Washington. "A Time of Unexampled Prosperity." *The Crayon Papers: The Great Mississippi Bubble*, 1819–1820. in Richard W. Fisher, Federal Reserve Bank of Dallas *Economic Letter* 3 (April 2008), 1–8.

Irwin, Douglas A. "Did France Cause the Great Depression?" NBER Working Paper Series, No. 16350, September 2010.

Isaac, William M. "The Fed and the Mortgage 'Crisis." *The Wall Street Journal*, May 22, 2008a, A15.

"The Deposit Insurance Funding Issue, Revisited." *American Banker*, October 7, 2008b, 7A.

"Viewpoint: Treasury Bill Gets It Wrong on 'Too Big.' *American Banker*, November 4, 2009.

James, Harold. "The Reichsbank 1876–1945." in Deutsche Bundesbank, ed., *Fifty Years of the Deutsche Mark*. Oxford: Oxford University Press, 1999, 3–53.

Jensen, Michael C. and William H. Meckling. "Theory of the Firm: Managerial Behavior, Agency Costs and Ownership Structure." *Journal of Financial Economics* 3 (October 1976), 305–60.

Jimenez, Gabriel, Atif Mian, Jose-Luis Peydro, and Jesus Saurina. "Estimating the Aggregate Impact of Credit Supply Channel: Evidence from Securitization in Spain." Bank of Spain, September 2010.

Johnsen, Terri and Forest Myers. "New Community Reinvestment Act Regulation: What Have Been the Effects?" Federal Reserve Bank of Kansas City *Financial Industry Perspectives*, 1996, 1–11.

Johnson, G. Griffith, Jr. *The Treasury and Monetary Policy 1933–1938*. Cambridge, MA: Harvard University Press, 1939.

Johnson, H. Clark. *Gold, France, and the Great Depression, 1919–1932*. New Haven: Yale University Press, 1997.

Jonung, Lars. "Knut Wicksell's Norm of Price Stabilization and Swedish Monetary Policy in the 1930s." *Journal of Monetary Economics* 5 (October 1979), 459–96.

"Lessons from Financial Liberalization in Scandinavia." *Comparative Economic Studies* 10 (2008), 1–35 (http://www.palgrave-journals.com/ces).

J. P. Morgan Securities. "US Fixed Income Strategy-Short Duration Strategy: Short-Term Fixed Income Research Note." August 16, 2007.

Kane, Edward J. *The S&L Insurance Mess*. Washington DC: The Urban Institute Press, 1989.

Katz, Ian. "FASB 'Close' on Off-Balance-Sheet Change, Herz Says." (Update 1), Bloomberg, April 30, 2009.

Kaufman, George G. "Banking Risk in Historical Perspective." in George G. Kaufman, ed., *Research in Financial Services*, vol. 1, Greenwich, CT: JAI Press, 1989, 151–64.

"Are Some Banks Too Large to Fail? Myth and Reality." *Contemporary Policy Issues* 8 (October 1990), 1–14.

"Bank Contagion: A Review of the Theory and Evidence." *Journal of Financial Services Research* 8 (April 1994), 123–50.

"The Financial Turmoil of 2007–09: Sinners and Their Sins." Loyola University, February 2, 2010.

Kaufman, George G. and Peter J. Wallison. "The New Safety Net." *Regulation 24* (Summer 2001), 28–35.

Keeley, Michael. "Deposit Insurance, Risk and Market Power in Banking." *American Economic Review* 80 (December 1990), 1183–200.

Keister, Todd, Antoine Martin, and James McAndrews. "Divorcing Money from Monetary Policy." Federal Reserve Bank of New York *Economic Policy Review* 14, September 2008.

Kemmerer, Edwin Walter. "Gold and the Gold Standard." *Proceedings American Philosophical Society* 71 (April 1932), 85–104.

Keynes, John Maynard. "The Economic Consequences of the Peace" (1919). in Donald Moggridge, ed., *The Collected Writings of John Maynard Keynes*, vol. 2. London: Macmillan, 1971a.

"A Tract on Monetary Reform" (1923). in Donald Moggridge, ed., *The Collected Writings of John Maynard Keynes*, vol. 20. London: Macmillan, 1971b.

A Treatise on Money (1930). in Donald Moggridge, ed., *The Collected Writings of John Maynard Keynes*, vol. 5 and 6. London: The Macmillan Press, 1971c.

"A Gold Conference (1931)." *The New Statesman and Nation*. in Donald Moggridge, ed., *The Collected Writings of John Maynard Keynes*, vol. 20. London: Macmillan, 1971d.

"Letter to Ramsay MacDonald, 5 August 1931." in Donald Moggridge, ed., *The Collected Writings of John Maynard Keynes*, vol. 2. London: Macmillan, 1971e.

Kocherlakota, Narayana. "Modern Macroeconomic Models as Tools for Economic Policy." Federal Reserve Bank of Minneapolis *The Region*, 2009 *Annual Report* 5–21.

"Inside the FOMC." Speech delivered in Marquette, MI, August 17, 2010.

Koller, Tim. "A Better Way to Anticipate Downturns." *McKinsey Quarterly*. The Online Journal of McKinsey & Company, October 2010 (https:/www.mckinseyquarterly.com/article_print.aspx?L2=5&L3=7&ar=2681).

Konishi, Toru, Valerie A. Ramey, and Clive W. J. Granger. "Stochastic Trends and Short-Run Relationships Between Financial Variables and Real Activity." NBER Working Paper No. 4275, February 1993.

Koopmans, Tjalling. "Measurement Without Theory." *The Review of Economic Statistics* 28 (August 1947), 161–72.

Koppenheffer, Matt. "Who's Really Getting Bailed Out?" "The Motley Fool.com," April 6, 2009 (http://www.fool.com/investing/general/2009/04/06/whos-really-getting-bailed-out.aspx).

Kozicki, Sharon. "How Useful Are Taylor Rules for Monetary Policy?" Federal Reserve Bank of Kansas City *Economic Review* 84 (2nd Quarter 1999), 5–25.

Krainer, John. "Commercial Banks, Real Estate and Spillovers." Federal Reserve Bank of San Francisco, July 2008.

Krugman, Paul. "Partying Like It's 1929." *The New York Times*, March 21, 2008, A23.

"Making Banking Boring." *The New York Times*, April 10, 2009a, A19.

"How Did Economists Get It So Wrong?" *The New York Times Magazine Section*, September 6, 2009b.

"The Old Enemies." *International Herald Tribune*, May 25, 2010a, 9.

"That '30s Feeling." *The New York Times*, June 17, 2010b.

Kydland, Finn E. and Edward C. Prescott. "Rules Rather than Discretion: The Inconsistency of Optimal Plans." *Journal of Political Economy* 85 (June 1977), 473–91.

"Time to build and Aggregate Fluctuations." *Econometrica* 50 (November 1982), 1345–70.

Lacker, Jeffrey M. "Financial Stability and Central Banks." Remarks before the European Economics and Financial Center. London, June 5, 2008.

"Prudential Stress Testing in Theory and Practice: Comments on 'Stressed Out: Macroprudential Principles for Stress Testing." 2011 U.S. Monetary Policy Forum, New York, February 25, 2011.

Laubach, Thomas and John C. Williams. "Measuring the Natural Rate of Interest." *Review of Economics and Statistics* 85 (November 2003), 1063–70.

Lawler, Thomas. Lawler Economic and Housing Consulting, LLC, February 17, 2010a, and October 1, 2010b.

League of Nations. Report of the Gold Delegation of the Financial Committee. Geneva, 1932.

Leffingwell, Russell C. "Letters to Senator Carter Glass." January 8, 1932a and February 3, 1932b, Leffingwell Papers, Box 3, Folder 66, Yale University, Sterling Library.

"Letter to George L. Harrison." December 18, 1932c, Leffingwell Papers, Box 3, Folder 66, Yale University, Sterling Library.

"Letter to Senator Glass." July 18, 1933, Box Number 4, Folder dates 1933–5, University of Virginia Library.

Leonhardt, David. "Pulling Back, Amid Echoes of the 1930s." *The New York Times*, June 30, 2010, A1.

L'Huillier, Jean-Paul. "Heterogeneous Information and Nominal Rigidities." Job market paper, MIT, November 2010.

Lucas, Robert E., Jr. "Expectations and the Neutrality of Money" (1972); "Econometric Policy Evaluation: A Critique" (1976); "Rules, Discretion, and the Role of the Economic Advisor" (1980). in Robert E. Lucas, Jr., *Studies in Business-Cycle Theory*. Cambridge, MA: The MIT Press, 1981.

"Nobel Lecture: Monetary Neutrality." *Journal of Political Economy* 104 (August 1996), 661–82.

"Interview." in Randall E. Parker, ed., *The Economics of the Great Depression*. Cheltenham, UK: Edgar Elgar, 2007, 88–101.

Lucas, Robert E., Jr. and Thomas J. Sargent. (1978) "After Keynesian Macroeconomics." in Robert E. Lucas, Jr., and Thomas J. Sargent, eds., *Rational Expectations and Econometric Practice*, vol 1. Minneapolis: The University of Minnesota Press, 1981, 295–319.

Macaulay, Frederick R. Some Theoretical Problems Suggested by the Movements of Interest Rates, Bond Yields and Stock Prices in the United States Since 1856. New York: NBER, 1938.

Mackay, Charles. *Extraordinary Popular Delusions and the Madness of Crowds* (1841). in Richard W. Fisher, "Comments on the Current Financial Crisis." Remarks before the Ninth Annual R.I.S.E. Forum, Dayton, Ohio, March 26, 2009. Federal Reserve Bank of Dallas Web of General Prices (1925)." in A. C. Pigou, ed., *Memorials of Alfred Marshall*. Reprinted by Kelley and Web site: http://dallasfed.org/news/speeches/fisher/2009/fs090326.cfm.

Macroeconomic Advisers. Monetary Policy Insights. *Policy Focus*. "Is Monetary Policy Working?" February 29, 2008a.

Monetary Policy Insights *Policy Focus*. "Inflation Expectations: Still Well Anchored?" March 19, 2008b.

Monetary Policy Insights *Policy Focus*. "FOMC Chatter Ahead of the September 2008 Meeting." September 12, 2008c.

Monetary Policy Insights *Policy Focus*. "Dueling Taylor Rules." August 20, 2009.

Maisel, Sherman J. *Managing the Dollar*. New York: W. W. Norton & Co., 1973.

Malysheva, Nadezhda and John R. Walter. "How Large Has the Federal Financial Safety Net Become?" Federal Reserve Bank of Richmond *Economic Quarterly* 96 (Third Quarter 2010), 273–90.

Marshall, Alfred. "Remedies for Fluctuations of General Prices (1925)." In A. C. Pigou, ed., *Memorials of Alfred Marshall*. Reprinted by Kelley and Millman, Inc., 1956, 188–211.

Marschak, Jacob. "Economic Measurements for Policy and Prediction." in Hood, W. C. and T. C. Koopmans. *Studies in Econometric Method*. Cowles Foundation Monograph No. 14, New York: John Wiley, 1953, 1–26.

Marsh, David. The Most Powerful Bank: Inside Germany's Bundesbank. New York: Random House, 1992.

McCallum, Bennett. "The Case for Rules in the Conduct of Monetary Policy: A Concrete Example." Federal Reserve Bank of Richmond, *Economic Review* 73 (September/October 1987), 10–18.

"Robustness Properties of a Rule for Monetary Policy." *Carnegie-Rochester Conference Series on Public Policy* 29 (Autumn 1988), 173–203.

McFadden, Louis T. *Congressional Record*, p. 12595, 1932.

McGuire, Patrick and Goetz von Peter. "The US Dollar Shortage in Global Banking." *BIS Quarterly Review*. March 2009, 47–63.

McKinsey & Company. "'Power Curves': What Natural and Economic Disasters Have in Common." *The McKinsey Quarterly*, June 10, 2009 (editorial@e.mckinseyquarterly.com).

Mehra, Yash P. "The Stability of the M2 Demand Function: Evidence from an Error-Correction Model." *Journal of Money, Credit and Banking* 25 (August 1993), 455–60.

Mehra, Yash P. and Brian Minton. "A Taylor Rule and the Greenspan Era." Federal Reserve Bank of Richmond *Economic Quarterly* 90 (Summer 2007), 229–50.

Mehra, Yash P. and Bansi Sawhney. "Inflation Measure, Taylor Rules, and the Greenspan-Bernanke Years." Federal Reserve Bank of Richmond *Economic Quarterly* 96 (Second Quarter 2010), 123–51.

Meltzer, Allan H. *A History of the Federal Reserve*, vol. 1, 1913–1951. Chicago: University of Chicago Press, 2003.

Mengle, David L. "The Case for Interstate Branch Banking." Federal Reserve Bank of Richmond *Economic Quarterly* 76 (November/December 1990), 3–17.

Mertens, Karel. "Deposit Rate Ceiling and Monetary Transmission in the US." *Journal of Monetary Economics* 55 (October 2008), 1290–302.

Metro-Goldwyn-Mayer. "Inflation," released June 15, 1933. See YouTube: http://www.youtube.com/watch?v=JUvm9UgJBtg.

Meulendyke, Ann-Marie. *U.S. Monetary Policy and Financial Markets*. New York: Federal Reserve Bank of New York, 1998.

Mill, John Stuart. *Principles of Political Economy* (1848). Fairfield, NJ: Augustus M. Kelley, 1987.

Miller, Adolph C. "Responsibility for Federal Reserve Policies: 1927–1929." *The American Economic Review* 25 (September 1935), 442–58.

Mincer, Jilian. "Some Options for Protecting Accounts." *The Wall Street Journal*, July 22, 2008, D6.

Mints, Lloyd W. *A History of Banking Theory*. Chicago: University of Chicago Press, 1945.

Mishkin, Frederic S. "Who Do You Trust Now?" in David Leonhardt, *Economic Scene. International Herald Tribune*, October 2, 2008, 1.

Morley, James. "The Emperor Has No Clothes." Macroeconomic Advisers' *Macro Focus*, June 24, 2010.

"The Shape of Things to Come." Macroeconomic Advisers' *Macro Focus*, April 27, 2009.

Morrison, James Ashley. "Keynessandra No More: JM Keynes, the 1931 Financial Crisis, and the Death of the Gold Standard in Britain." Unpublished paper, Middlebury College, 2010.

Mortgage Strategist. UBS, September 4, 2007, 37.

MSNBC. "Bank of America to Acquire Countrywide." January 11, 2008 (http://www.msnbc.msn.com/id/22606833/ns/business-personal_finance/t/bank-america-acquire-countrywide/).

National Public Radio. "Is the U.S. 'Nationalizing Banks?'" October 15, 2008 (http:www.npr.org/templates/story/story.php?storyId=95700786).

The New York Times. "Sindona is Convicted by U.S. Jury of Fraud in Franklin Bank Failure." March 28, 1980, 1.

"Big Cut in U.S. Deposits Hastened Fall of Freedom Bank in Harlem." January 29, 1991.

"Bank in Germany Posts Loss Because of Bad Stock Trades." August 31, 2007, C4.

"After the Fed." January 31, 2008a, A26.

"FHA Expects Big Loss on Home Loan Defaults." June 10, 2008b, C5.

"Seeing Bad Loans, Investors Flee from Bank Shares." July 16, 2008c, C1.

"Trouble at Fannie and Freddie Stirs Concern Abroad." July 21, 2008d, C1.

"A Lifeline for A.I.G. from State." September 16, 2008e, C1.

"Administration Is Seeking $700 Billion For Wall St.; Bailout Could Set Record: A Professor and a Banker Bury Old Dogma." September 21, 2008f, 1.

"As Stocks Rally, Credit Markets Appear Frozen." September 26, 2008g, C1.

"Nations Weighing Global Approach As Chaos Spreads." October 10, 2008h, A1.

"Plan B: Flood Banks With Cash." October 10, 2008i, B1.

"Struggling to Keep Up as Crisis Raced On." October 23, 2008j, A1.

"Greenspan Concedes Flaws in Deregulatory Approach." October 24, 2008k, B1.

"Tracking Firm Says Bets Placed on Lehman Have Been Quietly Settled." October 28, 2008l, A20.

"Where Did the Cash Go?" October 30, 2008m, B1.

"Fed Adds $21 Billion To Loans for A.I.G." October 31, 2008n, B1.

"U.S. Plans $800 Billion in Lending to Ease Crisis." November 26, 2008o, A1.

"Ex-Officer Faults Mortgage Giants for 'Orgy' of Nonprime Loans." December 10, 2008p, B3.

"1997 Tax Break on Home Sales May Have Helped Inflate Bubble." December 19, 2008q, A22.

"Obama Has No Quick Fix for Banks." January 21, 2009a, B1.

"Bank Crisis Deepens." January 29, 2009b, B1.

"Small Businesses Suffer in Crackdown of Credit." June 19, 2009c, B1.

"For Banks, Wads of Cash and Loads of Trouble." July 4, 2009d, A1.

"Germany Has Been Slow to Fix Its Banks." July 15, 2009e, B1.

"Bernanke, a Hero to His Own, Still Faces Fire in Washington." August 20, 2009f, A1.

"Lehman Had to Die, It Seems, So Global Finance Could Live." September 12, 2009g, A1.

"Tax Them Both." January 13, 2010a, A26.

"When the Fed Speaks." August 12, 2010b, A30.

"Report Details Wall Street Crisis." January 28, 2011a, A4.

"Europeans Reach New Deal to Fight Debt Crisis." March 12, 2011b, B1.

The Nikkei Weekly. "BOJ in Need of Some Maneuverability." October 13, 2008, 3.

Nocera, Joe. "A System Overdue for Reform." *The New York Times.* March 29, 2008, B1.

"Propping Up a House of Cards." in "Talking Business" column, *The New York Times,* February 28, 2009, B1.

Northwestern Banker. "Should Finance Company Paper Be Eligible for Rediscount?" January 1932.

Odell, Kerry A. and Marc D. Weidenmier. "Real Shock, Monetary Aftershock: The 1906 San Francisco Earthquake and the Panic of 1907." *The Journal of Economic History* 64 (December 2004), 1002–27.

Office of Federal Housing Enterprise Oversight. *2008 Report to Congress,* 2008 (http://www.ofheo.gov/media/annualreports/ReporttoCongress2008.pdf).

Organization for Economic Cooperation and Development. OECD Stat. (http://stats.oecd.org/index.aspx, item "B1_GE:VPVOBARSA.")

Orphanides, Athanasios. "Monetary Policy in Deflation: The Liquidity Trap in History and Practice." *The North American Journal of Economics and Finance* 15 (2004b), 101–24.

Patinkin, Don. "Price Flexibility and Full Employment." *American Economic Review* 38 (1948), 543–64.

Money, Interest, and Prices, New York: Harper & Row, 1965.

Pearlstein, Steven. "The Fed Should Stay Out of the Bank-Supervision Business." *The Washington Post,* February 27, 2010, A10.

Perri, Fabrizio. "Comment" on "Unsecured Credit Markets Are Not Insurance Markets." Carnegie-Rochester Conference, "The Causes and Consequences of Rising Income Inequality." April 25–26, 2008.

Pontzen, Martin. "The German Banking Crisis of 1931." *Central Banking* 9 (February 1999, 76–80.

Posen, Adam S. *Restoring Japan's Economic Growth.* Washington, DC: Institute for International Economics, 1998.

"Preface" in Ryoichi Mikitani and Adam S. Posen, eds., *Japan's Financial Crisis and its Parallels to U.S. Experience.* Washington DC: Institute for International Economics, 2000.

Reuters, "Dexia, Depfa Woes Led Them to Seek Fed Loans." March 31, 2011 (http://www.reuters.com/article/2011/03/31/usa-fed-lending-europe-idUSN3113160620110331).

Reynolds, Maura. "Legacy of Depression at Work Now: The Fed's Expanded Lending, a Salve for Current Crisis, Was Meant to Aid the 'Forgotten Man.'" *Los Angeles Times,* March 24, 2008, C1.

Richardson, Gary. "Categories and Causes of Bank Distress During the Great Depression, 1929–1933: The Illiquidity versus Insolvency Debate Revisited." *Explorations in Economic History* 44 (2007), 588–607.

Richardson, Gary and Patrick Van Horn. "Intensified Regulatory Scrutiny and Bank Distress in New York City During the Great Depression." *The Journal of Economic History* 69 (June 2009), 446–65.

Riefler, Winfield W. *Money Rates and Money Markets in the United States.* New York: Harper & Brothers, 1930.

Robbins, Lionel. *The Great Depression*. London: Macmillan, 1934.

Roberds, William. "Financial Crises and the Payments System: Lessons from the National Banking Era." Federal Reserve Bank of Atlanta *Economic Review* 80 (May/June 1995), 15–31.

Roberts, Priscilla. "Benjamin Strong, the Federal Reserve, and the Limits to Interwar American Nationalism." Federal Reserve Bank of Richmond *Economic Quarterly* 86 (Spring 2000), 61–98.

Robertson, Dennis H. *Money* (1928). New York: Harcourt Brace and Company, 1948.

Rogoff, Kenneth. "Interview." Federal Reserve Bank of Minneapolis *The Region*, December 2008, 20–29.

Rolnick, Arthur J. and Warren E. Weber. "The Causes of Free Bank Failures: A Detailed Examination." *Journal of Monetary Economics* 14 (November 1984), 267–91.

Romer, Christina D. "What Ended the Great Depression?" *The Journal of Economic History* 52 (December 1992), 757–84.

Romer, Christina D. and David H. Romer. "Does Monetary Policy Matter? A New Test in the Spirit of Friedman and Schwartz." in NBER *Macroeconomics Annual 1989*, vol. 4, 121–70.

Rudebusch, Glenn D. "The Fed's Monetary Policy Response to the Crisis." *FRBSF Economic Letter*, May 22, 2009.

Samuelson, Paul A. "A Brief Survey of Post-Keynesian Developments (1963)" in Joseph E. Stiglitz, ed., *The Collected Scientific Papers of Paul A. Samuelson*. vol. 2, no. 115, 1966, 1534–50.

   "Worldwide Stagflation" (1974) in Hiroaki Nagatani and Kate Crowley, eds., The Collected Scientific Papers of Paul A. Samuelson. vol. 4, no. 268, 1977a, 801–7.

   "What Jimmy Should Do." *Newsweek*, January 10, 1977b, 58.

   "Living with Stagflation" (1979) in Kate Crowley, ed., *The Collected Scientific Papers of Paul A. Samuelson*. vol. 5, no. 379, 1986, 972.

Samuelson, Paul and Robert Solow. "Analytical Aspects of Anti-Inflation Policy (1960)," in Joseph Stiglitz, ed., *The Collected Scientific Papers of Paul A. Samuelson*. vol. 2, no. 102, 1966, 1336–53.

Sargent, Thomas. "The Ends of Four Big Inflations." in *Rational Expectations and Inflation*, 2nd ed. New York: Harper Collins College, 1993, 44–115.

Scheiber, Noam. "Cycles of Doom." *The New York Times Book Review*, November 30, 2008, 17.

Schlesinger, Arthur M. *The Coming of the New Deal*. Vol. 2, *The Age of Roosevelt*. Boston: Houghton Mifflin Co., 1959.

Schnabel, Isabel. "The German Twin Crisis of 1931." *The Journal of Economic History* 64 (September 2004), 822–71.

Schumpeter, Joseph A. *History of Economic Analysis*. New York: Oxford University Press, 1954.

Schwartz, Anna. "The Misuse of the Fed's Discount Window." Federal Reserve Bank of Saint Louis *Economic Review* 74 (September/October 1992), 58–69.

Shiller, Robert J. "Interview." *Central Banking* 18, May 2008.

   "Animal Spirits Depend on Trust." *The Wall Street Journal*, January 27, 2009a, A15.

   "A Failure to Control the Animal Spirits." *Financial Times*, March 9, 2009b, 9.

Shizume, Masato. "A Reassessment of Japan's Monetary Policy During the Great Depression: The Constraints and Remedies." Research Institute for Economics and Business Administration, Kobe University, October 2007.

"The Japanese Economy During the Interwar Period: Instability in the Financial System and the Impact of the World Depression." *Bank of Japan Review*, May 2009, 1–10.

Siems, Thomas F. "Does Borrowed Money Lead to Borrowed Time? An Assessment of Federal Home Loan Bank Advances to Member Banks." Federal Reserve Bank of Dallas, October 2, 2008.

Silber, William L. "Why Did FDR's Bank Holiday Succeed?" Federal Reserve Bank of New York *Economic Policy Review* 15 (July 2009), 19–30.

Simons, Henry C. "Rules Versus Authorities in Monetary Policy." in Henry C. Simons, *Economic Policy for a Free Society*. Chicago: The University of Chicago Press, 1948, 160–83.

Sims, Christopher A. "A Simple Model for Study of the Determination of the Price Level and the Interaction of Monetary and Fiscal Policy." *Economic Theory* 4 (1994), 381–99.

Skidelsky, Robert. "The Remedist." *The New York Times*, December 14, 2008, 21.

Smets, Frank and Raf Wouters. "An Estimated Dynamic Stochastic General Equilibrium Model of the Euro Area." *Journal of the European Economic Association* 1 (September 2003), 1123–75.

Smith, Rixey and Norman Beasley. *Carter Glass: A Biography*. New York: Green and Co., 1939.

Solomou, Solomos and Martin Weale. "UK National Income, 1920–1938: The Implications of Balanced Estimates." *Economic History Review* 49 (1996), 101–15.

Sprague, Irvine H. *Bailout: An Insider's Account of Bank Failures and Rescues*. Basic Books: New York, 1986.

Sprague, O. M. W. *History of Crises Under the National Banking System*. Report by the National Monetary Commission to the U.S. Senate. 61st Cong., 2nd sess., Doc. 538. Washington, DC: Government Printing Office, 1910.

Sproul, Allan. "Money Will Not Manage Itself." The Second Annual Arthur K. Salomon Lecture delivered at the Graduate School of Business at New York University November 7, 1963. in Lawrence S. Ritter, ed., *Selected Papers of Allan Sproul*, Federal Reserve Bank of New York, 1980, 120–28.

Steel, Ronald. *Walter Lippman and the American Century*. New York: Knopf Doubleday, 1981.

Stein, Herbert. *The Fiscal Revolution in America*. Washington DC: The AEI Press, 1996.

Stigler, George J. "The Nature and Role of Originality in Scientific Progress." in George J. Stigler, ed., *Essays in the History of Economics*. Chicago: The University of Chicago Press, 1965.

Sumner, William G. *History of American Currency*. Henry Holt, 1874, 79–80, cited in John H. Wood, "The Stability of Monetary Policy: The Federal Reserve, 1914–2006." Working paper, Wake Forest University, December 20, 2006, 4.

Swagel, Phillip. "The Financial Crisis: An Inside View." March 2009 (http://www.econ. yale.edu/seminars/macro/mac08/Swagel-090409.pdf).

Tallman, Ellis W. and Jon R. Moen. "Lessons from the Panic of 1907." Federal Reserve Bank of Atlanta *Economic Review* 75 (May/June 1990), 2–13.

Tavlas, George. "Two Who Called the Great Depression: An Initial Formulation of the Monetary-Origins View." *Journal of Money, Credit and Banking* 43 (March-April 2011), 565–74.

Taylor, John B. "Discretion versus Policy Rules in Practice." *Carnegie-Rochester Conference Series on Public Policy* 39, 1993, 195–214.

"Monetary Policy Guidelines for Employment and Inflation Stability." in Robert B. Solow and John B. Taylor, *Inflation, Unemployment, and Monetary Policy.* Cambridge, MA: The MIT Press, 1998a, 29–54.

"Monetary Policy and the Long Boom." Federal Reserve Bank of St. Louis *Review*, November/December 1998b, 3–11.

"A Historical Analysis of Monetary Policy Rules," in Taylor, John B., ed., *Monetary Policy Rules.* Chicago: The University of Chicago Press, 1999a, 319–47.

"The Robustness and Efficiency of Monetary Policy Rules as Guidelines for the Interest Rate Setting by the European Central Bank." *Journal of Monetary Economics* 43 (1999b), 655–79.

Getting off Track: How Government Actions and Interventions Caused, Prolonged, and Worsened the Financial Crisis. Stanford, CA: Hoover Institution Press, 2009.

Temin, Peter. *Did Monetary Forces Cause the Great Depression?* New York: W. W. Norton, 1976.

Lessons from the Great Depression. MA: MIT Press, 1989.

"Transmission of the Great Depression." *Journal of Economic Perspectives* 7 (Spring 1993), 87–102.

Temin, Peter and Barrie A. Wigmore. "The End of One Big Deflation." *Explorations in Economic History* 27 (1990), 483–502.

Tett, Gillian. "German Move on Flexibility Opens New Can of Worms." *Financial Times*, July 9, 2009, 2.

Timberlake, Richard H. "The Central Banking Role of Clearinghouse Associations." *Journal of Money, Credit and Banking* 16 (February 1984), 1–15.

Monetary Policy in the United States: An Intellectual and Institutional History. Chicago: The University of Chicago Press, 1993.

Time. "Hold the Line." May 30, 1932.

"Governor, Senator, Dollar." July 23, 1934, 59.

"Person of the Year: Ben Bernanke." December 28, 2009–January 4, 2010, 76.

Tobin, James. "Macroeconomic Models and Policy" (1977). quoted in Raymond Lombra and Michael Moran, "Policy Advice and Policymaking at the Federal Reserve," Carnegie-Rochester Conference Series on Public Policy, "Monetary Institutions and the Policy Process," 13 (Autumn 1980), 9–68.

"Interview." in Randall E. Parker, ed., *The Economics of the Great Depression.* Cheltenham, UK: Edgar Elgar, 2007, 130–43.

Todd, Walker F. "The Federal Reserve Board and the Banking Crisis of the 1930s." in George G. Kaufman, ed., *Research in Financial Services: Private and Public Policy*, vol. 8, JAI Press, 1996, 97–139.

"The Bear Stearns Rescue and Emergency Credit for Investment Banks." American Institute for Economic Research "Commentary," August 11, 2008 (http://www.aier. org/research/commentaries/445-the-bear-stearns-rescue-and-emergency-credit-for-investment-banks).

Torres, Craig. "Bernanke Misses Baseball in Battle for Euro Debt with Fed LISCC." *Bloomberg Businessweek*, February 1, 2011 (http://www.businessweek.com/news/2011-02-01/bernanke-misses-baseball-in-battle-for-euro-debt-with-fed-liscc.html).

Torres, Craig, Bob Ivry, and Scott Lanman. "Fed Reveals Bear Stearns Assets It Swallowed in Firm's Rescue." Bloomberg, April 1, 2010.

Uchitelle, Louis. "Irrational Exuberance." Book Review in *The New York Times*, April 19, 2009, 18.

U.S. Congress. *Stabilization*. Hearings before the House Committee on Banking and Currency. pt. 1, 69th Cong., 1st sess., March and April 1926a.

Stabilization. Hearings before the House Committee on Banking and Currency. pt. 2, 69th Cong., 1st sess., April, May, and June 1926b and February 1927.

Stabilization. Hearings before the House Committee on Banking and Currency. 70th Cong., 1st sess., March, April, and May 1928.

Operation of the National and Federal Reserve Banking Systems. Hearings before the Senate Committee on Banking and Currency. 72nd Cong. 1st sess., March 23–25 and 28–30, 1932a.

Stabilization of Commodity Prices. Hearings before the Subcommittee of the House Committee on Banking and Currency (Goldsborough Committee) on H.R. 10517. *For Increasing and Stabilizing the Price Level and for Other Purposes*. 72nd Cong., 1st sess., Parts 1 and 2, March 16–18, 21–22, 28–29, and April 13–14, 1932b.

Restoring and Maintaining the Average Purchasing Power of the Dollar. Hearings before the Senate Committee on Banking and Currency on H.R. 11499. An Act for Restoring and Maintaining the Purchasing Power of the Dollar. 72nd Cong., 1st sess., May 12, 13, and 18, 1932c.

"Federal Reserve Policy and Inflation and High Interest Rates." Hearings before the House Committee on Banking and Currency, 93rd Cong., 2nd sess., July 16, 17, 18, 30; August 7 and 8, 1974.

Disturbances in the U.S. Securities Market. Hearings before the Subcommittee on Securities of the Senate Committee on Banking, Housing, and Urban Affairs. 97th Cong. 2nd sess., May 25, 1982.

An Analysis of Federal Reserve Discount Window Loans to Failed Institutions. Staff report of the Committee on Banking, Finance and Urban Affairs, U.S. House Of Representatives, June 11, 1991.

Hedge Fund Operations. Hearing. House Committee on Banking and Financial Services, 105th Cong., 2nd sess. October 1, 1998.

Congressional Budget Office. Peter R. Orzag letter to Honorable John M. Spratt, Jr., July 22, 2008, (http://www.cbo.gov).

U.S. Department of Housing and Urban Development. "HUD Prepares to Set New Housing Goals." *U.S. Housing Market Conditions Summary*, Summer 1998 (http://www.huduser.org/Periodicals/ushmc/summer98/summary-2.html).

"The National Homeownership Strategy: Partners in the American Dream," HUD Home Web site, April 27, 2000.(http://web.archive.org/web/20010106203500/www.huduser.org/publications/affhsg/homeown/chap1.html, etc. for the different chapters).

U.S. General Accounting Office. "Financial Audit: Resolution Trust Corporation's 1995 and 1994 Financial Statements." Washington: U.S. GAO, July 1996. U.S. Treasury. "Report on Foreign Holdings of US Securities." (http://www.treas.gov/tic/shl2007r.pdf).

University of Chicago. "Paul Samuelson, Nobel-Prize Winning Economist, 1915–2009." News Office Homepage, December 14, 2009.

Valletta, Rob and Katherine Kuang. Federal Reserve Bank of San Francisco *Economic Letter*, November 8, 2010.

Velde, François. "Poor Hand or Poor Play? The Rise and Fall of Inflation in the U.S." Federal Reserve Bank of Chicago *Economic Perspectives* (Quarter 1, 2004), 34–51.

Viner, Jacob. *Studies in the Theory of International Trade*. New York: Harper & Brothers Publishers, 1937.

Volcker, Paul A. "Statement" before the House Committee on Banking, Finance and Urban Affairs. *Federal Reserve Bulletin* 69 (February 1983), 80–9.

"Fed 'at Edge of Its Lawful and Implied Power.'" Speech at Economic Club of New York in *WSJ Blogs*, "Real Time Economics," April 8, 2008.

The Wall Street Journal. "Continental Bank's Planned Sale Caps Stormy History That Included Bailout." January 31, 1994, A6.

"Countrywide Continues Slide, Leaving Questions of Value." August 29, 2007a, C1.

"'Conduits' in Need of a Fix: Subprime Hazards Lurk in Special Pipelines Held off Bank Balance Sheets." August 30, 2007b, C1.

"Mortgage Fallout Exposes Holes in New Bank-Risk Rules." March 4, 2008a, A1.

"Lehman Is Seeking Overseas Capital, As Its Stock Declines, Wall Street Firm Expands Search for Cash, May Tap Korea." June 4, 2008b.

"Government Mortgage Program Fuels Risks." June 24, 2008c, A1.

"FDIC Weighs Tapping Treasury as Funds Run Low." August 27, 2008d, A11.

"Ultimatum by Paulson Sparked Frenzied End." September 15, 2008e, A1.

"U.S. Plans Rescue of AIG to Halt Crisis." September 17, 2008f, A1.

Economic blog. September 17, 2008g (http://blogs.wsj.com/economics/2008/09/17/barney-frank-celebrates-free-market-day).

"A Black Wednesday for the Credit Markets." September 20–21, 2008h, A5.

"Decade After LTCM, Meriwether Risks Another Fund Collapse." September 20–21/2008i, B6.

(European edition) "Bypassed Lenders Grouse About State Aid to Banks." October 3–5, 2008k, 1.

"U.S., Britain Up Ante in Fight to Stop Crisis." October 8, 2008l, A1.

"Deposits Are Flowing to Healthier Banks." October 16, 2008m, A6.

"A Money-Fund Manager's Fateful Shift." December 8, 2008n, A1.

"The Weekend That Wall Street Died." December 29, 2008o, 1.

"Banks Hit by Nationalization Fears." January 21, 2009a, A1.

"Top U.S., European Banks Got $50 Billion in AIG Aid." March 7–8, 2009b, B1.

"Town's Friendly Bank Left Nasty Mess." June 16, 2009c, A1.

"Fed's Lending Ebbs as Crisis Subsides." July 20, 2009d, A2.

"Request Seeks to Bar A.I.G. From Some California Deals." October 31, 2009e, B1.

"Jittery Companies Stash Cash." November 2, 2009f, A1.

"After the Bailouts, Washington's the Boss." December 28, 2009g, A1.

Recession Strikes Deep into Work Force." June 30, 2010a, A2.

"Fed Split on Move to Bolster Sluggish Economy." August 24, 2010b, A1.

Fed's Capacity to Stimulate Economy Is Limited." August 29, 2010, A16.

"Irish Crisis Shakes Europe." October 1, 2010c, A1.

"IMF Plan Sees Role for Fund in Crises." March 23, 2011, C1.

"Wall Street to Cut Reliance on Treasuries Amid Debt Ceiling Fears." June 13, 2011, p. 1.

Walter, John R. "Depression-Era Bank Failures: The Great Contagion or the Great Shakeout?" Federal Reserve Bank of Richmond *Economic Quarterly* 91 (Winter 2005), 39–54.

Walter, John R. and John A. Weinberg. "How Large Is the Federal Financial Safety Net?" *Cato Journal* 21 (Winter 2002), 369–93.

Wandschneider, Kirsten. "The Stability of the Interwar Gold Exchange Standard: Did Politics Matter?" *The Journal of Economic History* 68 (March 2008), 151–81.

Warren, George F. and Frank A. Pearson. *Prices*. New York: John Wiley & Sons, 1933.

The Washington Post. "Fed Leaders Ponder an Expanded Mission." March 28, 2008a, 1.

"How Lehman Brothers Veered Off Course." July 3, 2008b, D1.

"In Weekend Talks, New Rules Emerged for Navigating Credit Crisis." September 16, 2008c, A1.

"AIG at Risk: $700 Billion in Shareholder Value Vanishes." September 16, 2008d, A1.

"Stocks Plummet as Lawmakers Left on the Sidelines as Fed, Treasury Take Swift Action." September 18, 2008e, A1.

"A Joint Decision to Act." September 20, 2008f, A9.

"House Rejects Financial Rescue, Sending Stocks Plummeting." September 30, 2008g, 1.

"Global Rate Cuts Fail to Suppress Crisis." October 9, 2008h, A1.

"Bailout Expands to Insurers." October 25, 2008i, A1.

"Parsing the Bailout." November 26, 2008j, A10.

"Internal Warnings Sounded on Loans at Fannie, Freddie." December 9, 2008k, D1.

"Detox for Troubled Assets." March 10, 2009a, D1.

"Anger over Firm Depletes Obama's Political Capital." March 17, 2009b, A1.

"Rage at AIG Swells as Bonuses Go Out." March 17, 2009c, A5.

"AIG's Riskiest Bets Unwound Long Before Retention Awards." March 19, 2009d, A6.

"How Treasury Spent Its Bailout Funds." November 28, 2009e, A13.

"Aughts Were a Lost Decade for U.S. Economy, Workers." January 2, 2010a, A1.

"With Consumers Slow to Spend, Businesses are Slow to Hire." August 21, 2010b, A1.

Webb, Steven B. *Hyperinflation and Stabilization in Weimar Germany*. Oxford: Oxford University Press, 1989.

Weidner, Justin and John C. Williams. "How Big Is the Output Gap?" *FRBSF Economic Letter*, June 12, 2009.

Wessel, David. "Inside Dr. Bernanke's E.R." *Wall Street Journal*, July 18–19, 2009, W3.

Whalen, Christopher. "Viewpoint: Stop Blocking FDIC Securitization Effort." *American Banker*, March 9, 2010.

Wheelock, David C. *The Strategy and Consistency of Federal Reserve Monetary Policy, 1924–1933*. Cambridge: Cambridge University Press, 1991.

White, Eugene N. "A Reinterpretation of the Banking Crisis of 1930." *Journal of Economic History* 44 (March 1984), 119–38.

"'To Establish a More Effective Supervision of Banking:' How the Birth of the Fed Altered Bank Supervision" Federal Reserve Bank of Atlanta and Rutgers University Conference, "A Return to Jekyll Island: The Origins, History, and Future of the Federal Reserve." November 5–6, 2010, Cambridge University Press (forthcoming).

Wicker, Elmus. *The Banking Panics of the Great Depression.* Cambridge: Cambridge University Press, 1996.

Banking Panics of the Gilded Age. Cambridge: Cambridge University Press, 2000.

Wicksell, Knut. *Lectures on Political Economy* (1935). Fairfield, NJ: Augustus M. Kelley, 1978.

Wigmore, Barrie A. "Was the Bank Holiday of 1933 Caused by a Run on the Dollar?" *Journal of Economic History* 47 (September 1987), 739–55.

Willis, H. Parker. "The Future in Banking." *Yale Review,* December 1933, 233–47.

Wolcott, Susan. "Keynes Versus Churchill: Revaluation and British Unemployment in the 1920s." *The Journal of Economic History* 53 (September 1993), 601–27.

Wolf, Martin. "What the British Authorities Should Try Now." *Financial Times,* October 31, 2008, 13.

"The World Economy Has No Easy Way Out of the Mire." *Financial Times,* February 24, 2010, 11.

Wolf, Nikolaus. "Scylla and Charybdis. Explaining Europe's Exit from Gold, January 1928–December 1936." *Explorations in Economic History* 45 (2008), 383–401.

"Europe's Great Depression: Coordination Failure After the First World War." CEPR Discussion Paper Series No. 7957, August 2010.

Wolman, Alexander and Anne Stilwell. "A State-Level Perspective on the Housing Bust." Federal Reserve Bank of Richmond Pre-FOMC memo, June 17, 2008.

Wood, John H. *A History of Central Banking in Great Britain and the United States.* New York: Cambridge University Press, 2005.

"The Stability of Monetary Policy: The Federal Reserve, 1914–2006." Unpublished paper, Wake Forest University, December 20, 2006.

"The Great Deflation of 1929–33 (Almost) Had to Happen." Unpublished paper, Wake Forest University, January 29, 2009a.

A History of Macroeconomic Policy in the United States. London and New York: Routledge, 2009b.

Woodford, Michael. *Interest and Prices: Foundations of a Theory of Monetary Policy.* Princeton, NJ: Princeton University Press, 2003.

Woodward, G. Thomas. "Origins and Development of the Savings and Loan Situation." *CRS Report for Congress.* Congressional Research Service, The Library of Congress, November 5, 1990.

Yeager, Leland B. *International Monetary Relations: Theory, History and Policy.* New York: Harper & Row, 1976.

Yergin, Daniel. "A Crisis in Search of a Narrative." *The Financial Times,* October 21, 2009, 9.

Index

Printed in the United States
by Baker & Taylor Publisher Services